W. Adolphe Roberts

W. Adolphe Roberts in San Francisco in October 1908. MS353.6.1.

W. Adolphe Roberts
These Many Years
An Autobiography

EDITED BY

Peter Hulme

THE UNIVERSITY OF THE
WEST INDIES PRESS
Jamaica • Barbados • Trinidad and Tobago

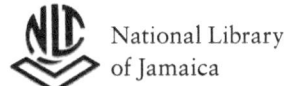

National Library
of Jamaica

The University of the West Indies Press
7A Gibraltar Hall Road, Mona
Kingston 7, Jamaica
www.uwipress.com

National Library of Jamaica
12 East Street
Kingston
www.nlj.gov.jm

© 2015 by the National Library of Jamaica
All rights reserved. Published 2015

A catalogue record of this book is available from the National Library of Jamaica.

ISBN: 978-976-640-511-3 (print)
978-976-640-517-5 (Kindle)
978-976-640-528-1 (Kobo)

Cover photograph: W. Adolphe Roberts, 1922
Cover and book design by Robert Harris
Set in Sabon 10.25/15 x 27
Printed in the United States of America

FOR ELEANOR

Contents

List of Illustrations *ix*

Acknowledgements *xi*

Introduction *xiii*

Bibliographical Note *xxvii*

These Many Years: An Autobiography

1. Tropical Boyhood *3*
2. Journalism in Kingston *20*
3. Baltimore and Northward *41*
4. Adventure *60*
5. San Francisco *84*
6. New York Heyday *101*
7. Pre-war Socialism *122*
8. Paris *142*

9 ▸ The Green Time Goes *163*

10 ▸ World War 1 *187*

11 ▸ *Ainslee's* and Its Legend *200*

12 ▸ Edna St Vincent Millay *215*

13 ▸ The *American Parade* *227*

14 ▸ The Lure of Travel *241*

15 ▸ Freelance *257*

16 ▸ The Author at Fifty *266*

17 ▸ 1939 *278*

18 ▸ The Act of Havana *300*

19 ▸ The Shaping of a Nation *311*

20 ▸ Full Circle *331*

Annotations *343*

Index *415*

Illustrations

Most of these photographs are taken from the W. Adolphe Roberts collection at the National Library of Jamaica (MS353) and are reproduced with kind permission. Photographers are unknown unless named in the caption.

1. Map of Jamaica 2
2. Roberts and his sisters outside Berry Hill, Manchester, Jamaica, about 1902 6
3. Adolphus S. Roberts in 1912 8
4. Knox Foster in 1921 9
5. Roberts, his sisters and his mother inside Berry Hill, about 1902 14
6. Clara Maude Garrett, "at about 18", so around 1898 22
7. W.P. Livingstone, writer and editor 23
8. Margaret Bourke around 1905 51
9. The American Felt Company, where Roberts worked in 1906 61
10. Florence Brochu, Roberts's first lover, in 1905 65
11. A sketch of Roberts by the artist John Butler Yeats, 1917 109
12. Charlotte Collyer (with her daughter Marjorie) 119
13. Polly Holladay's restaurant, New York 133
14. Roberts with Margaret Sanger and one of her sons, in 1917 139
15. Offices of the *Brooklyn Daily Eagle* in Paris 148
16. Roberts with Madeleine Lebourg and Aïcha Goblet in Paris, 1914 161

17. Roberts in 1917 201
18. Olga Petrova, one of Roberts's lifelong friends 203
19. Solita Solano, one of Roberts's lifelong friends 211
20. Salomón de la Selva being sworn into the British Army 211
21. Katherine Amelia Hickey in 1912 214
22. Edna St Vincent Millay 217
23. Roberts, Antonio Moreno and admirers 229
24. Cover of an issue of the *American Parade* 231
25. Eleanor Ramos, probably in 1922 236
26. Roberts in 1922 239
27. Roberts in Havana with Conrado Massaguer and Paul Milton 247
28. Muna Lee in 1930 269
29. Norman Manley in the 1930s 276
30. The flag of the Jamaica Progressive League 288
31. Rawcliffe, the house Roberts rented in Gordon Town, 1939 295
32. Roberts in Chicago in 1939 298
33. Cover of *The Caribbean: The Story of Our Sea of Destiny* (1940) 301
34. Looking down St Ann Street from Royal Street, New Orleans, c. 1940 307
35. Menu from the dinner held at the Myrtle Bank Hotel to celebrate Roberts's return to Jamaica in 1946 316
36. Drawing of Roberts collecting his Orden Nacional de Mérito, Havana, Cuba, 1950 321
37. Roberts in Washington Square, late 1940s 325
38. Celebration at the foundation of the Bolivarian Society of Jamaica, 1952 332
39. Cover of Roberts's last major publication, *Jamaica: The Portrait of an Island* (1955) 337
40. Barbara Ferland, in the early 1950s 339
41. "Nell", Roberts's daughter, c. 1950 341
42. The area of the Mandeville churchyard where Roberts's ashes are buried, unmarked 342

Acknowledgements

MY MAIN DEBT IS TO WINSOME HUDSON, LIBRARIAN at the National Library of Jamaica, and her staff, for enabling my access to Roberts's autobiography and for their wholehearted support in the task of preparing it for publication. In 2012 Rosie Dodd catalogued the W. Adolphe Roberts papers, greatly facilitating research on his life and work. I also thank the *Jamaica Journal* for permission to reproduce material from my essay on Roberts referred to on xxiv, n.4; and the Joint Initiative for the Study of Latin America and the Caribbean [British Academy] which provided some seed funding.

Others who have helped in significant ways and whom I would like to thank are Linda Speth and Shivaun Hearne at the University of the West Indies Press, Ann Rovere, Shirley Steele, Leah Rosenberg, John Aarons, Franklin Knight, Birte Timm, Kim Robinson-Walcott, Steven White, the late Stuart Hall, the late Richard Hart, Bill Schwarz, David Scott, Robert Hill, Owen Robinson, Faith Smith, Susan Gillman, Jonathan Cohen, Alycia Hesse, Peter Engleman, James Robertson, Sean Falconer, Luis Bolaños, Susan Forsyth.

Peter Hulme
Sedbergh
May 2014

Introduction

FIVE DAYS AFTER JAMAICA CELEBRATED ITS INDEPENDENCE ON 6 August 1962, Adolphe Roberts set off for a trip to Europe. He must have had mixed feelings. He had spent thirty years of his life working toward the day when Jamaica would be free of colonial rule, yet his contribution had not been honoured during the independence ceremonies and, as it turned out, the last part of his struggle – to defeat the idea of a West Indian Federation – had been waged against many of his former colleagues. In the event Roberts's trip was cut short. While dining with friends in London on the evening of 13 September he was taken ill and died early the next morning. Roberts had taken to London, to leave with his agent, his recently completed autobiography, *These Many Years*, a long account of his life, loves and careers as a writer and political figure, six pages of which, dealing with the onset of World War I, had appeared in *The Independence Anthology of Jamaican Literature*.[1] Roberts had had a long connection with the Institute of Jamaica: its director, Bernard Lewis, had been named as his executor and literary trustee. After Roberts's death, Lewis took advice about the feasibility of publishing *These Many Years*, and was told that publication might make the institute a target for criticism on the grounds of the rather abrupt judgements it contained on some of Roberts's contemporaries.

W. Adolphe Roberts had been a prolific and successful writer for nearly sixty years, both in the United States and in the Caribbean, and after his permanent return to Jamaica in 1950 he had become a prominent cultural figure, president of organizations such as the Jamaica Historical Society and the Poetry League of Jamaica, and chairman of the board of governors of the Institute of Jamaica. After his death, a commemorative volume collected warm tributes,[2] but Roberts's reputation then quickly faded. He had shown considerable versatility as a writer – poet, novelist, journalist, historian, travel writer; perhaps too much versatility for an age of growing specialism. The new nation certainly wanted literary heroes, but Roberts belonged to a generation and class whose time seemed to have passed. He became at best a marginal figure in the canonical postcolonial narrative of an independent Jamaica. The tenth- and twentieth-year anniversaries of his death brought short appreciations, and a few of his poems were anthologized,[3] but otherwise his writing was largely forgotten: all the novels remain out of print, as do the works of travel writing and history. Just recently, however, there have been some signs of a renewed appreciation of his achievements. In 2011, during the run-up to the fiftieth year of Jamaican independence, two journalists noted the importance of remembering Roberts's pioneering work for Jamaican self-government.[4] There have also been two analyses of *The Single Star*, his fine 1949 novel about the Cuban War of Independence and the US invasion of the island in 1898; one of his trilogy of historical novels about New Orleans; and good overall assessment of his pan-Caribbean achievements.[5] And now, more than fifty years after his death, with the original considerations that prevented its publication no longer an issue, *These Many Years* finally sees the light of day, bringing back onto the Jamaican stage a vibrant nationalist's own account of a full and fascinating twentieth-century Caribbean life, rich in detail, wide in canvas, and offering unprecedented insight into the development of the movement for Jamaican independence.

AS THE AUTOBIOGRAPHY EXPLAINS, ROBERTS had been educated by his talented but wayward father. Taught how to write well, Roberts worked as a teenager on local Jamaican newspapers before leaving for the United States in 1904 where, after a rocky start, he eventually made a living from his pen, working sometimes as a journalist, sometimes as an editor. He clearly never really relished life as a reporter, but as a feature writer he had a long, varied and distinguished career, interviewing figures as different as Alexander Bedward and Georges Clemenceau, and writing up the story of one of the first survivors of the *Titanic* to reach New York. Roberts is modest about his editorial work, though he takes pride in his spell in charge at *Ainslie's* magazine and in his own short-lived journal, *American Parade*. But from the start his aim was to be an author.

Roberts's first book of poems was published in 1919, his first novel in 1931, his first biography in 1933. *These Many Years* makes it very clear which of his books Roberts thought important. In the early 1930s, with his writing career launched and his finances relatively secure, Roberts embarked on his first major historical work, a biography of Henry Morgan, which he describes in some detail. Morgan was obviously an interesting choice: a controversial figure widely regarded as a pirate. His was certainly a colourful life and ultimately a Jamaican life, which allowed Roberts to raise issues of colonial governance and personal belonging alongside the telling of a rip-roaring story of plunder and intrigue in the seventeenth century. Greatest weight is then given by Roberts to his pioneering historical study, *The Caribbean: The Story of Our Sea of Destiny*, researched and written in the white heat of the late 1930s and early 1940s, and dedicated to Norman and Edna Manley, with whom Roberts had become close friends during 1939. The only one of his novels much discussed is *The Single Star*, set on Jamaica and Cuba during the late 1890s.

In her essay on "Regional Histories" in the UNESCO *General History of the Caribbean*, Bridget Brereton notes that Roberts and his Colombian contemporary, Germán Arciniegas, were the two historians writing in the 1940s whose approach "departed significantly from the imperial tradition".[6] In other words, they wrote their histories of the Caribbean *from* the Caribbean. Roberts was the pioneer: *The Caribbean: The Story of Our Sea of Destiny* appeared in 1940, the first historical expression of a pan-Caribbean political consciousness. Arciniegas's *Biografía del Caribe* was published in 1945, its English translation, *Caribbean: Sea of the New World*, one year later.[7] It would be a further twenty-five years before the appearance of books with a similar scope: Eric Williams's *From Columbus to Castro* and Juan Bosch's *De Cristóbal Colón a Fidel Castro*.[8] On most reckonings, Roberts's book is superior to Arciniegas's: its coverage of the region is certainly more even, and it takes its story up to 1940, while the Colombian stops at the end of the nineteenth century. But Arciniegas is an honoured figure in his homeland, so his book had a second edition in 2000 to mark the centenary of his birth, while Roberts's book remains out of print.[9]

ROBERTS'S FIRST CHILDHOOD MEMORY – he tells us on the opening page of *These Many Years* – is of escaping the house and running down the street. He would soon become an inveterate traveller and an accomplished travel writer. He wrote books about two of his favourite cities – Havana and New Orleans – but the autobiography also contains deft descriptions of many others: Kingston in 1904, San Francisco in 1908, New York in 1911, and Paris in the long summer of 1914, which ended in the end of a world. Most notably, however, Roberts had the great good fortune to arrive in Greenwich Village just as it became one of the most exciting places in the world to live. He rubbed shoulders and shared drinks with an extraordinary array of talents, many of whom dart in and out of these pages – Jack London, Edna St Vincent Millay, Margaret Sanger, Alan Seeger, Emma Goldman, Elizabeth Gurley Flynn, J.B. Yeats; while he also offers a series of fascinating sketches of Washington Square boarding houses and cheap *table d'hôte* restaurants. Roberts was a very young man at the time, struggling to earn a living, and so he does not feature in any of the classical accounts of Greenwich Village in its heyday, despite having clearly played a significant role in the establishment of one of its most important venues, the Liberal Club on MacDougal Street. In the last analysis, he was probably too much of an outsider to join in anything for long, although he was always interested, especially if attractive young women were involved – which they usually were in Greenwich Village at the time. So having helped establish the Liberal Club, he soon found it superficial; having joined the Socialist Party, he soon found it doctrinaire; having been intrigued by modern art, he soon found much of it fraudulent.

ROBERTS FOUNDED THE JAMAICA PROGRESSIVE LEAGUE in New York in 1936, an organization that pressed for Jamaican self-government. The founding declaration of the league, adopted on 1 September 1936, was a fundamental statement of Roberts's political credo: "Firmly believing that any people that has seen its generations come and go on the same soil for centuries is in fact a nation, we pledge ourselves to work for the attainment of self-government for Jamaica" (see below, 271). The stated ideal was a *national* one: national sentiment and national consciousness, created through political action and artistic fruitfulness. The Jamaica Progressive League's presence on the island in the late 1930s then brought Roberts into close contact with many of the emerging political figures of the time such as Norman Manley and Alexander Bustamante, respective leaders of the People's National Party and the Jamaica Labour Party, and therefore the figures who now tend to dominate the early chapters of the national story.

Roberts's involvement in politics came quite late in life: he was fifty when the Jamaica Progressive League came into being. The autobiography, however, points out that his indignation with colonial governance had its roots in his first experience as a young reporter in Kingston at the beginning of the twentieth century when he was sent to see the Legislative Council in action. Joseph Chamberlain, as colonial secretary, had made it clear that he did not support representative institutions for colonies where blacks were in the majority, and so Jamaica's painfully slow movement in this direction had, in the early twentieth century, entirely stalled.[10] If his father was Roberts's chief early influence on his literary tastes, then Sydney Olivier played that role in politics, the first of a number of powerful men whom Roberts saw in person over the next few years, Theodore Roosevelt, Lord Kitchener, Georges Clemenceau, all sketched in these pages with the skill of the political journalist that Roberts soon became. In New York in his twenties and thirties Roberts was a paid-up member of the Socialist Party: disillusionment came from its capitulation to patriotic fervour in Europe in 1914. One senses, however, even in his actions of the 1910s and 1920s the attitude of a lifelong liberal who was swayed to the left by the radical euphoria of the time, but who was reluctant to make political commitments – until he discovered the animating nationalist cause. Jamaica had always remained, he says, in the back of his mind, though after leaving in 1904 his returns to the island were few and far between before his re-engagement in 1937.

By this last date, however, Jamaica had clearly pushed itself to the forefront of Roberts's mind. To that biography of the rambunctious buccaneer Henry Morgan published in 1933, Roberts attached an appendix outlining the case for Jamaican self-government, an argument only tenuously connected with the body of the text, as if the author just had to find an outlet for his growing political frustrations. The five years that followed saw significant political achievements on Roberts's part, which did much to shape modern Jamaica: the founding of the Jamaica Progressive League in New York, the consolidation of a movement for self-government in Jamaica itself, the involvement with the establishment of the People's National Party. Recalling these years – and particularly the campaigning year of 1939 – Roberts conjures the vibrancy and excitement of that path-breaking moment, in which he was one of the central figures. The outbreak of World War II, which prevented Roberts settling in Jamaica as he had planned, cut short the possibility of him having a full political career on the island at the head of his own party, although a group with self-government as its main plank would perhaps always have been caught in the pincers of a Manley–Bustamante contest. Like so many countries, Jamaica's political life is incorrigibly divided into two – People's National Party versus Jamaica Labour Party, making Roberts's perspective particularly valuable.

ONE OF ROBERTS'S FRIENDS DESCRIBES him as "a ladies' man", a description from which he says he does not demur (below, 234). Of Austin Bride, the clearly autobiographical protagonist of his 1931 novel *The Moralist*, Roberts says: "Women had interested him to the point of enchantment", but also "that he shrank from responsibilities in love" (p. 11, p. 78). There were certainly plenty of women in Roberts's life, even more than feature in his autobiography. Two of relatively minor significance, though, were his mother and his wife. He clearly had scant sympathy for his mother's puritanical outlook on life and seems to have had relatively little contact with her after he left Jamaica as a teenager. He met Katharine Amelia Hickey in New York before leaving for Paris in 1914, and married her on his return – quite why, Roberts himself appears unable to explain. She leaves little trace. Three women stand out for their importance in his life. Shortly after his marriage he met Edna St Vincent Millay, on the threshold of her emergence as one of the most famous figures of her day. Like many of the young men of New York City, Roberts fell in love with her while realizing that she had no interest in being faithful to any of her many lovers. But he had helped her on her way as a writer and kept alive the memory of his passion by following her career, as one of his scrapbooks makes clear. Then, while still married but clearly leading a separate life from his wife, he met and fell in love with Eleanor Ramos, another aspiring writer, though one whose career would soon falter. Roberts openly admits that Eleanor Ramos was the love of his life, but one that he threw away because he mistook love for passion. Like Millay, Ramos had red hair, but whereas Millay's was wispy and golden, Ramos's was lush and flaming, clearly described here in *The Moralist*'s description of Beatrice Purcell: "she had the most bright, virile red hair he had ever seen. It luxuriated under her hat and looped down on either side as if it could not be controlled" (p. 136). In one of the passionate letters she wrote to Roberts during their affair, Ramos enclosed a lock of that hair which still, in the box of Roberts's correspondence in the National Library of Jamaica, blazes as brightly as the day Roberts opened the envelope nearly a century ago.

The third important woman in Roberts's life, but the one he knew least well, was his daughter. As far as one can judge, *These Many Years* is an honest autobiography, sometimes painfully so. The one obvious change Roberts makes is to some of the details regarding his daughter's birth, although there is no deception: his footnote indicates that he has changed names and circumstances. The fact remains, as he openly admits, that the daughter was born to a woman in a couple with whom he had been friends for many years, and when he finally met his daughter as a teenager – having seen her briefly as a baby – he was still unaware whether she knew that he was her real father. Although in the autobiography he moves the date of the birth forward ten years, Roberts was in fact nearly sixty when she was born and over seventy before he began, briefly and hesitantly, to get to know her. He died before any proper relationship might be established. Still living in New York, that daughter honours his memory. This book is dedicated to her.

THE RICHES OF CARIBBEAN WRITING are by now well known. Its poetry and fiction have long been outstanding, given the relatively small populations of even the larger islands. History-writing too has served the region well.[11] Oddly, though, there is a paucity of Caribbean biographies, and very few autobiographies.[12] Of Roberts's contemporaries as writers, there is Claude McKay's masterful *A Long Way Home* (1937), Alfred Mendes's posthumous *Autobiography* (2002), Jean Rhys's also posthumous *Smile Please* (1979), which is valuable, though too short and fragmented to be regarded as a proper autobiography, and Phyllis Shand Allfrey's unfinished autobiographical novel, "In the Cabinet"; but little else. Of Roberts's political contemporaries, Norman Manley tried to write an autobiography but left only a fragment; Alexander Bustamante was never likely to (though his wife wrote some memoirs); and others whose testimony would have had value did not: N.N. Nethersole, Wilfred A. Domingo, Ethelred Brown, Ken Hill, all of whom feature in *These Many Years*.[13] But, apart from McKay, who never went back to the Caribbean after he left Jamaica in 1912, Roberts may be the only Caribbean figure of substance in his generation (that is, born in the second half of the nineteenth century) to have written his own life-story – a fact which underlies the significance of this rare window onto Jamaican life, culture and politics.

From the perspective of 2015, Adolphe Roberts's career looks more typically Caribbean than it once did, with its youth and old age spent on the island, sandwiching a forty-five-year career in one of the world's metropolises. But even in the early twentieth century, movement back and forth between island and metropolis was not that unusual. Exact parallels with Roberts's career probably do not exist. Some of his friends and contemporaries – like Herbert de Lisser or Norman Manley or Luis Muñoz Marín – basically lived their lives on the island of their birth, though in Manley's case there were years at university in England and on war service in Europe, in Muñoz Marín's some bohemian years in New York. Others – like Claude McKay – left the island of their birth and never returned to settle. Still others – like the Nicaraguan poet Salomón de la Selva or the Dominican literary historian Pedro Henríquez Ureña – left when young and retained attachments to their homelands, but were prevented by political reasons from resettling there.

Three parallels seem worth pursuing in more detail. Roberts would not have liked the first parallel, but his career does have similarities with that of Alexander Bustamante, two years his elder. Bustamante had also left Jamaica as a teenager and travelled almost as widely as Roberts, doing all kinds of jobs to make a living. Cuba, Spain, Panama, New York: there are overlaps in their trajectories although they were working in very different areas. Bustamante kept the same intermittent touch with Jamaica as Roberts did, returning permanently in 1932. The temperaments of the men could hardly have been more different. Their politics, too; although ironically both eventually opposed Federation, with Roberts's final political involvement – discussed in the last chapter of *These Many Years* – being a series of radio broadcasts on the subject with airtime paid for by Bustamante's Jamaica Labour Party.

In the second case, "parallel" may be the appropriate word since Adolphe Roberts and Claude McKay had similar journeys, though their paths rarely crossed. They were certainly thought of together: in 1961 the pioneering critic G.R. Coulthard allowed McKay and Roberts to be the two twentieth-century West Indian writers of real stature.¹⁴ Both indeed had made prominent appearances in the landmark 1949 Langston Hughes and Arna Bontemps anthology, *The Poetry of the Negro 1746–1949*.¹⁵ McKay was just three years younger than Roberts. Both were brought up in rural Jamaica in relatively well-off families, though Thomas McKay's ascent into the position of "prosperous capitalist farmer" rather neatly and perhaps symbolically crosses A.S. Roberts's descent from son of a prosperous planter to intermittently alcoholic ne'er-do-well.¹⁶ During their formative years as writers, both had strong mentors: his brother in McKay's case, his father in Roberts's. Both were precocious writers, and both went as young men to live in the United States and ended up in New York, moving in some of the same circles in lower Manhattan around 1919 and 1921. Both spoke of their lust for travel, subsequently spending considerable time in England and France but returning to live in New York. In the early 1930s, after many years away from Jamaica, both returned to the island in their writing, Roberts with his biography of Henry Morgan, McKay with his novel *Banana Bottom* (1933). The one occasion on which we know they met was a party in Harlem where Roberts made the initial contacts that led to the founding of the Jamaica Progressive League. McKay could presumably have chosen to become involved in the nationalist movement, but he was now perhaps too long separated from his homeland and too well-established as a writer to make the necessary commitment. Or to put it another way, Roberts had less to lose. In fact, the contacts that Roberts made at that party with black West Indians such as Wilfred Domingo and Richard B. Moore were the same kinds of contacts McKay had made twenty years earlier during the heyday of the Universal Negro Improvement Association and the African Blood Brotherhood. McKay's New York had, at least initially, been black New York: he always lived in Harlem even when he worked in Greenwich Village. Roberts's never had been – until 1936, when he took the A-train north.

Jean Rhys was just four years younger than Adolphe Roberts. She left Dominica for England three years after Roberts left Jamaica for the United States. Both lived sexually adventurous bohemian lives in their chosen cities – London and New York respectively, though they also shared haunts in Paris. As they struggled to make careers as writers, both seemed to have left the Caribbean behind, but Rhys – like Roberts and McKay – was drawn back to it in the 1930s in her writing and her life. Both Roberts and Rhys prided themselves on their Welsh backgrounds, Roberts's more distant, Rhys's through her father, which allowed them to look aslant at their own position within the imperial hierarchy. Rhys's novel *Voyage in the Dark* was published in 1934, a year after Roberts's biography: both have a central character called Morgan, though Rhys's Anna Morgan is of course fictional. After these books were published, both writers returned to the islands of their birth for extended visits in a time of growing political turbulence, Rhys in 1936, Roberts in 1937 – though here the parallel starts to fade because Rhys found it difficult to make sense of what was happening on Dominica, while Roberts enthusiastically joined the movement for political change in Jamaica.[17] For both, the Caribbean would subsequently remain at the heart of their work, but *Wide Sargasso Sea* and *The Caribbean: The Story of Our Sea of Destiny* are very different accomplishments.

Roberts and Rhys both belonged to a privileged minority group: they were white West Indians, though neither family was particularly well off. However, whereas Rhys's work is marked by that Fanonian "terrified consciousness" that the critic Kenneth Ramchand sees as characteristic of writers in this group,[18] Roberts shows no signs of such an attitude, despite being apparently unaware that one of his great-grandmothers had been "coloured" (see below, 410). He no doubt shared some of the unthinking prejudices of his class and generation: so, for example, he writes openly of the child that his father had with the daughter of a black retainer on the childhood plantation without giving any indication that he might regard this child as a half-brother or half-sister: paternity across the racial divide does not entail kinship. But when the moment arrived to begin the nationalist movement, Roberts had no hesitation in heading to Harlem to find Jamaicans. It seems that nationalism really did trump all: to Roberts Jamaicans were Jamaicans, and that was good enough. That he was so warmly regarded by his black and brown colleagues suggests that his views were genuinely held.

IN AUGUST 1962, WHEN JAMAICA finally achieved independence, Roberts sent some of his final written words to his old colleagues at the Jamaica Progressive League in New York, congratulating them on twenty-five years' effort and recommending – true to his perspective – that Jamaica should seek to join the Organization of American States. Right after the independence celebrations, Roberts travelled to London on the first leg of what was to be a European trip. He had dinner with an old Jamaican friend, Lucille Parks, who had married a Tory MP called Tom Iremonger.[19] During dinner Roberts was taken ill and he died in his room (12A) in the Hotel White House at 17–19 Earls Court Square in the early morning of 14 September 1962. The death certificate gives the cause as cerebral haemorrhage due to hypertension. His body was cremated in London, with the West Indian writers Andrew Salkey and Vivian Virtue, and his last lover, Barbara Ferland (now Sheppard) present at the ceremony. After a funeral service at St Andrew's Church, Kingston, on 26 September, his ashes were returned to Mandeville for burial in the churchyard of St Mark's, the Anglican parish church. A memorial service was held at St George's Church, Kingston, on 18 November 1962. The prime minister, Alexander Bustamante, was invited to attend, but declined.

Note on the Text

The original of *These Many Years* forms part of the collection of W. Adolphe Roberts's papers held by the National Library of Jamaica at MS353.5.1.1 and 353.5.1.2. The first part of the autobiography ("The Tides of Spring") was started in 1944, with the bulk of it being written in 1951, in the early days of his relationship with Barbara Ferland. It was revised in 1954 and 1955. The second part ("Moonstones and Harvest") was started in the summer of 1961 and carries a completion date of 16 February 1962, although some of the pencilled additions may have been made in subsequent months. The first part – in the form of an almost clean typescript – is a more polished piece of writing, while the second part – typed but with many amendments and pencilled additions – shows signs of not having been fully revised and finalized. A full transcription was completed in 2011 and is lodged with the National Library of Jamaica. Since the autobiography was never published, this edition offers an edited text. The original typescript of just over 170,000 words has been shortened to just under 140,000. Only one chapter – about pets and animals – has been simply omitted. Other omissions involve long quotations from Roberts's own writing, some of his passages of travel writing, and a few anecdotes. Some chapters have been combined, so that this edition totals twenty chapters as opposed to the original's twenty-eight (divided into two parts). In other respects, normal editing procedures have been followed:

spelling and punctuation have been standardized, repetitions eliminated, wording occasionally clarified. Annotations, keyed to page numbers, mostly elucidate Roberts's references to people and events. This introduction has been kept brief so that *These Many Years* can speak for itself. The annotations develop points of more specialist interest. Cross-references lead to a main entry. Minor references can been found in the index. The absence of an annotation indicates that no information is available beyond what Roberts writes, or that no elucidation is judged necessary. The bibliographical note that follows this introduction contains a partial list of Roberts's voluminous writings. Other references in this introduction and in the annotations on the text are given in full at first mention, and thereafter by abbreviation.

Notes

1. Full references to Roberts's writings can be found in the bibliographical note at the end of this introduction.
2. *Bulletin of the Jamaican Historical Society* 3, no. 8 (1962).
3. Frank Birbalsingh, "W. Adolphe Roberts: Creole Romantic", *Caribbean Quarterly* 19, no. 2 (July 1973): 100–107; Wycliffe Bennett, "W. Adolphe: A Personal Recollection", *Jamaica Journal* 16, no. 4 (November 1983): 54–58; John A. Aarons, "W. Adolphe Roberts and the Movement for Self-Government", *Jamaica Journal* 16, no. 4 (November 1983): 59–63 (which drew on the autobiography); *The Penguin Book of Caribbean Verse in English*, ed. Paula Burnett (Harmondsworth: Penguin, 1986), 140–42.
4. Ken Jones, "W. Adolphe Roberts: 'Father of the Nation'", *Gleaner*, 31 July 2011, F14; Louis Moyston, "W.A. Roberts et al. and the JPL, 1936–1944", *Jamaica Observer*, 27 August 2011, 10. See also Peter Hulme, "W. Adolphe Roberts and Jamaica", *Jamaica Journal* 34, no. 3 (August 2013): 14–23, where some of the material in this introduction first appeared.
5. Peter Hulme, *Cuba's Wild East: A Literary Geography of Oriente* (Liverpool: Liverpool University Press, 2011), 260–66; Faith Smith, "Between Stephen Lloyd and Esteban Yo-eed", *Journal of French and Francophone Philosophy* 20, no. 1 (2012): 22–38; Owen Robinson, "North to the South: New Orleanian Identities in the Work of W. Adolphe Roberts and George Washington Cable", in *The (Un)Popular South*, ed. Marcel Arbeit and M. Thomas Inge (Olomouc, Czech Republic: Palacký University, 2011), 45–60; and Emilio Jorge Rodríguez,

"La visión pancaribeña del espacio cultural: Walter Adolphe Roberts", in his *El Caribe Literario: Trazados de Convivencia* (Havana: Editorial Arte y Literatura, 2011), 63–116.

6. Bridget Brereton, "Regional Histories", in *General History of the Caribbean*, vol. 6, *Methodology and Historiography of the Caribbean*, ed. B.W. Higman (London: UNESCO/Macmillan Education, 1999), 308–42, at 315.

7. Germán Arciniegas, *Biografía del Caribe* (Buenos Aires: Editorial Sudamericana, 1945) and *Caribbean: Sea of the New World*, trans. Harriet de Onis (New York: A.A. Knopf, 1946).

8. Eric Williams, *From Columbus to Castro: The History of the Caribbean* (London: André Deutsch, 1970); Juan Bosch, *De Cristóbal Colón a Fidel Castro: El Caribe, Frontera Imperial* (Madrid: Alfaguara, 1970).

9. Ironically, in 2004, Jamaica saw the reprinting of the English translation of Arciniegas's book: *Caribbean: Sea of the New World*, trans. Harriet de Onis (Kingston: Ian Randle, 2004). It had also been reprinted in 2003 (Princeton: Markus Wiener).

10. Ronald V. Sires calls the first decade of the century in Jamaica "a time of political stagnation" ("The Experience of Jamaica with Modified Crown Colony Government", *Social and Economic Studies* 4, no. 2 [1955]: 150–67, at 155).

11. A. James Arnold, ed., *A History of Literature in the Caribbean*, 3 vols. (Amsterdam: J. Benjamins, 1994); B.W. Higman, ed., *General History of the Caribbean*, vol. 6, *Methodology and Historiography of the Caribbean* (London: UNESCO/Macmillan Education, 1999).

12. Of Roberts's West Indian literary contemporaries, Claude McKay, Jean Rhys, Una Marson, Phyllis Shand Allfrey and Frank Collymore have had respectable biographies; those of political figures are in a few cases profuse – Marcus Garvey, C.L.R. James, Eric Williams – though sometimes lacking in personal detail and analysis, but otherwise thin on the ground. Neither Norman Manley nor Bustamante have yet had full biographies. See Wayne F. Cooper, *Claude McKay: Rebel Sojourner in the Harlem Renaissance* (New York: Schocken, 1987); Carole Angier, *Jean Rhys* (Harmondsworth: Penguin, 1985); Delia Jarrett-Macauley, *The Life of Una Marson, 1905–65* (Manchester: Manchester University Press, 1998); Lisabeth Paravisini-Gebert, *Phyllis Shand Allfrey: A Caribbean Life* (New Brunswick: Rutgers University Press, 1996); Edward Baugh, *Frank Collymore: A Biography* (Kingston: Ian Randle, 2009).

13. Norman Manley, "My Early Years: Fragment of an Autobiography", in *Manley and the New Jamaica: Selected Speeches and Writings 1938–68*, ed. Rex Nettleford (London: Longman Caribbean, 1971), xcv–cxii; Gladys Bustamante,

The Memoirs of Lady Bustamante (Kingston: Kingston Publishers, 1997). Richard Hart's papers at the Institute of Commonwelath Studies in London (GB 0101 ICS 122 [MF861]) are a valuable resource.

14. G.R. Coulthard, "The West Indies", in *The Commonwealth Pen: An Introduction to the Literature of the British Commonwealth*, ed. A.L. McLeod (Ithaca: Cornell University Press, 1961), 185–202, at 189.

15. *The Poetry of the Negro 1746–1949*, ed. Langston Hughes and Arna Bontemps (Garden City, NY: Doubleday), 1949. The anthology had three sections: "Negro Poets of the USA", "Tributary Poems by Non-Negroes" and "The Caribbean", broken down into countries. In this last section Jamaica had the biggest representation, and of the sixteen poets represented, only Claude McKay had a larger number of poems than Roberts. See Ifeoma Kiddoe Nwankwo, "More than McKay and Guillén: The Caribbean in Hughes and Bontemps's *The Poetry of the Negro*", in *Publishing Blackness: The Textual Constructions of Race Since 1850*, ed. George Hutchinson and John K. Young (Ann Arbor: University of Michigan Press, 2013), 108–35. Perhaps because of his prominent presence in this anthology, Roberts was – and sometimes still is – mistaken for a black writer.

16. The quotation is from Winston James, *A Fierce Hatred of Injustice: Claude McKay's Jamaica and His Poetry of Rebellion* (London: Verso, 2000), 11. James offers an excellent account of rural Jamaica in this period (3–51).

17. On Rhys in Dominica, see Peter Hulme, "The Return of the Native: Jean Rhys and the Caribs (1936)", in his *Remnants of Conquest: The Island Caribs and Their Visitors, 1887–1998* (Oxford: Oxford University Press, 2000), 204–43.

18. Kenneth Ramchand, "Terrified Consciousness", *Journal of Commonwealth Literature* 7 (1969): 8–19.

19. Lucille Iremonger (née Parks) (1919–89), author of several novels and biographies and a memoir called *Yes, My Darling Daughter* (1964). An extract from her novel *Creole* is in *The Independence Anthology of Jamaican Literature*, selected by A.L. Hendriks and Cedric Lindo (Kingston: Ministry of Development and Welfare, 1962), 155–63. Lucille Parks's father, Basil Parks, was a businessman who had co-owned with Walter Durie the *Jamaica Times*, for which Roberts wrote on occasion.

Bibliographical Note

The bibliography of W. Adolphe Roberts's writings is large and complicated. He wrote a great deal, much of it in ephemeral magazines. In addition, some of the books published under his name were not actually written by him, as notes in the copies he provided to the Institute of Jamaica library make clear. The list that follows is only indicative.

"Bedwardism: A Church with 6,000 Members". *Leader* [Kingston], 16 January 1904, 3.
> As "Our Correspondent". A considerable achievement for a seventeen-year-old reporter.

"The Love of a Woman". *Jamaica Times*, 23 December 1905, 2.
> Short story, as W.A.R.

"Across the Table". *Overland Monthly* 52, no. 1 (July 1908): 42–45.
> The first of a number of stories he published in California magazines.

"Tragedy of the Yaqui". *Overland Monthly* 53, no. 2 (August 1908): 119–21.
> Drawing on his experience working in Sonora.

"The Woman Rebel". *Birth Control Review* 1, no. 2 (March 1917): 12.
> A poem in praise of Margaret Sanger, first published in *The Masses*.

Pierrot Wounded and Other Poems. New York: Britton Publishing Co., 1919. 87pp.

His first book.

"What Ainslee's Stands For". *Editor: The Journal of Information for Literary Workers* 52, no. 4 (25 February 1920): 160.

A statement of editorial principles.

"Beautiful Spanish Screen Star Takes Paris by Storm – Will Soon Visit America". *Movie Weekly*, 19 May 1923, 4–5, 27.

About Raquel Meller. An example of the movie journalism he was keen to forget.

American Parade. Ed. W. Adolphe Roberts. 4 issues (January 1926–October 1926).

His proudest achievement as an editor.

"The Phrase-Maker and the Aztec: A Study of the Wilson-Huerta Episode". *American Parade*, no. 1 (January 1926): 35–47.

Showing his keen interest in foreign affairs.

The Haunting Hand: A Detective Story. New York: Macaulay, 1926. 309pp.

Written by Pauline Brooks Crawford from a synopsis by Roberts, but published under his name.

Pan and Peacocks. Boston: Four Seas, 1928. 79pp.

His second book of poems.

The Mind Reader: A Mystery. New York: Macaulay, 1928. 277pp.

"Island of Dreams", "For Poets Slain in War", "Villanelle of the Living Pan", "The Cat", "Peacocks". In *Voices from Summerland: An Anthology of Jamaican Poetry*, ed. J.E. Clare McFarlane, 285–90. London: Fowler Wright, 1929.

"The Most Spanish of Dancers". *Dance Magazine* (May 1930): 17 and 50.

His article about La Argentinita.

The Moralist. New York: Mohawk Press, 1931. 300pp.

An autobiographical novel about his relationship with Eleanor Ramos.

Mayor Harding of New York. New York: Mohawk Press, 1931. 271pp.

Published under the pseudonym Stephen Endicott and written by Paul Milton, Roberts helping with the plot.

Wisconsin Writings, 1931: An Anthology. Edited by Frank Shay, W. Adolphe Roberts, Loyd A. Collins, Stuart Palmer. New York: Mohawk Press, 1931. 229pp.

    Intended to be first volume of an inter-collegiate library.

The Strange Case of Bishop Sterling. New York: Meteor Press, 1932. 271pp.

    Published under the pseudonym Stephen Endicott and written by Paul Milton, Roberts helping with the plot.

"Dark Honey". *Harlem Stories* 1, no. 2 (August 1932).

    Perhaps significant as his earliest "engagement" with Harlem, though no copy has yet come to light.

Sir Henry Morgan: Buccaneer and Governor. New York: Covici Friede, 1933; London: Hamish Hamilton, 1934. 320pp. Abbreviated edition, Kingston: Pioneer Press, 1952. 165pp.

    The biographical study which first made his name as a writer.

"British West Indian Aspirations". *Current History* 40, no 5 (1934): 552–56.

    His first serious piece of political writing about the West Indies.

The Top Floor Killer. London: Nicholson and Watson, 1935. 319pp.

Self-Government for Jamaica. New York: Jamaica Progressive League of New York, 1936. 16pp.

    The first publication of the Jamaica Progressive League and one of the earliest statements of the case for Jamaican self-government.

Semmes of the Alabama. Indianapolis: Bobbs-Merrill, 1938. 320pp.

    His second biography, showing considerable sympathy for the cause of the Confederacy.

"Jamaicanising Jamaica". *Public Opinion*, 13 May 1939, 3.

    One of a series of articles for this new Jamaican publication, instrumental in the establishment of the People's National Party.

The Caribbean: The Story of Our Sea of Destiny. Indianapolis: Bobbs-Merrill, 1940. 361pp. Reprinted New York: Negro Universities Press, 1969.

    His major achievement as a historian.

The Pomegranate. Indianapolis: Bobbs-Merrill, 1941. 313pp.

    A novel about Latin American politics.

The French in the West Indies. Indianapolis: Bobbs-Merrill, 1942. 335pp.

The Book of the Navy. Garden City, NY: Doubleday, 1944. 302pp. [Selected with Lowell Brentano]

A compilation produced for the midshipmen of the US Naval Academy.

"The Future of Colonialism in the Caribbean: The British West Indies". In *The Economic Future of the Caribbean*, ed. E. Franklin Frazier and Eric Williams, 37–39. Washington, DC: Howard University Press, 1944.

Royal Street: A Novel of New Orleans. Indianapolis: Bobbs-Merrill, 1944. 324pp.

Brave Mardi Gras: A New Orleans Novel of the '60s. Indianapolis: Bobbs-Merrill, 1946. 318pp.

Lake Pontchartrain. Indianapolis: Bobbs-Merrill, 1946. 376pp.

In the American Lakes Series, but really an oblique history of New Orleans.

Creole Dusk: A New Orleans Novel of the '80s. Indianapolis: Bobbs-Merrill, 1948. 325pp.

Lands of the Inner Sea: The West Indies and Bermuda. New York: Coward McCann, 1948. 301pp.

The first of his travel guides.

The Single Star: A Novel of Cuba in the '90s. Indianapolis: Bobbs-Merrill, 1949; London: Herbert Jenkins, 1950. 378pp. Abbreviated ed., Kingston: Pioneer Press, 1956. 315pp.

"Great Men of the Caribbean. I: Toussaint L'Ouverture". *Caribbean Quarterly* 1, no. 2 (1949): 4–8.

"Great Men of the Caribbean. II: Simón Bolívar". *Caribbean Quarterly* 1, no. 3 (1950): 4–8.

"Great Men of the Caribbean. III: José Martí". *Caribbean Quarterly* 1, no. 4 (1950): 4–6.

Medallions. Kingston: Arawak Society, 1950. 16pp.

His third collection of poems.

"La historia de un retrato". *Carteles*, 11 February 1951. Translated by Armando Maribona.

"The Story of a Portrait", *Gleaner*, 8 April 1951. Backtranslated into English by Raymond C. Souza.

About a famous photograph of José Martí taken in Kingston in 1892.

"Boyhood Etchings", "The Captains", "San Francisco", "Villanelle of Washington Square", "Villanelle of the Living Pan", "Peacocks", "Vieux Carré", "On a Monument of Martí", "The Maroon Girl". In *The Poetry of the Negro 1766–1949*, ed. Langston Hughes and Arna Bontemps, 311–17. Garden City, NY: Doubleday, 1951.

Six Great Jamaicans: Biographical Sketches. Kingston: Pioneer Press, 1952. 122pp.

Probably his most widely read publication.

"Tiger Lily". Unpublished essay. 1952, 18pp. Vassar, Edna St Vincent Millay Papers, 11.16.

"Edna St Vincent Millay". *West Indian Review*, 12 June 1952, 28–29.

Havana: Portrait of a City. New York: Coward McCann, 1953. 282pp.

Jamaica: The Portrait of an Island. New York: Coward McCann, 1955. 247pp.

"Preface: Our Unique City". In *The Capitals of Jamaica: Spanish Town, Kingston, Port Royal*, ed. W. Adolphe Roberts, vii–x. Kingston: Pioneer Press, 1955. 112pp.

Anthology of the Poetry of the West Indies. Chosen and edited by W. Adolphe Roberts, OBE, and Wycliffe Bennett. With introductory essay and appendix by Wycliffe Bennett, c. 1955. Unpublished. 226pp.

"The Caribbean in the Pan American Movement". In *The Caribbean: British, Dutch, French, United States*, ed. A. Curtis Wilgus, 300–314. Gainesville: University of Florida Press, 1958.

Sign of his academic acceptance.

The Gleaner Geography and History of Jamaica, ed. W. Adolphe Roberts; rev. W. Adolphe Roberts and Keith D. Lowe, 17th ed. Kingston: Gleaner Co., 1959. 80pp.

Old King's House, Spanish Town. Kingston: Old King's House Restoration Committee, 1959. 24pp.

"The Act of Havana". *Jamaican Historical Review* 3, no. 2 (1959): 66–69.

"That Jamaica May Remember: The Visit of Bolivar, the Liberator". *Gleaner*, 22 February 1959, 8.

"All Caribbean League". *Pepperpot* 10 (1960): 66–67.

"How the War Came in 1914". In *The Independence Anthology of Jamaican Literature*, selected by A.L. Hendriks and Cedric Lindo, 190–95. Kingston: Ministry of Development and Welfare, 1962.
 "From the autobiography still in progress, *These Many Years*."

"Our Free Dominion" [August 1962]. In John S. Young, *Lest We Forget*, 39–40. New York: Isidor, 1981.

These Many Years
An Autobiography

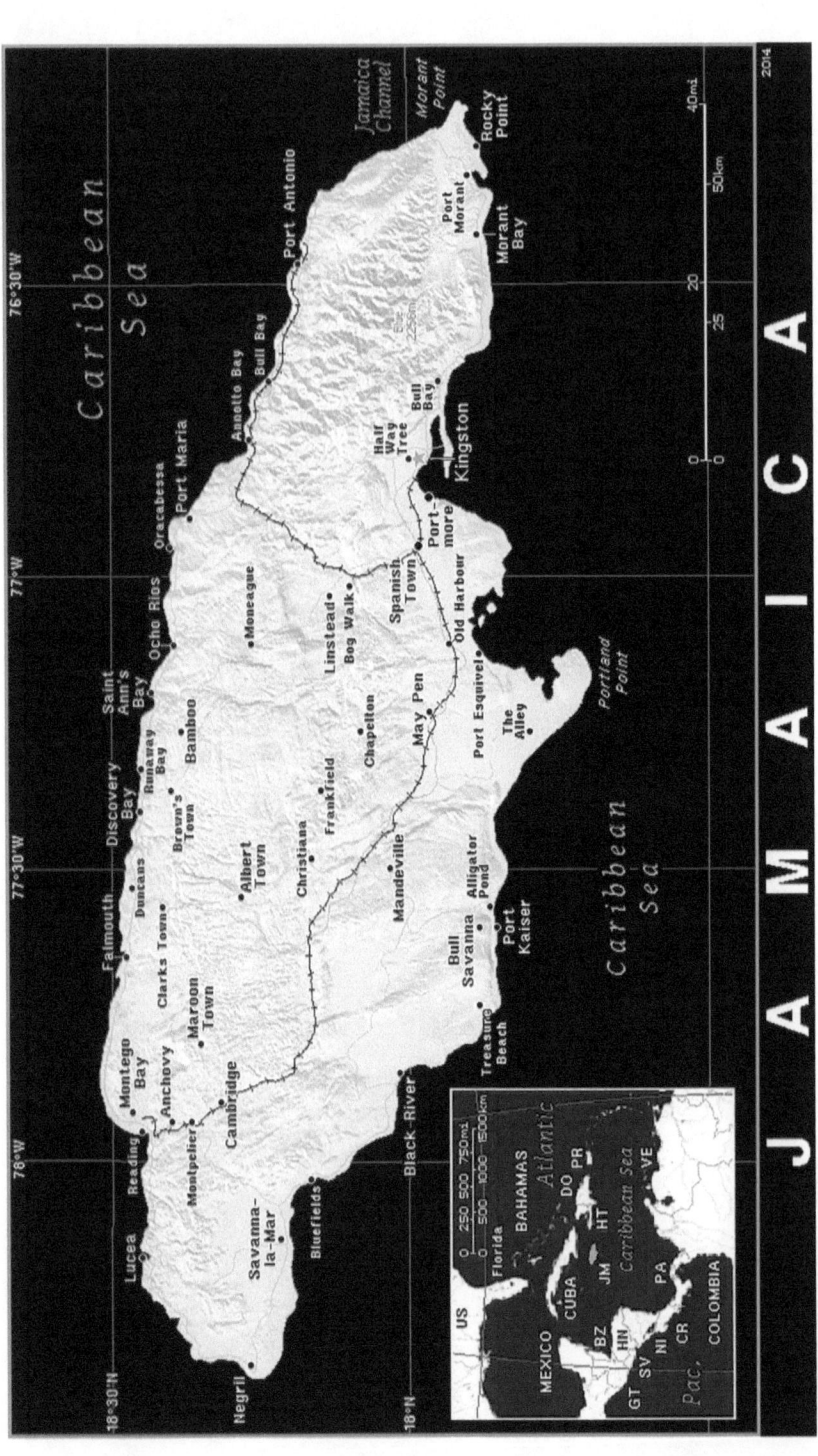

Figure 1. Map of Jamaica

CHAPTER 1 ❧ Tropical Boyhood

I HAVE ONLY TWO MEMORIES OF MY INFANCY in Kingston, Jamaica, where I was born on 15 October 1886, and where my father served briefly as a priest of the Anglican Church. The first is of escaping from the house onto the sidewalk and running. Nothing but that, yet the impression made upon me is as vivid as if it had occurred yesterday. I felt the inadequacy of my young legs, but gloried in the chance to use them to the utmost. The wind was in my face. I had a marvellous sensation of liberty, voluptuousness, and zest for life. The happening was a matter of minutes. I know I did not reach the next corner, though no mental picture survives of how I was caught and taken back indoors. I questioned my mother about it in later years. She said I was given to such flights between the ages of two and three, and she could not identify the particular one.

The second recollection is more realistic; it is longer, in fact episodic. We were living in a house on James Street, and I was not less than four years old. I recall dimly a bedroom where my cot stood, and where now and then my parents quarrelled. Much clearer is the backyard on the edge of a gully into which refuse was thrown. My father liked to potter about in the yard, and there was a tawny cat there which we both petted. One day the cat came pacing up from the gully. Its head had been almost severed from its body by the stroke of a machete. It went to an old sack under the steps and curled itself laboriously into a ring. The cat's journey is a motion picture which I have ever after been able to unreel at will in my brain. My father told me that the creature must not be disturbed, that it would lie there until it began to mend – or died. My visits to learn how it was getting along persist in fragments, at the end of which I see the cat miraculously recovered. And then no more of James Street.

When I was about five my father left a calling to which he was temperamentally unsuited and returned to the mountain parish of Manchester. Both he and my mother had been born in that parish, as had my father's parents and both his grandmothers. Various pieces of landed property remained in the family. The one to which we retired was called Berry Hill, a place of some three hundred acres at an altitude of a little more than two thousand feet. My conscious life began there. I had the advantage of being to all intents and purposes a country child, the special luck to develop against a background that was suited to my imagination.

The hills rolled in every direction, gently enough for several miles around us, but ending on three sides with steep descents – east and west to lowlands, and south to the sea. These Manchester mountains were a looped spur from the range that forms the backbone of Jamaica, but to the north there was a considerable depression through which the railroad ran. We lived on an island within the island, and we had spectacular views. On a fine day we could see the Blue Mountains to the east, their main peak 7,402 feet high, and get a glimpse in their shadow of Kingston harbour. From the nearby Hanover property, my mother's former home, we looked precipitously down to the St Elizabeth savannas and beyond to the next spur westward, while on the left the Caribbean shone. Far prospects glowed with strange and beautiful colours, a greenish gold in sunny weather, an unearthly purple after the rain. Because of the prevailing limestone formation there were no streams. Drinking water was collected in stone tanks, and ponds were scooped out for the livestock in spots where clayey soil occurred. Most years the rainfall was sufficiently heavy to keep the vegetation luxuriant. But there would be periods of drought which seared the face of things with an unwonted sadness.

Agriculturally the district had run to seed, from the standpoint of the big landowners, that is to say. It had been coffee country. Nearly all the plantation houses had barbecues in the rear, those long stretches of stone terraces where the berries had been pulped and the beans sun-dried. But mass production in Brazil and elsewhere had made coffee growing in Jamaica unprofitable. A similar difficulty applied to oranges and other citrus fruit, which flourished in our mountains. So the planters had converted their holdings into grazing pens, with cattle as the mainstay, the breeding of horses and mules a secondary interest, and an occasional flock of sheep as a sideline. Hogs and poultry were raised. Close to the house fruit trees grew half wild: avocado pears, oranges, guavas and others. A small coffee grove was generally maintained for personal needs, and there would be a patch of bananas in some hollow. Pimento trees were to be found scattered over the pastures, and although never cultivated were an important source of revenue, the spice being peculiar to Jamaica.

The name 'pen' for a place of this kind was of the simplest origin, meaning apparently a tract that had been fenced or walled in to 'pen' cattle from straying. It could have been self-sufficient in the matter of food, but few attempted to make it so. We killed our own meat to a large extent, produced our own milk, butter and eggs. Flour for homemade bread was bought, however, and some cornmeal. We did not grow tropical vegetables, but got them from the small settlers at derisory prices. It was tacitly understood that sweet potatoes, yams, corn, beans and so forth were in the domain of the peasant farmer, and that it would be infra dig to compete with him. If a white or a well-to-do coloured person planted a vegetable garden, it would almost unfailingly be robbed.

The whole community life and system of landholding was semi-feudal, anyway. Intertwined among the pens were the Negro villages which had come into being after slavery was peacefully abolished in the 1830s. The small individual lots had been sold, rented or conceded to squatters on the edges of the estates to enable freed people to support themselves, but the old human relationship had not altered radically when I was a boy. House servants, artisans and casual labourers came from the villages, and for the most part each pen employed the descendants of slaves who had been attached to the property.

Berry Hill house was a rambling building on stone foundations with a superstructure of wood, its shingled roof rising in three main peaks. Behind were two wings that flanked the upper reaches of the superfluous but delightful coffee barbecues where I and my sisters, Ethel and Ivy, loved to play. To the right stood the detached kitchen, and below that the coach house and stable. A walled flower garden, in front, gave onto a low parapet convenient for getting in and out of carriages, or mounting horses. The house

Figure 2. Roberts and his sisters outside Berry Hill, Manchester, Jamaica, the house in which they grew up, about 1902. MS353.6.10.

bore a family resemblance to the type that was built in Louisiana by the early French colonists. It had charming irregularities: a paved arcade on one side connecting with the narrow dirt yard on which the kitchen faced, a covered passageway behind, patches of garden in odd spots. The left wing contained a dairy and servants' quarters. The right wing, termed the bottom house, must formerly have been intended for the use of an overseer, or for guests, because it had its own living room and a row of three bedrooms. One of the latter was mine. Its window looked on a slope thick with orange trees above which an avocado pear towered, then a dale of pasture land, and on the further rise a stretch of woods.

Life at Berry Hill was simple, healthy and completely bucolic. We got up a little after dawn, had supper at sunset, read or played games for an hour or two by the light of oil lamps, and were in bed by ten o'clock. Our nearest railroad station was ten miles away, our post office four miles. Mail (for which a messenger had to be sent) was distributed three times a week, and the daily paper from Kingston was, in consequence, received only that often. A drive to Mandeville, the parish seat, five miles distant, was an event dedicated to sporadic attendance at the Anglican church, and shopping trips. There was not much visiting among the families in our part of the mountains. An outsider would have found existence dull. To my sisters and myself it was full of wonder, exciting, varied.

My passion for nature and books was intense, and my efforts at scribbling precocious. I read poetry and history with equal fervour. I wavered among the ideas of becoming a naturalist, an author or a man of action – the precise activity, in this last case, to be decided later. When, at the age of eleven, I ambitiously settled down to the writing of a book, it took the form of a history of a mythical country called Fairland, based on my school books on Greece and Rome but not devoid of personal notions about government, manners and customs. I also began to write verse and notes on birds, which I contributed to the local papers. It flattered me to see my words in print a few days after they had been penned, and I soon thought authorship the most romantic of callings.

I OWED MY EDUCATION AND individualistic development wholly to my father. There were no suitable schools within a convenient distance. The custom of sending planters' children abroad could not, for lack of funds, be observed in our case. So my father acted as tutor. He was a strange, contradictory man, scholar and periodic drunkard; physically courageous but weak-willed, inventive, artistic, and full of ideas for building a splendid future, but without the capacity for making his dreams come true. I loved him, and he was the first great influence in my life. He had been christened Adolphus Sigismund, names which had never been in the family and which his mother took from a romantic novel she was reading just before he was born. He received a formal education in England and began the study of medicine but abandoned it when an uncle of his in the China silk trade gave him a post in Canton. He spent twelve years there, comprising most of the 1870s and lapping over into the 1880s.

It was a mercantile opportunity which might have led him to riches, but he did not see it that way. Instead he made of it a fabulous experience, half sensuous, half intellectual, which coloured him permanently. The allure of Chinese civilization caused the West to be forever insipid to him. He studied Confucius and Lao Tse, drifted toward Buddhism and almost embraced it as a faith. He kept a Chinese concubine, as most of the young merchants did. The waywardness of my father, as his fellows saw it, lay in his sentimentality

Figure 3. Adolphus S. Roberts in 1912. MS353.6.2.

over the liaison and his expressed opinion that Chinese women made better wives than Europeans. Also, he was friendly with Chinese scalawags and went with them on smuggling expeditions up the Canton River. He drank more heavily than even a liquorish society could approve, which provided a simple excuse for damning him. I am surprised that he lasted as long as he did among the silk traders in the foreign concession.

Returning to England because his uncle would have no more of him, his disillusionment took the typical Victorian form of his trying to enlist in the army as a common soldier. Luckily they rejected him on the score that he had ruined his health in the East, a verdict which proved to be far from the truth. He came back to Jamaica and articled himself as a clerk to a lawyer in Mandeville. Of all the callings he tried, the law was the most distasteful to him. He sneered at its concern with precedents rather than equity, and he quoted the Chinese philosophers zestfully against it to the end of his life. That he would have resumed a course of bizarre adventure is probable, if he had not fallen in love with my mother. She thought a clergyman the elect among mortals, and to please her he turned to the Church.

His Greek and Latin were still good. The theological curriculum at the college in Kingston, knotty to many aspirants, seems to have been child's play to him and he passed his examinations spectacularly. No sooner had he been made a deacon than he married and was appointed curate of the Kingston Parish Church, as attractive a post as the diocese could offer a newcomer. Soon he was a full priest. I have been told that his sermons charmed the women members of the congregation and won approving chuckles from the worldly rector, Archdeacon George Downer. My father acted later as chaplain to the British garrison at Port Royal across the harbour, ancient haunt of the buccaneers. He was given a church of his own at Lluidas Vale. There is little doubt that his personality and talents sufficed for the building of a career in Holy Orders. Yet certain factors combined in six years to make a farce of it: orthodox Christianity bored him, he was not happy in his marriage, and to relieve the tedium he dissipated heavily. He resigned from the Church.

At Berry Hill he was supposed to be manager for his three old aunts, the Misses Lind, who owned the place and another pen called Mount Forest some ten miles southward near the sea. He merely made a show of inspecting the cattle and getting in the pimento crop. The real work was done by a remarkable black headman, Knox Foster, uneducated but shrewd, bearded like an Arab. Foster was the son of a former slave in our family. My father preferred to cultivate beautiful plants that had no commercial value, to graft rose bushes or orange trees with an almost magic touch, and to experiment in the crossbreeding of poultry with no particular end in view. He was a clever carver in wood – and treated this talent as the idlest of pastimes.

Figure 4. Knox Foster in 1921. MS353.6.8.

This was the man who opened the gates of knowledge to me. After grounding me in the first essentials of a grammar school education, he dropped the subjects for which I had no aptitude and concentrated on those that interested me. Thus I parted at the threshold with mathematics, which I abhorred. Latin was abandoned for French and Spanish, with emphasis on the former. It was not easy for me to learn any foreign language, but I had an intuitional urge in connection with French, and slowly mastered it. I ran to the opposite extreme regarding history, military and political, geography, zoology, and literature. I found these more fascinating than the games of youth, and my father did his utmost to develop such trends in me. He told me that the habit of self-education was more important than anything he could teach. One must be eager to enlarge one's store of information till the end of life. This I accepted, and this I have practised with the ardour he invoked.

My father went beyond any tutor of whom I have heard in making himself a partner in my enthusiasms and my efforts, and thus he led me subtly. If I discovered a good book for myself he would delve into it as though on my recommendation and discuss it with me. If he found me reading trash he did not reprove me, but would call my attention to superior works in the same field. I had a sudden passion for adventure stories, as exemplified by certain paperback books, mostly Westerns, that a visitor left at the house. My father said that exciting stories were a tonic after study. The better written, however, the more effective they were. The ones I had been reading were shallow, and he would demonstrate his meaning with some good examples. So he bought me H. Rider Haggard's *She*, *King Solomon's Mines*, *Allan Quatermain* and *Nada the Lily*. He pointed out a Sherlock Holmes series then running in the *Strand Magazine*. Instantly I was converted from Westerns.

More than that, my father paced me in my attempts at writing. When I announced my project for a history of a mythical country, he declared he would do one also. We agreed to compare our stints of manuscript each evening. I saw that his mythical country had a complexity unknown to mine. My inventions soon gained by the unconscious mimicry he had stimulated, though I coloured them according to my own fancy.

A little later he interested me in the contests which the *Daily Gleaner* of Kingston held to get material for its Christmas number. Cash prizes were offered for the best short story, the best poem, the best essays on various topics for which the titles were furnished. We must both try our hands at it, he said, yet not compete with each other. I decided to submit a short story and a poem. He offered to do whichever essay I selected from the list, and I chose the subject "Why Are the Churches Not Better Attended?" It probably amused him wryly, but he wrote and sent in the piece. I got an honourable mention for my short story. He won his prize. The next year I was a winner, both in the *Gleaner* and the *Jamaica Times*.

The side of me that loved the outdoors and all that lived there – birds especially – found a comrade in my father. During my early childhood he took my sisters and myself on picnics which he imbued with glamour. A camp for the day would be established in a grove of coffee shrubs, or some romantic woodland clearing, and he would show us how to start a fire Indian fashion by rotating a hard stick in a hollowed rotten log, how to enrich the pot with edible wild things, and how to fashion utensils from gourds and leaves. The pretence was that we were on a desert island. He made a wonderful scoutmaster before the scout idea for children had been born.

I felt an urge to wander alone, and my father at once agreed to this, making light of my mother's fears that at ten or so I was too young to be trusted in the woods. Then dawned a phase which gave me untold joy and stamped a lasting imprint on my personality. I roved the forested hills and gullies, the waste-lands or ruinates as we called them, and the wide pastures, delighting in the adventures of solitude. I was enchanted by the beauty of birds, their songs, the patterns of their flights: the audacious petcharies, a kind of tyrant flycatcher, which built their nests at the tip of a branch of some tall tree swayed by the wind, and which chased their enemies with shrill, exultant cries; the friendly mocking birds, garrulous between their bursts of melody, nesting in low trees; the golden-breasted banana birds with their flair for the glossiest foliage against which the contrast of their own rich plumage glowed; the equally lustrous spindalis, a species of tanager peculiar to the West Indies; the plump, stubby-beaked bluequits forever pecking at any fruits that were to be had; the 'hopping dick' thrushes, sober-clad but with a bright yellow bill, haunters of the outskirts of woods; the migratory John-to-wits, named for their sharp, incessant call which had such a sweet ring to it that it gave a special character to April, the month this visitor arrived; the red-headed woodpeckers; the glittering hummingbirds; the little green todies with scarlet throats which burrowed into banks of soft earth to nest; the ghostly nighthawks, flitters at twilight, which laid their eggs among the bare pebbles on a hillside.

I watched four-footed creatures also: the lithe mongooses with their narrow, spool-shaped heads, their cruel red eyes, and bushy tails; the timid wood rats which lived in trees and ate mostly fruit. There were numberless varieties of lizards, ranging from the brilliant green Venus that would change to a murky brown if frightened; the russet and bejewelled gallywasp with a serpent's head; down to the anoles of all sizes and colours that sprawled where the sunshine lay warm on tree trunks and stones. I was charmed by them, and by the background against which this wild life moved: the withes, the orchids, the parasitic plants like pineapple tops which grew upright on the branches of trees and collected rainwater at the base of their leaves for the birds to drink. But as I wandered and made notes I dreamed, and my dreams were of an existence for which I believed I was destined, far away from there. I wrote verses in my head. I toyed with my kaleidoscopic ambitions.

Horseback riding stands out among the memories of that period. I was not particularly devoted to it as a sport. But horses were part of my life, since they were the only means of making a journey. We did not use them for ploughing, for the simple reason that land was not cultivated that way in the mountains of Jamaica, the spade and the hoe being employed exclusively. Horses were considered too valuable for heavy draught work, which was done by mules. My father taught me to ride when I was ten or younger. It became second nature to me to approach and handle a horse skilfully, though not showily. I left such violent stuff as the breaking of colts to the experts, who as I remember were stockmen summoned on occasion from our other pen, Mount Forest. What I enjoyed was the feeling of companionship with a well-trained mount, preferably one of small build, smooth of gait for cantering, and with catlike agility on rough slopes peculiar to hill ponies.

For years I had a little chestnut, named Aster because of the white star on his forehead. I associate him with the red earth of the Manchester roads bordered by crimson hibiscus, or above which the great plumes of creaking bamboos met in a Gothic arch. I seldom rode in company. A trip to the post office for mail or to some house where I could borrow books was the usual motive. I went miles once on a dew-wet morning to gather orchids for a girl years older than myself, who seemed – briefly, alas! – the most desirable of living things, and who presently married an English surveyor. There were late returns through moonlight as pellucid and magical as daylight during an eclipse of the sun. I do not recall the wherefore of all these night rides, but know that my eyes were alert for the flapping, pale owls and the zigzag patterns made by the wings of bats.

I took great interest in our cattle, for the business of stock-raising struck me as being colourful. We had about a hundred and fifty head, of which there were never more than thirty or forty at Berry Hill. These comprised the best milch cows and a big roan bull. The weaned calves were sent to Mount Forest to mature for the market. The males had previously been castrated, this job being the specialty of a retainer called Brown Pitta – an odd name unconnected with his colour, which was black. He had been a member of the Moravian Church, a sect that had a fair following in Manchester, but had been expelled for practising obeah, the mild Jamaican form of voodoo. His disgrace sat lightly upon Pitta, and the white penkeepers thought it a joke. He was not primarily an obeahman, anyway, but a peasant landholder whose wife and numerous progeny cultivated for him while he did odd jobs more to his taste.

Where he learned his surgical art I have no idea. It was crude but effective. The fee paid him for calves was trifling – a shilling or two; the reward lay in the testicles, which by unwritten law were his. As calves were always done in batches, he would carry off a basketful of perquisites, his expression beatific, to an orgy of feasting with his cronies. He charged more for lambs and colts, in the first case because the penkeepers retained the 'fries', and in the second because the castrating of a horse was held to be difficult. Pitta joked caustically, and I regret that I have forgotten all his better sayings. My father had an illegitimate child with one of his daughters, which infuriated my mother but was taken carelessly by Pitta, who neither presumed on the fact nor complained about it.

Knox Foster, the headman, lived at Mount Forest, and several times a year he notified my father there would be a round-up there for branding, the passing of steers for sale or of heifers for permanent addition to the herd. I did not miss one of these exciting events if I could help it. Mount Forest represented adventure. It had no white residents. The grazing land was broad and wild. It was a thousand feet closer to sea level, and mangoes and other lush fruit trees, which were infertile at the Berry Hill altitude, flourished there. An orgy of mangoes fresh from the branch was a chief pleasure in visiting Mount Forest.

I DISLIKED TEAM GAMES SUCH as cricket, beloved of the British and taught by them as a sacred rite to young colonials, white, brown and black. As may be supposed, this caused me to be unpopular with boys of my own age. The feeling was mutual. I did not seek a single friend among the few I met. I indulged in a most self-complacent sense of superiority to the male runners in packs, who had to go to schools to get knowledge, and who batted balls around for amusement. On the other hand, I was a hero-worshipper of certain older men, beginning with my father, and I yielded early to the fascinations of girls. No doubt I was a terrible little egoist, but as

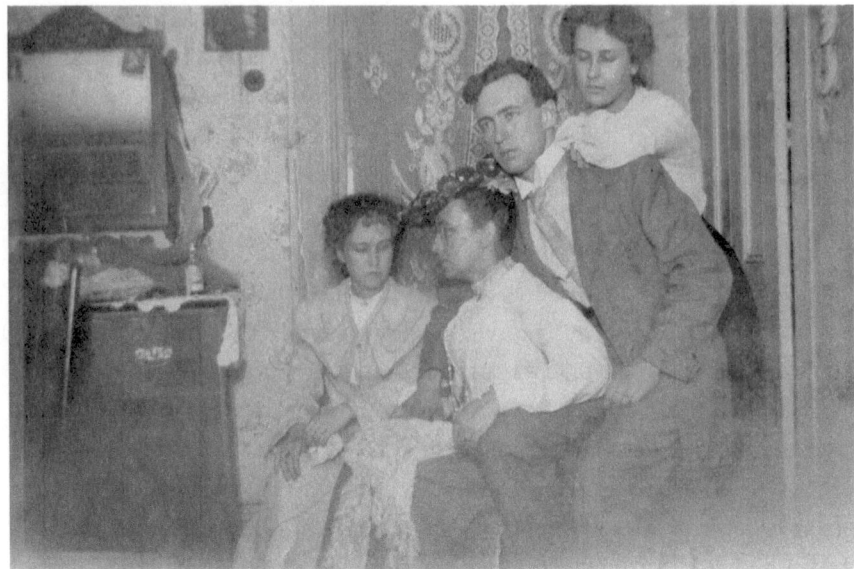

Figure 5. Roberts, his sisters and his mother inside Berry Hill, about 1902. Ellen is leaning over Roberts; Ivy is seated. MS353.6.10.

the objects of my admiration generally liked me pretty well I saw no reason to change my attitude. My mother's influence over me was slight, because of her puritanical nature.

While my father gave my sisters and myself a secular education, my mother undertook to put us through a sort of Sunday school of her own. As far as I was concerned, she succeeded only in making religion distasteful to me; but not the Anglican Church, that bland version in water colours of the imposing canvas of Rome. I loved our services with their noble rhetoric, their beautiful chants, the embellished altars, and the rich hues of the stained-glass windows. Centuries of the traditions of my ancestors had shaped that ritual into a structure of grandeur and doubtless of essential truth. Bishop Charles Douet, at Mandeville, in scarlet vestments, his white beard fanned out upon his chest, looked just as I thought God ought to look, though I forget every last word he uttered from the pulpit. Not, as I say, the Church and its ceremonial, but religion as expounded by my mother: that was what antagonized me.

My mother was not happy in her married life. All that I perceived as a boy was that she and my father had separate bedrooms and that she was often on bad terms with him. Unluckily she felt it a duty to make sex, as she saw it, abhorrent to me. She got wind somehow, when I was a little more than twelve years old, of my having ventured on the classic lubricities of puberty with a girl younger than myself, chiefly the game of "Show me and I'll show you!" as well as an attempt at coition with an older coloured girl. My mother extorted a confession from me. Then, with a frenzy that seems scarcely believable to me even now, she set to work to convince me that I was as vile a creature as had ever lived.

After adducing the Bible and Prayer Book, she rose to the height of setting forth her own interpretation of the "sin against the Holy Ghost" – the one for which there is *no* forgiveness. Even an archbishop of Canterbury would hesitate to define it. My mother informed me that as the human body was the temple of God, the "defilement" of it by sex relationships outside marriage was none other than the aforesaid dread offence. My physical incapacity had saved me so far, but if I ever deliberately committed the act I would be condemned to Hell for evermore.

She bullied me into taking vows that would have been suitable for a monk, and she set me long penances of oral contrition and prayer. A real sense of guilt about the girl children involved had been stirred in me, and this combined with a mother's lurid dramatization of Hell to keep me sunk in gloom and fear for weeks. But my nature did not permit me to respect puritanism and forced vows any more lastingly than it had accepted evangelical religion. When the reaction came, I passed into a mood of extreme romanticism about love. A psychoanalyst would probably conclude that I have since sought in every woman the mother with whom I lost emotional rapport in my boyhood.

THE FIRST WORLD EVENT THAT impinged on my consciousness was the Greco-Turkish War of 1897. I was only ten and a half years old when it started, yet I followed the newspaper accounts eagerly. Moved by my passion for ancient Greek history and mythology, I adopted the Greek cause. I still have a mental picture of the conservative headlines of the day announcing the defeat at Larissa, the failure to stand at Thermopylae, the disastrous recoil along a line studded with the classic names. My distress was keen. It was a consolation when the Powers, as they were then invariably termed with a capital *P*, intervened to stop the Turks from pressing home their victory.

About the same time I became aware of a struggle which had been raging much closer to me. This was the Cuban War of Independence, organized in 1895 by José Martí, the Apostle, and which by 1897 had reached a crescendo of terror due to the barbarities of the Spanish captain-general Valeriano Weyler, the Butcher. I had reason to take the business dramatically, for my father had a sudden impulse to fight for Cuba. He left secretly, intending to sail on a droger, run by the Spanish *guardacostas* if possible, and enlist under General Máximo Gómez, who had lived in Jamaica for two years as a political refugee.

But some sort of crisis existed at home. Foster was sent after my father posthaste on horseback, caught up with him in Kingston and persuaded him to return "for his children's sake". It may throw a light on this headman's feudal relationship to our family when I say that he talked to my father like a Dutch uncle, forced him to leave his hotel and cancel his engagement to sail, and then rode behind him respectfully the whole way back. As a matter of fact, though barely literate, Foster was the more masterful character of the two. The details were not explained to me until years later, but I knew that my father had been on a generous errand. If I had favoured the Cubans before, I was now their enthusiastic partisan.

The months wore on and the United States became involved. I read of the sinking of the armoured cruiser *Maine* in Havana harbour, and of the ultimatum sent to Spain. New names swam into my ken: Theodore Roosevelt, Sampson and Schley, 'Fighting Joe' Wheeler, Calixto García; Santiago, San Juan Hill, El Caney. The war was but a hundred miles from the northern shore of Jamaica. I strove to visualise what was happening over there. In May 1898, my sisters and I were taken to Kingston by our mother. I saw a Spanish ship lying in the harbour, interned. The thrill it gave me to establish this link with historical reality was something I did not understand then. I desired even more vivid contacts, but serious fighting by the North Americans had scarcely begun when it was all over.

The visit to Kingston had importance in another way. My infancy there being virtually a blank on the screen of memory, I was seeing a big town for the first time. I told myself solemnly that the country must be superior to any city, yet aspects of the new phenomenon enthralled me. The obvious things can be passed over: the massed buildings that appeared so imposing, the shops, the numerous horse-drawn cars, the rhythm of crowds in the streets. The impression made by colours, sounds and warmth proved to be more keen.

Kingston was completely tropical, which the pen in the mountains was not. Here breadfruit with thick, enormous leaves stood in many backyards, while in others were richer mangoes, ackees and almonds than those of the hills. Palms towered everywhere, their fronds as if cast in metal when the atmosphere was still, fluttering and clashing musically when the trade winds blew. Royal poinciana and lignum vitae decked the season with a pageantry of colour. Bougainvillea rioted in splendour above doorways and along the tops of walls. All hues stood out in intense relief. The languid air gave a dreamy quality to the tones of church bells, to the cries of vendors passing through the lanes upon which the yard doors of residences opened. Bathing in stone tubs where the water stood overnight to cool was a signal luxury. On that short visit the seduction of tropical towns entered my blood, never to be displaced.

A YEAR BETWEEN THE AGES of twelve and thirteen makes an immense difference, and more so when a boy is precocious. The news that came in 1899 was fully comprehended by me and stirred me profoundly. It was the Boer War. Rider Haggard's novels had attracted me to South Africa. I had read magazine articles about the diamond and gold fields of the Rand, the exploits of Cecil Rhodes, Paul Kruger, the big-game hunter Fred Selous, and various black kings from Tchaka to Lobengula. Now there was to be a coup to bring the whole country under the British flag, and for a moment that appeared glorious to me. I was a young Britisher uncritical of the eternal verities like Queen Victoria, the imperial system, and the Union Jack. The newspapers uttered jingoistic sentiments which I endorsed. Illustrated periodicals from England blossomed forth with coloured inserts of generals in scarlet tunics blazing with medals, and I thought them warriors of the first order. On to Pretoria!

But accounts of the mustering of the Boer commandos began to be published and my interest shifted its base. These men were stockraisers and planters with background similar to that of my own family. Fathers and sons reported together for war by taking down their rifles from the wall, mounting their best horses and proceeding to a rallying point, where officers chosen from among themselves assumed leadership. Their cause was what? Why, liberty pure and simple, as between them and the British. The right to maintain the small Transvaal and Orange River republics, to be an individualistic people. I asked my father about it, and he rather shamefacedly admitted that this time England was following an evil course. He said he could not help wishing the Boers luck. Most of our neighbours were unreflecting chauvinists, but there was one penkeeper who bluntly took the opposite stand and incurred some harsh criticism. A few objectors spoke out in England. A rising Welsh MP named David Lloyd George addressed meetings as a pro-Boer, was pelted with offal for it, but persisted stubbornly.

As for me, I had gone over to the side of the bearded farmers in their slouch hats, their bandoleers slung across plain hunters' coats, men of deadly marksmanship and hard riding. I studied their campaigns with ardour. The stinging early lessons they gave the blundering Tommies were a triumph of poetic justice. Aghast, the British poured a quarter of a million men under Roberts and Kitchener into South Africa, and the Boers were doomed. My sympathy remained with them, down to the last guerrilla raid by de Wet, who evaded every trap till the finish. Nevertheless, I was fascinated throughout by the figure of Rhodes, chief instigator of the rape of the republics, who died before the war ended, supposedly murmuring: "So much to do, so little done!" and left instructions for his grandiose burial on a summit of the Matopo Hills. There was no contradiction, really, in my dual partiality. I was temperamentally in favour of freedom for Boers no less than Cubans. But in Cecil Rhodes I saw genius concerned with large ends and working by means of the pursuit and exercise of power. About this time – there was, no doubt, an association of ideas – I began to muse on the role of my native island in the British Empire. Jamaica's story became one of my chief subjects. I read inadequate books treating of it, which were all that I could lay my hands on. I collected in a scrapbook every item of folklore and personal reminiscence I found in the newspapers.

When I was fifteen my father stopped giving me regular lessons. But he coached me further on the themes I wanted to pursue. As he was not a professional teacher and made no attempt to prepare me for college, I may be said to have left his care technically uneducated. I have had no cause to regret that I never sat in a classroom, never took a formal examination in any subject. If I decided in later life to learn a new language, or something else, I got the manuals and taught myself. It is worth noting that at fifteen I was more widely read in world history than I have found the average university graduate to be. My favourite book, apart from the English poets, was Macaulay's *Essays*, and I knew it backwards.

CHAPTER 2 ❧ **Journalism in Kingston**

IT WAS TAKEN FOR GRANTED AT HOME THAT I was not born to be a penkeeper, in spite of my boyish interest in the animals and crops. What, then, should I adopt as a calling? There were only a few choices for a white youth who had not had specialized training abroad. He could enter some branch of the colonial administration, in which case the appointment would be obtained by pull, after the form of passing a very easy examination had been observed. He could be articled to a lawyer and get admitted to the bar at the end of some years of dubious apprenticeship. The Anglican theological college that my father had attended would welcome him as an aspirant to the cloth. Commerce scarcely figured as a possibility, for it was regarded with scorn by all families with a plantation or professional background.

The Church had no attraction for me as a career. I played with the idea of joining the Public Works Department, because that seemed to promise adventurous roving about the island. My mother picked the law as the most genteel prospect and went so far as to open negotiations with a successful attorney in Mandeville who was the representative of the parish in the Legislative Council. At once I was seized with an emotion approaching panic. The things my father had said about the law had had a profound effect upon me. I conceived it to be the dullest of occupations, a bondage to the work of rooting among arid records. Later I became aware that I had done an injustice to a calling that has its philosophical and its picaresque sides, but at best it would not have suited my temperament.

Actually I had not swerved from my early resolve to be a writer. But I had assumed that in that small community I would have to make literature an avocation rather than a vocation. It now struck me that there was no reason why I should not have a try at the newspapers. I had been in frequent correspondence with the *Gleaner* and the *Times*, which never failed to publish the contributions I sent them. Payment had been confined to the Christmas contest prizes. A regular reporter would be placed on salary, however. I decided that journalism was the only work I could contemplate with any pleasure.

I clamoured against the law with such unexpected vigour that my mother gave up her plan. It was agreed that I should study shorthand, in view of the popular myth that all reporters took down public speeches verbatim and made exhaustive notes while interviewing celebrities. My father sent for textbooks and gave lessons to my sisters, too, on the theory that they might one day want to be private secretaries. I disliked shorthand and did not become fast at it, but my eagerness to acquire an open-sesame enabled me to stamp the chief symbols on my brain. The dream side of my existence was now dominated by poetry and romantic love, which may seem to pair strangely with my decision to be a journalist, but was not so regarded by me.

Following Shakespeare, whom my father had taught me to worship, and Keats, whom I discovered for myself, I was infatuated for a while with Tennyson, particularly the ardours and heroics of his *Maud*. Then Swinburne fell into my hands, and I was stunned with admiration of his extraordinary metres, the beauty of his rhymes and the pungency of his images. He was the great music-maker, the absolute lyrist, and I have so valued him ever since. I wrote more and more verse myself. Luckily an instinct saved me from attempting to copy the masters. I vied with our contemporary local poets, such as Tom Redcam, my pleasure being keener when one of us succeeded in doing well with a Jamaican rather than a general subject. Idealistically, silently, I fell in love with a girl in her early twenties, Clara Maude Garrett, who lived nearby and was one of our best poets. As it chanced, she was the first person to lend me a copy of Swinburne's works. She was like a Tennysonian heroine herself. Swinburne shocked her a little. But that made no difference to me.

The time soon came when I felt sufficiently well-equipped with shorthand to ask the editor of the *Gleaner* for an interview. My parents said that if he proved responsive I could go to Kingston to see him. A letter from me

Figure 6. Clara Maude Garrett, "at about 18", so around 1898. MS353.6.4.

was in the mails next day. Back came a friendly reply, and with what I thought dramatic and remarkable speed I was on my way. The single track at the Williamsfield railway station curved around a hill, so that I could hear the train coming before I saw it. A whistle blew, and a whorl of smoke shot above the lush fruit trees, the glittering palms. I watched for the appearance of the engine as for a portent. Standing at the edge of the platform, I let the wheels grind by, a prickly sensation running up and down my spine, my cheeks flushing hot. It seemed marvellous to evade the monster by inches, to feel its breath, and then with a sense of power in me to mount the steps that led to a coach. The train became a thing dominated, bearing me to an outside world of action.

It is curious that this should be one of the key memories of my youth, for I have not been charmed by the mechanized aspects of the century. The train, however, was a symbol of my innate unrest, and at the same time the only mechanical force with which I had had contact. I was sixteen years and two months old, and I had travelled on the railroad scarcely six times. Almost I could see in my mind's eye the interminable trains of the future that would carry me across continents, or that I would note as they went roaring by on the business of war.

Two half-sisters of my father lived in town at a house called Mon Désir on West Race Course. I slept the night there and started out early in the forenoon to find my editor. The *Gleaner*'s building was suggestive of a dingy warehouse. It stood rather far to the west on Harbour Street, where the city began to fray out into palm-studded slums, and the white dust lay thick. The business department occupied the ground floor. A short independent stairway led to the upper storey, and to reach the editorial offices screened off at the rear you crossed a composing room filled with men and a few women setting type by hand. I saw stacked rolls of newsprint and for the first time caught the whiff of printers' ink in my nostrils. The combination would never fail to excite me thereafter, in an odd way. It evoked the idea of a weapon that I longed to grasp.

I was self-conscious, a little awkward, that morning in spite of my eagerness, as a boy showed me to the desk of William Pringle Livingstone. A more kindly editor than this middle-aged Scotsman can seldom have existed. He wore a heavy brown moustache with short ends that cupped his lips. His eyes were sympathetic, and his low burred voice was calmly sagacious. He put me at my ease by talking about himself, telling me how greatly he loved newspaper work and what varied opportunities it had given him. In addition to running the *Gleaner*, he was the West Indian correspondent of the *Times*, a post that enabled him to make trips to all the Caribbean countries. I thought it the most fascinating career imaginable, as he described it to me. His hero, he said, was the explorer and missionary Dr David Livingstone, who I believe was not related to him; but his chief literary enthusiasm was for the work of Robert Louis Stevenson.

Figure 7. W.P. Livingstone, writer and editor, with whom Roberts travelled to the United States in 1904. MS353.6.8.

Livingstone then passed to the matter of my hopes. He asked me – perhaps slyly, to give me pleasure – whether I was the son of Mr Roberts who had won a recent prize contest. I let no false modesty deter me from assuring him that I myself had been the winner. He nodded several times warmly, said that my writing showed considerable precocity, but that I must not let that blind me to the difficulties ahead. I had practically everything about journalism to learn. The speed at shorthand which I claimed would not help me much. I should go on practising, for it was useful in some kinds of reporting. He was willing to put me on the staff as a sort of apprentice at the nominal salary of fifteen shillings a week, and after that we should see what we should see.

To be honest, I paid almost no attention to his homily, which was too wise and sober to fit my ebullient mood. It was my opinion that I could learn any technique with ease. The important, the exciting thing was to be accepted into the calling. Literally any assignment that one could be given on a newspaper was a chance to know the world and to write about it. Pay at the start was inconsequential, for wealth would follow success as a matter of course. I had derived only the vaguest notion of a wage-earner's financial problems from our life off the land at home.

The date for joining the *Gleaner* was set for a couple of weeks later. The second editor whom I was anxious to meet and to whose office I now hurried was Thomas Henry MacDermot of the *Jamaica Times*, he who wrote poetry under the name of Tom Redcam. I found him in a small, dark cubbyhole up one flight of stairs on Mark Lane in the heart of Kingston. His weekly paper was having a hard struggle to keep alive. It had been started a few years before by an Englishman named Walter Durie who managed the business end. The extent to which MacDermot bore the journalistic burden with only a couple of boys to help him was not then realized by me.

I introduced myself as one of his contributors and could hardly wait to tell him that I had just been given a job on the *Gleaner*. His lean zealot's face above the standing collar of a white coat cut like a soldier's tunic is among my clearest memories of the period. He was a very different type from Livingstone. This man in his early thirties was a Jamaican by birth, a pallid brunet, nervous and intense. Notwithstanding his Irish ancestry, he was as definitely Caribbean as any of his literary confrères in nearby Latin countries.

MacDermot gave me a welcome to Kingston that was phrased almost fervidly, and instead of talking to me about the difficulties ahead of me before I could become a good reporter, he complimented me on my choice of local themes for my poetry and said that it was the duty of rising talents to help create a Jamaican literature. He was fully as ardent as me, and along with it austere, which I have never been. I found his personality more moving than that of Livingstone.

Upon returning to Berry Hill, I set about packing my few treasured belongings, disposing of others, and bidding an almost ceremonious farewell to my youth of delight in nature. I went to certain loved spots in the woods and on grassy hillsides, where I built small cairns for remembrance. Parting with human beings was less difficult, for there was no doubt in my mind that I should see them all again. I visited my poetess, of course, and rejoiced when she promised to correspond with me. Her home was a bungalow where honeysuckle and jasmine festooned the railings of the deep verandas, and where the lawn was bordered by old-fashioned flowers: damask roses, tiger lilies, cannas, gladioli and love-in-the-mist. She was ethereal to me with her small bones, pink complexion and dreamy grey eyes. I felt sure that I would never love anyone else. The enthusiasms we shared might even bring about the miracle of her loving me, and then the difference in our ages would not matter at all. Ah, romance, romance! How wonderful it is at sixteen!

Finally I was off to Kingston again, full of zeal. It had been arranged that my aunts would board me at the house on West Race Course. I was given a room in a one-storey annex at the rear of the yard, a place where the sounds at night were the scuttling of geckoes along the walls and ceiling, the croaking of tree frogs in the garden next door, the crowing of cocks that started all over the neighbourhood long before the darkness lessened, the clap-clap of the bare feet of servants going about their tasks at dawn.

My first assignment was to a session of the resident magistrate's court. I mention it for the record. Doubtless most reporters have had their start with a Monday-morning docket of police cases. It gave me immense pleasure to see about a stick and a half, written by me, in the next morning's paper. Toward the end of the week Livingstone told me to go with one of the political reporters to the afternoon session of the Legislative Council and see what I could pick up. Headquarters House, where it sat, was a former private mansion of the plantation type of architecture on a grandiose scale, reached by an exterior flight of stone steps. The legislature met in what had been the ballroom, rather crowded now by the dais for the governor of Jamaica acting as Speaker, the desks for some thirty members, tables for the clerks and for the press, and a few rows of benches to which the public was admitted. I enjoyed marching in privileged fashion to the press table, where reporters were industriously transcribing the proceedings in the shorthand I detested. It took me several minutes to orientate myself and to grasp who was who.

A tall, imposing-looking figure had the floor. His aquiline features were strong, and he wore a dark, full beard. A man in his early forties and at the height of his powers, he spoke with assurance, a subtle note of arrogance, on some problem of the moment that has slipped my mind. I was looking at Sydney Olivier, a very early member of the Fabian Society of London, easily the most distinguished official that England has sent to Jamaica in my day, a future governor and the only one to rule the island to its indisputable benefit. He had arrived three years before as colonial secretary, the ranking subordinate post. I watched him and listened to him, fascinated, as he clarified points for his stodgy chief, Sir Augustus Hemming, and turned at intervals to lecture the members on the elected side of the House.

I knew how the Legislative Council was composed under the Crown Colony system, but it had not occurred to me until then to question its rightness or its dignity. The heads of certain departments, all Colonial Office career men, had ex-officio seats. So had the commander of the military forces. The governor added to their number, by appointment, sufficient resident Englishmen and Jamaicans in whom he had confidence to create an administration majority of one. The rest of the members, the submerged half, were returned by the parishes on a franchise severely restricted by property qualifications. The legislature that resulted was advisory only. It could not initiate anything, but debated and voted on the measures laid before it. Nor was it necessary for the governor to accept a 'decision' that might have chanced to go against him. He could veto or override.

The so-called people's representatives attracted my eye. They were planters, merchants, lawyers, doctors, clergymen – upper-class whites or coloured men of a light shade, with one exception. Most of them had heavy moustaches and were dressed, for this formal occasion, in serge or broadcloth most unsuitable for the tropics. The type was a matter of course to me; I would have found it hard to credit any other with being entitled to speak for Jamaica. That was why the exception, the black Alexander Dixon from the parish of St Elizabeth, moved me to a startled but not unfriendly interest. I looked upon him as a freak product of the system. In his modest ambition to be liked by his colleagues he had been successful.

When Olivier had finished his address, several of the white elected members made remarks. They spoke floridly, emptily, as even I in my limited experience could judge. The mild objections that they uttered were similar to those of pupils arguing with a teacher, and presently they were verbally rapped over the knuckles by the colonial secretary. Governor Hemming made some peevish observations from the chair. He struck me as being a stupid individual, with his vacant military type of countenance and claptrap phrases. I wondered why an official who had won no fame in the world should be governor of Jamaica, anyway. Olivier's presence was much more than that of a chief executive. The bill, whatever it was about, came to a vote and was passed with a smattering of nays from the opposition.

That routine episode was destined to influence my life. It might not have impressed me so deeply if Olivier had been less able, and had not been a man to whom I would later give a reasoned admiration. A session conducted wholly by nonentities would probably have been accepted by me at sixteen as the thing to be expected in legislatures, and I would have forgotten it. But the spectacle of the brilliant Fabian bullying men chosen to represent Jamaica stuck in my memory.

I asked Livingstone on my return to the office what sort of report I should turn in. He shook his head and replied that the political staff would attend to that. On the other hand, had I noted some human-interest point that would be worth a paragraph? Had I talked with any of the members in the lobby and sought personal news items? I answered that I had been too absorbed by the main business to think of side issues. He smiled tolerantly and said that he had intended the visit to be educational, but that I must remember a reporter's duty was perpetually to be on the lookout for news, great or small.

Sydney Olivier had seemed interesting to me, I ventured, and perhaps he would give me an interview for the *Gleaner*. But Livingstone said it would be some time before I was experienced enough to interview a high official. His voice very Scotch all of a sudden, he added that Olivier was a socialist. He didna hold that against the man, but there were people in Jamaica who did. This amazed me, for I had read of socialists only in connection with the 1848 revolutions in Europe, the Paris Commune and plots against the Russian Czar. In what sense could Olivier be a socialist? I noted mentally that I must find out.

There followed a varied list of assignments, most of them trivial: the meetings of societies, concerts, lectures and so on. I am sure that I performed inadequately. Sent to King's House to cover a ball given by the governor, I paid little attention to the names of guests and the details of costumes, but wrote a poetical impression of the human throng, the jasmine-scented verandas, and the swarms of fireflies competing with the Japanese lanterns amid the tropic shrubbery. That this story, pruned, should have appeared in the paper can only have been due to the good nature of my editor, who did not want to discourage me, for it was far from being a report of the social event in question.

Abruptly Livingstone tried a different approach. He ordered me to do a special article on the fishermen who operated out of Kingston harbour and supplied the public markets. My enquiry was to be thorough. That was something I could get enthusiastic about. I roved the waterfront at the east end of town and beyond, penetrating to stretches of untidy beach shadowed by coconut palms, where dugout canoes had been run up onto the sand, and sloops with reefed brown sails rocked alongside sagging wharves barely twenty feet long, while man-of-war birds wheeled overhead. I spoke with taciturn men who used a dialect of which no foreigner could have made anything. I climbed over their boats, examined their nets, and soaked myself in the atmosphere of the hard and ill-rewarded lives they lived. The result was a piece of a column and a half long that was featured in the paper, though without a signature. Others of a like nature succeeded it.

The truth of the matter was that I had very little instinct for the gathering of news as such, subconsciously esteeming it a labour I preferred to leave to the drudges. My interest was in getting to the bottom of things that made the world move, in analysing personalities and interpreting the news. I did not become a real reporter. I never have been one. Whenever I have seemed successful at the work, I was simply the beneficiary of a streak of luck. Instead of developing this, I reverted as quickly as possible to the methods of the feature writer. Jamaican journalism of the period ran to long-winded reports, and whether these dealt with foreign or local topics the events and persons had to be of recognized importance or outstanding as news. No attention was paid to the doings of the socially obscure. Headlines were most conservative. Special articles could branch out into the picturesque and the humanly significant, as in the case of my account of the fishermen.

GETTING ABOUT KINGSTON WITH REASONABLE speed was a problem in those days. The city stood on flat land, but except for a few of the downtown streets there was no attempt to provide continuous sidewalks. Each householder had done as he pleased about his communications. Some of the buildings had double exterior flights of steps running in the same direction as the street and leading to a platform in front of the gate. Others had level pavements. Between the two types of approach there might be a bank of rubble topped by a meandering path. Unless he kept to the thoroughfare, which had its disadvantages because of traffic and filth, a reporter was forced to do a deal of climbing in the course of his legwork. In the dry season an intolerable dust was kicked up at every step, the amenities of garbage-collecting and watering being very sketchily performed by the municipal council. Only the trade winds tempered the sunlight falling like a cataract. The shopping district was arcaded for the most part. It was pleasant to pass along the shadowy walks and breathe an air rich with tropical odours, such as things for sale do not give off in the present age of over-refinement and packaged goods. The scent of herbs from an apothecary's shop, for instance, the clean tang of leather, and occasional whiffs of rum, molasses and pimento from the warehouses of Port Royal Street.

A modest system of tram cars served Kingston and its environs. One line ran out along the Windward Road – a nostalgic name – to the far end of the harbour; a second to the Hope Botanical Gardens; and a third due north to Constant Spring. The cars were flimsy affairs painted a brownish yellow, open on both sides with curtains that could be pulled down when it rained. For short trips we depended upon an antique model of horse cab which we called a bus. They were really small buggies drawn by a single horse. They cluttered the busier streets and could cause traffic jams in encounters with commercial vehicles or some exceptional difficulty such as a funeral.

I recall arriving in a bus at a crossing where normal activity had been immobilized by an enormous and slow-moving funeral cortège. The hearse, nodding with black plumes, had just paced by, and the mourners' carriages stretched out of sight. My driver had promptly got himself entangled with other waiting buses, so that he could not even attempt a detour. I was in a hurry to reach the office, so I jumped out and seized an opportunity to dodge between two of the carriages to the opposite side of the street. An old mulatto touched my arm, horrified.

"Don't you know it's terrible bad luck to cross a funeral?" he said in a hollow voice, and added: "Most of all, *her* funeral."

"What's that? Who are they burying?" I asked.

"Madame Caesar."

Somehow the glare went pallid and an *ignis fatuus* appeared to flicker between the hearse and myself. Madame César, or Caesar, had been a noted voodoo woman, a Negress from Haiti, broad as a toad, whose clientele had not been confined to the illiterate. But I must have carried a countercharm, for the sense of menace subsided, and all that remained with me was an extraordinarily vivid memory of the scene.

In the pursuit of specials I did much wandering about the city at night. The peddlers interested me, the hawkers of country tobacco twisted in ropes, of peanuts and various sweets, of lemonade and ginger beer, and odds and ends of every description. Some had handcarts at fixed locations, others squatted on the ground and spread their wares on pieces of newspaper, and still others pushed barrows to the tune of traditional, sing-song calls. They were more numerous by day. The persistent ones who worked after dark, however, were better copy, notably on Saturdays when the markets and many shops kept late hours and life surged in the streets.

They had a hard lot. May their bones rest in peace. The background against which they moved is what dwells with me, and I doubt if its chiaroscuro effect could be paralleled in any big New World town today. Kingston had begun to use electricity for lighting, though not in the slums. The widely spaced street lamps were of gas, and they were left unlit on moonlit nights. Beyond the open windows of the poor an occasional gas jet without a shade flared starkly, helped out by smoking kerosene lamps and the primitive device of wicks anchored in a cup, or gourd, of coconut oil. Only a small radius around each spot of flame was illuminated. The rest was shadow in which vague forms stirred. Shops were even weirder than homes, because of the press of people in them. Often nothing was distinguishable of a black face except the eyeballs, then a flashing of teeth. The heads of women wearing folded kerchiefs bobbed in and out of the circles of light. These half-visible crowds chattered endlessly and broke into wild laughter. A hullabaloo issued from dim rum bars on the corners. Some blocks, as on Orange Street, would have seemed death traps to an outsider. But they were merely squalid and all too human. I roamed them without threat of harm. Recognized haunts of criminals existed, of course. I avoided these unless I were out on a news story.

IN WELL-TO-DO CIRCLES, SOCIAL LIFE outside the home was almost entirely confined to men. Kingston had been made the capital instead of Spanish Town only thirty-one years before; it still had the atmosphere of a city dominated by its merchants, with whom visiting planters hobnobbed. They met on the common ground of pessimism over business, a passion for horse racing and a taste for good rum and cigars. The Jamaica Club on Hanover Street was their chief rendezvous. I was invited there by a relative on rare occasions. But Burke's Geisha Café on Harbour Street, the sole place in town that could honestly claim to be a café, had more allure for me. Though I had not yet learned to take hard liquor, I would drop in at the Geisha with some reporter and feel grown-up as I sipped a glass of sherry.

There was nothing resembling a literary bohemia in Kingston, no restaurants or drinking spots where writers gathered. Parties at private houses were the means of contact, except for haphazard meetings at general cultural centres such as the Athenaeum and the Institute of Jamaica. Yet talent was effervescing, more of it I imagine than at any previous moment in the history of the island. I do not count the handful of British journalists among us, for they were birds of passage; until the eve of my arrival these had included a Scot with a Kiplingesque touch named Stephen Chalmers, who went on to a brief career of some distinction on New York newspapers, but who was invalided by tuberculosis and ended up as a writer of mystery novels.

The native-born were for the most part young men of mixed blood. A group of three inseparables struck me as being singular cards, their pose being a facetious cynicism and sophistication quite new to me. They were Herbert George de Lisser, the son of a former editor of the *Gleaner*, Walter Parker, and Gerald Hamilton. De Lisser and Hamilton wore short, curly beards that made them look like French colonials of the period. They wrote essays on exotic subjects, such as foreign literary trends and the role of the Roman Catholic Church in world politics. This virtuosity aroused my envy. Parker was the news editor of the *Daily Telegraph* and did not have much leisure for writing.

I was particularly impressed by de Lisser, a sound choice because he was the one marked for achievement. Hamilton left shortly to work on a Panama newspaper and dropped out of sight. Parker died prematurely. But de Lisser became by far the most powerful editor of his generation in Jamaica, as well as an author of parts. The friendship we formed at that time was never shaken by our clashes of opinion over large issues in years to come. When I met him de Lisser was full of enthusiasm for Sydney Olivier and he commended me for my interest. It appeared that the colonial secretary had upset the conservatives of Kingston by giving a series of lectures on Fabian socialism, which de Lisser had attended. To both of us, as we talked it over, the doctrine was less stimulating than the man. Here was a leader type who personified change, a word which it was easy at my age to confuse with liberty. Nevertheless, a seed rooted itself in my subconscious and its name was socialism.

The immediate inspiration by MacDermot held its lead, though he was so busy that he could give me but little of his company. This poet-editor had a touch of the saint about him; he did not know it, but he had been born too soon for the nationalist role he could have filled to perfection, and so he threw himself into compensating tasks. It was not enough that he should work himself almost to death on the *Times*. He gave his service at night to organizations that helped discharged prisoners and stranded sailors. Also, he did a prodigious amount of reading. I often passed him in the mornings striding down to his office, his nose and big moustache sunk in a book, while his feet mechanically steered a course for themselves.

At the institute, which included among its many activities our only public library, sat Frank Cundall, an oracle rather than a friend. He was an Englishman in his forties whose life had been, and would be to the end, devoted to the creation of a library, art centre and museum for Jamaica. His collection of reference works on West Indian history was particularly valuable. He was a bit aweing when one consulted him, and I think he liked to produce that effect. The information sought was always forthcoming, lavishly, with an air of the time spent on it being of no consequence. But it would have irked Cundall not to be acknowledged as the high court of appeal on historical facts. I knew one other Englishman who in a large way and without a backward look had cast his lot with Jamaica. He was Enos Nuttall, the Anglican archbishop, admittedly a giant of his order. He once commended to me the old saw about genius being an infinite capacity for taking pains. But there was an ironical glint in his eye when he said it. Nuttall assuredly went on the principle that genius was innate – with an infinite capacity for seeing to it that others took pains.

I ACQUIRED SOUND EXPERIENCE ON the *Gleaner* for the better part of a year, but got no increase in salary. Even my noncommercial spirit began to feel a little resentful. Then Livingstone disclosed a plan that had a place in it for me, and I found it much more dazzling than an ordinary promotion would have been. He intended to resign from the *Gleaner* and start a weekly paper of his own, to be called the *Leader*. I was to be his sub-editor and would be paid a pound a week at the start: one could live on that sum in the Kingston of those days. But what was that compared with the chance to help run a paper at seventeen? I was to write as well as do copy-reading and make-up. Livingstone had judged me carefully. He said that this sort of work would be my forte, yet I should not disregard the useful stepping-stone of reporting.

A couple of months were spent over plans, revamping dummies, soliciting advertisements and preparing special features for the first issue of the *Leader*. My chief contribution was an article on the prophet Alexander Bedward, a nine-days' wonder just then because of his sudden rise from petty notoriety to a fantastic success with the ignorant. His chapel was at August Town, a village within five miles of Kingston, but buried in a fold of the hills and hard of access. There he had baptized in the Hope River some six thousand converts, and more were flocking to him from all over the island.

I went in the streetcar as far as it would take me and got off at the Papine corner, close to the spot where the buildings of the University College are now being erected on the most beautiful site enjoyed by any university in the tropics. The mountains swept in a circle that formed an arena of almost perfect symmetry: mountains that soared in tiers, their peaks and valleys heaped in a close formation, blue merging into purple far away, a yellowish-green nearby mottled by the drifting shadows of clouds. I absorbed the visual impression for a moment, then turned down a footpath through the scrub to August Town.

From a scrapbook I find that I began my article: "A tall and broadly-built black man, with a round, somewhat mild and inscrutable face, moustache and side whiskers just beginning to turn grey; dressed in a rough suit of tweed with a collarless shirt and an old-fashioned black felt hat. Such is a hasty pen-portrait of the redoubtable Bedward." He said that he had founded a "free sect" of the Baptist Church to which he had given the name of Particular Baptists – the purest and only true branch, of course – and he was its bishop. Naive muddle-mindedness, I thought, since the Baptists had frowned from the start upon episcopacy. But the dark faces crowded about us, as we talked, and adoring comments referred to their shepherd, or their prophet, terms which evidently carried more weight with them than any churchly rank. If I had been there the previous Sunday, one member told me, I would have seen the chapel filled over and over, for the congregation had been so large the services had had to be repeated. Bedward smiled faintly like a bonze in ebony. The prophet of August Town was the first Jamaican popular leader in my times, and not altogether unconsciously there was a strain of political ferment in his revivalism. Others would take the same human material and brew a stronger draught. I saw him then simply as current grist for my most pretentious article to date.

The *Leader* made its appearance in January 1904. I walked about the streets with a pocketful of pennies and bought copies from every vendor I passed, this being one of Livingstone's canny ideas for stirring up interest. He was doing the same thing himself. Lethargic old Kingston took notice of that first issue, anyway, and I did not have the least doubt that we were going to be a success. Once launched, however, there would be only six days in which to get out the next number, and we really set to work.

Livingstone had arranged with the *Daily Telegraph* for composition and printing, and he and I shared a small office in that paper's building at 48 Church Street. It was a former private residence. In those days of handsetting of type and flatbed presses, the quarters sufficed. The printing was done on the ground floor. The composing room had been an upstairs front parlour, and the editorial offices had been bedrooms. Nooks and crannies were assigned to the business staff, likely enough the garrets and the outdoor rooms for servants that flanked the yards of ancient Kingston houses.

You mounted an interior staircase, turned to the left from a landing and went down three steps to reach the *Leader*'s office. The first storey did not remain at the same level for any distance. But we connected evenly with the composing room in which the cases of type stood too closely packed for comfort, each with an operator behind it. There were no labour unions in Jamaica then. The compositors were nearly all coloured, members of families that had long followed the calling, and had received their early training as apprentices. A fair number were girls.

The house was of stone finished off with a wooden superstructure. Its roof was pitched not too steeply and covered with cedar shingles. The walls of some of the rooms still carried paper in pretty designs like those of valentine cards, but dimmed by the moulds that formed in wet weather. Other walls had been stripped bare, such being the case in our office. To relieve the monotony, Livingstone hung a map of Jamaica and also a picture of his idol David Livingstone.

The whole place shook when the winds were high. A hurricane of secondary force, accompanied by torrential rain, held everybody marooned on a June day for hours beyond suppertime. I stood behind the front door that opened onto a typical stone platform and watched Church Street become a river that bore debris of all sorts, tossing and whirling, toward the harbour. The air was full of twigs torn from the trees. The water rose quickly until it almost lapped into the creaking house, and then started to recede. I told myself that it would not require much more pressure to bring the building down. Yet its frame proved stout. Two and a half years afterward, when luckily for me I was far away, an earthquake cracked and crumbled its interior walls at a stroke.

The *Leader* made little attempt to cover the news, except by rewriting important stories from the daily press. Our sixteen-page weekly was based upon editorial comment, general and literary features and correspondence from the country parts. I look back with a sort of amazement at my facility of production, the fanatic energy that possessed me. It was the full flowering of my precocity, and there was something frenzied about it. I did every job that came up at top speed, working by hand since typewriters had not reached Jamaican newspaper offices, and if we had had one I should not have known how to operate it. I dashed out to get interviews and wrote personality sketches of local worthies. I ran a literary column, invented a humorous character who held forth every week in dialect, reviewed books, did special articles, reported lectures and concerts. Finally, as it became more difficult to fill space because of our meagre showing of advertisements, I light-heartedly turned to fiction and each Sunday at home reeled off a long instalment of a serial.

Livingstone, of course, wrote the editorials and also did a great deal of the sheer drudgery. Getting out the paper became less a routine than a smoothly running effort that exhilarated me. But at the end of three months the *Times* ordered Livingstone on an assignment to Haiti, the Dominican Republic and Venezuela. This was a crisis for the *Leader*. Livingstone thought of resigning as correspondent of the *Times*, but could not bring himself to take that step. He asked me if I thought I could carry on alone for several weeks, with a cub reporter to help me and with Robert C. Guy, the editor of the *Telegraph*, to fall back upon in case of trouble. A Scot named Kirkpatrick would act as business manager.

Throughout my life I have been stimulated by responsibility, and the feeling was already strongly developed. I jumped at the chance offered. The fact that my salary would be doubled had little to do with my eagerness. So Livingstone sailed on his trip, and I was a managing editor at seventeen. The only check upon me was that Guy would write the editorials, or if I wished to try my hand at some they would have to be approved by him.

My curiously matter-of-fact friendship with Guy ran its brief course during the absence of Livingstone. Guy was still another Scot, I judged about fifty years old, short and stout, with a baldish head and a moderate moustache of the walrus type. Everyone agreed that he was a sound editor who took a forthright, liberal stand in public affairs. Of temperament he had not a sparkle, none of Livingstone's altruism, MacDermot's romantic ardour, or de Lisser's exotic cleverness. Guy had started as a Presbyterian minister, but was now wholly a journalist, well-read and a good talker.

I found that I often had to go to him for technical advice. This he gave cheerfully and tersely. When the rush was not too great he would ask me to stop a moment for a chat. I got the impression that if he had thought I was bungling the work he would have overruled me in a minute. On the other hand, the *Leader* was not his paper, and as he had consented only to act as a court of appeal, he refrained from hunting for trouble. He never remarked on my precocity either to warn or praise me. The closest he came to it was an occasional quizzical look when I mentioned plans for the next issue.

More than once he asked me what I had in mind for my future. Was I certain what I most wanted to do? I replied, with variations, that my ambition was to write books sooner or later, books growing out of my newspaper experience, and perhaps novels. Then Guy would throw himself back in his chair and discourse about the hardships suffered by those who attempted serious authorship. He told me of men and women who half starved in lodgings in the great capitals, gambling for the few prizes that fell to the profession. I would be astonished to know, he said, how little was actually earned by writers regarded as eminent. He cited some Scotch names, including that of Ian Maclaren who was then having a vogue. He was a friend of Ian Maclaren's and could assure me that most years Maclaren did not make as much out of writing as the editor of an average newspaper, or a feature reporter on a big one, received in salary.

I asked if there were not other rewards, and he answered: "Oh, yes! There are fame and influence of a different sort than the journalist enjoys. Myself, I prefer to jog along without worrying too much about cash."

"Do you think I ought to stick to newspaper work?"

"Yes. You'd do well enough at it. But if you're set on writing books, you'll probably write them."

He did not convince me of anything in particular, yet I learned much from the bland bonhomie of Guy.

The volume of my work for the *Leader* increased, for the assistant proved lazy. I was pretty well bound down to the office, and on the nights before we went to press I often corrected proofs until three in the morning. Yet I managed to find time for interviews. I thought of seeing the governor, whom I resented as a shallow-pated martinet, and doing an ironical sketch of him; but I decided that that indiscretion would not be fair – to my absent chief. As for Olivier, an article about him had been written for the weekly by Livingstone, much to my disappointment, because I had wanted the assignment. I did not get an opportunity to do more than exchange words in passing with the gifted colonial secretary. I recall writing a warm report of a lecture on Dante which he gave at the Athenaeum. That he was a lover of poetry, and moreover himself the author of some excellent sonnets, was to me additional evidence that lifted him fabulously above the level of his colleagues in our imported government.

There were other exceptions, of course, but the average English official in Jamaica was not admirable. I use the word *English* advisedly, for the Scots, Irish and Welsh among us were adaptable for the most part, and so one liked them. The Colonial Office had long since ceased to regard the island as being even a second-rate colony, this Jamaica that in the lush days of the sugar bonanza in the eighteenth century had been accounted the most valuable overseas possession of the British Crown. It had slipped into the third class, being no longer profitable *per se* to England and useful chiefly as a place in which jobs could be found for third-raters.

The heads of department were likely to be weary nonentities hoping for a last promotion to Ceylon or Hong Kong. The juniors were fellows who had not quite measured up to the standard required for India. Pro-English snobs among my contemporaries, of the kind that called England 'home' though they had never been there and turned up the cuffs of their trousers when they heard it was raining in London, would have been scandalized if I had told them how I felt. I was not ready to be aggressive about the matter in words. The fact remained that it was hard for me to bear the English civil servant in our midst.

As a reporter I had to see a good many of them in their offices. They greeted the pressman, as they called him, condescendingly, and seemed unsure whether a person who wanted to pry into governmental affairs should not be regarded as impertinent. They said they would rather I did not mention their names in my paper, yet yielded easily to persuasion on that score. Once I went to King's House at night on an important story and was stopped on the veranda by an aide-de-camp who refused me admittance to the precincts because I was not wearing evening dress. It happened that a ball was being held. After a long delay an individual of some note (in a swallow tail) came out, interviewed me under a poinciana tree, and with signs of marked distaste gave me the facts needed. These were trivialities. I hesitate to say how much incompetence existed in the administration, for I was too immature to judge; certainly there was a good deal of lethargy and ignorance of local conditions. Jamaicans in office might have done little better at the time, but as Kipling says somewhere, they would at least have talked my talk and practised the deceptions to which I was accustomed.

DURING THE FIFTH MONTH OF the *Leader*'s career Livingstone returned with beguiling stories of his journey. All went normally for a few weeks longer. When the blow fell it shocked me, for I had not given a thought to the business end of the venture. The paper had been losing money steadily and would have to be dropped. Livingstone made a point of assuring me that the editorial work had been competently done. The fault lay in his having begun with insufficient capital. It usually took at least a year for a new paper to show profits, and he had gambled on the hope of an immediate hit. We continued to publish until the end of the seventh month, in order to fulfil advertising contracts. Then the *Leader* quietly folded up. The action of my latest serial halted in mid-air, never to be resumed.

Now what? It felt strange to be suddenly without an occupation. De Lisser had been appointed editor of the *Gleaner*, and if I had asked him for a job I imagine he would have given me one. But ever since I had started in journalism I had planned eventually to go to the United States as the larger field would probably be rewarding. I had talked this over with my parents. True to form, my mother thought that Toronto, Canada, would be the safest place for me on the grounds that it was reputedly very law-abiding and English in spirit. My father suggested New Orleans, arguing that the climate was mild and that I would fit more easily into a life that did not differ radically from that of a Caribbean country. The New Orleans idea naturally was preferred by me, and it had come to be tacitly accepted in the family that that was where I would go. Livingstone had pooh-poohed Toronto, saying that the standard of literary work there was low and that all the good reporters cleared out for the United States as soon as they could. He regarded New Orleans, however, as a backwater.

I brought up the matter again with him after the *Leader* failed. He advised me to head for New York as the journalistic centre of the New World. The implied confidence in my ability to make good there was too flattering to be resisted. If I cared to wait until the latter part of August, he added, I could travel with him part of the way, and that was a stroke of luck that appealed both to my parents and myself. Livingstone intended to study the Negro question in the Southern states. He would write articles on it for the *Times* and perhaps work them up into a book later on. My mother's mind was relieved at the prospect of his acting as a sort of guide and protector of my inexperience. I knew that, apart from the pleasure of his company, the chance to see a little of how he went to work as a correspondent would be pure gain.

My farewells in Manchester were in some sort a repetition – though more hurried and self-centred – of those of a year and a half earlier. This time I was cutting loose to seek my fortune, and no mistake about it. I pictured myself as a colourful adventurer whom everyone should envy. No doubt my father felt just that way about it. But the others fussed sentimentally, and I was a little impatient with them. Years might pass before I came back, but

I swore in all sincerity that nothing should prevent me from returning to Jamaica. What are years to a youth under eighteen!

Money, as ever, was scarce at home. The smallness of the sum raised for my steamship ticket and expenses while hunting for a job worried the family, for apparently I would reach the United States with less than a hundred dollars. A postponement was discussed. I would have none of that. In my insouciance I would have started on a much narrower margin. However, I sold my chestnut pony Aster for forty dollars, and rising his amiable phantom, so to speak, I set forth.

CHAPTER 3 ❧ **Baltimore and Northward**

A BANANA FREIGHTER NAMED THE *BARNSTABLE* WHICH HAD berths for only six passengers sailed from Port Antonio on the north coast, bound for Baltimore. This route to the United States was unusual, for nearly all travel was from Kingston to New York, Boston or New Orleans. But Livingstone preferred to land as close to Washington as possible, and neither of us despised the bargain rates on the freighter. Sentiment choked me as we glided out of the lovely, verdure-clad little haven with the Blue Mountains towering behind. A few hours afterward I was deathly seasick, a calamity that has smitten me on but two of my many sea voyages. I rallied dizzily to look at Cape Maisí, Cuba, the first foreign place I had seen, and then at San Salvador, the landfall of Columbus. It was not until we were clear of the Bahamas that I could revel in the novelty of toying dolphins, flying fish and the gorgeous phosphorescence of the wake at night.

Landing in the United States in 1904 was so simple a matter that it must seem like a myth today. No passport was required. An official wrote down a few basic facts about the immigrant, collected an eight-dollar head tax and waved him on his way. My opinion of Baltimore after we left the pier – it was 4 September, I think – was not favourable. This could scarcely have been otherwise, because the heart of the city had been swept by a fire the previous February, and most of the twenty-five hundred buildings destroyed were still heaps of rubble. Livingstone and I shared a room in the Joyce Hotel at the edge of the burned district. I was depressed by the view from the window. My feelings began to change the next morning, largely because

I found the Baltimore *Sun* an animating accompaniment to breakfast and decided that that was the paper on which I would like to work. Too, I was captivated by sliced peaches with Maryland cream, a notable contrast to the fruits of the tropics.

Later that day I walked through streets in the Mount Royal district that had escaped the fire, and I was much attracted by the ivy-covered fronts of the houses, as well as the neat, low, narrow flights of exterior steps which by local custom were of white stone, or painted white. These steps suggested to me the paws of seated cats. In the evening I went to the editorial office of the *Sun* and confidently asked for a job. Some underling looked faintly puzzled, perhaps by my accent. He told me that there was nothing doing, that they were laying off reporters. I, in turn, had to think twice before I grasped the meaning of his phrases. I saw that I had a lot to learn about the North American idiom.

Livingstone and I moved to a rooming house at 606 North Calvert Street. We took separate rooms there, he paying by the day and I for a week in advance. He had started his work by visits to Negro institutions in Baltimore. I had missed these because of my fruitless rounds of newspaper waiting rooms. When he announced that he was ready to go on to Washington, I went with him by train, accompanied him to Howard University and other Negro centres, and did a lot of sightseeing for two days. We looked in at the White House, hoping to shake hands with President Theodore Roosevelt, a privilege open to anyone without an appointment in those free-and-easy times. But it was a campaign year. The president, a candidate for re-election, was out of town, and we contented ourselves with sauntering through the White House at will. It would be hard to say whether I rated this and a subsequent tour through the Capitol ahead of the Zoological Gardens at Rock Creek and the Smithsonian Institution. For the lure of natural history was still strong, and I had never before seen a big zoo or museum.

Abruptly, as it seemed, Livingstone left for the South. I said goodbye to him at the railroad station on a Saturday night and returned to Baltimore. Now I was strictly on my own. The following is etched deeply because of an acid, the name of which was loneliness. A torrential rain poured in the morning, and my shabbily furnished room was dark, pervaded by the first chill of autumn. I dressed, temporized at the front door, then plunged across the street into the nearest restaurant. It was a second-rate place, with seats at a counter and a few tables. Buxom girls manipulated heavy crockery, and though they smiled at me kindly I had no heart to flirt with them. A boy came in with the Sunday papers. I bought one and pored over it while I ate peaches and cream.

Back in the room I pushed aside the shadows by writing letters to Jamaica, using a thin paper on which the ink ran and made many of the words illegible. This was to prove hard on my correspondents, but I thought only of killing a gloomy day and forgetting the naive chromos on the walls, the fly-specked mirror. The rain did not stop. I darted through it for lunch and again for dinner. I remained sad, ineloquent with the blonde Germanic-looking waitresses, not realizing that one of them would probably have been pleased to comfort me. So there was nothing memorable about the restaurant, or the dreary evening in my room. Yet I remember them.

The one place where I did not feel lonely during the next week was Druid Hill Park, on the outskirts of the city. The squirrels and the bronzing September leaves enchanted me. But I could not become a haunter of Druid Hill Park. A city-desk man at one of the newspapers gave me an idea. He asked if I could run a typewriter, and on my answering 'no', he suggested that I learn, since that would be an advantage in job hunting. I objected that it would be difficult and would take more time and money than I could spare. "Not at all," he said. "Any of the typewriter companies will teach you for nothing, or allow you to pick it up on their machines."

This unlikely sounding beneficence proved to be a fact. The typewriter was only just beginning to register as an office necessity, and the makers pushed it in every way possible. They ran free employment agencies for stenographers and typists. They had rows of desks in their salesrooms where any aspirant could come and practise. The teaching consisted of handing out printed instructions. I have never had an aptitude for machines, but I realized that this one was basically simple. Accuracy in hitting the keys was what mattered, and it could be acquired by doing the exercises over and over. So I went at it toilsomely. How I hated it. At the end of a week I could produce a clean page of typing, though at very moderate speed. I saw an advertisement for a reporter in a small city, unnamed, and I sent in an application describing my exotic merits. That I should have received a reply was due, I think, to the singular point of my letter being typed.

The editor of the *Daily Press*, Plainfield, New Jersey, wrote that he was willing to take me on trial for two weeks, at ten dollars a week. If at the end of that time I had not turned out to be satisfactory he would refund my train fare. I consulted a map and learned that Plainfield was quite near to New York. That was in its favour, though my eagerness to get a start was so keen that I probably would have gone to any town in the United States. I left at once, having spent fifteen days in Baltimore, arrived early in the evening and reported at the *Press*. A round-faced chap, who looked more like a bookkeeper than an editor to me, glanced up from a neat desk and gave me a casual welcome. He said that the work would be just routine. Better come in at eight the following morning when I would be given a list of places at which to call regularly for news. He jotted for me the address of a boarding house, recommending it as preferable to the dollar-a-day hotel near the railway station where I had taken my bags.

The *Press* was a morning paper, and I thought it odd that its workday should start at the ungodly hour of eight. But I showed up as instructed and presently found myself the worst misfit that could be imagined. My list of calls included the marshal's office, the firehouse, two undertakers' establishments, three florists' shops, the studies of five ministers of the gospel and the YMCA. There had been no specific leads. These places were perpetual sources of information: a lawsuit now and then, or a two-alarm fire; but for the most part personal chit-chat about the citizens of Plainfield and their guests from out of town; who was courting who, what engagements had been announced, who was planning to give a party, who was ailing or dead. It irked me beyond reason to go around collecting such stuff about nonentities. That it was regarded as news appeared absurd to me. I simply could not get into the spirit of the American small-town paper as a gossip shop of what the folks were doing. By the end of the week I was miserable.

The police reporter and the men assigned to politics were the ones I envied; particularly the last-mentioned. But I knew that it took some familiarity with the life of a country, and even more so of a town, to write convincingly about its politics. Why should I be trusted to do it? I had a broad idea of the issues between Republicans and Democrats, and not the least notion of how the campaign was being fought in Plainfield, who was important and who unimportant. It was easy to discover that the community was heavily Republican, a faith shared by the *Press* whose editorials shone with that light diffused by a smug majority organ, though I believe it called itself independent. When, however, a courtly gentleman looked in at the newsroom one morning and happening to find me alone offered details of his activities as the Democratic candidate for Congress, I thought I had a story. Carefully I took down everything he said. His name was James E. Martine, and he had a statesmanlike air, with his full head of iron-grey hair, his broad forehead and goatee of the kind worn by Southern colonels in the cartoons. He vaunted his platform and he announced a large number of meetings to be held that month.

A copy-desk man and a reporter came in while we were talking. They watched impassively, but after Martine had given us each a cigar and left, they shook with merriment. "Old Jim's been taking advantage of you because you're new," the desk man said. "Why, he couldn't be elected to anything. He runs for a different office every election year. Cut that hot air of his to a stick, not a line more."

I agreed that the laugh was on me, while privately appraising the attitude toward a regular party candidate as queer. Surely the Democrats would get their turn in New Jersey someday? The joke wore another face when I was at last given a respite from the firehouse-undertakers-YMCA beat and sent to cover a church fair. Be sure not to overlook any names, I was told. James E. Martine was the sole individual I recognized, and he genially identified the rest for me. In return I wrote a complimentary paragraph about him, which somehow escaped the blue pencil. No other paragraph in my small quota of printed material in the Plainfield *Daily Press* afforded me the slightest satisfaction.

Of course, if I had been a natural reporter I should have adapted myself quickly and perhaps held the job. There was no Livingstone to nurse me along as a special-article man, and it did not surprise me when at the end of the fortnight the editor shook his head sadly and gave me my time. A fellow on the staff – Hackett was his name: I can see his lean, hawklike face – remarked: "Don't worry. We'll be hearing about you." I asked why he said that, and he answered carelessly, "Oh, you're clearly not one of the real ducklings!" Remembering the fairy story, I was grateful.

Plainfield left certain impressions that had nothing to do with the newspaper. Autumn marched in while I was there, making the first tang and flush of changing colour I had known in Baltimore seem petty. Now the trees, especially the maples, were a conflagration of scarlet and gold. Flowers such as chrysanthemums, which blossomed feebly and were lost against the tropical background in Jamaica, dominated the gardens with peculiar splendour. This was the fall about which I had read so much, the most vivid season of the North American year. I loved it when the days were sunny and soft, but these alternated with waves of a cold to which I was unaccustomed and gave me forebodings about the winter to come. The chittering of sparrows as they flocked, their feathers ruffled, on twigs from which leaves were falling had a sad sound to my ear. The half-rural town with its monotonous frame dwellings did not attract me. I felt that I would always prefer the opposite extremes of plantations or of cities.

On the same Sunday afternoon late in September I had my first ride in an automobile and my first jaunt in a birchbark canoe, the newest and oldest forms of transportation in North America. Acquaintances at the boarding house had driven me out to a park where there was a lake. Half of the friendly fun for them was the initiating of a confessed greenhorn. The experience taught me things about my own nature. It was exciting, of course, to start away in the Oldsmobile, a wonder for its time and not the clumsy, primitive vehicle it would seem today. But I took almost no interest in how it was operated. The noxious fumes it gave off, the rattling and the jerky motion soon irritated me. Unlike the thundering steam engine of a train, it did not convey a sense of might, and I thought it just a trivial invention. Why should anyone travel by choice in such a contraption? I asked myself. The current japes about motor cars in the newspapers were fully justified. If nothing else, the snorting, smoking wagons marred the scenery through which they chugged, both for passengers and passersby.

Then we came to the lake, a tranquil mirror under the pale, bland sunshine of autumn, while a blue haze hung suspended among the encircling trees. My friends' canoe was alongside a small landing stage. I followed instructions and stepped in carefully, taking the seat in the middle with a girl in front of me and a young fellow behind. They gave me a paddle, but told me not to use it until I had observed what they did. We shot across the surface of the water, the canoe like a living creature under me, fragile and perilous. I was enchanted. A few minutes later I was given a lesson in paddling, and I learned quickly.

A FRIEND I HAD MADE casually took me to New York one night in the middle of my Plainfield stay. For some curious reason, the memory is blurred, reduced to a phantasmagoria of crowds and lights. I was guided here and there on streetcars, my friend telling me that I was now on Broadway, now on Fifth Avenue, now on Fourteenth Street, and at the entrance of Brooklyn Bridge. We strolled for a distance along the bridge. We stopped at a number of saloons and had beer. But it might as well have been in Baltimore. My first true impression of New York was obtained on the morning that I went there from Plainfield to live.

The same friend was with me on the train, for he had a job in the city and commuted. At Jersey City we transferred to a ferry. We walked to the front of the ferryboat, and through pale October sunlight I saw the silhouette of downtown New York. My companion pointed out a structure in the form of two linked up-ended oblongs with rounded caps, which he said was the tallest skyscraper. It had thirty-two storeys and was called the Park Row Building. Next in height were the nearby St Paul Building and the New York World Building with its gilded dome. The zigzag skyline ending at the Battery may have been closer to the earth than it is now, but resembled nonetheless the chart of a fever patient. I found it ugly, hard and exciting. Ships lay ranged at their piers. An infinity of small craft moved here and there under plumes of smoke. It was these manifestations of a port's life that had beauty for me: these and the slender spire of Trinity Church, gothic and dark against the disorder of the skyscrapers.

The ferryboat docked at the foot of Liberty Street. I walked with the Plainfield man to the door of the office building in which he worked. Broadway lay one block beyond, he told me as we shook hands. I could take a trolley car there and ride uptown to about Twenty-Third Street, the best centre from which to look for a furnished room. But by way of greeting and orientation I decided that I would mount Broadway on foot. An arduous project, as I soon discovered, for I had no notion of the distance involved.

The environs of City Hall Park were an architectural jumble. A station of the elevated railroad crouched like a spider, obstructing the view of Brooklyn Bridge, standing guard over the approach to the Bowery. The City Hall itself had good proportions. But the southern tip of the park had been marred by the Federal government with a building of surpassing ugliness, an enormous dirty chateau masquerading as a post office. The old Astor

House on the left had a commonplace facade unworthy of the fame of its lush interior. To the right were the newspaper buildings – the *World*, the *Sun*, and the *Tribune* side by side, and looming down narrow streets the *Press* and the *Times*. At the moment these newspaper fortresses were all that mattered to me. They were dramatic in my eyes, and I noted every outward detail of Park Row as the background of my future career. Metropolitan journalism, it stood to common sense, would be free of the banalities that had plagued me in New Jersey.

A room being the first consideration, I tramped north and covered endless business blocks that I disliked because of their sameness and lack of beauty. Big skyscraper or little factory, the designer had seldom gone beyond the conception of a series of boxlike floors, the front conventionally ornamented but the flanks, wherever they protruded, as crude as raw steak. Here and there a shop front held me, especially the display of the Bannerman Company, dealers in second-hand arms and other military relics, the mass of their stock still deriving from the War of Secession.

At last Broadway slanted northwestward, and at this point began a section half residential, half given over to hotels, theatres, department stores and luxury shops. Grace Church stood at an angle. Union Square showed ahead. I was glad to see again the brownstone houses to which I had been introduced in Baltimore, a heavy type of residence to be sure, but one so universally built in the eastern cities of the United States during the decades of their most rapid growth that it is impossible to escape from brownstone, impossible not to have a sort of affection for it. A block of these houses with their high stoeps, with ivy about their window ledges, and sumach trees along the kerbs is the very essence of old New York, and the last traces of the style will not vanish for many a day.

I did not go the whole distance to Twenty-Third Street and so missed the Flatiron Building, lately completed and which had been commended to me in Plainfield as a wonder of the big town. Instead I turned down Eighteenth Street, looked at several rooms and ended, out of sheer weariness, in taking on trial an unpleasing room between Eighth and Ninth Avenues. It was very like the one in Baltimore. My recollection is that I stayed there less than a week. I have no intention of tracing every step that I took. Enough to say that I soon moved to 246 West Twenty-First Street, a typical boarding house of the period. For meals and an attic room ventilated only by a skylight, I paid five dollars and fifty cents a week. I had to live as cheaply as possible and did not expect to be comfortable. But why I preferred at a glance my terrible little room to the one on Eighteenth Street is an obscure point. The new house had a role in my fate, that was all; I was to feel many such convictions about dwellings in the future.

Starting on my second day in New York, I knocked for admission at the doors of all the newspapers. A reporter on the *Times* whom I had been advised in Jamaica to look up told me that it was good psychology to be so persistent that after a while you could not be ignored. Make the rounds every day, he said, no matter how bluntly you had been refused the day before. I tried his tactics, but they were ineffective for me. I also made friends with the typewriter companies and resumed practising. An employment agent in that quarter astonished me one morning by handing me a slip and directing me to apply for a job at the address given. I answered that I was a reporter, not a typist. He laughed and said it would not do me any harm to pick up a few dollars. The firm in question wanted some copying done; it would be a temporary job. I concluded to take a shot at it, since I was running short of cash, and the man who hired me completed the surprise by dictating a few letters to me on the assumption that I wrote shorthand. In this casual way I discovered a crutch that was to be of service through a long spell of freelancing as freakishly irregular as any that have been described to me. For though that first employer growled over my errors, I got his work out after a fashion and was paid for a week. I knew I must improve. There would always be the typewriter to fall back upon.

Arduously I tapped out one day a copy of a youthful poem of mine, a description of tropical scenery, and mailed it to the *Sun*. It appeared several mornings later at the bottom of a column on the editorial page. I was delighted. My future seemed clear. While looking out for an opening on the staff of a paper, I would write verse and articles, and doubtless make enough to pay my expenses. The reporter on the *Times* had told me that everything printed, no matter of what nature or how short, would be paid for at the end of each week. The *Sun* required local contributors to call at the cashier's window with the proper identification. I did so, was handed three dollars in cash and felt like a New York professional.

That was the only acceptance of a poem that I was to have for two years. I did prose pieces, mainly about Jamaica, which were rejected with complete apathy on the part of the editors. Then a few of the shorter, trivial ones began to be printed in the Sunday magazines of the newspapers, never anything that drew as much as ten dollars. I had to resort more and more to the typewriter employment agencies. Briefly, I worked in the business department of the *Times*, hoping in vain that this would prove a back door to the city room.

I LOOKED FORWARD EAGERLY TO my first sight of snow. It might come any time in November, I was apprised, though there were years when it did not fall until December. After the passing of autumn the New York weather rapidly turned grey with frequent chilly rains. A certain afternoon about the middle of November was leaden and still, a portent which I did not recognize. And in the morning there was snow, fluttering steadily down. I ran out on the stoep and caught up a handful of it. To my amazement it was crisp, and where it touched my skin it melted instantly. What had I expected? Why, that it would be soft in the manner that cottonwool is soft, smooth and malleable; cold of course, and slow to melt. The prickly sensation when the flakes drifted against my cheeks and neck did not cease to be a surprising novelty all that season.

As the winter advanced I found it increasingly difficult to write. I could see that the preference was for local subject matter handled in the American idiom, and my approach was fumbling. The winter played a part. My first turned out to be a very severe winter. I detested the cold that seemed to paralyse my brain as well as chill my body. The trouble, however, went deeper. Suddenly I had a breakdown such as I had not heard about or imagined. It was not what the doctors call a nervous breakdown. My capacity for ordinary work and my enjoyment of life were in no way diminished. Rather, my precocity as a writer had shrivelled, and my drive toward a career had been checked. If this was the result of mere discouragement I cannot read my own character. I found it literally impossible for the time being to compose a serious article. I became just a hack. In the terms of my original impulse, I had fallen behind schedule at least five years. Yet I clung tenaciously to an ambition that I believed would finally attain its end.

I set out consciously to know New York for its own sake and to crowd my life with events. The future would show what use I could make of my experiences. This was a reversal of my Kingston attitude, which had been to approach all things for the purpose of writing about them immediately. Who knows, the new state of affairs may have been a salutory release from tension. The sorry boarding house was the hub of my doings. It stood in a brownstone row, but was of brick darkened by the weather. Two pillars crowned with pineapples of hollow iron flanked the stoep and supported metal railings. The sandstone stoeps were worn in the middle, with thin flakes curling upward on either side of the furrow. The small vestibule had a paving of chipped black-and-white tiles that were seldom washed, and dust rose at a touch from its fibre mat. At mealtimes you did not have to use the front door, but could reach the basement dining room by way of the narrow areaway and a gate under the stoep.

A long table ran down the middle of the basement front. Most of my fellow boarders did not interest me. Two Irish girls, however, lit up the place. They were sisters, Kitty and Margaret Bourke by name, from County Mayo. Their hair was of a brown so dark it was almost black, yet they had bright complexions and clear blue eyes. A touch of brogue made their speech musical. Kitty had been in New York for three years and was already superficially Americanized. She was the smaller physically, the less beautiful. But Margaret, who had arrived recently, glowed in a bewildering exuberance. She had a lovely body, salient health, a plenitude of all the more obvious charms.

Figure 8. Margaret Bourke, to whom Roberts never quite proposed, about 1905. MS353.6.8.

Anyone who lived in the same house as these girls was their friend without formalities. Evenings of simple entertainment resulted, such as no group in a city today would conceivably think worthwhile in competition with motion pictures, the radio or motoring. A sample from the naive past should be worth preserving.

"What will you be doing after supper?" Margaret called to me across the table.

"Why, nothing in particular," I answered.

"Would you look in at our room? We can have a little singing, maybe."

"I'd like to very much."

At about eight o'clock I knocked at the door of a double room on the second floor rear. Kitty admitted me, smiling a greeting, and offered excuses for the fact that both girls were sewing on fine work they had brought home from their jobs. Their industry was something to wonder at. Throughout the evening they bent over stitches as delicate as those used by lacemakers.

"Sure, the lad won't mind that we keep on working," cried Margaret, her gay voice filling the room. "We can sing and have a grand time all the same." She made a place for me on the sofa beside her, while Kitty sat in an old leather-covered armchair. The bed was flagrantly visible, its double width jutting three-quarters of the way from wall to wall. An innocent freedom of manners, an acceptance of boarding-house life as they found it, saved the girls from embarrassment. They received in their bedroom as a matter of course.

"Mr Forbes and Mr Connolly will join us soon," said Kitty. "Then we'll all sing. Five voices are better than three. But you are looking real serious. Are you sure you're not fretting for an old sweetheart?"

"No, no," I protested. "There's been nothing like that in my life."

"Go on! A fine-looking lad like you! Well, you're missing your pa and your ma, maybe."

"Not so much."

"Tell us about that grand place you come from. I've forgotten its name already. I've no head at all for names."

Before I could say anything about Jamaica there was a knock at the door and Margaret got up, remarking: "It's Mr Forbes and Mr Connolly, for the singing."

Two young men entered breezily. Forbes was a mechanic from Scotland via Boston, and Connolly worked, of all unlikely places for one of his race, in an Eighth Avenue pawnshop. As soon as the newcomers had found seats, Kitty brought out a cheap paperbound book of Irish songs and suggested that Forbes and I hold it between us. "The rest of us know the words by heart," she said. "Why wouldn't we, with the names we have?"

We ran through number after number, our eyes alight with pleasure at the Celtic melodies. Kitty and Margaret sang with a piercing sweetness, devoid of artifice. Forbes and Connolly had tolerable voices. Only I was a hopeless amateur, but I kept pace with the others and they did not seem to mind. There was a pause, and stories were told. We turned to American popular songs of the moment: "In the Good Old Summertime" and "In the Shade of the Old Apple Tree". Connolly announced that he would treat everyone and went out for refreshments to a corner store. The men paid compliments as we dallied over the ice cream, and transparent flirtations started. I was falling in love with Margaret when I said goodbye at eleven o'clock.

The city was not bounded for me, however, by the walls of the boarding house and the route to and from a shop, as it seemed to be for my new friends. I had a vast curiosity about the city, and I began to develop an attachment that was not precisely love, but a sense of having won adoption by the most exciting stepmother imaginable, in whose world anything might happen. The city differed widely from modern New York. It was O. Henry's "Bagdad-on-the-Subway". It was George M. Cohan's "Little Old New York". Also, it was the city of flashy spenders drinking in hotel bars, of French and Italian *table d'hôte* restaurants, of the roaring Tenderloin centring about Sixth Avenue between Twentieth and Thirtieth Streets, of a Bowery that had seen its rowdiest days but was still pretty tough, of a Chinatown reputed to be more mysterious than the facts merited, and of the Great White Way.

The population, including Brooklyn which had been annexed six years before, was around four million. Nightlife in its most pretentious form had already moved up from Union Square. The core was now at Herald Square and stretched southward to Madison Square, northward to Longacre Square. The last-named was rechristened Times Square that winter when the paper shifted from downtown to its new white building at Broadway and Forty-Second Street. The area between that point and Columbus Circle was chaotic, with many vacant lots. To the right Fifth Avenue flaunted the chateaus of the millionaires, and otherwise was almost solid brownstone. Harlem seemed far enough away to be thought of as a suburb, its inhabitants mainly German and Irish.

My exploration of nightlife was timid at first, because I had little money to spend. I had learned to drink whisky, but rated it expensive at fifteen cents a glass. Entry to certain wild spots could be had for a few beers at a nickel a glass, and if one were willing to be a spendthrift and pay ten cents a glass it was possible to visit even the garish Haymarket in the heart of the Tenderloin. I began with Tom Sharkey's saloon on Fourteenth Street in the same block as Tammany Hall. It was not unique, for its like flourished in every city on the westward trails of the frontiersmen, and up and down the Pacific Coast. But it was a late survival in New York. The ex-heavyweight pugilist who ran it had come close to winning the championship from Jim Jeffries. He had been a sailor. His battered countenance, huge hands and thick neck made of him a gargoyle. Flocking about him, a profitable branch of his business, were scores of harlots all much of a grade, not the first or the next best obviously, yet still above the level of the drab majority that haunted the sidewalks and the rear regions of barrooms. The girls at Tom Sharkey's swarmed along the bar, asked any man who would return a wink for their smile to buy drinks, manoeuvred him to a table where prices were higher, and ended by leaving the premises with him if possible. The house rules did not permit them to plague a customer who kept a poker face and reordered for himself with average frequency. So I played the role of spectator. I was neither shocked nor tempted, but the impact of troops of questing females created a certain inner turmoil.

I had read a lot about the Bowery and of course went to see for myself. Its resorts were a disappointment because of their unrelieved squalor. The atmosphere of gargantuan follies, of violence and sudden death, which had existed if one were to believe the books, had given way to panhandling, manifest disease and the cheapest forms of entertainment. The singing waiters about whom some chroniclers have written nostalgically did not amuse me. I quailed with nausea at the drunks flattened on the muddy pavements like dead fowls, and at the lobbies of ten-cent hotels where male derelicts huddled, their rags steaming, as they awaited their turn to go to dormitories alive with vermin. Only the Salvation Army made a strong emotional appeal on the Bowery. It was really an army of rescue in those days, not a charity organization with expensive headquarters and an efficiency system. The lassies clashed their tambourines in rain or snow, exhorters shouted in uninhibited language, hymns were bawled to famous military tunes. Then the lowest of the low were collected and marched off in files to temporary comfort, and no questions asked. The Bowery understood that sort of benevolence.

The glamour of the stage allured me, naturally enough. A seat in the top balcony could be had in almost any theatre for a quarter. I saw a few plays and a great deal of vaudeville. Early in my round of odd jobs I was sent on an agency call to the Fifth Avenue Theatre, a variety house on Twenty-Eighth Street. It appeared that the press agent's typist was ill and he wanted a substitute for two weeks or less. He asked me some questions in a bored tone, but when I said I had been a reporter he clucked, "That's swell!", dismissed the other applicants, and gave me the job. I was handed some rough notes in pencil and a large number of photographs of actors. The press agent instructed me to type the notes in multiple copies, padding the text as I worked, paste the result to the bottoms of the right photographs, and that afternoon deliver sets to the dramatic editors of all the newspapers. He dictated a few letters in halting phrases, ending with the remark: "You see what I'm driving at. Put it into good English."

He made a dozen telephone calls, mostly to girls, smoking cigarettes incessantly the while. Then he clapped on his hat and announced he was going for a drink and didn't know when he would be back. At the door he remembered something. "Looka here," he said. "You'll want to drop in at the different shows." He fished passes out of his pocket and scrawled his name on them. "These are good for all the Keith and Proctor houses. S'long! Be seeing you tomorrow, if not before."

I thought myself in clover. It was revenge of a sort to appear in waiting rooms where I had been often rejected and ask for the dramatic editor on business. I never saw anyone more important than a dramatic editor's second assistant, but that was all right. The truly delectable thing was my freedom of the vaudeville theatres. I caught the tail ends of matinées here and there, and for several nights in succession saw full shows from orchestra seats. The slapstick acts were tiresome, but I revelled in the sing-and-dance acts, the gymnastic novelties, the animal numbers and the strange hard-boiled patter of the monologists. An usher happened to ask me whether I was going backstage after the show, and I grasped that as the press agent's representative this privilege was mine. Thereafter I always went backstage, where hurried beings in greasepaint pressed additional photographs upon me and boasted shamelessly about their successes. The experience was telescoped into so short a period that I did not reach the point of untangling the details.

The offices at the Fifth Avenue Theatre were presided over by B.F. Keith himself, the organizer of the circuit. He was oldish and pudgy, a quiet man who snoozed at intervals on a couch in his private office. Erratic underlings careered about the premises, and players looking for engagements came and went in a constant stream. My press agent seldom remained at his desk for longer than an hour. He continued to use me as a rewrite man and assistant rather than a typist, and I asked nothing better. I told him I hoped he could make it a permanent job. He twisted his features into an exaggerated grimace intended to show goodwill and said: "Gee whiz, I wish I could! You're okay, but the other guy will soon be back, and there isn't work for two." The "other guy" appeared relentlessly at the end of ten days and I had to go. I was cast down, though there is reason for an earnest suspicion that I had a lucky escape. The life of vaudeville and vaudevillians was alluring in a superficial way, and it would have been easy then for me to sink myself in it. I have nothing against theatrical press agents and in after years I made some good friends among them; but to have joined the calling at eighteen might have been a perilous detour, in view of my real interests.

I HAD DISCOVERED ANOTHER STIMULANT, one that could be courted endlessly and without costing me a penny. As I have said, 1904 was a presidential campaign year. I reached New York early in October and the final frenzied month of electioneering was underway. Plainfield had given me my first ideas about United States politics. Now I made up my mind to study the matter and attended many of the rallies held by the two parties. It is odd to think that I should have heard Theodore Roosevelt speak in a little hall on the West Side that seated barely a thousand persons. But those were simple times. The president had been touring the city and making appearances at district meetings with the informality of a candidate for sheriff. A hundred first impressions of him have figured in memoirs, so excuse this one.

He crossed the platform with a vigorous lurch, as if his frockcoat hampered him. I had been prepared for a personality, and his took violent hold of me. The eyeglasses struck an incongruous note on that pugnacious face. He tore at a subject as though he were worrying it, shooting out his jaw and striking his palm with his fist in a manner that was a relief from Anglo-Saxon repression. At the end of some phrases his voice soared thinly in the celebrated falsetto. He was very Dutch in appearance. I found a resemblance to pictures of the younger Boer commandants. Handsome, no. Deliberately histrionic, yes. Withal you felt a man born to lead and jolly well determined to brush rivals out of the way. I could not have become a blind follower of Roosevelt, for he was so much of an extrovert that he dispensed with subtlety. Compared with prosy Judge Alton B. Parker on the Democratic ticket, however, the advantage of magnetic pull lay overwhelmingly with the Rough Rider. Theodore Roosevelt stirred an enthusiasm in the crowd and won a loyalty to his person such as no other president, or presidential candidate, has equalled in my lifetime. That first year I saw men jump up with their fists clenched to defend his name against the least slur. It was not a campaign, mind you, in which the issues were tense, and few doubted that Roosevelt would win. Sheer hero-worship was in play, and to me that was extremely interesting.

On election night I went to Herald Square to watch the posting of the returns. Dense mobs blocked every inch of space that commanded a view of the bulletin board extended across the facade of the *New York Herald* building. The board was reached by ladders and a catwalk. Operators scrawled on its surface with large sticks of chalk. The outpouring of the public was an institution in North American life, a sort of political carnival that only the crippled or the very lazy allowed themselves to miss. You battled for a foothold even on the outskirts of the crowd, and if you were energetic you steadily bored your way forward until you stood wedged at a desirable spot, from which at long intervals you could read clearly that your favourite had either carried or lost so many districts out of so many in Brooklyn, Boston or St Louis. Idiots blew tin horns and yelled raucously. When you could endure the constrictions no longer, it was almost as arduous to worm your way back to a side street as it had been to advance. Yet the excitement was genuine, much keener than the present generation works up over returns heard by radio. Until changing customs killed them, I never was able to resist the bulletin boards as the climax of an election in New York.

A calm so absolute that it was like a repudiation of politics succeeded the Republican victory. I knew better. Now was the time to take a look at the workings of the local groups. I had heard Tammany denounced as a nest of unredeemable villains, and I had not been convinced. The organization sounded to me as if it might be liberal, imaginative and at all events picturesque. Having no excuse to ask for interviews as a reporter, I just dropped in at Tammany Hall and talked with anyone who came along. There was absolutely no difficulty about that. The place resembled a series of hotel lobbies of the third or fourth order of cleanliness, where hosts of job-seekers and charity cases waited for attention from the offices. The stamp of the Bowery was upon it. If you wanted to come in and sit, nobody cared. You were presumed to be there in hopes of a chance to sue for favours. If you left without having been summoned, doubtless you were tired of waiting and would come another day.

I went often when I had nothing else to do. Soon I got to know Boss Charles F. Murphy at sight. He looked like a boiled fish, this ex-trolley car conductor and actual saloon-keeper, famous for his taciturnity and regarded as being the shrewdest organizer the Hall had ever had. He was a Catholic puritan who would not allow women in his saloon and who called it his 'shop' because he had a sneaking feeling that it was immoral to make money out of liquor, but who did not balk at taking revenue for the Hall from Tom Sharkey's across the street and countless other chippy-joints as they were called. Hangers-on told me tales of Murphy's goodness of heart and extolled the merits of the Sullivans, Big Tim and Little Tim, of whom I had a few glimpses. The pair were decidedly of a more genial Celtic type than the Boss.

More than half of Tammany's members at that period were Irish. I thought it a pity that their concerns were so utilitarian, their politics those of immigrants who had put the memory of Ireland behind them. This was a shallow judgement, as I discovered when I visited a middle-aged woman doctor named Garnier who had been in Jamaica and had invited me to call on her if I ever came to New York. I went on a lonely Sunday and she introduced me to her colleague, Dr Gertrude Kelly. They had a parlour floor in the East Thirties. What I remember are the full, kind features of Dr Kelly, her blue eyes and her greying sandy hair as she served tea and asked me a host of questions bearing on the Celtic race.

Was I of Irish descent? Oh, chiefly Welsh! Well, the two peoples were closely related. . . . Did the Irish in Jamaica have cultural organizations? No! That was a pity, surely. . . . Had I studied the Welsh language? No! It was said to be difficult. Perhaps I should prefer to take up Gaelic, and if so she could arrange to have me admitted to a class gratis. . . . Had I met any Irish here from the Old Country? Ah, two girls from County Mayo, and they loved to sing! It was to be hoped that they knew many of the ancient Gaelic songs. . . . Had I heard about the great renaissance in Ireland? I must join a group that discussed it and which she often entertained at the house. Yes, a number of the Tammany politicians were interested.

I did not follow up the friendship, largely because of my material worries that winter, I think; afterwards I felt embarrassed at having stayed away so long. It was a pity. I would be deeply moved one day by Sinn Féin, and some of its early activities in New York centred about Dr Gertrude Kelly.

Drifting with any wind that blew and doing haphazard work which it would be tedious to catalogue, I struggled through my first winter in the North. I had a dreadful attack of bronchitis followed by a cough that hung on for weeks and led to morbid predictions at the boarding house. "You must be careful or it's consumption you'll be getting, and you so young," Margaret had said, as she and Kitty dosed me with soothing syrups. My eyes held a feverish glitter. I had lost a good deal of weight. The alien climate certainly had not been kind to me. Then there was a change in the weather, with sudden thaws, the icicles on lintels running like waterspouts, and the dirty crusts that had formed on the sidewalks crackling underfoot and merging into puddles. Pale sunlight that seemed miraculously warm gave a comfortable feeling to the back of one's neck and set the sparrows to chirping gaily.

Never have I been so glad of a change of season as I was when I hailed the spring. The very sounds associated with it remain sharp-cut: the calls of men pushing handcarts loaded with flowers in earthenware pots, of old-clothes men, of Italians grinding out operatic airs on barrel-organs – typical urban sounds that the winter had banished. *Incipit vita nova.*

CHAPTER 4 ❧ **Adventure**

MATERIAL WORRIES LED ME IN 1905 NOT ONLY to take a typist's job offered on a permanent basis, but to hang onto it for month after month. The firm was the American Felt Company, old-fashioned and easy-going, with wholesale offices on East Thirteenth Street. They paid me ten dollars a week and presently raised the figure to twelve. I called myself a craven, a quitter and other opprobrious epithets. The fact remained that I had been doing poorly at writing, and with board and lodging to pay each week the irregularity as well as the smallness of my income had been bad for my nerves. Twelve dollars a week meant solvency, with a nice margin for amusements.

In thinking back to the merrymaking of those days it is impossible to omit Coney Island, the prototype of all the rowdy, crude, fantastic summer resorts that the mob loved. Modern Coney Island is but a decorous shadow. The change began under a reform administration forty years ago. But when I first saw it the Island, as it was affectionately called, was uninhibited and tolerantly policed. To get there from Manhattan you changed at the Brooklyn Bridge and rode interminably by elevated railroad or streetcar, jammed in with skylarking crowds. An alternative route was by excursion boats from a pier on the Hudson River, but that cost all of fifty cents round trip whereas you could go on the cars for nickel fares. The Saturday and Sunday trippers weighed the consideration, for they demanded that each item of their jaunt must be cheap, no matter what the total amounted to. I far preferred the boat, on account of the cool breezes and the lordly panorama of New York harbour. The Statue of Liberty, however, I did not admire. It

Figure 9. The American Felt Company (110–112 East Thirteenth Street, New York), where Roberts worked as a typist in 1906. MS353.9.18.

was too lumpy a figure, smothered in draperies. Only the uplifted arm with the torch was beautiful to me.

Supposedly you went to Coney Island for two reasons: to bathe in the surf and to sample the novelties of its famous Luna Park and Dreamland. But you were also lured by the thought of minor low-class attractions, as well as the legend that at Coney Island you met stranger people, had stranger adventures, than anywhere else.

The accepted ritual on arrival was to push your way along Surf Avenue, eat hot dogs from open-air stands, and if you had a girl with you, to buy her popcorn and a bag of the meretricious candy known as salt-water taffy. Myself, I disliked hot dogs and usually had instead a soft-shell crab, a North American delicacy of the first order which sold in those happy days for a dime. Secondly, you roamed through the side streets and alleys to see what had been thought up since the last time. Many of the concessions preferred to do business outside the big amusement parks, and they went to ludicrous extremes to attract attention to shows that promised much but were in fact complete rubbish. Acrobatic barkers howled to the passersby to have their fortunes told, or to inspect hairy women and two-headed babies. There were rooms full of peep-show machines, in which for a cent suggestive pictures could be run off and seemingly merged by the use of a hand crank, in an anticipation of the cinema. Men alone or in parties would visit the concert saloons, where the liquor at minimum prices was villainous, and where shopworn females plastered with tinted chalk sang hoarsely and promoted engagements with the customers. The salt, clear air and the breaking of the surf were a paradoxical accompaniment to all this. Early or late, the tripper went to bathe uncomfortably on the most congested beach in the world, and then made the rounds of the parks with their switchback railways, their booby traps and their sensational shows.

I learned at that time to enjoy café life, which for a youngster with a thin pocketbook was to be found chiefly in the *table d'hôte* restaurants. Latin immigrants ran them, providing a most savoury meal of several courses and red wine for about sixty cents. A decent cigar could be had for five cents. The waiters never rushed you. Even in those liberal days, some of the places were speakeasies. By dodging the cost of a retail liquor licence, they could sell both the food and drink more cheaply, and of course the customers enjoyed being initiates who knew which bells to ring on houses that bore no signs. Names come back to me: Guffanti's, Gonfarone's, Renganeschi's, the Lion d'Or, among the open restaurants.

Inside, they were all fairly similar, consisting of the front and back parlours of an old residence thrown into one, with the backyard occupied in warm weather. Tables for two or four were set close together, the wine bottles and the baskets of French bread or Italian breadsticks creating an atmosphere of luxury. So it seemed to the generation. A *table d'hôte* once a week, as a change from the boarding house, made me feel expansive. That I was earning the wherewithal as a typist, however, wounded my vanity.

The clerical yoke could be readily evaded compared with a temptation that now beset me. I desperately wanted to marry Margaret Bourke. This last phrase is used advisedly. I was not in any profound sense in love with the Irish girl. She had stirred me to great admiration of her sweet character and her physical beauty. I needed to mate. She had begun to be tender with me, allowing me to hold her hand and even to slip my arm about her waist as we sat side by side. A situation of this sort was bound to come to a head.

One evening I asked her with assumed carelessness whether she would not prefer marriage to the slavery of long hours at needlework.

"I would so," she replied frankly.

"And would you think it necessary for the man you married to have a position in the world – money, and all that?"

"I'd take a likely, hardworking lad I loved before any old millionaire. I'd not ask for riches when I was young," said Margaret, her voice softening.

She had as good as told me that I might propose to her. I was on the point of doing so. There were married men at my office who earned as little as fifteen dollars a week. I knew without asking that Margaret would gladly continue to work at her shop until I got another raise. Then a realistic demon went to work in my brain. Good God! I thought. It would mean sticking indefinitely to the job at the American Felt Company, and even if I succeeded later in finding a post as a reporter I would be chained to that. With a wife to support – and children: who could doubt after glancing at Margaret in her radiant health that there would be several children? – I would not be able to experiment, to travel. When would I ever get a chance to write books?

I remained silent that evening. Not that I had reached a decision so quickly. I tormented myself for weeks, swaying between common sense and the terrible emotional need I had for Margaret. The snobbery of whether it would have been wise to tie myself to a comparatively unlettered girl did not enter my calculations. And who knows, this aspect might not have mattered at all. She had a very quick mind, which could have adapted itself to my interests. As a social being, her fidelity to a pure Gaelic type was poetical and had unalterable charm. But my dread of shackles finally prevailed, and it was a logical instinct at my age. Marriage before twenty is almost invariably a folly.

To go on flirting with Margaret was dangerous, and deliberately to cool off to her was beyond me. I decided to move. I was sick of boarding-house menus anyway and wanted to try eating all my meals in restaurants. So I took a small furnished room on the top floor of a house on West Twenty-Third Street. With this break, my adolescent dreaming about love came to an end. The poetess in Jamaica had receded to a place in the world of precious romantic memories and, I may add, of lasting friendship. Margaret was the first woman I had intended to ask to be my wife, and I had given her up. I knew I could be enamoured from now on, but not boyishly sentimental.

ABOUT A WEEK AFTER I HAD moved in I heard a girl singing lightly in the adjoining room. The tune was exotic, and I made out after a while that the words were French. She stirred here and there at some task, ending by a window where her voice fell to a hum. I looked out of my window at the rear of the house and saw her leaning with both arms on the sill. She was a dark brunette with heavy eyebrows and a wide mouth, her undone hair gathered with a ribbon at the nape of her neck. She had a quaint, happy expression rather than good looks, and when I smiled at her she smiled back.

"I think that's a very pretty song," I told her.

"It is nice you like it. Then I know when I want to sing it will not disturb you," she replied, with a mere trace of accent.

She drew back into her room. But we both took the attitude that we had introduced ourselves, and when we met on the landing the next day we stood and chatted. Her name was Florence Brochu. She was a French Canadian from Montreal, a milliner who had come to New York by way of New Bedford, Massachusetts, and had a job in a shop off Broadway. She was twenty-two or twenty-three years old. A more amiable, informal personality than hers could not be imagined. We scarcely made appointments, but exchanged notes on our favourite restaurants in the neighbourhood and met there as a matter of course. Soon we were taking all our meals together.

One evening we saw the Cohans in *Little Johnny Jones* from balcony seats and walked arm in arm from Times Square. When we reached our top floor Florence invited me into her room. She had some cookies and would make coffee on a naphtha burner.

We drank the coffee and then suddenly were in each other's arms. I knew instinctively that this would be no episode of repressed desires, and I began to tremble. Florence gave a low, kind laugh. "I think it is the first time in all your life," she said. A sort of banal masculine conceit led me to

Figure 10. Florence Brochu, Roberts's first lover, in 1905. MS353.6.8.

protest that such was not the case. She only chuckled tenderly and wrapped me about with caresses. It was indeed the first time for me, my age being then six weeks less than nineteen years.

I experienced a perfect delirium of joy in the days that followed. But it was to be a brief interlude. It did not occur to me to wonder at the impermanent way in which Florence took our affair on the practical as well as the amorous side. She made no plans for our future and told me that I did not realize the difficulties when I suggested that we might take a big room together. In this she was much more the male of the liaison than me. Without warning, she declared that she was leaving right away for San Francisco. It was a move she had long intended to make, for she had been assured that milliners earned good money on the Pacific Coast. She would write to me often.

Though I begged her to change her mind, I was youthfully offended and not so very urgent about it. Besides, I found it hard to believe that she would really go. It had happened almost before I was aware of it, and at the end of ten days I received a letter from her giving an address on Mission Street, San Francisco. We corresponded irregularly, for I had decided to play an injured role, and I marked this by delaying my replies.

Florence had been a creative adventure for me. By leaving she had symbolized adventure in another form, and although I had no idea of following her to San Francisco, her example helped to bring to a head a feeling that had been growing in me. I wanted to know more of North America than the city of New York, to go to extremes in fact, in hunting for new sensations, new knowledge of people and places. What better way of spending my time until I should be able to write effectively again!

I had been doing some steady reading in the public library, mainly on American history as told in memoirs and novels. Two interests had been sharply aroused. The first and more lasting was in the Southern states, particularly the reasons for the unsuccessful war that they had waged with the North for their independence. I recalled that my father had always spoken of Dixie as though it were a separate country, where conditions were similar to those in Jamaica and with which a Jamaican with a plantation background would naturally sympathize. But he had never lived there and did not attempt to go into details. Now I grew animated over the stories of the generals, starting with Beauregard of Louisiana. The second interest was in the Western frontier, and this was because of its current potentialities for furnishing excitement. The California of Bret Harte was gone, I knew that. I was influenced, however, by Frank Norris's recent novels, *McTeague* and *The Octopus*, and by one of the brilliant Stephen Crane's short stories called "The Blue Hotel".

A choice between the South and the West was not very difficult. The first-named would always be there, and I would assuredly pay it a long visit someday. The West might change radically and should be seen before it was too late. I decided to go to California. As I had no money for the journey, it would be necessary to continue at distasteful jobs and save enough. I hoped to leave by the summer of 1906, but unexpected happenings delayed me.

On 18 April San Francisco was wrecked by earthquake and fire, with a loss of life most conservatively put at seven hundred. My heart sank when I thought of Florence, who had arrived there five months before and had not changed her address so far as I knew. The district through which Mission Street ran was reported to have suffered heavily. I watched the mail deliveries for a letter from her, and none came. A letter I wrote was returned after several weeks bearing the notation, "Not found". I wanted to get to San Francisco and look for her. Insufficient funds made this impossible. I rationalized that if she had escaped she would have let me know, and that I probably would not be able to find work in the damaged city.

Besides, my mother would be in New York with my two sisters that spring.

She had broken off her unhappy marriage, though it did not enter her head to ask for a legal divorce, and she was making plans to live in Nova Scotia. I rejoiced at seeing the three of them again. As it turned out, my eldest sister revolted against apartment-house life in the North and soon went back to Jamaica. My mother and younger sister lingered in New York.

IF A MAN WHO WAS young at that period swears that he never picked up a streetwalker, he is probably not telling the truth. Companionship with home girls was, to put it mildly, on a stricter basis than it is now. Public women by the hundreds drifted at night along Broadway and the important crosstown streets, and many a youth who would have thought it brazen to go to a bordello yielded to the allure of a girl who spoke to him on the sidewalk. It seemed personal in comparison with taking what was offered in a 'house', though it was every whit as commercial a transaction and riskier from a health standpoint.

I succumbed at times, when not involved in some love affair. The procedure was to register as man and wife at a complacent hotel, of which there were scores, chiefly those quaint New York institutions know as Raines Law hotels. A pious legislator named Raines had fathered a bill requiring saloons to be taverns in the old sense of the word, that is to say places that served food as well as drink for those who sat at tables, and that provided rooms for transient guests. This was supposed to make the saloons virtuous, but they got round the law by putting a plate of dusty bread and cheese, like a theatrical prop, on each table and renting the otherwise unwanted bedrooms to lechers.

One evening I was accosted gently by a slim red-haired girl. She said her name was Marjorie. Instead of parleying in the usual way, I smiled and nodded, curiously moved by her personality. She slipped her arm in mine without affectation, and chatting like old friends we went to the nearest hotel, which happened to be one on West Thirty-Fourth Street that had formerly been chic. Our room had a high ceiling with mouldings that still bore traces of gilt, and the flowered wallpaper was of a delicate pattern. She declared it was grand, a nice room to come to, her plebeian voice touched with a sort of romantic sadness. Then she drew my head down and kissed me.

I asked Marjorie, as young men nearly always do in such circumstances, to tell me about her past life. She answered gravely that she had been brought up in a country home that had a garden full of flowers, and she added trivial details. There was no pose that she was not a regular prostitute. She had put the customary three dollars in her purse with a quiet "Thank you." Later she remarked that there were good and bad times in the calling.

But she caressed me with a dreamy intentness. As we lay side by side, she proposed suddenly that we spend the whole night in the room. "You mustn't think I'd let you pay me any more for it," she added.

"It would not be fair of me to take so much of your time, Marjorie," I answered, my eyes held by the red hair spread upon the pillow.

"And if I want it so!" she countered. "I was very tired when I met you, and now I am in a happy mood."

The pity of it was that, for reasons that have completely slipped me, I did not do as she asked. But I have never forgotten Marjorie, not the least expression or curve of her kind, wistful face. On many evenings after that, I hunted vainly for her on Thirty-Fourth Street and up and down Broadway.

There presently occurred a stunning shock. I was walking in Union Square late on the afternoon of 14 January 1907, when I heard newsboys shouting, "Kingston, Jamaica, destroyed by earthquake!" Coming on top of San Francisco, this seemed too melodramatic to be true. But so it was. I seized a paper and read that most of the downtown part of the city had been devastated, and that over a thousand had been killed. We heard promptly from members of the family. None of them had been hurt, though the entire island had felt seismic tremors. In Kingston many acquaintances were dead. T.H. MacDermot had suffered grave injuries through having been pinned to the floor of his office by falling beams and debris. The best official move was that Sydney Olivier was soon appointed governor, to handle the crisis.

I had a wild feeling that I was more uprooted than when I had left Jamaica. Exaggerating the damage done to Kingston, I thought of it as a dead place to which I might never have cause to return. And the money to finance my mother's move north had been obtained through the sale of Berry Hill. The family had only one holding left in the mountains. Yet this sense of instability enhanced my eagerness to go West and seek adventures. I wrote and told my father about it, and I was not much surprised when he answered that he, also, had made up his mind to cut loose. He intended to try the Isthmus of Panama, where the canal was then being dug and where he had heard that anyone could ease in as a sub-contractor and make a fortune. In a year or so he might be able to visit me in California. This would have been the clincher, had I needed a final impetus, and in any event it pleased me greatly.

The American Felt Company had served its purpose long since, but profits from freelance writing were still elusive. I took a last job as a typist, tempted by wages of fifteen dollars a week. The partners for whom I went to work might have stepped out of the pages of a nineteenth-century humourist. The obvious cliché would be, 'out of the pages of Dickens'. But Wildman and Treherne were uniquely American, and Frank Stockton would have understood them even better than Mark Twain. They dealt in prescription bottles, jars, corks and other such accessories needed by drugstores, and as a special line they imported cork from Portugal. Their office was in a corner of a warehouse floor they rented on Desbrosses Street, a name pronounced by them with a nasal sounding of all the *esses*.

Both men were bachelors, with which fact resemblance between them ended. Wildman was a timorous, greying individual with watery eyes and drooping moustache that partly hid a weak mouth and a still weaker chin. What his value to the firm might be – the larger contribution of capital, or a special knowledge of glass and cork – I did not know; he was very lazy and ineffective. Treherne, who was some years younger, ran to the opposite extreme. His rugged face was adorned with a piratical red moustache, and baldness did not detract from his round Celtic skull. He held himself erect, moved with assurance, was continuously active in every phase of the business. These queerly matched partners seemed to detest each other, or rather Wildman was afraid of Treherne, while Treherne scorned Wildman. Day after day saw the same comedy enacted. The energetic partner snapped questions at the weak one, ridiculed his failure to do things he had said he would do and issued peremptory orders. The other defended himself in a whining singsong, his manner a plea to be left alone.

I observed them with considerable surprise. They treated me, each in his own way, with old-fashioned courtesy. But Treherne might just have finished asking me in almost flowery fashion to write a letter when he would turn on Wildman with a brusque complaint. Then I began to see below the surface. Nothing that they said altered the routine of the office; their relationship did not worsen an iota; they called each other by their first names. In short, they were like a husband and wife who disagreed on almost everything, but would have felt lost if forced to part.

With a purpose to stiffen me I could lay by seven dollars a week from the fifteen I earned from Wildman and Treherne, and this despite the fact that shortly afterward I discovered bohemia. There was a little basement restaurant on East Eleventh Street, between Fourth and Third Avenue, a speakeasy kept by a Signora Volanti, the memory of which is still a password among certain veterans in New York. We called the proprietress Madama, dodging the Italian form and yet recognizing that she was neither Madame nor Madam. Her pretty young daughter Emma served us meals at extraordinarily low prices and red wine at ten cents a glass. I met more artists than writers there, visited among them, became excited over pictorial art, and acquired a taste for the life of studios. Madama's will figure again in my story.

The chief characteristic of that generation was romanticism. I mean among those who regarded themselves as being artists, or adventurers in the good sense. Youth today is solemn, virtuous and level-headed by comparison. We passionately admired such notions as bohemianism and the wanderlust. The romantic embroiders wonder upon the world as it is, unlike the sentimentalist who demands that the world measure up to a preconceived ideal. So we zestfully sought experiences, and we delighted for their own sake in exotic faces and strange shores.

MY MOTHER AND SISTER WENT to Halifax, Nova Scotia, in the summer. There was nothing further to hold me, and exactly three years after I had sailed from home I left New York on a second-class ticket covering transportation by ship to New Orleans and thence by day-coach on the Southern Pacific Railroad to Los Angeles. When I stepped aboard the *Comus*, I discarded my old self for the time being. Career became inconsequential. Like a person starting on a long holiday, I was ready to swing with any tide and do anything that amused me. Perhaps because of my very assurance I did not have a single qualm of seasickness. The second-class was full of emigrants seduced by the cheap rate to California, and I made casual friends among them.

There was a little Cockney who averred that he had been around the world three times, visited every continent, and sailed the seven seas before the mast, as a steward or as a passenger, but who struck a false note by persistently wearing a bowler hat in his walks on deck. A sad Swiss admitted to turning tramp whenever he was short of cash; he had paid only for his steamship ticket and he would hop a freight train for the rest of the journey.

Too, there was Gertrude, a pretty German girl who said that she worked as a maid but had restless feet and tried some new part of the world whenever the notion struck her, "yust like a man". I drank beer, played penny poker and swapped lies with them all, including Gertrude. My hopes regarding her were thwarted by the miserable crowding of our respective cabins, never free of some victim of *mal-de-mer*.

The pilot took us across the bar of the Mississippi at nightfall in the face of lashing gusts, and we lay at the anchorage called Head of Passes. Before noon the next day we docked at the foot of Bienville Street in the Vieux Carré, New Orleans. My curiosity about the city was intense on account of my boyhood plans for going there, and I had decided to spend the day. Alas, the rain was pouring in torrents, and the balconied houses of which I had heard so much looked dismal. I made my way along the Levée, then turned up to Royal Street, keeping under the arcades as much as possible. I had no guidebook and was not so lucky as to stumble upon any of the famous restaurants or bars. The old French Quarter of New Orleans is picturesque under even the worst conditions, and I felt its charm. It is impossible, however, to do sightseeing happily in damp clothes. I gave up the attempt after a few hours and drove to the railroad station, just in time to catch the 'tourist' express. I now suspect that if I had spent the night in New Orleans I should have remained for a while and might never have gone on to the Coast.

Gertrude and the Cockney were in the day-coach where I found a seat. We agreed to stay together for the transcontinental run, and for the first two days it worked well. The train did not have a diner. It made stops for meals and we rushed for the lunch counters, treating it as a great lark to eat quickly, take a look at the Texas town in question, and dart back at the last minute. At San Antonio we had a long stopover and saw the Alamo. But forty-eight hours in a day-coach will exhaust the attractions of most companions. I found the Cockney insufferably garrulous. Gertrude began to look frowsy, and to mumble as if she were half asleep all the time. Alone, I'd have made shift to offer her my shoulder as a pillow and got some fun out of it. The grubby Cockney made this impossible. So by the third day I was interested only in the stupendous desert scenery through which we passed.

Above all I remember colour of a very different quality from that of the tropics. A note jotted at the time records that during the day everything "shimmered in a white and palpitating heat". The whiteness is what dwells with me, culminating in a pageantry of sunset built up not with clouds – for we had reached the desert and clouds seldom form there – but with the mountain ranges and the scattered rocks themselves. The tones were so piercing and dry that the heaped masses appeared soaked in colour. Those far off were semi-opaque battlements of amethyst, jasper, red coral and onyx, while the ones nearby seemed transparent as if made of crystal dyed lemon-yellow, rose or green.

We pulled into Los Angeles early on the fifth day, and I went by myself to a modest rooming house. The city had a population of well under half a million, but already showed all the characteristics of boosterism and devotion to cults and fads that afterward became so inflated. I tried hard to like it, but could not. The buildings were ugly, and the much-vaunted climate a disagreeable alternation between hot days and chilly nights. One of the first persons I met was a retired doctor living next door who urged me to abstain totally from salt because it was the cause of all human ills. Another man, encountered in a cheap restaurant, did his utmost to sell me a lot in a new suburb called Hollywood. The price was fifty dollars and the down payment would be only three dollars, he said; if I pyramided the investment I would certainly make a fortune. These two exhortations show how hard it is for a greenhorn to judge the truth. The second man, as it happened, was right. But I had no taste for business, nor did I feel that I could spare three dollars. What I wanted was a job that would set my feet on the trails of adventure.

Employment agencies were a much larger factor than in New York. They advertised jobs of every description in the newspapers and on blackboards in their waiting rooms. The market was fluid. Men were being shipped in gangs up and down the Pacific Coast, to work at picking fruit or on various construction projects. I almost decided to sign up for no matter what, so long as it would take me into the wilderness, but glanced at my soft hands and thought better of it. Early one morning I saw a notice posted for a timekeeper on the Mexican border, at seventy-five dollars a month and everything found. That sounded attractive, though my ideas about a timekeeper's duties were vague. I went inside to interview the labour agent.

He questioned me carelessly and nodded approval when I told him I could run a typewriter. "That's good. They want a fellow who can make clean monthly reports," he said. "By the way, can you talk Spanish?"

"Yes," I answered.

"Then you'll do. The fee to us will be twenty dollars, payable in advance."

I demurred in alarm, informing him that twenty-five dollars and a few cents was all I had.

"Don't let that worry you," he said. "We give you a railroad pass to go down there. Even if they don't like your work, they can't replace you inside of a month. You'd come out ahead."

His happy-go-lucky talk sapped my honesty, for to tell the truth I knew only a few words of Spanish and had claimed the contrary on an impulse. Since the bluff had worked, so be it. I paid him the twenty dollars and he gave me credentials. The firm to which he was sending me was Grant Brothers Construction Company, engaged in building a spur into Mexico for the Southern Pacific Railroad. That was why I could have a pass to Nogales on the border, near which the headquarters camp was located. So a couple of weeks after my arrival in Los Angeles I retraced my route as far as Tucson, Arizona, where I changed for a local running south.

There was a stopover of several hours in Tucson. I had no sooner stepped out of the railroad station than I perceived I was taking the right detour in my quest for novelty. The blank-faced adobe houses in the narrow streets were Navajo modified by Spanish, and people with leathery dark skins peered from the doorways. But the town was the chief crossroads in thousands of square miles of desert, and as such was bedizened with anachronistic frontier saloons. I dropped into several of them. The rows of hard drinkers appropriately armed and costumed for the Arizona Territory of 1907 may be imagined. I had been prepared for them, more or less. I was thunderstruck, however, at the poker game I watched in one barroom where five men gambled with a sinister venom, the tall stacks in front of them being twenty-, ten- and five-dollar gold pieces instead of chips.

The local train, aptly called El Burro, passed through sagebrush country that looked as if it had never been inhabited. It did not bore me, and I regretted that it was after dark when we reached Nogales, a small town that straddled the border between Arizona and the Mexican state of Sonora. I went to the Montezuma Hotel on the American side, where I took a room for the night. My situation seemed a doubtful kettle of fish, for I had barely enough money to pay for the room and breakfast the next morning. But I learned that a buckboard from the construction company's camp always came to town for supplies on that day of the week. The driver was pointed out to me, a lanky Southwesterner who grunted that I was expected and told me to hop up. We crossed the border without formalities of any sort and rattled along a bad road for three miles, skirting the single track of an old Mexican railroad, and then diverging a short distance to the camp. The latter comprised a rough frame and corrugated iron warehouse containing an office and bunk rooms, a canteen and a cook tent, a dump heap of equipment, and a corral for horses and mules.

At once I was plunged into a bizarre existence in which luck was with me. The superintendent, harassed by a thin, restless wife who should never have been brought to such a spot, was about to be transferred. He did not speak a word of Spanish. His assistants in office and warehouse were equally ignorant of the language, with the exception of an ancient white-bearded Canadian employed as a labour scout who used a jargon, a pidgin-lingo that even I realized was inadequate. But I was supposed to be fluent in Spanish. I do not know whether this or my lack of experience at timekeeping worried me most.

Then I discovered that I would have to keep time for only about twenty persons, half of whom were Americans, for this was the administration centre and not like the labour camps, which were strung out at intervals farther down. My chief duties would be in the canteen, where I found a Mexican clerk who spoke English, and in the office. With the clerk's help I made a list of the essential words and before long I was getting by easily enough.

An early question asked me was whether I had a revolver. I said 'no' and was advised to get one. It was not prudent to go about with a gun at your belt, I was told, because this was Mexico and the people resented the idea that North Americans were seeking to overawe them, but precisely because it was Mexico a gun in your hip pocket or desk drawer amounted to a sage precaution. So I charged myself with a .38 Smith & Wesson at the canteen, the first revolver I had ever owned, and on occasion when I felt sure no one would follow me I went out among the stark rocks that lay to the north of the camp and practised target shooting. I proved a wretched marksman, but the activity earned me credit for knowing how to handle firearms.

Sparse sagebrush and a very few stunted trees, mostly chaparral, were the sole vegetation that relieved the monotony of the rocks. Bird life was rare, except for that desert member of the versatile cuckoo family which looks like the awkward Caribbean lizard cuckoo but has developed the faculty of running with amazing speed. It is called the road runner, or more properly the chaparral cock. Jack rabbits were occasionally seen, and as I was certain of missing with a revolver I did not mind taking shots at the uneatable brutes, to stimulate their grotesque leaps. I discounted larger game so near to camp and was wary only about snakes.

Then one afternoon, as the declining sun was throwing long shadows, I turned into a hollow and saw a great dun-coloured cat stretched out on a ledge about twenty-five feet from me. It was a cougar, or puma, known in the West as a mountain lion. What a lie it would be if I were to write that I was not scared! I had never before been alone in the open with a dangerous wild beast. Yet a sound instinct caused me to stand still. The worst policy in such circumstances is to bolt, for this invites pursuit.

Memories of lore I had read about cougars flashed through my mind. The creature is supposed to be the least pugnacious of its race, indeed somewhat faint-hearted in an encounter with man. This one gave no such impression. It lay easily, its two paws extended and bulking like those of the Sphinx. It stared at me fixedly, and when I moved its eyes followed me, which was not pleasant. My .38 revolver would have been ludicrous as a weapon if the cougar had decided to attack. The beast's indolence, however, was complete. I edged around a spur of rock, and as soon as I had put it between us I hurried my pace with progressive energy until I was at a safe distance. Afterward I found beauty in the episode, whereas, given my atavistic repugnance for the dog tribe, a meeting with a wolf would have left me horror-stricken.

In camp I gave a nonchalant account of the cougar and was commended. I needed to appear not too much of a tenderfoot if I was to avert hazing by my companions, a notably unpredictable lot. Even the hen-pecked superintendent, who ordinarily talked like a school-teacher, and the glum Chinese cook were given to sudden bursts of temper. The sub-contractors, section bosses and foremen from the other camps represented a type new to me, for they were surviving tough boys of the raw West. One man was said to be wanted in Kansas for murder. Another had the reputation of never taking a bath, and it was true that if you stood leeward of him he smelled like a neglected birdcage. Also there were the Mexican labourers ebbing back and forth, hundreds of them, dark little full-blooded Indians or *mestizos*, accompanied by their women to cook and wash for them, ill-paid peons whom I afterward learned were delivered like cattle by local authorities who collected a bonus of so much a head. It was still the period of the dictator, Porfirio Díaz. No wonder our antique labour scout could be such a faker. All he had to do was to jabber his requirements, illustrated in the sign language, to the nearest *jefe político*. My first two weeks were a chaos, which I convinced myself that I enjoyed mightily because of the setting and the unique experience I was gaining. Actually the show started for me when the superintendent left and his successor, Bill McKee, took over.

It is too bad, in a way, that I never cared to specialize in the Western novel, that popular feature of American mythology. For in McKee I had a character who would have stood out vividly in spite of the mock heroics and false virtue which tradition demands of a Western hero. He was small and lean, standing straight as a lance, not a day under sixty-five, with sweeping sandy-grey moustaches and only one steady blue eye. His attitude toward the work was realistic, lenient, a little cynical, but there was absolutely no fooling the man. He inspected everything within twelve hours of his arrival. When he came to me, he seemed to like my account of myself. "How good is your Spanish?" he asked finally.

"Not very good," I answered. "But I'm learning."

"The damned lingo stumps me most of the time. I hear you haven't made any serious mistakes. You'll be all right," he said and turned away.

McKee was from Nashville, Tennessee. He had served through the war in the Confederate army, and had then had difficulties at home which he would not discuss. He may have ridden with the original Ku Klux Klan under General Forrest, for all I know. Then he had come West, where he had drifted for almost forty years and where he expected to die. He knew practically everyone, at least by reputation, in the far-flung worlds of southwestern railroading, construction and mining. McKee swore constantly in a biting, sarcastic, ingenious way. But if you laughed at one of his queer blasphemies he would laugh with you and generally give a fanciful account of the origin of the curse. He liked to tell things about himself, some of them strangely candid, and others with a flippancy that you knew was intended to mask the true version.

For instance, he asked me if I had noticed that he kept no liquor around and refused to drink whenever a visitor offered his flask. I replied, "Yes," adding that I supposed he did not like the stuff. "Ha, ha!" he cackled in his dry, railing fashion. "Why, man, I'm the greatest booze-fighter you ever heard of. I've piled up a stake a dozen times and then cut loose on liquor until the last red cent was gone. I've drunk myself into jails and hospitals. If I don't touch it now it's because I don't dare to, seeing as how I'm getting to be as old as God and feel I oughta save another stake. The first slug would set me off."

I looked incredulous, whereupon he rooted in his desk and pulled out a snapshot of himself slouched on a stool, his clothes disordered, his hair hanging over his eyes, and wearing the idiotic expression of a man blind drunk. "That was taken at Santa Monica, California," he said. "Some son of a bitch took it and gave it to the woman who was trying to watch out for me. When I sobered up and she showed it to me, I couldn't remember anything I'd done for a week, much less the taking of the Christless picture. But I'm glad I have it. It's funny." In doubt as to what it would be prudent to say, I shrugged. "You'd be surprised to know how many men there are in this outfit who can only stay off liquor by not drawing their pay," McKee continued. "I haven't drawn mine for a year. We all hope to quit with a couple of thousand or so and buy a farm. Ha, ha! Wonder which of us will be the first to fall off the wagon with a bang."

One morning he handed me a cheque for a hundred and fifty dollars on the little Mexican bank in Nogales. He told me to ride in and get the money, which was needed to settle with some minor employees. The regular payroll, running into thousands of dollars, was made up once a month and the cash fetched by the superintendent himself in a buckboard with a guard carrying a rifle. My errand seemed trivial to me. I cantered the three miles, left my horse among several others hitched outside the bank, and presented the cheque.

Paper money was scorned in the West in those days. The cashier gave me two small canvas bags, one containing gold and the other silver, which I crammed into the side pockets of my coat. As I walked out of the building, two idling Mexicans whom I had not noticed before did likewise. They waited for me to mount and ride away. Then casually they swung themselves onto their horses and followed at a distance. I was still unsuspecting. But when we were a good mile out of the town, with nothing visible except mesquite and rocks, it struck me that the men had drawn much nearer, and I became alarmed. They had seen me cash the cheque, and I realized that I should be a fool in this lawless frontier country to assume that they were harmless travellers. I rode a little faster, and they promptly speeded up. I slowed down, and they imitated me. I stopped, and they did so too.

We were now close enough for me to turn and see their faces plainly, a pair of dark countenances with black eyes fixed upon me very coldly. I was not carrying a revolver in sight, and neither were they. But someone at the camp had told me that Mexicans preferred to attack with knives, having no confidence in themselves at gunplay with foreigners. Furthermore, they believed every North American to be a dead shot. I had the inspiration to draw my revolver quickly from my hip pocket and fire once, not at either of the men but in the air, a gesture that did not betray my poor marksmanship and could be taken as a warning. The men started, looked at each other, hesitated for a minute, then turned their horses' heads and loped off. I went straight to McKee, gave him the money and described exactly what had happened. He stared at me owlishly with his one eye. "Why, you're a tenderfoot, damn you to hell!" he said without malice. "I figured you'd look out in Nogales for somebody to ride back with." He slapped me on the shoulder. "Can't say you didn't handle the Greasers smartly, though."

THAT WAS MY FIRST BRUSH with danger on the border. My second had complications and spun itself out. I had many chances to go to Nogales, on errands during the day to make purchases or to the post office, and at night with groups of men who lusted after the bars and bordellos of the shabby little town. I was by myself one afternoon when I noticed a comely Mexican girl behind the counter of a small haberdashery shop. Being in the mood for a flirtation, I entered, bought a handkerchief from her and lingered to chat. She spoke fair English. Her type was extremely sensuous, with full red lips against an olive skin, masses of jet black hair and prominent breasts. I could not penetrate her reserve that day, but she told me her name was Concha Martínez, and I said I would look in again.

The next time, I came with a hoary subterfuge. My Spanish was very poor, I said, and I needed practice in conversation. Was she willing to exchange lessons with me? Concha gave me an enigmatic look that touched me to flame. Her physical exuberance reminded me of Margaret. I did not stop to make comparisons with the limpid honesty of the Irish girl. When Concha scribbled her home address, murmuring that it would be all right for me to call the following evening after supper, I was enchanted.

Camp rules forbade the use of the horses at night for private purposes. But a little extra effort meant nothing to me. I had walked into town before with parties, and this time I struck out by myself without leaving word where I was going. The walk was uneventful. The street to which I was bound proved to be several squares from the international line, a street of huddled adobe houses looking primordial and secretive in the moonlight. I thought it a romantic setting.

Concha answered my knock and admitted me to a living room into which the front door opened directly. The moment I entered a very old woman came tottering and took an armchair that had been placed in the doorway connecting with the rear of the house. Concha did not offer to present me, and when I glanced curiously at her she shrugged a shoulder and smiled. We sat beside each other on a sofa. For about a quarter of an hour we gravely discussed the Spanish language. Then the old woman, whose head had been sagging onto her chest, began to snore rhythmically. Concha chuckled. "My grandmother," she explained. "Always she must be the duenna if anyone comes to visit me, and always she falls asleep. It would take the letting off of firecrackers to wake her."

The rapidity with which our dallying progressed after that astonished me. I felt it was love at first sight for both of us. But I could not quite get the old woman out of my mind. I threw oblique looks at her slumbering form, though Concha fairly hissed at me to pay no attention and ended by becoming so annoyed that she flounced off to make coffee. I was annoyed at myself. On the occasion of my next visit, the duenna's routine being exactly as before, I concluded that Concha must know her own grandmother, and I behaved more courageously. The girl's parents were dead, I learned. The crone was her sole guardian.

I came back several times in the course of the next two weeks, always footing it both ways. The liaison assumed for me an aspect of permanence. I asked nothing better than to love and be loved by this wild girl of the country. Then a young Mexican who worked in the canteen asked, with many apologies, if I would object to his warning me about something. "Of course not," I answered carelessly. "What is it?"

"If you keep going to Nogales alone at night, I think you will not live much longer," he said.

"Why?"

"Juan Saya, of Number Two Camp, is very angry at you for taking that young lady, Concha Martínez, away from him. They were engaged to be married, and Juan has sworn to kill you. He trailed you the other night."

My informant's words rang true, but I did not want to believe him. I had an appointment with Concha that very evening. Dramatically I decided that if I failed to keep it and Juan was really after me, he would be encouraged by my cowardice to knife me at the first opportunity. So I checked my revolver to make sure that it was fully loaded and, with private qualms, I started after supper. There was no longer a moon. The road beside the railroad track was villainously hard to navigate in the pitch darkness, and to make matters worse there chanced to be a string of freight cars on the track itself. It would be easy for a killer to dodge among the cars and strike from behind.

Soon I felt sure that I was being followed. I interpreted certain noises as being a man's foot scraping the ties and rattling the cinders. I did not see anyone, but I repeated the tactics I had used on the ride from the bank and fired one shot in the air. No attack developed and I strode into town at record speed. By then I was in a great fury at Concha.

When she opened the door to me I at once denounced her. "It's no thanks to you that I'm alive," I said. "You might at least have told me to be on guard against Juan Saya."

She recoiled, biting her lip, disconcerted for a moment. "If you thought there would be no man to be jealous over a girl like me, you were a fool," she countered. "It was your business to find out and protect yourself."

"Suppose I hadn't found out in time! You wouldn't have cared a rap, eh?"

"Of course I would have cared, *chico*. But why do you go on complaining? Nothing has happened to you."

My next impulse did me no credit. Resolved to make her feel guilty, I boasted: "Juan tried to stab me out there by the railroad track, and I shot him dead."

"It is not true," she breathed, her eyes dilating.

I took out my revolver, broke it and showed her that one shell had been discharged.

"You murderer!" she screamed, and jumped straight at me. Her fingernails scored my face deeply before I shook her off.

I walked home, my ego badly deflated. Yet I found at camp the next day that the Mexicans considered me a devil of a fellow for having gone into town in spite of the warning and avenging myself, as they saw it, by shocking the girl out of her wits. The details, naturally, had circulated over the grapevine.

McKee's comment on my scratched cheek was typical. "By the jumping Jesus Christ! It beats all, the price a fella your age will pay for a skirt," he exclaimed. I could not help grinning, for I had not heard his expletive before, and immediately he put on a solemn air. "That's no cussing. It's a pious reference to the Ascension, the highest and longest jump in history," he said. A month later I heard that Concha and Juan Saya were married. My period of disillusionment having ended, I rated this a good ironic joke.

THERE WAS MUCH SERIOUS VIOLENCE in northern Sonora that winter, especially just southwest of Cananea, the terminus of the railroad spur Grant Brothers Construction Company was building. Yaqui Indians had risen, and the *rurales* led by a Russian adventurer named Colonel Kosterlitzky waged a running fight with them. Near Magdalena, about fifty miles from our headquarters camp, Yaquis killed twelve Mexican civilians on a ranch. As the mutilated bodies were found naked and lashed to the trunks of trees, the worst horrors could be presumed. Kosterlitzky moved swiftly, but when he failed to catch any of his quarry he descended on the construction company's camps and charged that Yaqui warriors had taken pick-and-shovel jobs as a means of hiding. The notion was preposterous. Nevertheless, all the peons had to be lined up, along with their womenfolk. Kosterlitzky inspected them personally, declared that some twenty of both sexes were fugitive Yaquis and marched them away to Hermosillo, the state capital.

The Mexican border was prodigal of strong men. The life threw them up, or attracted them to itself. They were needed to control the rank and file of brawling, carousing roughs, and the dull dogs. Bill McKee, to a certain point, was a strong man, but under a cloud because of his past lapses with liquor, and trusted only tentatively. It would have been permissible for him to be a heavy drinker, but not to become incompetent for days on end as he had admitted to doing. The complete strong man was a type that I suppose must exist today. It could not have vanished from the American strain when the border was tamed. So different are its physical appearance and its activities, however, that I fail to recognize it. Two figures from my Nogales days will be sufficient as examples.

James Cashion, the head of Grant Brothers Construction Company, had been a pick-and-shovel labourer, a foreman, a sub-contractor – in brief he had gone the whole route on his relentless way from the bottom to the top. His office was in Los Angeles. He could seldom have been there, for a dozen interests kept him swinging on a wide circuit through the West. When Cashion came down to us on a tour of inspection, the string of camps felt his presence like an electric shock. He needed only a glance to detect a flaw in a section of grade, and the offender took his judgement as gospel.

A burly extrovert in the prime of life, Cashion's brunet skin was as clear as a woman's, his voice an impressive growl. He wore an enormous black moustache. Catching sight of me in the lobby of the Montezuma Hotel, Nogales, he recognized me as an employee he had seen at the headquarters camp and waved me to join the party he was leading to the bar. That kind of bonhomie with a youngster was part of his social technique. I had two drinks on him, listened to him talk like an empire builder, and was at one with his camp superintendents in rating him a 'big guy'.

Tom McCarty was something quite different. I heard of him when I first arrived and was made to feel that his personality was legendary. McCarty had lived for years among the Yaquis, in the heart of Sonora where Mexican pressure upon the Indians was most severe. He spoke Spanish and the Yaqui dialects perfectly. He was the only white man allowed to pass in and out of the Indian strongholds at will, and he acted as a go-between for the exchange of prisoners and other amenities. Both sides trusted him. Grant Brothers had thought it wise to pay him a bonus simply to explain their activities to the Yaquis and advise the latter not to attempt raids on the construction camps.

"What is his stake in the country?" I asked. "What is the source of his power?"

I was told that he was believed to be working a secret mine. Then he had a Yaqui wife, a chief's daughter, and it could be presumed that that had been a factor in his acceptance by the tribe. He brought her to the towns to shop for silks and jewellery whenever he felt like it, and although the regulations provided that every Yaqui must be arrested, the Mexican soldiers did not touch her.

McCarty came to our camp one day. I had never seen such a man. He was tall and lean with the features of a raptorial bird, his whitish-grey eyes like pebbles against a skin tanned to the colour of saddle leather, his sweeping moustache bleached by the sun. He spoke to no one, except McKee in private conference, and when he headed back alone it was by a side trail into sheer wilderness. In a subtle, inexplicable way, Tom McCarty seemed the master of his world, far more powerful than Kosterlitzsky, the colonel of *rurales*.

I decided that five months of the border would be enough, and that at the end of that time I would go to San Francisco. Shortly afterward I received a letter from my father saying that he was about to sail from Panama to California. He would stop over in Los Angeles, and he asked me to write him at General Delivery there. I was delighted, though a little saddened on his account, for his early move from the Isthmus probably meant that he had had another financial failure. It fitted in with my plans to meet him the first of the next month, and I gave my notice to Grant Brothers Construction Company.

But before I left Mexico I got leave from McKee to spend a couple of days in Guaymas, the seaport on the coast of California. It was about two hundred miles from Nogales. I did not have to buy a ticket, for the Mexican line gave me a pass on the grounds that I was a railroad builder. All new country was of interest to me, Sonora more than most, and in Guaymas I found a dream place unspoiled as yet by tourists. It was a small port enclosed on three sides by mountains like brooding wings, and it had an improbable sailing-craft commerce with the peninsula of Lower California and in rusty tramp steamers with Japan. Fishing boats rocked at the indigo-blue anchorage.

The town was primitive Spanish colonial. Important buildings around the plaza, including my hotel, the Almada, had colonnades, balconies and thick walls enclosing patios choked with flowers. The rest was adobe, monotonous in form but of many tints. All sounds were muted in the still, warm air. The band in the plaza on Sunday toned down its brass and played romantic Mexican airs – "Sobre las olas", "La Paloma" – and the young men and girls took separate paths, crossing each other in a figure-of-eight, flirting cunningly the while.

Guaymas was my first Latin American town of any size. At the Café Gambrinus I watched a girl dancer, savage and sad, whom I afterward put into a story. On the central street I saw Tom McCarty for the second time, riding a beautiful mustang, with his Yaqui wife behind him on another pony. He looked straight through me. Guaymas gave me no more than those few pictures: enough to make a piquant, fruitful memory.

CHAPTER 5 ❧ San Francisco

THAT I SHOULD BE GOING to an appointment with my father in Los Angeles did not seem quite real. Jamaica apart, his stories of China and London gave me the only convincing backgrounds for him, and nowise could I associate him with a boom town of the American Southwest. Indeed when I saw him waiting in the lobby of the Post Office, his thin suit rumpled, his fine head slanted, and his spectacles on his nose under a misshapen felt hat, he looked like a tropical planter and nothing else. What a good meeting it was, all the same. We shook hands, chuckling, asking the most haphazard questions, telling the first reminiscences that came to mind, as if we were pals of the same age. He interrupted to say that in the three and a half years since I had left home I appeared to have picked up the experience of seven years, and of course that pleased me. We took a walk, saw a vaudeville show, and continued our talk until late into the night.

It soon came out, as I had feared, that my father had made a mess of affairs in Panama. His latest enthusiasm was for Oregon where he had been informed there was big money in apples. I could not imagine a more visionary scheme, for he had no knowledge of apple-growing or selling apples, and labour problems in Oregon differed radically from those of the West Indies. He conceded that it might be better to practise his hand first at any venture that turned up, but he was resolved to try the Northwest sooner or later. I told him that Los Angeles, in my opinion, was a miserable town and that I had settled on San Francisco as the place where I hoped to get back into newspaper work. He replied jauntily that he would go there with me, San Francisco being, so to speak, on the road to Oregon.

At Redondo near San Pedro, the port for Los Angeles, we boarded a decrepit tub named the *Santa Rosa*, which a couple of years later went to pieces with considerable loss of life. She wallowed lamentably, and for the second and last time I was seasick, recovering just before the beautiful approach to San Francisco. The fog that had wrapped the Farallon islets parted and we saw the Golden Gate, the morning sun directly behind it, on the one hand the city of many hills sloping down to rocks on which sea lions basked, on the other the Sausalito heights with Mount Tamalpais in the distance. The waterfront where we landed had preserved its Spanish name, the Embarcadero. Although downtown San Francisco was still partly in ruins from the earthquake, I found the city as romantic in its utterly different way as New Orleans. In fact I am an early member of the school that proclaimed, and still proclaims, that only three North American cities have ever been romantic in the literary sense: New York, New Orleans and San Francisco.

My father and I took rooms in an old frame house south of Market Street, not far from where the fire had stopped. One of the first things I did was to go to the block on Mission Street where Florence Brochu had lived. I had hoped the house would be standing and that I could get some news of its occupants of two years earlier. But the whole block had been levelled by the earthquake and then burned over. A policeman told me that the casualties there had been very heavy. I turned away mournfully, convinced that Florence was dead. But the heart is resilient at twenty-one, and I did not mourn long.

For several days after our arrival, I roamed with my father about the city. It pleased him better than any place he had seen since leaving Jamaica. The obvious signs of contact with the Orient set his tongue to wagging of his youth in the Canton silk trade. He thought San Francisco's famous Chinatown a garish travesty of a typical shopping district in Canton, but it entertained him. Chop suey was a fake of a dish, he said, a hash invented to delude Americans into supposing that they were getting the real thing. Nevertheless, he ate large quantities of it. I have no doubt that he would have liked to remain in San Francisco, unsuited though he was to the life. The Northwest would be still more impracticable for him, but he was committed to that dream, and away he went before the end of the week.

I now set about my own projects. My attitude was altogether different from the one with which I had faced New York. Perhaps I had been too intense then, too resentful at the failure of editors to acknowledge my talent. The winter on the border had done me good. I was light-hearted and took it as a matter of course that I would get my share of recognition. To the devil with the policy of trying to force myself upon anybody. I would mix with people in the profession, and some of them were bound to meet me halfway when they realized what my experience had been.

The San Francisco newspapers of the period were the *Chronicle*, *Call*, *Examiner* and *Bulletin*, as well as a Scripps daily of small significance. I called on all the city editors, was turned down, grinned and told them I'd be back sometime. There were also a literary weekly, the *Argonaut*; two weeklies that flourished on scabrous gossip, the *San Francisco News-Letter* and the *Wasp*; the dignified old *Overland Monthly*, which had been founded by Bret Harte; and the *Sunset Magazine*, a monthly, published as a sort of glorified house organ by the Southern Pacific Railroad. I dropped in at their offices, spun yarns about Jamaica and Mexico, and promptly was asked to write articles for almost all of them. The *Argonaut* suggested that I give a fictional treatment of my Sonora adventures, and before long I sold two short stories to that paper. I did some factual pieces about the Yaquis for the *Overland Monthly*.

The amounts paid in every instance were extremely small. My name was publicized, however, and it became simple to place stories with the Sunday magazines of the newspapers. In New York it had been difficult for me to handle the local material. Here it was much less of a problem. San Francisco seemed the capital of wild regions that I had been exploring, and I wrote easily about the life that effervesced both on the border and in the city.

The earthquake had ripped San Francisco apart in other respects than the physical, but if ever there was an example of a community rallying from disaster in devil-may-care spirit this was one. Stupendous energy had been shown in rebuilding. People were sensitive, however, about admitting that the crisis had been caused by an earthquake. They referred to the calamity as 'the fire', on the theory that a city subject to earthquakes was no fit place to do business, whereas a fire was an accident that might occur anywhere. To this extent they fell into line with Californian boosterism, a revolting propaganda from which they were comparatively free and which they ridiculed when practised in more obvious forms by the people of Los Angeles. It was the contention of the San Franciscans that there had been of course an earthquake, but just a little one that would not have disturbed anybody if the fire had not chanced to break out. Those who had been through it knew better. It was a case of telling a good story and sticking to it. As a matter of fact, the seismic shock had been of great violence, and by disrupting electric and gas conduits it had started not one but a hundred fires.

The tremors had continued at irregular intervals and markedly diminishing force for over two years. They were still occurring when I arrived. The citizens pretended not to notice them, or at the most said, "Ah!" I had never before had the experience and found it more disconcerting than any other natural phenomenon. The variations were very strange. Early one morning the bed in which I was lying rolled easily a few inches away from the wall. On another occasion, as I sat in an office, the whole building shook noisily. No matter how harmless the tremor, one knew that it might be repeated and that even a slight increase in power would send things crashing.

Politically, commercially and socially the city was steeped in scandal, and it manifested little inclination to change its ways. The municipal government at the time of the earthquake had probably been the most picturesquely corrupt that the United States has ever seen. Chicago certainly had been as shameless, but not so colourful. A boss of Franco-Jewish ancestry named Abe Ruef had outmanoeuvred both Republicans and Democrats in 1901 and elected an independent ticket in the name of union labour. The choice for mayor of San Francisco had been priceless. Ruef felt that he needed a candidate who carried a union card, yet he did not want to ruffle the middle class by offering a horny-handed carpenter or bricklayer. So he had picked a musician, Eugene Schmitz, who played in the orchestra at the Tivoli Theater, a strikingly handsome man of his period, with melting eyes and a glossy black beard, admired by the ladies and regarded as a good fellow in sporting circles.

Schmitz was no sooner in office than vice burgeoned on an unexampled scale in a city that had always enjoyed being lawless. Every source of revenue was squeezed for personal profit by the boss and his friends. The mayor, who was twice re-elected, was credited with having a financial interest in many shady enterprises including a huge bordello nicknamed the 'municipal crib'. Things that everybody knew, or at least had guessed, were dragged into the open by the sheer disruption of the earthquake and the temporary regime of martial law that had followed. The Grand Jury had returned indictments. When I reached San Francisco the famous graft investigation was underway, conducted by the reform lawyer Francis J. Heney, with Hiram Johnson as assistant. Schmitz had been superseded as mayor by the highly respectable Dr Edward R. Taylor, a university professor and poet. But these evidences of virtue had scarcely affected the underworld. A tenderloin district shaped like a half-moon curved from Chinatown and its adjacent alleys, around Portsmouth Square and along the lower blocks of Pacific Street, this latter section being the Barbary Coast proper. The dance halls and concert saloons crowded with women entertainers made those of New York seem prim.

The present generation in the United States has never seen anything faintly resembling the old red-light districts of San Francisco and indeed of all the towns of central California. Few books have attempted to describe them frankly. Yet so brazen were their methods, so lurid their glow, that the record of them is important as Americana. Leave aside the Barbary Coast with its concert saloons, which can easily be imagined from the prettified versions offered by the motion pictures. Leave aside the standard bordellos at the opposite end of the scale, run by elegant madames such as Tessie Wall, whose name has lived on. Leave aside even the dives of Chinatown which were largely conducted as shows for sightseers. What I have in mind were the cheap houses known as cribs, cow-pens and other opprobrious names, which filled whole blocks on Commercial Street, Morton Street, Jackson Street, Bacon Place and other nearby San Francisco thoroughfares.

Hordes of men milled in these streets, especially the dead-end alleys which were closed to wheeled traffic by iron chains on posts. They chaffered with the girls through open windows, or pushed into sitting rooms where they could stare at the talent for a minute or two and then, if they had not made a choice, were eased out through another door. The men's faces were commonly more repellent than those of the money-hungry harlots; jowly porcine faces, the weak-chinned faces of pimply boys, simian faces, rat faces, the grimy faces of ditch-diggers, and the sooty faces of stokers from ships. The majority on any given occasion did not intend to take a girl, were perhaps broke. They were window-shopping while others bought, and there was a weird touch about the shifting pattern. Arnold Genthe, the early camera artist, who was a San Franciscan, should have photographed one of those scenes as a companion piece to his marvellous *Street of the Gamblers*, which shows a swarm of pigtailed Chinamen in black, bewitched by their particular lust.

Astonishingly, the most grotesque single establishment that I saw was in the capital, Sacramento. At the foot of one of the slopes of the hill on which stood the neo-Roman building where the laws of California were enacted there could be found a large, low wooden barracks that housed fully a hundred women. It may have had among its customers the less squeamish and prosperous of the legislators, for all I know. Parodying the Frisco term 'cow-pen', it was called the Bull-Pen. The women displayed the upper parts of their bodies nude on shelves formed by letting down panels in the doors of their cubicles. There were several corridors of them, divided into sections – one North American, one supposedly French and fancy, one Mexican, one Chinese, one Negro, et cetera. Race prejudice did not enter the matter. Variety was the watchword. Prices, which dropped as low as half a dollar, were governed by myths of freshness and aptitude for passion. The traffic ebbed and flowed ceaselessly by the light of gas flames in globes of red glass.

The countless bordellos of San Francisco itself were of a staggering diversity, ranging from the foulest dens to luxuriously furnished houses, or apartments, the parlours of which were patronized as cafés by a certain nightlife elite. Tessie Wall's mansion on O'Farrell Street was a favourite. Reporters called regularly at some of these places after midnight, to drink and to pick up news rather than to practise bawdry. For those who preferred games of chance, San Francisco was wide, wide open.

I learned the intricacies of this whirlpool and turned everything to journalistic account. But I felt no urge to be on the side of reform. The crusading newspaper was the *Bulletin*, edited by the gifted Fremont Older, and its furious attacks on the ring caused plenty of dynamic action. Its reporters went in peril of their lives. Once Older was kidnapped and held for days. Assuredly I was not scared off from working for the *Bulletin*, for I have always enjoyed danger. Reprehensibly, perhaps, I simply preferred to be one of those allowed behind the scenes, instead of having to behave like a detective in hostile territory. I was on the staff of the reactionary *Chronicle* for a few weeks. Then I found a soft spot on the house organ of the Pacific Gas and Electric Company, which left me time for freelance articles and fiction.

I was on my way to the courtroom to take notes for an impression of

Heney in action when he was shot from the floor and wounded so seriously that he was never able to resume. A young reporter thinks it a great misfortune to be cheated of such a spectacle, and I was no exception. I wrote instead about Johnson, who took over the graft investigation on the spot. His personality did not appeal to me, and I erred by making light of him. The assassin's bullet had started Hiram Johnson toward the governorship of California, a seat in the United States Senate and a chance at the presidency, which he missed by a hair.

MY SIDELIGHT ON THE GREAT Biggy mystery was fortuitous. I have never before told it in print. William J. Biggy had been appointed chief of police shortly after the earthquake and fire. He was a moderate who had closed a few blatantly evil resorts while apparently holding the line for Ruef on major issues. There was considerable surprise when Biggy was ordered removed from office at the height of the graft investigation, for reasons which the police board did not announce. Biggy refused to accept dismissal, and in this he was upheld by a minority of the commissioners. The rumour ran that he intended to go to Johnson and tell all he knew. The possibility infuriated the ring. It was stated openly that if the chief wanted to enjoy good health he would make a sweeping denial. Clamping his jaws under his black moustache, the chief said nothing.

On the night of 30 November 1908, I dropped in rather early at one of the superior uptown bordellos near Van Ness Avenue and ordered a drink. The place was a flat. My seat in the parlour happened to command a view of the corridor, and when four or five police officers walked past I recognized the man in the middle as Chief Biggy. It was the first time I had seen him there, but his presence was no cause for wonder. He often visited bordellos on tours of inspection, or for private conferences with his cronies. The last-named possibility was of interest to me, and I edged my way to a spot from which I could see to the end of the corridor. Two civilians were standing in the doorway of a bedroom. I could not identify them, because the solid forms of the officers blocked off their faces. They stepped backward, and Biggy and one of his men followed them. The door closed. The other officers had the air of standing guard over it. Fifteen minutes later Biggy lumbered out, his features set wrathfully. I did not think it prudent to ask him for a news tip, for it had been known for days that he was ready to bite off the head of any reporter who approached him. He and his officers departed the way they had come. The civilians remained out of sight; there was a back entrance which they probably used.

The incident seemed a San Francisco commonplace. As I had no assignment to cover, I went home at midnight. The morning paper, however, plunged me into a state of excitement over the scene I had witnessed. Four-column headlines declared that Chief Biggy had vanished from a police launch in the Bay. Judging by the time schedule given, I decided that he had gone straight from the bordello to the ferry at the foot of Market Street. There he had taken a launch to Oakland and had visited the home of Hugo Keil, one of the police commissioners friendly to him. Several persons had seen him re-embark in the launch. According to the man at the wheel and a policeman who was aboard, the chief's absence was not noticed until they had almost reached the San Francisco side. Then they had cruised frantically in search of him, to no avail. "Poor old Chief! Wonder why he should have committed suicide!" they hazarded.

I felt sure that I had, if not a scoop, at least what we called a hot angle that might lead to a solution of the case. Not one of the papers had mentioned that Biggy had been at the uptown bordello, so I appeared to be the only reporter who knew it. I rushed straight to the city room where I had a connection as a space writer and told my story. The city editor heard me out stonily, then said with a curious acid inflection:

"Hot stuff! Now you just go away from here and forget you ever saw that."

"You mean you're not going to use it?" I demanded, amazed.

"Hell, man, if I *could* use it I'd give you the break. I'd let you write it. But I'm telling you, bury the whole thing so deep that you never even talk about it. You must have been recognized at that joint. So don't sell the story to the *Bulletin*. If you do we'll be running a stick about your funeral."

He may have been exaggerating. Clearly it was the policy of his reactionary paper to call me off. No doubt he could make a good guess at the identity of the two civilians at the bordello. In view of what had happened, I knew that they must have been top-rank politicians who had hoped to persuade Biggy not to give evidence in the graft investigation. But the other police officers counted for more in the riddle than any politician. If Biggy had talked on the witness stand, his own department would have been hardest hit. It seemed plain to me that his escort had herded the chief to his rendezvous, and that when he had proved intractable a police ringleader playing the Judas role had passed the word that he must not return from Oakland.

I did not work up a keen interest in any of the political figures I met in San Francisco. The state had been ruled for some time by henchmen of the great railroad systems, the Southern Pacific and the Union Pacific. The governors had been chosen from this ring, which was constituted of smooth manipulators, mostly lawyers, who did not make very good copy when they came to town. Before the earthquake and the graft investigation, the city obviously had had colourful rogues in power; but these now kept in the background, worried lest they might be sent to prison. Abe Ruef, a little fellow with a manner so subdued that my colleagues said it was comical, would occasionally see the reporters *en masse*. Ex-Mayor Schmitz simply could not be interviewed, not at least by a freelance of my standing. This was a pity. I should have liked to study Schmitz at first-hand.

No leaders worthy of the name had taken charge politically. Those in the limelight were all brigands or prosy reformers. Except Fremont Older. The editor of the *Bulletin* could have been a leader, but he preferred to confine himself to newspaper crusading. No one could have bumbled along more ineptly than the interim mayor, Dr Taylor; he was at least honest. The men who got out the vote and held the lesser offices were mere hacks. I can spare no space in these memoirs for the gamblers and lords of the tenderloin who financed campaigns and took the largest slice of the profits. It is enough to say that when 'Pin Head' McCarthy was elected mayor, he at once telegraphed to certain notorious gamblers who had been driven out of the city by Taylor: "Come back. We have won."

The city was impassioned about sports, especially prizefighting. Heavy betting was done on star events. I found myself drawn into this feverish current, though not deeply. As I have said in connection with my Jamaican days, I had been unable to take the least interest in the British national game of cricket. My apathy had extended to football and other team sports. In New York enthusiastic friends had dragged me to one or two baseball games, which had left me cold if not downright bored. Now I experimented in other directions and worked up a fair taste for bowling, not as a looker-on but as a player. On a much higher level I placed fencing. Unfortunately it took money as well as a lot of time, and I did not go very far with this most skilful and beautiful of contests.

Boxing as a spectacle really stirred me, and I realized that what I enjoyed was struggle between two individuals, whereas an effort that simply fitted into the pattern of teamwork did not excite me. The first bout that I saw was one of twenty rounds between Owen Moran and Eddie Hanlon, which Moran won on points. There were many others. Stanley Ketchel, the Assassin, billed as a cowboy and actually a bouncer from the concert saloons of Butte, Montana, was easily the most colourful figure of the moment. He had torn through the middleweight division like a hurricane; then, doubtless because he had been dissipating, he had been stopped by the blond, soft-seeming Billy Papke. I watched Ketchel training for his second fight with Papke, saw him weigh in at Tom Corbett's with the gamblers swarming in the room, yelling the odds against him. He was lean and taut, apparently drawn too fine, yet he went out and reversed the verdict beyond debate, carrying Papke along for round after round, so that he could maul him deliberately, cutting his face to tatters before he sketched a jeering signal to the crowd and knocked him out.

LURID POLITICS, NIGHTLIFE AND SPORTS by no means constituted all of the San Francisco that emerged above its substratum of solid wage earners. The era was that of the California literary movement, which had produced a score of names, some crowning their success by migration to New York, some like Jack London, the poet George Sterling and the ageing Ambrose Bierce preferring to remain in or near the city by the Golden Gate, the city they loved and celebrated with passion in their work.

A lively little bohemia existed in the studios of Telegraph Hill, and in French, Italian and Mexican *table d'hôte* restaurants scattered from the Embarcadero to Van Ness Avenue. I enjoyed going to Sanguinetti's, where the meal cost fifty cents and a glass of red wine ten cents; to Coppa's, and to many similar places, ranging up to The Poodle Dog and the Pup which seemed very expensive at a dollar and a quarter a cover; and not least to certain saloons, where perfectly incredible 'free lunches' could be sampled by anyone who bought as little as a glass of beer.

The term 'bohemian' was much in vogue. Several resorts used it, in addition to the bar on Market Street. There was the famous Bohemian Club composed mostly of businessmen with unconventional tastes, but which really welcomed writers and artists as members and lionized the clever ones.

I never felt prosperous enough to join the club. All its celebrities were pointed out to me and I shook hands with some, though I did not get to know any of them well at that time. I was involved too completely with reporters and the obscure applicants who hung around such offices as that of the *Overland Monthly*. Jack London's first sale of a story, years before, had been to the *Overland*. He had grown too busy and successful to keep up the contact.

The strangest of the *Overland*'s coterie in 1908 was Diego Estrada Cabrera, a son of the then dictator of Guatemala. He was attending the University of California, and since women and gambling kept him perpetually short of money, he dropped in to talk about writing articles of which he never did a line. Once he seriously proposed to the rest of us that he would disappear, leaving it to us to launch a good hoax to the effect that he had been kidnapped and was being held for ransom. His father would pay up in a minute, and we must promise to divide the money with Diego. Needless to say, this brilliant plot was never executed.

George Sterling was eventually to be my friend. He paid small attention to me in San Francisco, mainly, I think, because my current pose was to exalt glittering journalese above literature, adventure above art. Sterling seemed to me, nonetheless, the most romantic of the local bohemians, far more so than the recognized chief of the young San Franciscan writers, the vigorous Jack London, who was riding the wave of his gigantic popularity and making money hand over fist. Sterling's profile was often said to resemble that of Dante. A shrewder pen-portrait described him as "a Greek coin run over by a Roman chariot." Actually, there was nothing of the sorrowful Florentine about him except the long, fine nose. Sterling looked, felt and lived like a pagan. His verse was pure Hellenic beauty-worship and hedonism.

He made a cult of women, another and associated cult of San Francisco, which he called "the cool, grey city of love". I was astonished by the perfection of the tragedy of his relations with the young poetess Nora May French, who the year before my arrival had leaped to her death like Sappho from a cliff while Sterling's guest at Carmel, California, though not for love of him. Men who had been of her circle extolled her to me with boundless enthusiasm. Somehow there was no trace of affectation when they called her "the swift-souled one". They were collecting a volume of her poems, which they published locally not long afterward.

Oddly enough, I did not fall in love in San Francisco despite the fact that it was there I began to perceive how great an influence women were to be in my life. I formed a number of light attachments instead, and possibly that was the normal first-result of my shifting mood. My father's part in moulding my boyhood had led me to think subconsciously that in life I would meet a succession of men who would inspire me. Something of the sort had prevailed in Kingston, though in a diluted form. Thereafter I had not attached myself to any man. I had felt myself to be in competition with men. I wished to be, whenever I could, the one among them whose ideas dominated; instances of profound friendship I believed would be rare. On the other hand, I needed the company of women more and more.

THE PHYSICAL SETTING AND CLIMATE of San Francisco were unique, and while I was charmed by the first I was not at all sure that I agreed with George Sterling about the climate. It was neither subtropical nor temperate, but a singular combination of the two which resulted in a mild winter, no true summer, and an arid fall. During most of the year a fog drifted in from the Pacific, crept about the streets at night and banked them solidly by dawn. Warm clothes were needed for nocturnal roving or for starting out to breakfast and the office. But before noon brisk winds swept away the fog and a topcoat became a burden. Even in July it was cooler in the morning than I have known midsummer to be anywhere else. September was the hottest month, for then the fog shredded itself away. I never got accustomed to such eccentricity on the part of the weather. Only the region of the Bay and the coast northward were affected. So I used to make trips up the Sacramento Valley, or down to Santa Cruz or Monterey, to enjoy a little consistent warmth – a motive which my associates found quaint.

On one of these forays I met a peculiar character, an undersized but sturdy man of about thirty-five named Al Hughes. His hair was sandy, his eyes a cold grey. The skin of his face was corrugated, with a high polish between the ridges and permanently red, as the outcome of a severe case of frostbite. Hughes struck up a conversation with me on the beach at Santa Cruz and in less than two minutes had started to tell me about the Alaskan gold rush, which in its second decade was still a bonanza. He was a veteran, of course. I was informed that Indians named Taggish This and Skookum That had been, along with a certain squawman, the real discoverers of the Klondike diggings. The fortitude of the 'sourdoughs' was lauded to me, the hardships of mushing it over the passes glowingly described. Rex Beach, who had lately published a best-seller called *The Spoilers*, had been no sourdough, Hughes said scornfully, but a drifter who had found a tenderfoot's way of cashing in. The gold was the thing. That and the life, which was wonderful. He, Al Hughes, had made and lost a couple of fortunes, and he was eager to take another shot at it. Didn't I want to join a party that would be leaving soon?

Now, despite my flair for adventure, I had never been stirred by the idea of Arctic exploration. As I have just written, there were times when I found even San Francisco a bit too chilly. I said as much to Al, but tactfully, for he was giving me novel information that day and I did not want to discourage him. If I had only known, it was utterly impossible to discourage Al. He retorted that I looked like a regular fellow who had done some knocking about on his own. I answered by telling him briefly about my months on the Mexican border.

"There you are, pal," he exclaimed. "You've had experience. You'd do fine in Alaska."

"Not at all," I protested. "Mexico is my kind of country. I wouldn't know how to cope with snowdrifts above my head and frozen rivers, not to speak of sub-zero cold for half the year."

"Them troubles are nothing. You get accustomed to them, same as you do to snakes in Mexico. Let's go and have a beer."

We crossed the boardwalk to a saloon, where we drank several beers and where Al continued to discourse with an inexhaustible garrulity. I felt presently that I had heard more about Alaska than it was necessary for me to acquire at the cost of my mounting ennui. The rest of the afternoon – indeed the rest of my stay in Santa Cruz – would be, I feared, devoted to the subject unless I got rid of Al. Hints or pleas might do no good. He had already snatched a moment in which to announce that we would dine together at a certain seafood restaurant and then go to a dancehall where the drinks were cheap and the girls attractive. So I bided the time when nature forced Al to leave the bar for a few minutes and walked out on him. I hid myself in one of the many small hotels behind the boardwalk.

Earlier I had incautiously given him my San Francisco address, but thought he would be too offended to use it. I answered a knock four days afterward, and there was the shiny, frostbitten countenance of Al. He did not even refer to my sudden disappearance in Santa Cruz. It was apparently his philosophy that a man was entitled to act on any impulse that seized him. I asked him to have a seat, and he proceeded to dispense the lore of the Klondike as if there had been no interruption. This, I opined, was going to be terrible. I took a strong hand, said that since our meeting I had done nothing but read books about the far North, was weary of the topic and would prefer to change it. Did he, by any chance, know the underworld of San Francisco better than I did? To my surprise, he at once altered his monologue to an account of the Barbary Coast "before the fire", adhering to the Californian pretence that there had been no earthquake worthy of the name in 1906. The material interested me, though his delivery was monotonous to the point of tedium. That evening he showed me some curious dives.

It turned out that Al Hughes was not quite the blockhead that I had taken him for. He had a one-track mind. Conclusions he reached slowly, but when he reached them they had a sort of thick logic. Accusing himself at last of being too talkative, he explained it by saying that he was often alone for weeks in Alaska and stored up the words. Then he turned his powers of analysis upon me and concluded that after all I was not the type for the Klondike. Some men were best suited for the hot jungles, some to be desert rats, and some for the lands of the Northern Lights – the damned finest lands of the lot. Now that he looked at me closely, I had a marked resemblance to a man he knew who had done well with pearl fisheries in the Solomon Islands. Perhaps that would be my game. But while I hung around San Francisco I really ought to try to get myself better fixed financially.

"What would you suggest?" I asked.

Without a trace of sarcasm and judging doubtless from the fact that I had proposed the underworld as a livelier subject than Alaska, Al said that I should pick a girl in a house who showed a fancy for me and make heavy love to her, just as if she were not a whore. This would flatter her so much that she would become my slave. It was no trick at all at my age, he added, to get kept in luxury that way. A week or so later, I saw Al off on the steamer to Seattle and Nome, my opinion of his tip unexpressed.

I have described this individual at some length because, in a negative manner, he had an effect upon my life. Though I liked San Francisco, I knew that I would not remain there. It was one of the world's crossroads and my fate seemed to urge me on to more positive extremes, either of the primitive or the civilized. I had been playing with the idea of going to Tahiti, a name that was a catchword of romance as yet unspoiled by the tourist trade, and then working my way around the world. But the great European capitals also lured me. I intensified my reading on London, Paris, Rome and Vienna, and found myself held most by the glamour with which the writers had invested Paris.

It is not too much to say that Al Hughes turned me against a further spending of my youth in wild places. Whether I were to travel to the Arctic or the South Seas, Al was the characteristic drifter with whom I would find myself involved. Dreams of 'going native' surrounded by beautiful brown-skinned girls were probably only dreams. My companions on voyages, in cheap hotels and bars, would be repetitious he-men without a single aesthetic taste. So it had been in the construction camp on the Mexican border, when I came to think of it. Among those I had known well down there, only Bill McKee had had enough salt to give a memorable tang to his personality. True, I had enjoyed the camp as a novelty, but one such experience was enough. My decision was to return to New York, with Paris as a goal to be reached as soon as possible.

San Francisco stands for youth to me. It was where I first felt like a young man who knew approximately what he intended to do with his life, rather than a precocious boy convinced in Jamaica that the world was his oyster and then brusquely checked. All is not comprised, however, in the accident of finding myself at the Golden Gate when the development took place in me. San Francisco itself was the very spirit of youth. Its darker exuberancies did not alter that fact. Los Angeles was younger as an Anglo-Saxon city, but I could not have responded to the pseudo-religious virtue of Los Angeles.

A wine of life ran strongly in the veins of San Francisco. There was magic there. Lotta's Fountain, at Market and Kearney Streets, erected by Forty-Niners to an actress who had charmed them, was beautiful in the curling fog. Beautiful, too, the delicate little monument in Portsmouth Square to Robert Louis Stevenson, who had lingered in the city on his way to the South Seas. The flowers seemed more brilliant to me than in any other place outside the tropics. They made Golden Gate Park worthy of its name. And who that has seen them can forget the blaze of California poppies on the slopes behind Sausalito in the spring!

Al Hughes had just gone when I had an encounter, a brief one, with another queer character. I was standing after midnight on Mason Street, between Eddy and Ellis, when an oldish man, very drunk, lurched up to me and opened a conversation. He said his name was O'Connor. I admitted that I was a writer, but did not mention my country of origin. In the next breath the other declared that he had been a lieutenant in the British navy and had been cashiered at Port Royal, Jamaica. Just before that event he had taken part in suppressing the rebellion at Morant Bay in 1865 and had witnessed the hanging of George William Gordon, the member of the House of Assembly arbitrarily accused of having been the instigator.

O'Connor (the ranking commander of troops in the Jamaican affair, mind you, had been of that name) would not tell me why he had been cashiered. He went on to say that after leaving the navy he had gone to Europe and lived in most of the great capitals. When the Franco-Prussian War broke out he enlisted in the French army, was with Bazaine at Metz, but escaped, subsequently served under McMahon and was through the siege of Paris and the Commune. He saw the Emperor Wilhelm I crowned at Versailles. After the war he tried the United States and, as he had spent whatever money he had, he dropped into what he called an irregular way of life. The Boer War drew him to South Africa, where he fought on the Boer side. He had come in now from Tonopah, Nevada, with the idea of going to Cananea, Mexico, to work in the mines there, but had blown in his stake and found himself that night drunk and absolutely broke. He ended up by asking me for the price of a bed.

It was most improbable that one man could have done all the things he claimed to have done. The discrepancies in his statements about the Franco-Prussian War were manifest. He seemed too old to have fought in the Boer War. I felt sure that he had made up the kind of story that should impress a young reporter. But the Morant Bay part of it might well have been true, for few Englishmen would have heard of the episode and none would have thought it worth bragging about to a stranger, unless there was a basis of fact in a personal experience. What a coincidence that O'Connor should have met a Jamaican in San Francisco and told it to him!

Shortly after this my father came back to San Francisco. He had never got to Oregon, his farthest stage north having been the vicinity of Mount Shasta at the upper end of California. Nor had he done anything about apple-orcharding, except make enquiries. Bizarre and unprofitable hazards had taken up most of his time and left him with scarcely a penny in his pocket. He was now in a hurry to go to Belize, British Honduras, on a wholly chimerical project. His route was to be via New Orleans, and incidentally he did not take a ship to Belize from that port, but sailed home to Jamaica instead. The first week of May 1909, at the end of a year and couple of months in San Francisco, I also departed, having bought a coach-car ticket to Vancouver, across Canada to Montreal, and thence to New York.

CHAPTER 6 ❧ New York Heyday

MY SWING UP THE PACIFIC COAST, THEN THROUGH the mountains and across the interminable plains of Canada, was an experience that can be passed over briefly since it left no mark upon my life. The detour was made in the spirit of seeing as much of the world as possible, and until I reached Montreal that was all I got out of it. A ceaseless drizzle blurred the atmosphere of Seattle and Vancouver, at each of which I stopped over one night. The northern Rockies were imposing enough, but the second week of May was still winter there. Snow was banked along the railroad tracks, and in some places was deeply crusted upon mile after mile of sheds built of solid timbers slanted against the mountainsides to protect the train from avalanches.

Montreal was an exciting contrast with western Canada. Except for my glimpse of New Orleans, I had never been in a city founded by the French and where the language survived. Montreal was at least fifty per cent Gallic, which modern New Orleans was far from being. I spent almost a week there and felt a pronounced affinity for the tastes of the people. The cafés of the Boulevard St Laurent struck me as a more civilized form of resort than the North American saloon. The eighteenth-century Norman architecture, cast in a heavy mould against the severity of the winters, seemed elegant, almost gay, in the balmy weather that had come to town overnight. On the commercial Rue St Catherine the shopgirls flirted with an unabashed flair for intrigue. I thought of Florence, who had been a modiste on that very street, and somehow her blithe personality would not allow me to be sad.

But Montreal, provincial at best, could not have held me even if I had been offered a good job there. The immediate goal was New York, to which I hurried with an enthusiasm that proved not to be mistaken. I roomed at first in a succession of houses in the Chelsea district where I had lived before. Then I became attached to Washington Square South, the core so to speak of New York's current bohemia. This is a jump ahead in chronology, but to avoid marking every change of address it may be as well to state that for the most part my life at the period centred about 42, 60 and 61 Washington Square.

I wrote industriously, concentrating on the Sunday newspapers, and made a fair living at it. A kindly old gentleman named Taylor, who had been in the War of Secession, was Sunday Editor of the *New York Tribune*, a paper that clung to the attitude and format created for it by Horace Greeley. In an offhand manner Taylor took me up. I had submitted a filler, and across a proof of it which he mailed me he simply scrawled, "Come in for an assignment." For about a year he was my most generous patron on Park Row, sending me out on feature stories that he wanted treated with old-fashioned gravity and at considerable length. I investigated for him the domestic habits of New York horses and the social routine of a certain communal group of radicals. I found sprightlier topics for other editors. Before long I was selling to a few of the less pretentious monthly magazines.

New York, as I have known the city, was at its absolute best during those last years preceding World War I. It was huge and growing fast, yet not so huge that its old way of life had been swamped. There were still leisurely meeting places for writers and artists. Prices were still modest. The theatre flourished as never before or since. With the unique William Jay Gaynor as mayor and Charles S. Whitman as district attorney, local politics was interesting. Above all, there was an enthusiasm in every art and profession for the exchanging of ideas: not on a purely utilitarian basis as in the whole United States at present, but more in the European mood for the sake of the ideas themselves.

I had gone for companionship straight back to Madama's restaurant on East Eleventh Street. If anything it had improved, and without artificiality, this being its great virtue. Madama had not tried to attract bohemians, a breed she probably could not even have defined, and she met the oddities of her clientele with a sort of rough humour. She was a large woman built like a German and, as is the case with many northern Italians, of a rather light complexion. But her daughter Emma was a black-haired brunette, slender and ripe at sixteen, a pure type of the Roman artists' model. Madama did not mind when her boys, as she called us, flirted with Emma. Sometimes she encouraged it verbally, though behind the banter she was a stricter duenna than I had found the old woman in Nogales to be. At last, inevitably, the girl fell under the influence of one of the crowd, and in the opinion of all the rest of us he was the least likely of the lot.

Strange how vividly the scenes in that obscure basement recur to me. The room was unadorned, the equipment very plain. It would have been difficult to seat thirty persons there. Emma waited on us in a cloud of smoke, more from cigars and pipes than cigarettes in those days. At every table there were eager faces, young faces, of both sexes. It was on the whole a noisy place, for we all had theories to expound, or tales to tell. In winter sleet rattled on the two low windows, the steps down into the areaway were clogged with snow, and the wet overcoat of each new arrival thawed visibly, adding to the murk. It must have appeared a cheap, congested little eating house to the passerby. Yet I assert that it had a potent identity. I have yet to meet an old customer who has forgotten it.

Many of the artists there had been to Paris and others were planning to do so. A minority swore by the recent art movement in Munich that was being widely accepted as a school. None of the writers gave importance to German literary influences, and among us those who wished to go abroad divided their allegiances between England and France. I was strongly with the French clique.

The illustrator T. Victor Hall had been an acquaintance of mine at Madama's before I went to California. Now we became good friends. Accident as well as choice thereafter threw us together in nearly all the important chapters of my life. We were dissimilar personalities, except for the fact that we both liked bohemianism, and such is the case in more spontaneous friendships than one might think. The others I met at Madama's need not be named, for although I was close to some of them, including a girl with whom I was infatuated to no avail for several months, they meant less to me as time passed. Nor did any of them become celebrities. The place was more significant than the individuals who composed it, a rare variation.

Through friends there, however, I got to know Henry Gallup Paine, who was organizing the editorial end of a syndicated periodical called the *Monthly*

Magazine Section. This was to be in competition with an older weekly venture which amounted to a Sunday magazine put out simultaneously as an insert by newspapers all over the country. Better reading matter than the separate papers could afford was provided, and the subscription rate was low. But Paine's idea, or rather that of his publishers, Abbott & Briggs, was to furnish the supplement free of charge and depend upon advertising for revenue. It would be a monthly at first, as an experiment, with the hope of turning it into a weekly.

I listened to some of the talk at Paine's apartment and hoped I would break in as a contributor. A likely chance, I corrected myself, when I heard that he intended to go after big names and pay top prices. He was an urbane man of fifty, very much the New Yorker and related to the Roosevelts, whose air suggested the 'Gay Nineties'. That he was short and bald, that his clean-shaven face was rather fleshy and his nose prominent, seemed to make no difference. He was extremely dapper in his way of dressing. His eyes twinkled perpetually. If ever there was a good fellow, he was one. An advocate of simplified spelling, perhaps the best known in the United States, he had not allowed his hobby to interfere with his jobs. It was surprising that I had never run into him at the *New York Tribune*, where he had been literary editor for years.

Without a preliminary hint, Paine sent for me and offered me the position of assistant editor. He mentioned twenty-five dollars a week as the salary at which I would start. If he had said fifteen dollars I would have accepted. I joined the staff of the *Monthly Magazine Section* on 1 April 1911, feeling that I was back on the course I had intended to follow when I came to the United States. It had taken me six and a half years. I at once found myself in a professional milieu that counted, and my personal circle enlarged greatly. There were only three of us in the office at first, the third being a plain, clever girl named Blanche Schrack, who read proof and acted as a secretary. One issue of the magazine had been set up, others had been tentatively planned, and already Paine was jockeying for contributors to a star number he had designed as propaganda with our list of newspapers and those that might become subscribers. All this brought a flock of literary agents to the office, often accompanied by their stars. Other authors dropped in to make their own contacts. So did artists, for everything we published was to be illustrated and with only a sparing use of photographs. When Paine noticed that

I was pretty familiar with the world of illustrators, he made me art editor as well as general assistant.

Magazine and book illustrating had had its golden age in North American publishing. I came along just as it was about to decline. Periodicals of any importance still felt that it was *de rigueur* to have pictures drawn for their fiction, decorative initials, tailpieces and so forth. The full-page drawings, often in colour, in popular novels were going out of fashion. Many illustrators had turned to the advertising agencies to supplement their income, and some of the newcomers set out to be nothing but advertising artists.

I paid little attention to the trend. The state of affairs as I found it seemed permanent enough to me, and I was elated to find myself somewhat of an influence in an art that I admired. Men and girls with portfolios came to the office and showed me samples of their work, in the hope of being given an assignment. Those who were well established left it to editors to seek them out at their studios. In one way or another, I greatly increased my circle of acquaintances among illustrators.

Critics probably give the palm to those who were then middle-aged – to men like A.B. Frost and Charles Dana Gibson – on the theory that they exemplify the best period. I do not agree with this. There were a few in their thirties and younger whom I thought superior artists to, for instance, Gibson. They had not achieved so wide a popularity as his with the 'Gibson Girl' and the 'Gibson Man', but they were sounder illustrators and their draughtsmanship was finer. Franklin Booth performed marvels with a pen-and-ink technique that enabled him to capture any nuance. His handling of trees in this medium was incredibly beautiful. He was famous for his purely decorative work, but he could apply his manner equally well to a landscape and a life-size portrait. Booth was a great artist, and it cannot be said that either the publishers or his own colleagues failed to appreciate him. An illustrator of Czech ancestry, Charles Sarka, was another who loomed above the average. He preferred to work in wash, but was effective also in pen-and-ink. He had a dramatic touch. His best pictures were nobly composed and looked as if they should have been salon pieces in oil. A sort of Eugène Delacroix in reverse, for it has been shrewdly said that Delacroix's chief impulse was to illustrate. I knew both Booth and Sarka, but saw more of the former.

Two intimates shall be mentioned so that I may lay sprigs of myrtle on their unlucky tombs. Robert G. Vosburgh, middle-aged, and Albert L. Scherzer, pathetically young, were products of the Munich renaissance. Each in his manner was a gifted draughtsman. But Vosburgh simply never had the touchstone of success. He died obscurely by his own hand. Scherzer, a curious racial mixture of German, Spanish and Guatemalan Indian, had begun to do well when he developed acute tuberculosis and succumbed in a few weeks. Scherzer gave me on his deathbed a little framed drawing of his, showing a nude nymph sitting in the woods with her back turned and resting on the palm of one hand. It hung above my desk for thirty years until it became imprinted on my brain – a symbol of what? The original was stolen finally, but I had photographed it.

The special number of the *Monthly Magazine Section* was a revelation to me. Six of the authors who commanded the highest rates of the period – Rudyard Kipling, Richard Harding Davis, Sir Gilbert Parker, Jack London, Rex Beach and Gouverneur Morris – were engaged to furnish short stories at not less than a thousand dollars apiece. Kipling, if I remember rightly, was paid three thousand dollars and Richard Harding Davis two thousand. Moreover, full-page pictures were bought from popular artists such as Howard Chandler Christy and Harrison Fisher, the price in each case being a thousand dollars. For some it was the largest amount they had ever received for a single piece of work. The total of the issue, including fillers, came to around twenty thousand dollars, which for those days was staggering. Paine had talked Abbott & Briggs into the project on the score that in addition to pleasing our newspapers it would impress advertisers, but I overheard Lynn Abbott, the head of the company, muttering comments that showed he regarded it as a wild gamble.

Jack London and Rex Beach were among those who visited the office in connection with our publishing jamboree. London was blond with a half-tough, half-humorous, blunt-featured face that gave him somewhat the appearance of a Scandinavian sailor. Part of his he-man pose was to go even to formal gatherings hatless and wearing a blue flannel shirt. He recalled having met me in San Francisco, which led him to chat boisterously about the doings of Sterling and other bohemians there. Rex Beach, his features juvenile, suggested nothing so much as a robust member of a college football team.

NOT LONG AFTER I JOINED the magazine I was asked by Paine, or it may have been Blanche, whether I knew the Maison Petitpas, a restaurant on West Twenty-Ninth Street frequented by John Butler Yeats, the father of the Irish poet. I had not heard of it, but the particular mentioned was beguiling to me. I greatly admired the work of William Butler Yeats, and it would be a treat if I could get his father to talk about him. That was my first thought, little knowing that Petitpas's had become virtually a salon over which the elder Yeats presided as the undisputed attraction. It was a private *table d'hôte*, and one had to telephone in advance for a seat and give credentials, I was told, a proviso usual enough in those days when many small places sold drinks without a licence.

The house stood in the middle of a neat brownstone block. Summer had just begun, so the front basement dining room was empty, and I was taken through the kitchen into the backyard. An awning left space for a tepid breeze to sigh over the top of a board fence. A table stretched along the far end, and smaller tables, set closely together, filled the rest of the floor. The effect was leisurely, bland, in comparison with Madama Volanti's. A hundred other French and Italian *tables d'hôte* were like this. Yet I carry a picture of dark wine bottles against white cloth, of browned roast chicken and lettuce salad, of a pool of faces and costumes now outdated, which I associate with no other restaurant and which time does not erase. It was the unforgettable Maison Petitpas, run by three Breton sisters, where Marie cooked in obscurity and Joséphine and Célestine, brunette, corsetted, slim, served the diners with tireless industry.

As I had asked for Mr Yeats, I was led to the long table at the head of which he sat. He shook hands and waved me to a chair near him, treating me like an old acquaintance. He was a tall, spare old man with a broad forehead, blue eyes and a white beard. In a general way he resembled the standard portrait of Charles Darwin, but he had a more pronounced nose and a more genial expression. As he talked he fingered his beard, and his glance roved from face to face. Silent, he reached automatically for pad and pencil and sketched an impression of someone nearby. Then, as later, he freely gave these drawings to the subjects, and a great many of them must be extant.

He took me at once into the talk, which was continuous with an odd, warm glow to it, and moulded by himself. He liked to hear the opinions of others and listened intently. Yet it was his answers and his way of bringing up new topics which were memorable. That evening, I recall, he said that the *Marseillaise* owed its eternal appeal to the fact that it freed the crowd by giving it a soul. He also remarked that personality, not temperament, was the important thing in art as in life. We are gregarious creatures, he said, and are moved by the nuances of personality, whereas temperament is nothing but a mania or sickness conveying little to those who are not similarly afflicted.

The story behind his presence at Petitpas's was an unusual one, as I discovered by enquiry from others. J.B. Yeats was a portrait painter who had had a middling career in Dublin and London. Scorning the fads of the moment, he had gone his way, an honest craftsman who knew how to catch a likeness and interpret character shrewdly. His professional standing was secure, but that was the least of it. He was a bohemian and a good conversationalist who knew everybody. His London studio was a rendezvous of all the talents. With two famous sons – Jack, the younger, was an artist – no man seemed less likely to emigrate than he.

The year before I met John Butler Yeats an exhibition of Irish arts and crafts was held in New York. His own work was represented, and John Quinn, connoisseur and patron of all that was both Irish and excellent, induced him to be present. He arrived fussing; a rough ocean crossing had upset him. He had made up his mind that he would have nothing to do with hotels, nor would he live as a guest in a private house. Lodgings such as might be had in Soho would suit him, he declared. So Quinn found for him the Maison Petitpas, then quite unknown to fame. There were rooms to let upstairs, and Yeats settled himself in the third-floor back. He was over seventy – just how much was uncertain, for he was given to underestimating his age. When the time came for his expected return to London he shrugged the idea aside, saying that he wanted to see more of New York and would stay it out until the spring. He had simply turned the key of his studio door in London, but the paintings and books left behind did not seem to worry him. In the spring he declined to use his steamship ticket. He said: "I'll be going in the autumn – or maybe next year."

He was no sooner installed at Petitpas's than the world had begun to come to him. Night after night he sat at dinner in the same chair at the head of the table and talked with fluent fascination to those within earshot. Artists and others who had been attracted by the Irish exhibition formed the earliest group. Then young writers joined the symposium. It became the vogue with half the literary generation in New York to go to Petitpas's. The little restaurant had flourished because of the presence of Yeats.

Having discovered the place, I returned more times than I can tell. There were periods when I went there every night for weeks on end. The coterie included the painters Robert Henri, George Bellows, John Sloan, and Boardman Robinson; the poets Alan Seeger, Joyce Kilmer, Shaemas O'Sheel and Jeanne Robert Foster; Van Wyck Brooks, Allan Benson and Michael Monahan; Robert W. Sneddon and a host of other short story writers; women who were interested in Irish questions, such as Dolly Sloan, the painter's wife. John Quinn dropped in now and then and brought distinguished guests.

Figure 11. A sketch of Roberts by the artist John Butler Yeats, made in 1917. MS353.6.1.

Jack London came of a winter evening, with a party of editors and satellites. We of the *Monthly Magazine Section* had been included in the former classification, and I sat beside London. As usual, he was dressed like a workman. The conversation was mostly about a voyage around Cape Horn which he proposed to make in a sailing ship. He was drinking heavily, cheered on by the satellites. His dynamic ego interested Yeats, who called him a wild man. At midnight London turned to me as the nearest auditor, raised a glass of whisky, and announced loudly that it was the last drink he would take for at least two years, perhaps for the rest of his life.

Everybody mocked the statement; but London, suddenly serious, vowed that he meant it. He had decided to write a book concerning a drunkard's struggle to overcome the habit. How could he be realistic on paper unless he had been through the experience? It would be a struggle, because he liked drinking, and it chanced that he had long ago fixed this night as the night on which to quit. London swallowed the whisky and refused to have another. In due course the book appeared, a best-seller entitled *John*

Barleycorn. It purported to be the confession of a sincere and spontaneous act, and not the journalistic device he had vaunted. Yeats often referred to the episode, which he wondered at and disapproved of. It was American in the bad sense, he said.

Very different was the first visit to Petitpas's of William Butler Yeats, who arrived unheralded, still the bohemian with tumbled hair and in a dark cloak that, according to George Moore, gave him the appearance of a rook with trailing wings. The old man magniloquently abdicated for the evening, but saw to it that Willie, as he called him, did not flag as animator of the salon. "Tell those good people about the Abbey Theatre, Willie," he would say, plucking his beard. Or again, "You'll be giving us *Innisfree*, maybe." I was moved by the artistic verity of the poet's way of chanting rather than reciting his verses.

On ordinary evenings, J.B. Yeats would occasionally shout, "Stuff and nonsense!" when some idea exasperated him, but he was by nature a tolerant critic. He emphasized the genial qualities in men and things he wished to praise. "Ireland is kind," he was fond of saying – a kind mother to her children, who in turn had warm hearts for the newcomer and a receptivity to beauty. And, "Shakespeare was a kindly man," he said time and again in discussing the plays. Standardization and a hard, cold attitude toward life were detested by John Butler Yeats.

For all his sweetness, he had a biting tongue when he encountered humbug or crudity. On hearing that a young poet who had talked boastfully to him had tried to commit suicide with rat poison, but had recovered because the dose had been too small, Yeats plucked at his beard, growling, "If ye ask me, it would be mouse poison he chose." A noisy fellow once told him in my presence that since visiting the Bronx Zoo he understood why an Irishman should be portrayed in caricature as a monkey; it was that they both had such long upper lips. Yeats, whose thick moustache concealed any possible resemblance, flushed scarlet. "Monkeys are we, to you?" he exclaimed with startling ferocity. "Get away from my table, and never sit here again."

The only time I ever knew the old man to be stumped for an opinion in words was the day he returned from the huge exhibition of 'modern art' at the Sixty-Ninth Regiment Armory. He merely shrugged his shoulders and muttered: "Tush, tush! The divil and all!" This show was the first big one of its kind in the United States. A total of some sixteen hundred items had been assembled, among them a canvas by Marcel Duchamp, a Frenchman, that had already had a lot of publicity. It was titled *Nude Descending a Staircase*.

The Armory show had far-reaching effects. The size of it, the large attendance and the heed paid by the newspapers launched 'modern art' in the Western world. No serious New York critic thought that the fad would last long, or that there would be an established circle calling itself a school. The masses went to gasp and jeer, and commonly ended by holding their heads. Art lovers went to look at curiosities, and they did not feel at all hostile. The motto adopted by the exhibition was "The New Spirit", but we regarded that as being just part of the comedy.

Nude Descending a Staircase had caught on with the mob, and to get a look at it you had to stand in line. There was, of course, no nude, but in the mass of angles you could vaguely distinguish five featureless marionettes that might have been hacked out of tin, one behind the other to give an impression of motion. I thought it worthless. Some of the exhibits went much farther than this in distortion, perversion and senselessness. The cult of the ugly extended to colours, which were jumbled without regard to harmony and often suggested putrefaction in a dunghill.

The apologists are in the habit of explaining away anyone over forty who condemns 'modern art' by calling him a fossil; they say that his mind is incapable of accepting anything new. I want to make the point that I saw *Nude Descending a Staircase* when I was twenty-six years old, thought it a rotten egg then, and still think it a rotten egg. I have never liked a single example of this school. From Picasso down, the stuff is charlatanry – or the product of minds suffering from infantilism or lunacy.

CELEBRITIES DID NOT COMPRISE MY sole grist of friendships at the Maison Petitpas. Unattached women went there in larger numbers than to Madama's, and instead of the empty-headed models that flocked about illustrators these were for the most part writers, painters or women who held interesting jobs. The type stimulated me. I was in accord with the feminist trend among young intellectuals of both sexes and felt sure that I could love only a thinking, free-minded woman.

If you go on an assumption of this kind it will bear fruit, real or counterfeit, and there will probably be quite a number of fruit unless a great love should occur, this last being a marvel to which preconceived theories do not apply. A girl of Norwegian descent, Hedda Sars, was the first to allure me. She was not at all pretty. Her complexion was swarthy for a Scandinavian, and she had blunted features, dark brown hair without the trace of a curl in it, and a thin, restless body. But she had a good mind, talked well and was attracting notice as an interviewer on one of the morning papers. A series of her interviews with authors had impressed me, partly because she had adroitly shown that she despised the current namby-pamby attitude of American publishers toward a realistic portrayal of life. Even the success of Jack London had not converted most of the publishers.

The seats close to John Butler Yeats were in great demand, and by an unexpressed agreement we all took turns at them. Little cliques would form for a few days at a time at the middle of the table and at its foot. I often was in a group about Hedda Sars, and on those occasions she would generally ask us to come up to her apartment after dinner for drinks and a prolonging of our talk. A poetical young Englishman, frail in the pink-cheeked way that points to tuberculosis in so many cases, appeared to have her favour and I began to feel jealous of him. One night we two were the last to linger at her place. Without having intended to do so, I found myself determined to outsit him. It grew to be two o'clock in the morning. Hedda had been glancing cryptically from his face to mine, but she said nothing. She prowled to the kitchen and back again, smoking many cigarettes, and at that time none but the boldest bohemians among American women smoked. Presently the Englishman stood up and spoke a mild farewell. Hedda laughed as soon as he was beyond earshot.

"Why, I've never been attracted to him," she said. "I didn't realize I was to you either until you started this game with him tonight. Then I hoped you'd win."

I thought her words a proof of sophistication, and the incident a thrilling adventure. Naturally I did not go home until the morning. Neither of us had slept as much as an hour on that night of early summer, a night with a tepid breeze rustling the branches of the sumach tree outside the bedroom window. The liaison continued for several months, during the course of which the poor Englishman actually died, though not for love.

My experience with Hedda was full of surprises. In utter contrast to her rather pedantic manner of discussing general ideas, she was extremely vain in the love relationship, commending her own charms and requiring a constant flow of tribute from me. Nor was it a tourney of mere words, or words used to fill the spaces of physical languor. I have never known anyone so frenziedly amorous as Hedda of the drab exterior. If not a nymphomaniac, she was very close to the type. It is illuminating for a man who is deeply attached to women to have an affair with an extremist in his salad days. The chance to gourmandize seems wonderful to him at first. Then he perceives, more quickly and surely than he would have otherwise, that a love depending wholly upon climaxes can become the least revelatory of loves.

When I began to weary of Hedda, I flirted with a girl at Petitpas's who did not at all resemble her. The new one was of a Boston Irish family and had been educated in Europe, mainly in Italy and France. Her name was Katharine Hickey. Purely Celtic in appearance, her hair mahogany-brown and her eyes blue-grey, her complexion bright, Katharine suggested Mediterranean culture to me, and in no way the poetical dreaminess of the Celt. She was, if anything, a modern Roman by adoption, but I gave more value to her fluent command of French. She had acquired all the necessary accomplishments, read all the right books – up to a certain point in her post-scholastic education. Then she had stopped bothering to keep in touch with trends, and her attitude gave her somehow an agreeably old-fashioned air. Her favourite amusements were the opera and plays, about which she talked effectively. She treated the Catholic faith of her ancestors as an influence she had outgrown since childhood. To my astonishment, however, she attended Christian Science lectures and averred that she found them helpful. She was several years older than me. I did not weigh the possibilities as I paid effervescent court to her, but Katharine Hickey was to be in my life for a long time.

MADAMA VOLANTI'S AND THE MAISON Petitpas were not the only café-restaurants of old New York that I enjoyed in those days, and some of the best should be mentioned. There were the Brevoort on lower Fifth Avenue and the Lafayette a block away on University Place, both run by Raymond Orteig in connection with his local French hotels. Luchow's on East Fourteenth Street, and Allaire's – also called Scheffel Hall – on East Seventeenth Street and Third Avenue, were German resorts famous for their imported beer. Joel's, on West Forty-First Street, had a strange Spanish Jew who had lived in Mexico City as host, and was the headquarters of a theatrical bohemia. The Monopol, on Second Avenue, was Hungarian and the rendezvous of chess players.

But Volanti's and Petitpas's were two of the trio of places that meant a great deal to me. The third was Mouquin's, on Sixth Avenue near Twenty-Eighth Street. The original Mouquin's was founded in 1857, downtown on Fulton Street, and it still flourished. I was there once or twice and it was a fine restaurant, a resort chiefly of newspapermen and politicians. But the uptown house, opened in 1898 in what had been the Isaac Varian homestead, had a character all its own. It was the best French restaurant in New York, with the best wine list, yet a succulent *à la carte* meal could be had there, including drinks, for about two dollars. When bohemians were solvent, this was their headquarters. In using the name Mouquin's, I mean the marvellous spot on the Avenue, particularly the ground-level café with its cosy *banquettes*, its mirror-covered walls, its marble tables decked with pale green absinthe as well as the reds and ambers of the wines, the bluish-black of steamed mussels, the brown of roasted poultry and of crisp French breadcrusts.

I seldom went alone. You took a girl to Mouquin's and made a rite of it. A notable difference between that generation and the present one, as I see it, is that we dramatized more, sought out the places that had the fame and were consciously romantic ourselves while we enjoyed them. The young people of today are much too literal to acknowledge any such frailty, though the time will doubtless come when they, too, will think back with nostalgia to their haunts. I believe ours was the happier way.

It was good to revel in Mouquin's, to point out the celebrities at other tables, to feel the connoisseur and a gay spendthrift for a night as you recommended *bouillabaise* or onion soup, perhaps broiled quail with tiny peas, a salad in a bowl that had been rubbed with garlic; along with these a bottle of Château Margaux at seventy-five cents, and afterward the carefully chosen cordial at twenty-five cents or less, the cigar for a dime. Money has been devalued by two wars, to be sure. Everything has been marked up, including salaries. Yet there is a fascination in dwelling on those old-time prices, because relatively they were much more within reach of the small pocketbook than are the bloated prices now charged for the same things.

To revert for a moment to chess, the Monopol was not the only meeting spot for players on Second Avenue at the period of which I write. The most dignified and important matches were often held there; but in some of the nearby coffee houses the game was featured with more verve, albeit with a certain degree of commercialism. One place in particular – I wish I could remember its name; let us call it Karl's – was always filled with Germans, Slavs and Jews, who when not actually playing, debated wordily the fine points of chess. Among the patrons were experts who made a sort of living out of it. They would take on any comer with the understanding that if he lost he must pay twenty-five cents, whereas if they should lose they were exempt from paying. My father had taught me the moves and given me a fair conception of chess strategy. But he was no devotee of the game and I did not get much practice with him. I felt that I could become enthusiastic about it and welcomed the opportunities on Second Avenue. Though I never became a really strong player, I improved and added a resource to my stock-in-trade for the enjoyment of life.

The chief expert at Karl's was Charles Jaffé. He was a lesser master, good enough to have taken part in international tournaments and therefore to have contested games with most of the great men. He had never won a title, however, and the ordinary money rewards of chess being small he was glad enough to make twenty-five cents a game from amateurs. I played him dozens of times, and I do not believe I ever won. He taught me a lot, nonetheless. He would discourse over the board like a professor. "Now that was the move with which Lasker broke up a powerful defence by Schlecter at Berlin in 1903," he would say after he had applied it airily to me. Or: "That reply was invented by Janowski against Marshall in the last tournament at Ostend." He was more terse than the rest of the patrons. They knew who had played whom, and how, in every important tournament for the past twenty years, and they clamoured the details with exact dates.

Jaffé was a thin, poorly dressed young Jew who seemed to have Mediterranean Gentile blood. Once Janowski, who was on a visit to New York, appeared at Karl's and caused great excitement. He was a dapper Frenchified Pole, bald and with a curled black moustache. No one could persuade him to accept a challenge, not even Jaffé, and he soon left. "Here he treats me like a coffee-house player," said Jaffé sadly. "But he may be different at the Monopol. Let us go there." Janowski was not to be found at the Monopol. Jaffé played me instead, and I lost another quarter.

IN OCTOBER 1911, I HAD moved to 61 Washington Square South, for reasons that were altogether romantic. To get in I had to take an attic room with one long window that came down to the floor. I wanted to live there because it was the most celebrated rooming house in downtown bohemia. Many writers, many artists, and at least one singer, the sublime Adelina Patti, had been among its lodgers. It was called the House of Genius, and I felt that I must absorb some of its inspiration. The landlady, Mme Catherine Branchard, was a remarkable woman of Swiss birth who had come to the United States by herself at twenty with the express object of seeing the Centennial Exposition at Philadelphia. After working as a hotel maid, she rented the four-storey house on the Square and took in lodgers, her guests from the start being chiefly persons engaged in the arts. Her second husband, dead for four years when I met her, had been an erratic French adventurer, Colonel Alexandre Casarin, who had fought in Mexico and painted as an avocation. Strangely enough, she did not use his name, although her back parlour was cluttered with relics of him, including a good portrait he had made of her. Casarin had won brief success with a bust of President McKinley, and Madame spoke about him proudly.

She was a heavily built, dark woman, none too sociable, but capable of sudden confidential moods. Her attitude toward her tenants, past and present, was one of amused cynicism and tolerance. She thought bohemians crazy, but liked them all the same. Her favourite had been Frank Norris, whom she often extolled to me for his courteous manners and good looks. He had been unwell when he left her house to go to San Francisco, where he had died after an operation, and she could never quite forgive herself for allowing him to go. Tears came into her sombre eyes when she spoke of Norris's end.

She had kind words for the humourist Gelett Burgess, too, and for Thompson Buchanan the playwright, and further back for Eddie Townsend, of the "Chimmie Fadden" tales, who seems to have lived in the house longer than any other literary lodger. I could never be sure whether Stephen Crane had been of her company. Sometimes she said that he had; at others she would ask me what he had looked like, would shake her head, and say it could not have been the same man.

In the West I had got hold of the partly fossilized skull of an American Indian which I put on the top of my bookcase. This was a matter of great interest to Mme Branchard, though she took it enigmatically. Had I ever seen the ghost of the Indian? she enquired. I replied solemnly that I had, whereupon she gave a short, sceptical laugh and said no more. But she glanced at the skull whenever she came to tidy the room. One evening a knock at the door was followed by the entry of the tall figure of the poet Alan Seeger. I had talked with him several times at Petitpas's, but did not know until he casually announced it that he had taken a room on the same floor in the rear. His errand was to look over my books. If I remember rightly, he had written a poem in an odd metre and wanted to compare it with some ancient model. He prowled up and down in front of the shelves, failed to find exactly what he sought, and threw himself into a chair.

Seeger was an arrogant personality, a poet of an ivory tower, contemptuous of whether the average run of humanity approved either of his verse or of him, and extremely handsome. He was then twenty-four. His features were classic, his complexion of a singularly luminous brunette tinge, his black hair thick but already flecked with grey. He wore closely clipped side whiskers in front of his ears, and a shirt open at the neck. The effect was distinctly Byronic. There was a reason. Byron was one of his heroes; another was the Renaissance aesthete and scholar Pico della Mirandola.

Our conversation turned on Paris, the preoccupation of so many of us at that time. Seeger remarked that he had spent much of his boyhood in Mexico, and it was clear to him that the Latin conception of the artistic life was a great deal more sympathetic than the Anglo-Saxon. But Mexico was comparatively primitive. The solution for him would be Paris, since the United States was not as yet a civilized country. "I have only a small allowance to live upon, and I refuse to do commercial writing," he added haughtily. "But I shall find a way to go to Paris."

I declared that I agreed with him on general principles, yet was less of an extremist since I enjoyed myself in New York. He shrugged. Then his eye fell on the Indian skull and he asked for its story. I told him how I had obtained the skull, passing from that to Mme Branchard's rather furtive interest in it. A mischievous smile flitted across Seeger's face. It was one of the few occasions on which I knew him to break his pose of lofty reserve.

"Let us have some fun out of this," he said. "Suppose we tell Madame, separately and in a careless way, that we drank wine out of the skull tonight, that you keep it for toasts when writers visit you."

The Byronic precedent was plainly in his mind and was not to be resisted. I got the first chance at Madame. She looked at me then with a touch of real horror.

AT THE OFFICE THE WORK had rapidly increased in significance for me. More newspapers had signed contracts to issue our supplement. The first expansion on our part was to put out a new monthly called the *Family Magazine Section*, aimed at women, and which alternated with the original periodical. But this did not work out so well. Presently the two were combined as the *Semi-Monthly Magazine Section*, which was liked by the subscribing papers and the public, and which helped to make periodical history for a few years. It was an upstart competing along irregular lines with *McClure's*, *Everybody's*, the *American* and others during a time of great vitality among magazines that did not pretend to the dignity of the seemingly eternal 'big four': *Harper's*, *Scribner's*, the *Century* and the *Atlantic Monthly*.

I had some useful experiences in connection with special articles, of which two will suffice. In April 1912, the world was appalled by the sinking of the White Star liner *Titanic* on her maiden voyage, as a result of collision with an iceberg off the Grand Banks of Newfoundland. Humanity was not shock-proof then. Mechanical devices supposedly had made ships safe. The *Titanic* had been the last word in construction. How could she have gone at the first contact with danger, in an instant so to speak? How could hundreds have been drowned, including beauties and millionaires, as well as the common herd? There were rumours of inefficiency, even of cowardice, on the part of her officers. Great crowds gathered, as on election night, to read the dispatches on the bulletin boards of the newspapers.

Every editor wanted a feature article about the *Titanic*, by an eyewitness if possible, and clearly the bigger names involved would not go around. Paine was struck by a good idea. The largest number of survivors had been picked up by the Cunarder *Carpathia*, bound for New York, and Paine arranged with the line to offer the chance at quarantine to some woman, preferably a second-class passenger, who had lost a member of her family. The article would be written for her in the first person, but she would be paid.

If the story were done immediately, we could make the next issue with it. The assignment fell to me. I was lucky in my survivor. The Englishwoman, Charlotte Collyer, widow of a Hampshire grocer who had been taking her to an Idaho valley to grow fruit, awaited me in the Cunard offices with her eight-year-old daughter Marjorie. The mother was wearing the nightgown and dressing robe in which she had been rescued, and she used a blanket from the *Titanic* as a shawl. Her hair was down her back. The child had on

Figure 12. Charlotte Collyer (with her daughter Marjorie), interviewed by Roberts shortly after her arrival in New York after the sinking of the *Titanic* in May 1912. MS353.6.8.

a skirt that had been roughly made for her aboard the *Carpathia* from the blanket in which she had been wrapped. The two were straight from the sea, and this was no premeditated costuming. The first thing I did was to have them photographed.

In a stunned voice and employing the simplest of language, Charlotte Collyer told me what she had been through: the great ship reeling back from the iceberg, the struggle over the lifeboats, the surface littered with human wreckage and loose ice, the *Titanic* ablaze with electric lights from end to end as she tilted forward, then reared her stern into the air and went down while the band played "Nearer My God to Thee". The scores of newspaper columns about the disaster that I had read could not lessen the impact of this woman's story. There was a tragic grandeur in her laconic phrases.

I took very full notes. After I left her I phoned the office and said I would prefer to do the article at home. I was worried about it. There appeared to be much more material than I could possibly get into the five or six thousand words allotted me. But I went to my attic room at 61 Washington Square, sat at the typewriter and almost without hesitation wrote the piece in a single afternoon and evening, and at the length wanted. It was like a dress rehearsal for my future journalistic work. The thing made a hit. We printed a note at the end of the article that if readers wished to help Charlotte Collyer, individual contributions of five dollars would be accepted for her by the magazine. Thousand of dollars poured in, and many of the cheques were for a good deal more than we had mentioned. She went on to Idaho, as she and her husband had planned, and was able to buy a splendid orchard.

The other article was different indeed in character and was not written by me. A youngish, black-bearded Russian had come unannounced to the office. He gave the name Ivan Narodny, which was probably an alias since it meant, roughly, John Patriot. We did not question it at the time, because none of us knew Russian. Our caller said that he had been in the Kronstadt revolt of 1905, had been named by a committee provisional president, had been captured and suffered long imprisonment. Of course he wanted to place selections from his memoirs. After several tries, he sold us an account of prison experiences. To help build up confidence, he had once brought in a comely Slav girl whom he introduced as a princess, a member of the Galitzin family. I was naive enough to believe her authentic; likely enough she was a café artiste.

Then, early in 1913, the Russian appeared with a more singular offering. This purported to be an unpublished document by Count Leo Tolstoy, who had died in 1910. It was in the form of a statement by Countess 'Nastasia Tolstoy, grandniece of the late illustrious author. She averred that she had been asked by Czar Nicholas II to get a personal message for himself and his royal cousins, George V of England and Wilhelm II of Germany, from the old sage of Tsarskoe Selo. 'Nastasia had dutifully broached the matter. Tolstoy had gone into a sort of trance and made a prophecy which she had taken down verbatim and which constituted the body of the article. It forecast a war that would start in the Balkans and plunge all Europe into flames in 1913. Empires and kingdoms would be swept away, and the world would form a "federation of the United States of Nations". A strange figure from the North, a writer and journalist rather than a soldier, would be the crucial influence. There was much vague and theatrical stuff besides. A handwritten letter in French, signed by 'Nastasia and dated from Russia, authorized publication in America.

Paine had me read the manuscript and then asked me whether I did not think it was a hoax. I answered that I did, that I could not believe the Czar, the Kaiser and the King would jointly have sought a message from Tolstoy, and that even if he had received such a request the author would have expressed himself differently. Paine chuckled. "Well, Tolstoy's name is a drawing card for any magazine. Ask our Russian friend to give a local reference and investigate it yourself. If it holds up, we'll take a chance on this, though it's absolute bunk to predict a general European war." Narodny promptly furnished me with a polysyllabic name and a good address in the East Eighties. I was received by a suave foreigner who said that he was a colonel in the Czar's army, that he was a close friend of 'Nastasia Tolstoy and could swear the letter I showed him was in her hand.

So we printed the article. It was heatedly discussed, came to life a few years later when it was quoted to prove that Tolstoy had prophesied World War I and the rise of Lenin, and is by no means dead yet. It remains a classic example of how magazine myths are born. So far as I have been able to discover, Tolstoy never had a grandniece who can be identified with the Countess 'Nastasia of the article.

In spite of being prolific of ideas, Paine lasted only about two years as editor. The publishers felt, I think, that he spent money too lavishly. He was succeeded by William Griffith, a Missourian, a shrewd bargainer with contributors, and a poet in his spare time. I remained for a short while under him, but a change of editors often means a change of assistants, and so it proved in this case. I did not mind much, because I wanted to move on to France.

CHAPTER 7 ❧ Pre-war Socialism

I DELIBERATELY LEFT OUT OF THE LAST CHAPTER my increasing political bent, for it requires a separate approach. Certain friendships overlapped from my literary work, but fewer than one might suppose. The majority of journalists in Anglo-Saxon countries, and especially in the United States, seem to think that no matter how much they may write about politics they should avoid it as a personal activity. I have always felt that this attitude is mistaken. There are good opportunities in the calling to study the theory and art of government. Why should we not be rather more effective than the next man in putting our ideas into practice?

As early as my San Francisco days, I had begun to look seriously into socialism, the Fabian as well as the orthodox variety. To say that I read Karl Marx's *Das Capital* with enjoyment or any sense of having been converted by it would be false. It is, in fact, a most unreadable book, turgid and unbearably dull. But I accepted it as a scientific work on the management of human affairs, to which radical thinkers went for new principles, historical evidence and useful speculations. The French and Russian socialists were certainly more exciting. The Fabians had a simpler doctrine; my interest in them was enhanced by their leadership, comprising as it did men and women like the Webbs, Bernard Shaw, and Sydney Olivier, who had so impressed me as a boy and who was now governor of Jamaica.

There were two kinds of socialists then: those who cared mainly about reforming economic conditions, and those who saw in the movement a means for the triumph of all generous ideas, of liberty over oppression, of youth over conservatism. Both schools put great emphasis upon the cause of labour and favoured strikes as a means of getting justice. I was no welfare worker by temperament, and I did not find the methods of the unions inspiring. What I became, more or less, was a politico-revolutionary of the second school mentioned above. Like many of the age, I believed that that brand of socialism must impose itself intellectually and at last take over the governments of the world. Socialists would refuse to fight in international wars and thus render all military machines helpless. A better society would be created by popular mandate and, we theorized, bloodlessly. We regarded certain other isms – feminism, syndicalism; even philosophical anarchism, which objected to any form of government – as natural allies in the realization of our bright dream.

To smile at these as the illusions of a green Arcadian past is easy. But to do that is to misunderstand them. They were not so innocuous as their protagonists made out to themselves. Western civilization had been free from major wars for a good deal longer than a generation and was growing bored, though the solid middle-class element did not perceive it. Those who had nothing were in a mood to listen to any new doctrine. The young with a flair for leadership wished either to be dashing members of an elite like that rising statesman in England, Winston Churchill; or they swung to the opposite extreme as socialists. The period was subconsciously preparing itself for violence. I recall with what glee, in spite of our pacific talk, we heard rumours of a possible upheaval in Russia, or how nobly tragic we found the martyrdom of Francisco Ferrer in Spain. The lure of ideological radicalism was that we really knew it might lead to action.

I never attended a socialist meeting in San Francisco, though I was beguiled by Jack London's activity in the party. Freelance reporting furnished me with stimulation enough. In New York the subject took on immediacy through chance contacts. Several of the younger people I met at the Monopol and other Second Avenue cafés were socialists; some few were anarchists. I began to go to the lectures and public dances they recommended. Practically no one at Madama Volanti's cared a rap about politics. But the contrary was true at Petitpas's. Notable intellectuals of the left wing, particularly Irishwomen who dabbled in socialism, were attracted to John Butler Yeats. This seemed queer at first blush, for the old gentleman held socialism in genial contempt and would say so to anyone. I learned before long that his leftist countrywomen had their ideas mixed, being half-nationalists in the confused manner of the times and working for an Irish republic.

For its colour and total flouting of middle-class values an anarchist affair put all others in the shade. It was generally a propaganda meeting held in some East Side hall and followed by a dance. The price of admission to both would rarely be more than twenty-five cents. Emma Goldman, the high priestess of anarchism, a woman with a coarse face, an ugly, squat body, and a vigorous mind, would make a speech in which she scourged Church and State with scorpions. She had genuine eloquence. Goldman on liberty was often worth hearing. But Goldman on God made you uneasy. How, you asked yourself, could a nullity (that was what she called God) move anyone to such fury?

Then Ben Reitman, a big fellow and handsome in a crude way, would mount the platform and utter Rabelaisian blasphemies. He might be succeeded by the shuffling and paltry figure of Alexander Berkman, who years before had fired a bullet into the steel magnate H.C. Frick, though you found it hard to believe that he had been capable of the act, and had served a long term in jail. Berkman droned on about his anguish behind the bars. His *Prison Memoirs of an Anarchist*, ill written, would be hawked meanwhile on the floor. It was the thing in those circles to pamper him as a martyr and hide your ennui. There was almost certain to be the reward of several buxom and fiery young Jewesses who, in short harangues, would breathe the deaths of kings and extol free love with equal fervour. Nearly all the New York anarchists were Russian or Polish Jews, with a sprinkling of Italians.

The ensuing sociable provided strenuous dancing, beer-drinking at five cents a glass and a deal of wild talk, and it lasted until an hour or so before dawn. The utmost licence in words prevailed. Any sort of story could be told, any topic brought up, and this included the sex lives of individuals. Well and good. If your dancing partner knew that Ben had been sleeping with someone else, she would tell you about it in a minute, even if she had been the woman. When these people said free love they meant the word 'free'. But they had their own standards of morality. You had to be sincere about it. You must believe yourself infatuated, if only for the occasion. Your impulse must not be exclusively physical.

The anarchists were great readers, and they preferred art to economics or history. They maintained a pose of having the whole list of disruptive philosophers at their fingertips, but were familiar only with those that were stormily eloquent, like Nietzsche, or romantic in the manner of Kropotkin. I admit that Emma Goldman could quote all the dullest dogs and make them sound interesting, that being part of her equipment as leader. The rank and file were engagingly devoted to poetry, the drama and fiction, providing the technique was masterly and the spirit rebellious.

Their favourite English poets were Shelley, Swinburne and Oscar Wilde, the first for obvious and almost traditional reasons, the last chiefly for the sake of *The Ballad of Reading Gaol*. With Swinburne they were infatuated. I supposed at first that this was on account of such poems as *Before a Crucifix*, *Dolores*, *Faustine* and *Anactoria*. But no. While they relished the impious sentiments and voluptuous descriptions, it was Swinburne's metres taken in connection with what they termed his lawless ideas that enchanted them. They said it was in the spirit of pure anarchy. This seemed fantastic to me, since Swinburne's metres are severely disciplined and his thinking negligible. But as I had never ceased to delight in his lyrical magic, I zestfully exchanged favourites with the prettier anarchist women.

Dostoyevsky was, of course, a giant among novelists in those circles. They introduced me to *Crime and Punishment*, and I acknowledged its power, though I found Raskolnikov the most unlikeable, in fact downright annoying, character of major fiction. Joseph Conrad had just published *Under Western Eyes*, which in my opinion is a deliberate satire on *Crime and Punishment*. I had been reading Conrad since 1904, and I much preferred his genius to that of the Russian. Maliciously I extolled Conrad among the anarchists until a few of them tried him. The uproar may be imagined. The cult of duty, the sense of Fate in the Greek sense, the noble austerity of Conrad: those qualities were not for the devotees of Dostoevsky, Gorky and Strindberg.

Politically it was out of the question to take the anarchists seriously, except as dangerous fanatics who might break loose suddenly with an assassination. They knew how to make philosophical anarchism sound attractive to a liberal. But the next moment they would be entangled in sophistries. The members of the New York group openly defended the recent killing of the Grand Duke Sergei of Russia, of the perfectly harmless Empress Elisabeth of Austria and of King Umberto I of Italy. The last-mentioned crime gave them great satisfaction because it had been planned in Paterson, New Jersey. They were a bit more prudent, be it noted, about discussing the shooting of

President McKinley, which had caused them to be watched as never before by the police.

The Socialists had realistic plans, a working organization, and were on the upward surge of the best prestige they have ever enjoyed in the United States. I attended several meetings and then joined Branch One of Local New York, which had its rooms, if I remember rightly, on East Twenty-Eighth Street. I still have my copy of the famous 'red card' of membership, an international certificate among Socialists which could get you into the outer circle of the Russian revolutionists in Europe headed by Nicolai Lenin, though I attached slight importance to that and did not so use it. The leading spirit of the branch was Max Eastman, poet, essayist and editor of *The Masses*, which last made him a name to conjure with among leftist writers and artists. Another important member was Allan Benson, also a man of letters but a more pedestrian one, an analyst of economic and political questions for the big periodicals. Norman Thomas probably attended, though I do not recall meeting him then. The membership, largely proletarian, was sufficiently weighted with teachers and social workers to make it the 'highbrow' branch of the city. Many women belonged. They voted on party questions, as was not the case with the Republicans and Democrats.

I found the business meetings tedious. The problems dealt with were much the same as those that troubled the big parties: the choice of delegates to conventions, how to get out the vote and train watchers at the polls, and the raising of funds. Socialists had supreme difficulty in financing a campaign, and there is no more tiresome subject unless you happen to be a born treasurer. Even the debates over principles and platforms were not exciting if you had already been through the textbooks. The public meetings were better, for at them the authentic thunder from below the horizon was sometimes heard. The movement had a number of good orators, including Eugene V. Debs who had run three times for the presidency. Debs, a tall, lean man, excessively bald and with an angelic expression on his thin-lipped shaven face: he could fill Carnegie Hall any evening. Enemies joined with friends in calling him one of the best speakers of his age. Yet I admired him with reservations. There was a broad sentimental streak in him that I thought incompatible with the leadership of a radical cause.

A Congressional district on the Lower East Side furnished the largest Socialist vote in the city. It could be carried, and indeed this was accomplished before long by an indefatigable Jewish party worker named Meyer London. So it was a favoured district for meetings, convivial and otherwise. The most typical Socialist balls were held there, and what they lacked in bizarre jollity in comparison with anarchist balls they repaid with the circulation of ideas. The disputes around the tables foamed like the froth of the beer we drank. Members of the older Socialist Labor Party, whose idol had been Daniel DeLeon, came and accused us of being really bourgeois moderates. Heavy Germans visiting from Milwaukee, Wisconsin, where they had elected Victor Berger to Congress, countered with the charge that the Laborites were "red-flag madmen." At an East Side dance I heard straight talk for the first time about the plans of the IWW (Industrial Workers of the World), a devious union that had been spreading disorder in the Western states.

Bill Haywood, the leader of the Wobblies, this being a sobriquet derisively adopted by the IWW, was present, but followed his usual practice of saying little except from a platform. The empty socket of one eye added disfigurement to a leaden, glabrous face. He had done time in connection with the murder of a governor of Idaho, and his admirers naturally said that he had been railroaded. Haywood nodded his approval while one Thompson, a big, ruddy man with a thick moustache, ebulliently set forth the beauties of applied treachery.

The class struggle was on, and there must be no qualms, said Thompson. He used expressions about sabotage that have since become catchphrases – boring from within, the slow-down, scamped production. He exulted over the notion of boring from within, cupping a huge hand and thrusting his index finger into it with a rotary movement, as he compared the IWW workman to a weevil in a nut, breaking down the nut's structure and opening the way for the entry of other weevils. Anything to destroy capitalist property until conditions were ripe for the dictatorship of the proletariat. A mild-looking Englishman put in that his contribution was to walk through orchard country at night and slash young fruit trees.

Now I had never fancied those two key propositions of Karl Marx's, the class struggle and the dictatorship of the proletariat. I swallowed them as meaning less than they said, 'classes' being interpreted, I suppose, as the worthy and unworthy in a community, and 'the proletariat' as an alliance of honest workingmen and intellectuals. But there was no getting away from what the IWW meant. Their methods were despicable to me. I found them as venomous as those of the anarchists, without the palliating ideals of philosophical anarchism.

If I did not reject them openly it was because of our leftist theory that all forms of rebellion were useful. We held that they would be sifted out in the final reckoning. 'Rebel' was our favourite word. We glorified it as a badge, and even the mildest socialists laid claim to it. That was why *The Masses* had so broad a following. Everything in the pages of that curiously effective monthly upheld the rebel in labour and politics, in love and art, or satirized the docile herd and the oppressors of rebels. The note enchanted American youth in the 1910s, whatever might prove to be the case in the 1960s. The editing of *The Masses* was brilliant, and the cleverest writers and artists were glad to contribute their work free. Many a future star sparkled there for the first time. But paid advertisements were scarce. The magazine used good paper and sold for only ten cents. Its success in at least breaking even on most numbers was a nine-days' wonder in publishing.

Periods of change bring casualties. There began that depreciation of the liberal attitude which was to gain an unforetellable momentum and sweep away in most countries the long-established parties that bore the name. The very term 'liberalism' became a sneer on the lips of radicals. Conservatives were rated as the enemy and in that degree respected. Liberals were held to be fools or weaklings, doomed to be crushed between the opposing forces.

I TOOK GREAT INTEREST IN the presidential campaign of 1912. It is said that Colonel Edward M. House, scouting for a candidate to back for the Democratic nomination, chose Mayor Gaynor of New York ahead of Woodrow Wilson, but changed his mind after meeting and observing Gaynor, on the grounds that his forthrightness of behaviour as well as language would shock the majority sentiment of the country. If that is true, House vetoed a genius. Gaynor was a reformer in his own way: the most original, realistic, unpuritanical reformer in the annals of New York. He detested crimes of violence, the oppression of the helpless, malingering by public servants, bribery and the stealing of votes. But he made no bones about his disbelief in the possibility of enforcing virtue by statute and changing human nature in the process. He wrote scintillating counterblasts against hypocrites. His steady, blue-grey eyes, firm mouth and severely clipped grey beard gave him a cold appearance, but nothing could have been further from the truth. He was a passionate, self-willed person.

He liked to walk home from City Hall over the Brooklyn Bridge, and when his police commissioner begged him not to risk a physical assault in that way during the uproar over the Herman Rosenthal murder, Gaynor pooh-poohed the danger. The troubled commissioner assigned two plain-clothes men to shadow the mayor on his walks, so that they could rush to his help if necessary. Gaynor's keen memory identified them one afternoon. He stopped, denounced them in a voice that could be heard for a quarter of a mile, and forbade them as their commander-in-chief to follow him again. I went with a party of reporters to Gaynor's house on Eighth Avenue, Brooklyn, to hear a statement he had promised to issue. An impudent question from a man on a hostile paper caused the mayor to blow up. He hurled an inkpot at the offender. Yet few officials have been so well-liked and respected by reporters. He knew when not to throw inkpots.

It will be remembered that Theodore Roosevelt split the Republicans in 1912 and founded the Progressive Party. Though I did not admit it at the time, my real preference was for him. I gave Debs lip service, but as I have said I could not become personally enthusiastic about him. President Taft, of course, was a hopeless reactionary in my eyes. I felt an antipathy for Woodrow Wilson. He was incurably the schoolmaster in politics, a Presbyterian do-gooder and a political prig. Ordinarily I would have found some appeal in the fact that he was a Southerner; but no man of Virginian birth ever seemed less a Southerner than Woodrow Wilson.

The individuality of Theodore Roosevelt loomed above those of his rivals. He was a colourful ego, a fighter, a leader, a man, and with interests so broad that they included a passion for natural history. I knew perfectly well that he was no reformer at heart. A progressive, yes; for that signified energy and movement, giving him opportunities to express himself. He praised the 'heroic virtues'. He hated trusts in the degree that they resisted his ideas, and as it happened his ideas were superior to those of the trusts. If Big Business had been shrewd enough to support him, it would have been the gainer in the long run. Along with this, he might easily have been encouraged to become a beneficent dictator. I was convinced of it all, and yet I would have been glad to see him win. And a Socialist victory was out of the question anyway.

Much cant attended the third-party movement with its talk of a crusade and its hymn-singing. But TR knew how to turn the emotional fervour to account without appearing too evangelical himself. He rode his new party like a steed – or like a bull moose, to use his own picturesque epithet. When he stood at Milwaukee with a would-be assassin's bullet in his chest and delivered the speech he had come to make, I thought him unbeatable. His frustration would have been less of a shock if Gaynor had been his opponent. That a Wilson could slip in on the divided Republican vote simply proved that 1912 was too placid a year for a revolution.

I treated myself to a trip to Washington to see James E. Martine, my old acquaintance from my fortnight in Plainfield, New Jersey, who had unexpectedly become a United States senator. At that time senators were not elected by popular vote, but by the state legislature in joint session. Some Southern and Western states had adopted a primary system under which it was mandatory to elect the majority party candidate who had been previously successful in winning nomination at the polls. As a concession to the progressive trend, New Jersey, too, held a primary, but it was advisory only and looked upon as the biggest joke in the world. No one expected the legislators to give away the valuable prize of a senatorship for such a reason. No serious aspirant troubled to campaign for an endorsement. James E. Martine had entered his name in the primary. He had received a very light vote. The fact remained that more ballots had been cast for him than for his nearest rival. A Democratic legislature had been swept in along with Wilson, and to its horror he shook his schoolmaster's rod and required the election of Martine.

It is unlikely in the highest degree that Wilson esteemed the jovial perpetual candidate, Martine. The Presbyterian conscience that Wilson had brought into statesmanship from Princeton University was the deciding factor, or at all events received the credit. An electoral law must be observed in the spirit as well as the letter, he insisted, and he was given a favourable country-wide press. Whimpering with anguish, the New Jersey legislature had covered its eyes and passed the toga with a left-handed gesture to Martine. Later, under pressure from Wilson, it had enacted a real primary law. I heard that Martine could scarcely believe his good fortune at first. Then he staged a hilarious victory party for his supporters of many a bygone campaign. The fairy-story reward that had come to him delighted me. When I reminded him of my contacts with him in Plainfield, the good-hearted old boy professed himself ready to do anything on earth for me. He assuredly looked like a senator and had assumed the mannerisms.

THERE EXISTED IN NEW YORK an organization called the Liberal Club, headed by the suave, aesthetic rector of the Church of the Ascension, Percy Stickney Grant, who enjoyed some fame as a minor poet. He had good social connections, preached in a mood of graceful but prudent scepticism, and his women parishioners adored him. The Reverend Mr Grant conducted the Liberal Club as a forum where any subject could be debated decorously. The atmosphere was pleasant if you had no strong convictions one way or the other.

A fairly large number of us were inspired to join the Liberal Club with the express intention of capturing it and turning it into a revolutionary club. True to their precepts, the old membership received us and allowed us to operate as we pleased. We soon won seats on the board of directors. Then was launched a ruthless heckling of Grant, which the elegant clergyman could not endure. He and his supporters resigned. Ernest Holcombe was elected president, Leigh Holdredge treasurer, and Berkeley Tobey a member of the board. Holcombe, jaunty and hirsute, looked like a moral dissenter, while the short, round-faced Holdredge did not. Both were businessmen who withdrew in time from our suspect company. Tobey, bald and snub-featured as a gnome, wearing a long chin beard, was to be an amusing minor rebel for many a year. I mention them all as a contribution to the marginalia of New York history because they, along with myself – I having been chosen secretary of the Liberal Club – became inadvertently the founders of Greenwich Village in its present incarnation.

This is what happened. The club was functioning in a fourth-storey apartment, where it could not become the large social centre that we wanted it to be. We decided to move to a house in some picturesque quarter. Washington Square was favoured on account of its artistic traditions, but some other downtown neighbourhood would have been acceptable. Holcombe, Holdredge, Tobey and I were authorized to look for a place. The underground telegraph spread the news and Paula Holladay, better known as Polly, called to see us. She was a robust young woman with prominent eyes and chin, a frequenter of rebel balls given by all the factions.

She announced that she was going to start a restaurant, and for the sake of mutual advantages was willing to locate it in any building chosen by the club. We agreed that this was a fine idea.

The house, 135 MacDougal Street, just below Washington Square, was discovered by Tobey. The rest of the committee visited and approved it. The first floor was reserved for club purposes. A hardwood parquet floor for dancing was put down, and a player-piano was bought on the instalment plan. Polly opened her restaurant on an exceedingly modest scale in the basement. It would have been difficult for anyone to forecast that a Latin quarter had been born. Yet so it was. The date was early in 1913.

At that time Greenwich Village proper, which may be defined as south of Fourteenth Street, west of Sixth Avenue, and west and south of the Square, did not contain a single nightclub, dance hall, tea room or novelty shop. There were a few isolated studios in the correct meaning of the term. The remodelling of houses into two-room flats described as studios had not commenced. The only restaurants were a few Italian *tables d'hôte*, a bakery or two, and I think one chop suey place. The population was partly middle class and old New York, living in houses that the families had long owned; partly Irish and Italian immigrant.

Polly's restaurant had more to do with the change at first than the Liberal Club did. Her basement was a big success. Down flocked the anarchists, the more festive of the socialists, and along with them many of a type that apparently had had no place to go till then: students, would-be artists recently arrived in New York, and sheer sensation-seekers. They crowded together in a thick pall of tobacco smoke, drank red wine or coffee, and argued half the night. An invitation upstairs to dance was a highly regarded privilege. Other restaurants opened in competition, and that was a development to which there has been no end.

The Liberal Club staged a number of meetings on controversial questions. How well I recall Elizabeth Gurley Flynn, slender in her brunette beauty then, a Celt astray in the thickets of syndicalism. She addressed us with passion on mill conditions at Lawrence, Massachusetts, which had led to one of the great strikes of the period. A milder programme got up by the entertainment committee of the club promised weekly lectures and debates through the winter season, to discuss the New Drama, the New Fiction, the New Poetry, the New Art, the New Journalism, the New Music, the

Figure 13. Polly Holladay's restaurant, underneath the Liberal Club at 135 MacDougal Street, New York. Courtesy World Museum of the City of New York: Polly's Restaurant, Greenwich Village Image Number: 95.74.3. Maker: Jessie Tarbox Beals.

New Sociology, the New Politics – in fact, the new everything. I recall being somewhat depressed by it. Apparently nothing was to be rated exciting or valuable unless it were new. The members of the committee might have hesitated to affirm that the mere state of newness made a form good, but I haven't a doubt in the world that that was what they subconsciously believed.

First-class minds were willing to lend themselves to the illusion. It was in the air. Lincoln Steffens, for instance, came and talked to us pungently about the new something-or-other. I cannot suppose that that keen intelligence thought his subject was having its first workout in history. The new interest gave him a chance to ring the changes, that was all. At the end of the club's programme there was even a lecture on the New Forestry, a topic so remote from the cares of that urban throng that its inclusion caused cries of amazement. But there was a reason. The prominent female member who was down to lecture on the New Pedagogy was having a love affair with a forester, and she did not want him to feel neglected. The Liberal Club could claim no immunity from the wire-pulling that took place in bourgeois organizations.

Our next bright idea was to hold a ball to raise funds. The name given the jamboree was the Pagan Rout. It was held in Webster Hall on East Eleventh Street, outdid previous affairs of the kind in costuming, gusto and unconventionality, and made money. Pagan Routs thereafter became the chief activity of the club. One of the most successful and certainly one of the most beautiful was based on a Spanish musical and dancing show, *La Tierra de la Alegría* [The Land of Joy], then playing in New York. The club members and their friends wore approximately the correct costumes, and so the eye was satisfied. The orchestra industriously rendered Spanish music, not too badly. Doloretes and Bilbao, the female and male stars of *La Tierra de la Alegría*, danced as guests of honour. The efforts of the merry-makers to go Spanish themselves on the dance floor were heavy-footed, to be sure. But everyone had a good time.

I recollect it mainly on account of Doloretes and Bilbao and the vivid pageant, half *zarzuela* or light opera, half popular dance recital, in which they had been brought from Spain. New York did not appreciate them at their true worth. My love of the Spanish dance had been kindled by a few good acts I had seen in vaudeville, had fed on glimpses I had had at such places as the Café Gambrinus in Guaymas, Mexico, and was to become a major ardour. After great poetry, painting and sculpture, nothing excels for me the patterns created by the human body within the framework of a tested cult. I delight in all traditional dancing, including ballet of course, but particularly Spanish. And only in Spanish is the male dancer as well worth watching as the female. He never gives the impression of being emasculate.

Charming *La Tierra de la Alegría* with its gay, piercing tunes, its wealth of *flamenco* and regional measures. Brown Doloretes, a Triana gypsy undoubtedly, with her marvellous figure and ugly face. Poor Doloretes, who died in New York, of an abortion I was told, leaving Bilbao to carry on impeccably, his features expressionless like a mask of stone, until the company disintegrated in a flurry, because no one worthy to take her place could be found.

The Liberal Club had set out to establish a focus of rebel thinking, and it had succeeded, with the assistance of Polly Holladay, in creating a new bohemia that at the beginning had a political motivation. I wasted a lot of energy over the Liberal Club. Polly's was fun, though it lacked the charm of Madama's and Petitpas's; as the unpretentious Greenwich Village Inn of later days and at another site, it never was the equal of Mouquin's.

MEANWHILE – AND HERE I jump back to when I was first active in the Liberal Club – I was seized by a profound nostalgia for Jamaica. A vacation was due me at the *Semi-Monthly Magazine Section*, and I decided to go home. I would only have three weeks, of which four and a half days each way would be spent at sea. But the prospect of twelve full days on the island filled me with joyful anticipation. I took the *Almirante*, a United Fruit Company passenger ship which carried bananas on the northward voyage but was luxuriously equipped compared with the old *Barnstaple* on which I had left Jamaica. Also, it was a more seductive experience physically to sail down into the tropics than to depart from them. The flying fish and the man-of-war birds reappeared like boyhood friends off the Bahamas. The colours of the mountainous cumulus clouds at sunset surpassed those of the Arizona desert. In the Windward Passage the soft winds at night brushed my face like feather-down, and the Southern Cross wheeled back into view. The next morning we were off the south coast of Jamaica, running in the shadow of the Blue Mountains toward Kingston. Since I had sailed from Port Antonio in the north, this visual effect was new to me, new and yet known. The pilot boat that came off to us at Plumb Point on the Palisadoes was a canoe, in which a half-naked Negro sprawled like a figure in a Winslow Homer painting.

My sister Ethel was in from the country to meet me, and we spent the night at a guest house on Hanover Street. She had with her Helen Fulford, the eldest daughter of one of our Manchester neighbours and who had been a child in pigtails when I left eight years before. Helen's honey-blonde prettiness, her soft Jamaican speech, instantly touched a romantic chord in me. The three of us drove about town, and I was glad to see how much rebuilding had been done in Kingston since the earthquake, often at the cost of the antique atmosphere but serving to quell my fears that the city had been lastingly crippled. Then we hurried off to our parish in the hills.

The house where my father lived with two of his surviving Lind aunts was called Fairview, a less attractive place than Berry Hill. Fairview stood on an exposed spur of the ridge overlooking the savanna in St Elizabeth parish. As its name implied, it commanded a fine view that took in an expanse of the sea ten miles distant, but it was scourged by winds concentrated upon it by unlucky oddities of the terrain. The square two-storey house with no balconies shook in weather that did not even approximate a storm; the trees and the garden shrubs were bent over at a permanent angle by the pressure of the wind. I did not like Fairview and, curiously, I remember my contacts with my father less clearly on the occasion of that visit than at any other time of my life. Perhaps this was because I was eager to talk socialism to him, and he gave the subject a faintly mocking reception. Socialism was contrary to human nature, he said; it would never master the world.

My crowded stay in Jamaica, anyhow, was like a spinning kaleidoscope. I went on successive days to Helen's house. We rode together on sunny afternoons and by moonlight, with Ethel along as a chaperone. Afterward Helen and I were permitted to be alone together on her back veranda, and before the end of the week I was formally engaged to her. Little more can be said about this incident. Helen was a sweet girl. We responded to a mutual flush of sentiment, poetizing each other in the broadest terms, but undoubtedly she would not have been happy in the life I was committed to leading. She wisely and tactfully ended the betrothal in a few months.

Ethel and I had been invited to spend the better part of a week at Hopewell in the parish of St Ann, the home of Charlie [Charles L.] Walker, an uncle by marriage on the maternal side. He was both a penkeeper and a banana planter, a zestful racing man in his young days, a good representative of the successful native-born developer of landed property. The average Englishman in the tropics was a bungling tyro beside him. And Charlie Walker called anyone who drifted and dreamed, as my father did, a "poor Christian", to quote his own peculiar expression. In boyhood I had visited at Hopewell and enjoyed the greater luxury than prevailed at Berry Hill. A brief return was now a pleasant prospect.

On the way over, Ethel told me a story that I found diverting. It appeared that a married woman of the conservative penkeeping set in St Ann had been, a couple of years earlier, on the same liner that brought Sir Sydney Olivier back from a trip to England. The sight of him had enraged her, and one morning she unburdened herself to a friend in the adjoining deck chair. "Imagine having that socialist and nigger-lover as governor of Jamaica. He's a menace," she ranted. "His land settlement plan aims at turning Quashie [the poor illiterate type of black] into a landowner. It's a state of things that will end in the Negroes taking over the island, and we'll be forced to give it up to them." Olivier had emerged from a companionway behind the two women just as the speech started. He heard it through with a cryptic smile, then deliberately took the chair on the other side of Mrs . . . and made a courteous remark to her about the weather. She had been flustered, but had not apologized.

Ethel added that the upper-class whites had more against Olivier than his political faith. They objected to his going about the island on horseback without ceremony, and alone when he felt like it. If night caught him or bad weather delayed him, he would accept lodging as readily in a peasant's cabin as in a plantation house. This, too, was resented by his critics. They were horrified by the fact that when one of his daughters said publicly that she believed in free love and the governor had been asked about it, he had replied that she was entitled to hold any views that she pleased on the subject.

My interest in Olivier had not flagged. I had read most of his Fabian essays, and I understood him better than had been possible for me in boyhood. He had arrived at socialism by way of the positivist philosophy of Auguste Comte, which has been defined as dealing only with the natural phenomena or properties of knowable things, and he was the only one of the Fabians so to arrive. This had preserved him from much of the claptrap of Marxism. A truly strong man, he did what he thought necessary, no matter who was in the way. During the very period when I first observed him as colonial secretary and compared him more than favourably with Sir Augustus Hemming, his chief, Olivier had written to a friend in England that he was the actual administrator of Jamaica, though the system provided a governor who was paid five thousand pounds a year for living in the King's House and giving a dinner party now and then. Olivier also stated openly that the break-up of the British Empire would scarcely be the end of the world.

Naturally I was delighted that the accidents of Crown Colony hierarchy had sent such a man to my country. His colonial secretary assuredly was not running him. I wanted badly to talk with Olivier, but this was impracticable in the short time at my disposal. Instead I lauded him at my uncle's dinner table and cockily professed my own belief in socialism. Charlie Walker was not edified, but said that my youth excused me.

Hopewell was less than a thousand feet above sea level, and the surrounding countryside of rolling grass lands and thickets teemed with more tropical fauna than we had in Manchester. Herons stalked on the margins of the ponds dug for cattle. Parrots were to be seen, and big cuckoos called Old Man Birds did their awkward tumbling in the underbrush. My feeling for birds revived sharply; odd moments were all that I could give them. Picnics had been organized, and there were social calls to be made. The visit to Jamaica ended in a trice, it seemed. I sailed back, as I had come, on a white-painted fruiter.

THEREAFTER I BUSIED MYSELF WITH the Liberal Club while following a parallel course of literary bohemianism and dallying as an amateur in the studios of artists. The illustrators had a club, the Kit Kat, in an East Fourteenth Street house that was pure bohemia. Antedating by many a year the Pagan Routs of the liberals and in fact all such fiestas in New York, the costume ball given by the Kit Kat Club was one of the liveliest events of the winter. Its special character derived from the combination of artists and their models.

The strike of silk operatives at Paterson, New Jersey, was launched and quickly became the labour struggle that most aroused the sympathies of New York intellectual radicals. They saw it as a cause sacred to all the isms, though why this one over and above other strikes I could not make out. Perhaps it was simply a matter of the moment in time. Aid committees were formed, those run by women being particularly active. Volunteers invaded Paterson, marched in parades that the police had forbidden and paid fines for it. A young writer fresh from Harvard, who lived a few doors from me on Washington Square, was one of the demonstrators. Reporters liked his poise and a certain steely vigour in the things he said. Their stories made him celebrated overnight. His name was John Reed. Set his case, if you relish the irony, against that of Pat Quinlan, a fanatical socialistic Irishman, ugly as a lephrechaun and sentimental as a schoolgirl, with no friends except among the extremists. The New Jersey courts made Quinlan the scapegoat for better-connected trespassers, his jail sentence being a stiff one. Personally I kept aloof from the Paterson strike. I would have been unable to speak the economic lingo of the strikers, and so I did not see how I could be useful to them. Their claims, no doubt, were just. I hoped they would win, and let it go at that. But I attended city mass meetings held in their support and met some people who ordinarily did not give time to feverish manifesting. I thus got to know the important feminist leaders, including Margaret Sanger, a singularly gallant personality, who had started to promote her birth-control movement and risked the most dire persecution for it. She was the mother of three young children then, and she had been a nurse, which should have

Figure 14. Roberts with Margaret Sanger and one of her sons, in 1917. MS353.6.7.

been proof of her sane outlook but which conservatives twisted to mean that only a perverse mother could wish to thwart the mechanism of life. She published shortly afterward a lustrous little magazine called the *Woman Rebel*, which adventured far beyond birth control, and which ran for nine issues in the face of grotesque legal obstacles. I felt honoured to become her friend.

I had reached the breaking point with the *Semi-Monthly Magazine Section* and had made my plans to go to Paris. The engagement to Helen had ended months before. My easy-going attachment to Katharine showed no signs of taking a positive turn. I was growing disgusted with the Liberal Club. Those were the conditions under which I fell in love with Camilla Farr, and many details about New York as the city was for me that winter are vivid in consequence. Unless I was in love I found it hard to capture mental pictures of uptown New York, where all takes place on a checkerboard of numbered streets.

Camilla Farr was one of the non-bohemian feminists whom the Paterson affair had brought out, a Celt with bronze hair and that quality of cream-white skin that is enhanced by a faint freckle or two. Everything seemed unfavourable to our growing to be other than casual acquaintances. She was married, and though her husband was away she had not said she was separated from him. A busy woman with varied interests, absolutely cool on the surface, several years older than myself: the effect she had on me at first was to make me feel rather callow. She did not go to restaurants like Madama's and Polly's, and I imagined that she thought me a time-waster for frequenting them. But no rules apply to paradoxical attractions between the sexes, simply none.

She was staying with a sister on a street that is now in the middle of Negro Harlem, but was then mainly Irish and German. An elevated railroad station at the corner, its four crooked stairways straddling apart like the legs of a spider; the wide block sprinkled with flurries of snow; the tall building with a plain front of yellowish stone; and the apartment featureless except for many books. Nothing could be more ordinary – or have in my memory a more personal significance.

Camilla and I had been out together several times before the evening I took her to Mouquin's. Her ideas and ways of expressing them, her wit, her balance – in short her ego – were a revelation to me. She believed in the same things that I did, but for righter reasons and without blind partisanship. Socialism was worth supporting, she said; it seemed to have both a rational and a noble programme, yet until one had seen it in power who could tell whether it would not restrict liberty beyond the endurance point. The IWW were shock troops of revolution, with all the brutish qualities that went with the merits of such fighters. Anarchism had some appeal to the heart, none to the brain. Camilla had gone far beyond ordinary political liberalism. Rather she was a libertarian, especially where her own sex was concerned, and it was the substance itself that she cared about. She was a friend of Inez Milholland, the suffragist, whose husband Eugen Boissevain afterward married Edna St Vincent Millay.

I observed that night at Mouquin's that anyone meeting Camilla, even in radical society, would take her for a conventional woman.

"But darlin', I believe in the conventions," she said. "They preserve good manners."

"At the cost of repression," I argued.

"They don't have that power. They're superficial, and you're mistakin' them for convictions." She smiled. "Think it over, darlin'."

I compared her with some blatant feminists I knew, and much to their disadvantage. I was quite gone on Camilla, though I prudently discounted her calling me "darlin'"; dropping her *g*'s the way she did, the word became her. But a wonderful surprise awaited me. After dinner I took Camilla home in one of the pleasant hansom cabs that had not yet been entirely replaced by motor-taxis, and she asked me up for coffee. Her sister threw a queer look of disapproval at me, served the coffee with cake and vanished. Noting my faint discomfiture, Camilla said lightly: "She objects to you only because you are a man. She is a dragon about my career, whichever career it is she means."

"I hope you get to like me to the extent she fears," I ventured.

"I do already, or you would not be here," Camilla answered softly.

Hours later I was stricken with dismay at the thought that I was booked to sail for France in just one week. This could not be. Unthinkable that I should have found Camilla and then leave her almost instantly. I would cancel my passage.

To my astonishment she resisted the suggestion with the utmost firmness. It would be a weakness, affecting her as well as myself, she said. She was planning to leave New York at about the same time on important work. If I stayed she would no doubt be tempted into doing the same thing. We must not try to alter our luck, our fate, or whatever we chose to call it. It was not as if we had to squeeze dry a fleeting passion. We would correspond, see each other once more, remain close through the years. In the meantime we had a week. It was a very special week. All that Camilla said was true, except for a reservation of which neither of us could have dreamed. The setting could never be the same again, for the gods were about to change the world – including New York.

CHAPTER 8 ❧ **Paris**

ON 24 JANUARY 1914, I SAILED FOR FRANCE on the *Niagara*, a one-class ship of the Compagnie Générale Transatlantique. It was a reckless journey, for I had not been careful with my savings and would land with about forty dollars, less than the price of the fare back. I forget the exact figure, but I paid some seventy-five dollars for a west-to-east passage that would take ten days. No passport had been required, no health certificates, no proof of financial solvency. It was a free world. The second-rate ship had attractions that I had not found on any other: a café-bar that could produce cognac and absinthe, a cuisine like that of a French *table d'hôte*, and the lavishness of litre bottles of both red and white claret between each two places at table, to drink in any quantity or to leave alone. The stewards were frivolous instead of servile; they seemed bohemians of their trade and offered tips about the girls aboard. It mattered nothing to me that the Atlantic was in boisterous winter mood. I was not seasick and would not have changed any aspect of the voyage.

Most of my fellow-passengers were French. The young fellow who sat beside me at meals was a clerk in a Paris bank. He had spent a vacation in New York to improve his English. His regular military service had ended five years before, but as soon as he got back he would rejoin the colours for brief exercises in the form of manoeuvres near the German frontier. I asked him what he would have to do if France got into a war. He answered cheerfully: "I'd be just a plain foot soldier and have no idea where they would send my regiment. But I imagine you mean about mobilization, if I were at home. Look." He slipped his *carnet militaire* out of his breast pocket. "This tells me where to report – the very day and hour – after my class is called."

I found it bizarre to be talking to a man who took compulsory military service as a matter of course, especially as war would almost certainly not come to France in our lifetime. He agreed with me that the era of great wars was ended. "Yet there are many who still talk of revenge for 1870," he added pensively.

Travelling with us was a coal operator from Pittsburgh who gossiped to me, as we leaned on the rail, that he was going to Brest on what he thought was a queer errand. The French government was in the market for large supplies of coal for its navy and would consider American anthracite.

"What's there so queer about that?" I asked.

"If you were in the business –" he began. "Well, the French mine coal of their own, and they usually piece it out with cheap stuff from Cardiff. I've as good as sold them a hundred and fifty thousand tons, which will cost them plenty. They must fear an emergency."

I nodded, without paying much attention to the coal merchant's shop talk.

Then there was my cabin-mate, a sleepy-eyed, middle-aged Belgian who grumbled now and then about the nuisance of having had to take so slow a boat to Europe. He admitted he was a gambler, and he lost to us all at penny poker because, he said, such small stakes could not be taken seriously by a professional. "The connections in winter are bad," he explained, "and I must get home by a certain date. The family want to do something foolish about property we have in Liège. It is not the moment to start a lace workshop in Liège." This, too, seemed a commercial worry of minor interest to me.

The high seas rolled and surged, buffeting the *Niagara* with mid-winter power. I could easily have run into such weather in the Caribbean or the Pacific, but I had not chanced to do so, and now it seemed grandly congruous with a voyage to old Europe. I would go forward at night, cling to a stanchion, plunge with the plunging bow and dream at the same time of Paris and Camilla Farr. I associated them together because they were my two most intense desires, and I refused to admit what a deep gulf ran between them. Diverging from our course on the ninth evening, we raised the Lizard light in the murk, my first glimpse of Europe. We were due at Le Havre the next afternoon.

It was probably the least attractive port in France, with its series of artificial basins under a film of coal dust. Liners and tramp ships threaded their course through devious channels, as if they were trains being shuttled. At the pier I noticed a sign above one of the entrances which announced in English, "Baggages Visited Here". On this note of Gallic confusion over foreign tongues, I landed smiling. I bought a Parisian paper at the newsstand, struck by the headline, PAUL DEROULEDE EST MORT, and the accompanying drawing of a gaunt bearded face suggestive of Don Quijote. Who was Paul Déroulède? I found out from my newspaper. He was a poet, the late chief of the Ligue des Patriotes, the great irreconcilable in the matter of Alsace-Lorraine, the enemy of the Republic because it had acquiesced, the man who had been condemned to banishment for ten years for plotting the overthrow of the moderate President Loubet by force of arms. The obituaries treated his memory with mingled reproof and pride. I felt in all this a sense of political drama such as I had not known in the United States.

But the charming Norman landscape distracted my attention from Déroulède. Though it was winter, the fields and orchards were not entirely bare. A soft haze lay upon them, and a tinge of green showed through. Cattle browsed in the open amid the russet stubble. The detached country houses, of an antique architecture, stood out among the leafless trees. The compact little towns were reminiscent of the Middle Ages. As we approached Paris my ebullience grew. Night had fallen when we left the suburbs and crawled through a deep cut into the Gare St Lazare, a smoky barn of a station rendered gay by stands heaped with books in yellow, pink and blue paper bindings, and by extraordinarily artistic posters advertising the products of France from liquors and perfumes to pneumatic tyres. An illustrator friend, Adrien Machefert, had gone over several months earlier and had promised to meet me. I found him presently, standing in an attitude typical of him with his head tilted on one side, looking very bohemian in a baggy overcoat and a felt hat, a slim Scots girl at his side. He grinned amiably, introduced me to Peggy, and led the way to a cab, which in those days was still by preference a horse-drawn *fiacre*. There were plenty of motor-taxis in Paris, but bohemians scorned them.

We clip-clopped across the Grands Boulevards, through the Place de la Concorde, and over the Concorde bridge to the Left Bank. Machefert took me to the modest Hotel des Ecoles, 15 rue Delambre, a few doors from the boulevard du Montparnasse. He waited while I had my things carried to a room on an upper floor, and then we strolled over to the Café de la Rotonde on the boulevard for a drink.

Suddenly my observations became as clear as if etched. I could be sitting at this moment on the terrace of the Café de la Rotonde with Machefert and Peggy. It had only a small vogue then among certain writers and artists who had turned against the much better known Café du Dôme across the street. The Rotonde had a zinc bar scarcely twenty-five feet long, an adjoining room with a cushioned divan around the walls, and under an awning a goodly share of the broad sidewalk. There were more girls than men at the round marble-topped tables, girls of many nationalities. The lone ones, as well as some of the escorted, were models, Machefert said, the Rotonde having come to be recognized as the café in the neighbourhood into which you looked if you needed a model. The well-dressed wore hobble-skirts and little velvet toques with frail black plumes, but most of the girls had on shirtwaists and plain skirts, and were hatless. The running fire of talk was meaningless to me, for the Parisian inflection baffled my ear. The boulevard seemed dark, mysterious compared with a New York street. I rocked on a current of interest that was almost passionate, and I told myself that of all the cities I had ever seen this was the one that promised most.

The next morning I was up early and looking romantically from my back window across the rooftops of Paris. For four days I explored on foot, making my own discoveries. I grew attached to two spots: the gardens of the Hotel de Cluny with its Roman ruins and the courtyard of the Palais Royal. The history of fifteen hundred years appeared to me to vibrate between them with singular profundity. Walking from one to the other on an evening dark with mist, I heard a clatter of hoofs on cobblestones, and as I stood back against a wall in a narrow street dragoons fully accoutred thundered by me. They had tall helmets with horse hair sweeping down to their shoulders and capes lined with scarlet, and they all wore great black moustaches. I had only seen pictures of French dragoons until then. In the flesh and in that setting, they were an incredibly colourful legacy to the Third Republic from imperial times, and in some subtle way they added a link to the harmony of Cluny and the Palais Royal.

After my initial orgy of roaming about Paris, I began to frequent the Montparnasse cafés. Machefert had me meet a number of his friends of both sexes, and we were expecting T. Victor Hall from New York. It may seem a mad waste of time on the part of one who had come to Paris with only forty dollars and had already spent ten of them, but I passed the better part of a week in the cafés without sparing a thought as to how I was to earn some cash. Two desires obsessed me. I wanted to get the feel of the life, and I wanted to break though the barrier of spoken French. To these ends I breakfasted in a café for a few sous and read the newspapers obligingly furnished by the house, took a walk and dropped into another café before lunch and still another after lunch, did the same thing before dinner and after dinner. The drinks were marvellously cheap; they cost me no more than three or four francs a day, since it was permitted to nurse a single order indefinitely. Soon I decided that the Rotonde was my favourite place and seldom went anywhere else.

I listened intently to conversations at neighbouring tables. When given the chance I joined in. It was quite easy for me to make myself understood, but almost impossible to cope with the replies unless pronounced clearly and slowly. The girls, of course, were my best bet, because it amused them to combine teaching and flirting. To jump ahead a few weeks, I overcame the difficulty at a stroke. Without being able to tell the minute or the hour when it happened, I found myself hearing everything that was said and answering without hesitation. I think that sufficiently remarkable to put it on record, for I have never had another linguistic experience with similar abruptness. I had had no real practice in French before, not even with Florence Brochu, who preferred to speak English, though my book knowledge of the language was fair.

ONE DAY A YOUNG AMERICAN writer asked me what I expected to do in Paris. I answered that I had a mind to call at the offices of the United States and English newspaper correspondents, in the hope of getting a job. He made no bones about assuring me that I would be disappointed. "Dozens of us here have had the same idea," he said. "There aren't any jobs of that sort for us. The home offices send across their favourites."

His words struck me as alarmingly reasonable. The next morning I went early to the right bank of the Seine and started a round of the correspondents. I began with the *New York Herald*, which published a Paris edition in English, and then tried the *Chicago Daily News* and the *New York Times* because they maintained lavish services for visiting Americans. I was treated amiably, but warned that my quest was just a bright dream. Other papers, including the London ones, were equally unreceptive. My first days in New York recurred to me, but though the present quandary was every bit as serious as that one had been, I somehow could not feel pessimistic.

At the corner of the boulevard de la Madeleine and the rue Cambon a sign announced that the *Brooklyn Daily Eagle* ran a bureau on the first floor. I knew the *Eagle* of that period to be a dignified literary paper, but I shared the average New Yorker's feeling of indifference toward Brooklyn journalism. In Paris it was well worth a bid. I climbed the stairs and found a large and comfortably equipped reception room for tourists. A clerk named Thomas J. Smith took me to the inner office, and as if by wizardry my fortunes changed. The man sitting there was Hans von Kaltenborn, later eminent as the pioneer commentator in American radio. He was then an assistant editor of the *Eagle* and had been rushed over from Brooklyn to handle an emergency. The Paris correspondent had died suddenly, and while the home office hesitated as to whom to appoint in his place, the junior in Paris also died, of pneumonia. Kaltenborn told me this, and added: "It would not have done to send two reporters who did not know the background. I know the game here, so it fell to me. I haven't had time yet to study our needs and make recommendations." Although born in the United States, he spoke with an accent and rapped out his words in a curt German way. I wondered at his frankness with me, decided that it promised well, and played up to it by telling him with what fervour I had been studying the Parisian scene.

"So the thing you want most is a chance to stay here. Good. I had thought of shopping for a man already on the spot. Why should it not be you – on trial, you understand."

Ordinarily I am not helped by the element of luck, if such there be. It would have been more like me to have called at the *Eagle* bureau twenty-four hours too late. But that time the die fell true, and when I reported it at the Rotonde the young American who had lectured me could scarcely believe that I was not lying. After I had written some columns of acceptable stuff and there had been negotiations with Brooklyn, I was definitely given the job at a modest salary. It might have seemed to many a recession from my assistant editorship in New York. To me, no. I had a psychic conviction that it was an advance.

My duty was to read the French papers and choose articles for translation,

Figure 15. Offices of the *Brooklyn Daily Eagle* in Paris, where Roberts worked from 1914 to 1916. MS353.7.2.6.

or that could be adapted, in some cases developed by the unearthing of new details. I enjoyed it, and almost at once I had a sense of penetration behind the scenes. Something new to me was in the air. It involved the whole of Europe, and if I thought this of no more immediacy than one might expect from the greater complexity of an old civilization, I was simply taking the stand common to all Americans and most Englishmen in the spring of 1914.

Perhaps the first thing I noticed was the quizzical surprise shown by Frenchmen to whom I went for news, that the *Eagle*'s latest correspondent was a German. I said that Kaltenborn was born in the United States. No doubt, the answer came; but surely he was very Prussian in manner. I had the feeling that he was not precisely resented, only looked upon as a peculiar choice. Kaltenborn was aware of this himself. He remarked to me that Parisians clung to their stubborn foolishness about Alsace-Lorraine and regarded everyone with a German name as a possible spy.

The best news stories of the moment had to do with the catching of spies, who swarmed about the fortresses, the naval bases and the arms factories of France like an insect pest. The death penalty was not in question; people had as good as forgotten that it was exacted in time of war for espionage, a crime which now seemed an archaic nuisance, an impertinence that no powers but Germany and Czarist Russia would practise. Names that mean absolutely nothing today flash back to me: Eva Ortner, who was given a year in prison for the indiscreet inquiries she made at Antony; and pretty Clara Poniersh, alias Sonia, a Silesian adventuress who drew six months for corrupting young naval officers at Toulon.

On the Grands Boulevards one day, a French reporter pointed out to me a woman with a voluptuous figure, tawny and lithe, and a face of no great beauty, who had had a vogue, he said, for her exotic Oriental dancing. She was still popular in Germany. Paris had ceased to take her seriously, except as a cocotte who charged fabulous prices. My informant did not connect her with espionage. Her stage name was Mata Hari.

Political intrigue formed the subtler background of events. Few correspondents bothered to know it well, because of the indifference of their readers. I found it keenly interesting, and I went beyond what was required of me in gathering material for the second-string dispatches I was then writing. I haunted the press gallery of the Chamber of Deputies and manoeuvred for contacts, however fleeting, with statesmen in the lobbies, so that I could observe their oddities.

The chief issue was the proposed reduction of the term of compulsory military service from three years to two, a measure which would have weakened the army. Louis Barthou, astute politician, man of letters and collector of erotica, had been forced from office the preceding December for resisting the change. His successor was Gaston Doumergue, put forward by the unified radical groups whose real leader, Joseph Caillaux, became minister of finance. Doumergue was my first French premier and I retain a clear mental picture of him. He was a little dark man of fifty, with the singsong accent of the Midi, black hair which he plastered into a cowlick on his forehead, moustaches curled at the ends and touched with brilliantine, and a penchant for loud checked suits. Politicians regarded him as a tough fellow, a sort of Gascon district boss. It was commonly and correctly supposed that at all events he was honest. Doumergue's backers expected him to fight for a two-years conscription law. But on studying the matter from within the circle of power he had his doubts. The life of the current Chamber of Deputies would run out in April, and he decided to await the verdict of the electorate. His premiership, however, did not escape the test of a resounding public scandal.

Caillaux had been under attack for alleged financial irregularities dating back three years. His chief critic was Gaston Calmette, the editor of the *Figaro*, who suddenly announced that he would print certain letters written by the minister, while still living with his first wife, to the woman who had become the second Mme Caillaux. The rumour cropped up and would not die down, that the destruction of the man politically was not the only object, that Calmette wished to avenge himself upon the woman for a wound to his self-conceit inflicted by her years before. His possession of the letters at issue was itself a mystery. Paris awaited agog for the first chapter of the indecorous serial.

On the evening of 16 March, Mme Henriette Caillaux appeared at the *Figaro* building and sent in her card to the editor. Calmette expressed his amazement that she should come to him, but with the remark that he "could not decline to receive a woman", he ordered that she should be shown into his private office. He stepped behind her as she entered, to close the door. They were alone in the room – the fighting journalist, middle-aged, robust; and the sleek beauty whose influence in official circles was so great that she was called the 'ministeress'. Incidentally, she knew the office. Her first husband had been Leo Clarétie, the literary editor of the *Figaro*. Mme Caillaux had both her hands plunged into a muff. Calmette waited for her to speak, but she did not waste a moment in preliminaries. She drew an automatic revolver and fired five shots into the body of the editor. He collapsed across an armchair, mortally wounded.

The assassination of a president could not have caused a greater sensation. As soon as the newspaper extras were out, the morbid of both sexes flocked about the *Figaro* building, the St Lazare prison for women where Mme Caillaux had been taken, and the Ministry of Finance in the north wing of the Louvre. I visited all three scenes of uproar and heard the mob calling in a high-pitched chant for blood. Not the blood of the killer, who had become a heroine of melodrama, but that of her husband. The charge had been instantly framed: "He used her finger to pull the trigger, knowing that a Paris jury never sends a woman to the guillotine."

I had been on the *Eagle* staff for about a month, and here to my hand was the most exciting case I had ever observed as a reporter – the curtain-raiser, had I but guessed it, to incredible exposures and torrents of blood. My assignment was simply to translate French comments on the murder, but I could not resist going into the thing for my own satisfaction. Joseph Caillaux had at once resigned his portfolio and the fall of the government seemed imminent. I watched Doumergue's cabinet stagger visibly in the Chamber, while the besmirched Caillaux sat bolt upright in his seat as a deputy, his bald head shining and his lips grey under the cropped moustache. But the Gascon premier singsonged his way out of the trouble. Caillaux's disgrace was personal, not political, he said. The elections would show how the country felt about it, and until then it was his, Doumergue's, duty to serve. He was upheld in this view by a vote of confidence.

Under the French system a magistrate, instead of a grand jury, weighs the evidence for an indictment. The procedure is called a court of instruction. Thousands wanted to see the ministeress on the preliminary rack. There were few seats, and the press box had been expanded to take in most of them. With journalists from all over the world competing, I gained admittance once. A curious memory. Henriette Caillaux, plump and brunette, her charm of an Italian type, was in fact playing the role of a stage favourite rather than a sinner. Her every word was precious to the reporters, and her every gesture. I was told that she had sobbed only at her first glimpse of the grey, grimed walls of St Lazare, built as a leper hospital in the Middle Ages by the monk St Francis Xavier, and used during the great revolution as a death-house for aristocrats condemned to the guillotine. But interest was soon postponed to the actual trial, which was set for July.

PARIS HAD MUCH ELSE TO offer me, as its early spring broke in a cloud of tender green and the blossoming of chestnut trees. There were three notable bohemias: the old Latin Quarter centring about the Sorbonne and with the boulevard St Michel as its main street; the Butte Montmartre sloping down to the Place Pigalle; and that part of the fourteenth arrondissement known as Montparnasse. The third was the newest. I lived there because I had been taken to it by Machefert. Sometimes I wondered whether I ought to make a change in order to draw closer to more ancient traditions. But I concluded that Montparnasse was a very good centre. University students still dominated the café life of the Latin Quarter, and Montmartre was half tenderloin in the American sense. Montparnasse had both these aspects, while being mainly the quarter of foreign writers, artists and musicians. We were not overrun by tourists then, and it was the liberty allowed to residents from all over the world, rather than bohemianism among the French themselves, that made Montparnasse so amusing in 1914.

The artists' models certainly offered the spice of variety. They were in such numbers that they could not hope to make a living at their calling and had to rely on lovers, permanent or temporary. Only a Puritan extremist would have termed them harlots, seeing that they followed their fancies as much as possible and did want any given affair to last. If they accepted five or ten francs after a single night, it was from hard necessity; they knew how to pretend prettily that the money was a gift. They were smitten easily, let us say, and at the least excuse they made their feelings clear without inhibitions. A few reached the status of acknowledged mistresses, kept house for the man and were generally faithful. This was the ideal of all.

T. Victor Hall – Tom to his friends – arrived on the boat train from Le Havre, and we took him straight to the Rotonde for initiatory drinks, as I had been taken. A French-Portuguese girl named Anita, ugly to the point of enjoying a kind of vogue among artists as a type, had been an habituée of the Rotonde for some weeks. She had often hailed me with gamine hilarity, but had shown me no favour otherwise. Within ten minutes of Tom's appearance I observed her giving him a rapt attention. The presence of Machefert's Peggy at our table seemed to hold her off; I doubt if it would have been for long, had the problem not been simplified by the early departure of Machefert and his girl. In a moment Anita had crossed the room, gambolling like a calf, making a show of knowing me well and saying she wanted to meet my friend.

I invited her to sit down and have a drink. She told Tom at once that he was the handsomest man she had ever seen – "such an eagle's nose, such piercing eyes, such a fine face generally". He knew very little French at the time and did not catch a word of her speech. I translated literally, at which he muttered in annoyance that she must be a madwoman.

"She's nothing of the sort," I answered. "Just an exaggerated species of Parisian model."

"Well, I don't like her," he growled.

"What does he say? What does he say?" Anita clamoured.

"That your compliments make him feel bashful," I said.

"Tell him for me . . ."

That was the beginning of an endless chorus, "What does he say? . . .

Tell him for me (*Qu'est-ce qu'il dit? . . . Dites lui . . .*) which marked the pauses of the most bizarre of attempted seductions at second-hand. If Tom had understood what was being said and had treated it with raillery, even in broken French, Anita might have been discouraged. But the language obstacle drove her wild. Using me as an automaton, she made me ask Tom to take her where he pleased that very night and added her pledge that she would follow him to the ends of the world thereafter. He replied distractedly that he preferred to be able to talk to his sweethearts. I rendered this as a statement that he was exhausted by his long journey to France, but would see her at the café the next evening.

So there was a second act in serio-comedy, which Tom cut short by leaving in haste and refusing to go back to the Rotonde for several days. Anita migrated to the Latin Quarter and was seen no more. The other girls found it dramatic. "A real *béguin fou* (an amorous mania)," one of them commented, sighing. "Your friend must be in love with another. What a shame for Anita." Tom was soon introduced by me, however, to flirts who spoke a little English and who made efforts to improve his French before proposing anything more complicated. He and I took them on sweet, inexpensive trips: by Seine excursion boats for a few sous to St Cloud or the woods of Vincennes; by train to Versailles, or the country ranging from Moret-sur-Loing to Fontainebleu that landscape painters loved.

There were no stunning beauties among the models of the Café de la Rotonde, for such a one would soon have made an advantageous match with or without a wedding ring. Few were intellectual and none markedly so; the quality would have been a drawback in the life they lived. They did read more poetry than a similar group in the United States or England would have read. A good many, of course, had lovely bodies. But a girl plumed herself upon standing apart as a physical type, and generally she was also highly individual in the matter of temperament.

The girl who called herself Reine (probably she had been christened Renée) wore the title well. She was tall, dignified yet amiable, and had good taste in clothes. Several men longed for her and she appeared to be loyal to one without losing the friendship of the rest. At the opposite extreme was Suzanne, whose unflagging gaiety caused you to forget that she was a dumpy little creature, and who had no more constancy than a guinea pig. Aïcha was the sole Negress; she wore a semi-Moorish costume and wanted it to be supposed that she was a Muslim from North Africa. I judged her to be a Senegalese. She was in demand by painters, and she figures in canvases that have survived. Her sullen, prognathous countenance may be seen on the walls of the Musée du Luxembourg.

Some of the models were amusing because they were total, professional crackpots. There was Gabrielle, fancifully lachrymose, who was always asking to be taken somewhere, anywhere, as far away as possible. "Take me with you to New York, I implore you," she would cry. "It would change my mood to one of happiness, for the buildings touch the sky." Or to Rome, or to London, or to Jamaica, though in the last instance I doubt if she even knew where the island was. We teased her with half-promises. Then a misguided Slav actually took her to Majorca for a few weeks, a place about which she had nothing particular to say on her return.

Alice was a buxom, lymphatic damsel who invariably took off all her clothes the moment she arrived as a guest, whether at a studio, a flat or a single room. She said that clothes oppressed her. But she would hasten to add that the state of her health was poor, indeed perilous. I concluded that that was her way of maintaining fidelity to some unknown, while indulging herself as an honest nudist. But Germaine was easily the daftest girl of the lot. She credited herself with weird adventures which she described in a patois, not the *argot* on the streets; and she translated into prompt action whatever impulse struck her.

Tom and I foolishly went on an excursion to the country with Germaine and Suzanne as companions. The former behaved as if she had never seen a cow or a fruit tree before. She screamed over them, charged into the fields and trampled the crops, and generally speaking made such a nuisance of herself that we cut the trip short. But Suzanne felt personally insulted at having her day spoiled by the crazy Germaine, and returning to the railroad station she got into a fist fight with her. It was necessary to put them in separate compartments on the ride back to Paris.

How different was our jaunt to St Cloud with the graceful Reine and a half-Irish friend of hers named Lizette. It was obvious to me by then that a wise bohemian discriminated among models. Some were charming in the country. Others should have been shot dead if discovered beyond the purlieus of the Café de la Rotonde.

The two large spring salons, that of the Artistes Françaises and that of the Beaux Arts, were interesting to me. The work as a whole was monotonous and not very good, being dominated by uninspired nudes and subjects from French history that were mere illustrations. I recall a canvas of the *Revanche*. A dragoon was shown, lance pointed, staring across the frontier, while about the hoofs of his horse the dead of 1870 arose from the soil – skeletons still clad in tattered uniforms, with their bony fingers crooked. On the other side of the boundary post a group of jeering Prussian officers mounted guard over two shackled women wearing the peasant costumes of Alsace and Lorraine. Literal was the word for it. Reproductions enjoyed quite a vogue a few weeks later.

But the salons did contain some fine pieces, especially of sculpture. And the manifestation of the vast amount of work being done by artists of all nationalities in the studios of Paris was valuable on that account alone. I understood bohemia better after I had spent days in the endless galleries of the Grand Palais, and at the same time I was depressed to feel that this output was certainly in excess of the demand by buyers, that only the smallest fraction of it would bring fame to the artists. The year-long competition was to get hung in the salons, and too often no further reward materialized. At least the exhibitions were fiestas for the craft and tests with the critics.

Then there was the Salon des Indépendants, for post-impressionists, cubists, futurists, and indeed for any one who wanted to be represented in it with anything. No jury barred the way. You paid twenty francs for space on the wall and hung what you pleased. A popular name for it, in consequence, was the Salon à Vingt Francs. It was a comparatively new institution, and with memories of the Armory show in New York fresh in my mind I hurried to see this one. The grotesque hodge-podge of 'modern schools' was varied by some outright nonsense. I noticed, for instance, a canvas daubed with multi-coloured, patternless lines, to which a little off centre a plain tin kitchen-utensil was glued. But it should be realized that in those days Parisian artists looked upon the independents as being mainly practical jokers. They called them *fumistes*, the dictionary meaning of which is chimneysweeps, but which in slang implies mystification and buffoonery.

Unfortunately the critics insisted on taking the crackpots and the *fumistes* seriously. A story that year in Paris was to the effect that a well-known painter hired his vegetable man's donkey, smeared its tail with every colour on the palette, and then prodded the beast into swishing the tail over a clean canvas.

The result was framed and sent to the Salon des Indépendants under the title *Sunset on the Dunes*. It was chosen for praise by a critic. The painter thereupon published a statement of what he had done, backed by affidavits.

One afternoon in that spring of 1914 two artists, one of whom was an Italian American named Lascari, invited me to go along with them to visit the painter Henri Matisse. He had been a good draughtsman and colourist, they said, but he had made no great success and was now involved with modernism and considered the leader of a group called *Les Fauves* – the Wild Men. It would be curious to note how far he had gone.

We went to a building on the Left Bank not far from the boulevard St Michel, facing the river, and climbed to the top floor. Matisse received us amiably, said he was always happy to meet artists and writers. He was approaching middle age, a handsome bearded man, conservatively dressed. The pictures he showed us were marked by flat, crude forms and a distortion of perspective, but they were not extreme. Modestly he averred that he was experimenting, that there were grounds for the theory that the human eye did not actually see things in the shapes that had been accepted as conventional. He was now looking at the world from fresh angles, and possibly might work out a satisfactory technique. He asked us to judge these rough sketches of his accordingly.

After we had been there about half an hour, Matisse's bell tinkled. He stepped out on to the landing and peered down the well of the staircase. "Tourists!" he muttered to us. "I must get ready for them. They buy the modern stuff." He ran behind a screen and reappeared in a moment, wearing a paint-stained smock and carrying a palette. The tourists arrived, and he proceeded to talk a fantastic jargon about the 'new art' to them. He seemed well on his way to a sale when we left. I think Matisse had been sincere in what he said to us. We ran into him at a café the same evening, and he did not even refer to his behaviour with the tourists. He expected us to understand that a painter must live.

Meanwhile I had been going behind the scenes in Montmartre with the most singular guide to Paris whom I have known. This was T.J. Smith, the clerk at the *Brooklyn Eagle* bureau, a fellow about thirty years old. He was a New Yorker, and he both looked and spoke in English like the average New York clerk of the period. He had worked his way over on a cattleboat a year before, just for the trip, and although quite ignorant of French he decided not to go back. How had he managed? Simply because he had an amazing, instinctive aptitude for foreign tongues. He took no lessons, read no books in French, but picked up the language as he went and used it with unparalleled fluency for an alien. His was the *argot* of the streets, and of Montmartre in particular, that being the company that Smith liked to keep. He scarcely knew there was a difference between good French and *argot*. His pronunciation of the latter was faultless, according to his admiring French pals.

Smith saw to it that I did not miss much in his adopted world, if we except the poets who recited their own verses at the Lapin Agile and Aristide Bruant's; he had a poor opinion of them. But he took me to the Moulin Rouge where the public would still have served the brush of Toulouse-Lautrec, and to versions of the Moulin Rouge and the Moulin de la Galette more modern, more outrageous. I saw bouts between girl boxers in which the punching was not faked. The dancing had progressed beyond the can-can, however. That spring the dreamy Argentine tango held first place. Smith and I sat up whole nights, and an anomalous parade of friends greeted him in the different cafés: prostitutes, apaches, actresses from neighbourhood fairs, soldiers and crooks. To think we had the verve to follow the dawn through streets that were being watered afresh, drink a cup of coffee, and report to the office for work! Such is youth.

I had been living a secret romance in my letters from Camilla, which came regularly and glowed with affection. It was nonetheless plain to me that she was wrapped up in her own work, and that there was no psychic connection between her and this Paris to which I was becoming devoted. I reasoned that she belonged to some unpredictable future that would take care of itself. Interesting things were happening to me at every turn, and I must make the most of them all. Camilla would understand when I told her about them someday. Kaltenborn went back to Brooklyn and the post of correspondent was filled by a Swedish American named Naboth Hedin. My position was confirmed by a small raise. I got along very well from the start with Hedin. He encouraged me to write whatever appealed to me and had me sign my more important articles.

THE ELECTIONS WERE HELD, ACCORDING to custom, on two Sundays, toward the end of April and the middle of May. Was three-year-conscription to stand? That was the vital question. But the Caillaux scandal made itself felt in the fortunes of the left-centre, which called itself Radical Socialist though decidedly middle class in its composition and hostile to Marxist doctrines. Joseph Caillaux held his own seat and so did Doumergue. They controlled the Chamber with a diminished following, the indication being clear that it would not be wise to alter the military service law. The true Socialists, led by Jean Jaurès, were the only extremists to register important gains. But the conservative groups also had added to their strength.

I had hoped to see a Socialist sweep. The personality of Jaurès had attracted me. He was forthright and strong, an admirable orator, with much of the humanist poet in the way he expressed himself. Controversies between him and the independent liberal, Georges Clemenceau, had seemed to me fascinating expressions of current French political thought. I was not sure, really, which of the two men had impressed me more. Another side of me was moved by that voice of the elite, the author and deputy Maurice Barrès.

When the Chamber reassembled, Doumergue caused general astonishment by resigning the premiership. He simply announced that he had done all he could for the groups that had placed him in power and would withdraw, a stand rarely taken by a politician in any country. In ordinary circumstances this would have meant a turning over of the office to Caillaux. The bullets fired into Gaston Calmette's body made the bald financial juggler impossible for the moment. There followed ten days such as only the mazes of French parliamentary democracy could provide.

First choice fell on René Viviani, who had been one of Doumergue's ministers. He formed a cabinet resembling that of his predecessor, but so intractable under his leadership that it could not agree on a programme to offer the Chamber as the basis for a first vote of confidence. It was never officially a cabinet, for Viviani disbanded it and notified President Poincaré that he had failed. Four eminent leaders were then asked in turn to try, but after a few pourparlers all refused the honour. The materials for a bloc existed, but they could not build it. In despair the president appealed to Senator Alexandre Ribot, then seventy-two, a name of vast respectability, an influence from the past. He had the remnants of a party, the Progressive. Clemenceau had ended a similar jam a few years back by appealing to the public over the heads of the deputies and dragooning their support.

Perhaps Ribot could do as well. It was a vain hope. This patriarch was not a Clemenceau.

The manoeuvring enthralled me, and from a café across the way I kept a close watch on white-bearded Ribot's house in the Luxembourg quarter. All the old war-horses of French politics came there and conferred until late into the night. The expressions on their faces as they departed, their gestures as they crowded muttering into cabs, enabled me to make for the *Eagle* a fair estimate of what would be attempted. This was to be a cabinet with a small following on the floor, but which would appeal to the good sense of the deputies – if they had any. Just such a cabinet appeared at the Palais Bourbon. Ribot uttered platitudes in his shaking voice, submitted the budget for 1914 and asked for a vote of confidence. He was swamped by the left-centre, aided by the Socialists under Jaurès. His government had lasted for just three days.

But the crisis had been allowed to go a little too far. The country was indignant, and the sarcasm of the foreign press, notably that of Berlin, caused the politicians to be alarmed at their own recklessness. Opposition to the ideas of Viviani evaporated. The president asked him to resume his interrupted task, and in twenty-four hours he had organized practically the same cabinet he had had before. He got the vote of confidence which had been denied the veteran Ribot. With thunder on the verge of becoming audible over the Balkans, Viviani celebrated his triumph, day after day, with an almost uninterrupted flood of the oratory which was his chief claim to fame.

Odd little incidents were happening in various parts of Europe, but although the newspapers played them up as proofs of international enmity this was not taken seriously by the public. I recall as typical the Hansi case in Alsace-Lorraine. Jean-Jacques Waltz, known as Hansi, was a round-faced, gentle satirist, the voice of French traditions in the annexed provinces. Artist as well as poet, he was of that pure Alsatian stock which, although Teutonic, had long been antipathetic to the Prussian way of life. Hansi had chosen to address his propaganda to children. His early books had been modern fables written in language as simple as that of Hans Christian Andersen and illustrated with drawings in which goose-stepping soldiers, policemen with wooden faces, functionaries with no backs to their heads and waddling German tourists were ridiculed outside the scope of official censorship. Then, in *Mon Village*, Hansi had gone a step farther. Still speaking to the young generation, he had hinted wistfully at revenge. "O stork, stork, flying from the West!" he made the pupils at an Alsatian school sing. "Bring back to us in your bill a little toy soldier from France."

Harmless talk enough, had he been living in a free country. But in Germany it was treason. The local judge before whom he was first brought decided that he should not be let off with a fine. The case was transferred to the High Court at Leipzig and the date of the trial set for July. It would overlap the trial of Mme Caillaux. Drama was assured for July, though in what measure we were far from dreaming. The first result was to make *Mon Village* a best-seller in France.

I had become enmeshed in an incident of my own. Tom had rented a studio on the rue de la Grande Chaumière, and I had moved to a pleasant little hotel on the rue du Montparnasse. But it was agreed between us that I should have the freedom of the studio and take it over when he left. We gave joint parties there for our friends of both sexes. One day my attention was caught by a new model at the Rotonde, a brunette of some charm in a wild way. Her eyes were her best feature, being large and greenish-grey. She talked with verve, dropping often into *argot*. Her name was Madeleine Lebourg, and she had been an habituée of a Montmartre café, an acquaintance told me. He asked casually whether I wanted to meet her. I said I did.

Madeleine's attitude was more subtle than that of the half-Portuguese Anita. She made up her mind, nevertheless, almost as quickly. After we had seen each other a couple of times, she whispered in her husky voice that all other men had ceased to interest her. This was a plain hint that I should take her home with me. She made the appeal of a symbol rather than a girl. I confess that bookish comparisons with Mimi and Musette, of Murger's *La Vie de Bohème*, were in my head. I thought this a romantic experience I'd be a dolt to miss. A latterday Mimi who talked *argot* and had a broad, gay smile. If not true love, the stuff of dreams was there.

The hotel offered no difficulties. My *patronne*, indeed, had once asked me whether I was in good health, and according to Machefert her solicitude had been aroused because I had not yet brought a girl home. That was as it might be. Her expression remained genially noncommittal when she saw me with Madeleine. But the latter had surprises in store for me. I discovered first of all that she was broke to the point of destitution. She owned nothing

Figure 16. Roberts with Madeleine Lebourg and Aïcha Goblet in Paris, 1914. MS353.6.7.

except the clothes she was wearing and the contents of her handbag. When I enquired how such misfortune could have come about, she sighed and answered that she had had to pawn and sell her things because it was so hard to make a living as a model. I bought her a few necessities, of course, and rented a very small room for her with the understanding that she could be with me a good deal of the time. I was touched by her helplessness behind the jovial mask she wore in public.

Then one night I woke up and saw her pacing the floor, her hands held to her head. It took much urging to get her to come out with the truth. She needed cocaine and believed she would go mad, she said, if deprived of it any longer. I demanded rather roughly what she supposed could be done about it at that hour of the night. She answered humbly that if I would give her five francs she knew where to go. An artist for whom she had worked had taught her to take the stuff, but she was not a real addict. One dose would straighten her out for weeks, and it was her intention to break the habit entirely for my sake.

Up till then I had had no experience with drug victims. I gave her the five francs, thinking that the next day I would send her packing. In the morning, however, I found her at the café in an apparently normal state. She spoke about her trouble with great earnestness, vowed that her explanation the night before had been truthful and begged me to give her another chance.

Madeleine had been an amusing companion nine-tenths of the time, and if the marks of cocaine had ever been visible I had not recognized them. Drug addiction horrified me as an abasing weakness. The more cause for self-congratulation, I told myself, if this girl should be cured of it through me. I stroked her cheek and said that if another breakdown on her part did not occur, all would be well.

"Have confidence in your little apache," she replied, a tear showing in each eye.

I scarcely heard her. For I had picked up a newspaper and was thinking about the article I would write that day. The news of Europe had taken a startling turn.

CHAPTER 9 ※ The Green Time Goes

ON 28 JUNE, THE ARCHDUKE FRANZ FERDINAND, HEIR to the Austro-Hungarian throne, had arrived for a state visit to Sarajevo, Bosnia, near the Serbian frontier. He was accompanied by his wife, Sophie, the Duchess of Hohenberg, a former Bohemian countess for whom he had with difficulty obtained recognition at Court, though without the right of succession for their children. The day was the feast of Saint Peter and Saint Paul, portentous for a good many centuries. The Christians had routed the Muslims on that day outside Antioch, in the First Crusade. To the Serbs it was the anniversary of Kosovo, or the Field of Blackbirds, the most disastrous battle in their history, and which after five centuries still aroused thoughts of vengeance.

The Austrian imperial party was not disturbed by ancient omens. More to the point, Franz Ferdinand bore in mind that the provinces of Bosnia and Herzegovina had been seized six years before, ahead of the wars in which the Balkan nations had conquered Turkey. The Bosnians were Slavs, and the Serbs were always reminding them of the fact. It was partly to counteract disaffection that he had come to Sarajevo. Was he not known to be friendly to the Slavs in the Austro-Hungarian Empire? Had he not married a Slav? He was nettled to find the crowded little city feebly patrolled by the military. Then, while he was on his way to the City Hall for a reception, a bomb was thrown in the street, wounding two officers.

Franz Ferdinand had shouted at the burgomaster, "So you welcome your guests here with bombs!" Yet he decided to go ahead with the planned tour in automobiles, ordering only that the route be changed. A freakish blunder occurred. There were four cars, the one in front being a pilot vehicle containing officers. In the second car sat the Archduke, gloomy, square-faced, with a heavy moustache, and beside him the plump, amiable Duchess of Hohenberg. At a cross street, which had been on the original route, the crowd had opened a wide lane automatically. The chauffeur in the lead thought that this must be the result of a new ruling, turned down the cross street and was followed by the Archduke's car.

The terrorist Gavrilo Princip, a young student of Serbian race but Austrian citizenship, had taken his stand on the sidewalk of that street. He would never have been near Franz Ferdinand if the chauffeurs had not blundered. Two revolver shots rang sharply. The cars had actually started to turn around before the Duchess was seen to collapse against her husband's breast, and he, who had been bolt upright, sagged in the middle. Both had been mortally wounded. They died within half an hour. Princip had attempted to swallow poison, but was taken alive.

I read the story heedfully, filling in some of the historical details for myself. It lent itself to interpretation, and the more space the French press gave it the more it would be worth to me. But editorial comment in the next few days was disappointing. No great importance was attached to the killing of Franz Ferdinand – on his own soil, after all, and by a fanatical boy. Hapsburg scandals and tragedies of the past were dragged out of closets. The octogenarian Emperor Franz Joseph had been scourged by suicides and assassinations in his family. Yet to be honest he had never liked his late nephew, and now the handsome Archduke Karl was heir apparent. Why forecast an incident between Austria and Serbia because of the crazed Princip's parentage? Serbia was not a big enough country to cause a European war. So the talk ran loosely, and we slipped into a July of gorgeously fine weather with the deed of Sarajevo already taking on a false aspect of inconsequence. The approaching trials of Hansi and Mme Caillaux were held to be more interesting by the journalists. To the Parisian masses the coming celebration of Bastille Day, 14 July, was the prime event.

THE FOLIAGE OF THE CHESTNUTS and plane trees was unusually dense that summer, and the sky had never been clearer in the soft climate of the Île de France. All the stately parks took on added charm from the dappled shade that enticed the world to linger, but none more than the Luxembourg Gardens near which I lived, with its statues of poets and nymphs and queens. On the other side of town the Champs Elysées seemed the perfect urban avenue, bearing an endless tide of horse-drawn carriages and a few cars, the promenade on either side overarched by greenery and bordered by the terraces of cafés. I was a familiar in an apartment on the left bank of the Seine from the windows of which the view was magical: the winding stream in the middle, the dome of the Invalides on one hand and the Arc de Triomphe on the other. But every boulevard had sorcery, in the bland sunlight or the blue dusk of Paris. I loved the plumes and gay scarves worn by the models on Montparnasse, the opalescent tints of absinthe in tall glasses, the bright nosegays of the flower-vendors. These, and much else.

The Quarter was full of writers and artists from the United States, the majority of them on short trips. Among those who had taken root the symbolic figure, to me, was Alan Seeger from my New York days at Mme Branchard's rooming house and the Maison Petitpas. I ran into the poet at the Café Lavenue. He had changed both in appearance and manner. His intellectual arrogance was undiminished, but he seemed happier than I had before known him, and notably more mature. He now affected a severe style of dress, his black coat buttoned tightly under an unstarched stock collar. The music was good at Lavenue's, and I often saw him there, sitting like a rapt aesthete in the company of a very beautiful blonde woman whose name he did not tell me. Sometimes he went alone to the Rotonde, or to the Closerie des Lilas where Paul Fort was the presiding French poet. One day Seeger came up to me in the Rotonde and solemnly asked me how I made my living. It must have been around the first of July, for well before the middle of that month he was in London trying to get a publisher for a book of his poems. I told him about my job on the *Eagle*, and I have not forgotten my amusement at the lofty way in which he answered me. "Daily journalism, eh? I have never fancied it as a calling," he said. "But I believe I could adapt myself, could stomach a little of it. I need money. If you hear of an opening, I wish you would let me know."

It was a season when young poets wrapped themselves in cloaks. Rupert Brooke, the Byronic Englishman, had been looking for romance in Tahiti; I never met him. I was taken to shake hands at the Bal Bullier with Charles Péguy, the Catholic mystic, incongruous in that resort of student-frolicking near the south end of the Luxembourg Gardens. There was a link in the destiny of Seeger and Brooke and Péguy, perhaps dimly forecast by them, however disparate their temperaments may appear to be.

To mention a place like the Bal Bullier is to want, as with all the aspects of Paris in 1914, to etch its identity. Easier said than done. It was nothing but a barn of a dance hall, situated above the Catacombs, though few of its habitués knew that. Admission of a few francs was charged, varying according to the day. You went down a short flight of steps from the boulevard and found yourself in a throng that combined the groups of a dozen bohemian cafés. You went there to dance, yes; but you also went to dispute about ideas, to find a radically different girl, or to catch a glimpse of some admired girl who had abandoned your circle for occult reasons. In an Anglo-Saxon country it would have been a hotbed of brawling. No one fought at the Bal Bullier, except with words. The prevailing perfumes were *chypre* and *santal*. The band played Viennese waltzes and Argentine tangoes, but the favourite local tune to which you hopped and whirled, singing the naive words as you danced, was "Sous les ponts de Paris"

As July wore on, the newspapers uttered a faint uneasiness about Austria-Hungary and Serbia. It was rumoured that there had been diplomatic warnings from Vienna that there must be a strict accounting for the terrorist Princip, for he had been in Belgrade a few weeks before the assassination and was believed to have obtained weapons there. Well, an inquiry and the labelling of abettors would be logical enough. Only the Socialists were worried. At their party convention in Paris they passed resolutions: "A general strike, in the event of war, would be particularly efficacious. . . . It would constitute popular agitation and action in its most virile form . . . the most rational answer to the menace of imperialism." But such resolutions were part of their stock-in-trade; they rarely overlooked an opportunity to pass them. There was to be an international meeting of Socialist leaders in Brussels later in the month, and what they might have to say should be more pointed. Paris shrugged it all aside and swung gleefully into the ceremonies of Bastille Day.

I am glad that I saw Bastille Day of 1914. It was completely nineteenth-century in character, because only national catastrophes alter the ways of Paris. The generality of the workmen wore corduroy trousers, peaked caps and sabots. Many of their women also had on wooden shoes, with black cotton stockings and voluminous skirts. The national fête has always been of and for the people, in the first place. I had a feeling that the well-to-do joined in it and were welcomed, just that.

All classes danced in the streets to the music from little bandstands set up by the municipality, sang patriotic songs, provided ready-made audiences for impromptu harangues, and knew how to be friendly with every stranger without degenerating into rowdyism or drunkenness. Informal parades marched and countermarched, and there was of course a huge formal military review. Fireworks began at dusk, to last all night in the Place de la Bastille itself and other centres. The gendarmes were treated as carnival heroes. Their dignity broke down at times, and they danced with the rest. The city was vibrant with the tempo of a festival that actually prolonged itself for two more days.

THE JUBILEE ENDED, AND GENERAL European affairs came back into perspective. In Germany, where they did not care a rap about Bastille Day, they had been trying Hansi the caricaturist. He was found guilty of treason and sentenced to a year's imprisonment in a fortress. But he was given three days in which to settle his affairs, and no one was greatly surprised when he used this respite to escape into France. It had doubtless been intended that he should do so, for the German newspapers made capital out of the point that France had given asylum to an Alsatian "traitor, a fugitive from justice". To meet the venom of the comments, the brothers Guy and Paul de Cassagnac, co-editors of a right-wing journal and incidentally two of the most noted duellists in Paris, declared that they would drive out all the German correspondents by forcing them to choose between a meeting on the field of honour or social obloquy. They issued several challenges and intimidated one journalist into fleeing to Berlin. The others simply kept out of the way of the Cassagnacs.

Kaiser Wilhelm II was cruising in his yacht off the Kiel Canal, where he held a naval review attended by a British squadron. President Poincaré of France announced that he and Prime Minister Viviani would leave at once to pay state visits to the czar and the kings of Sweden, Norway and Denmark. A conference of peace societies from all over the world was about to meet in Switzerland. These appeared to be good signs, and Paris settled down to enjoy the raffish drama of the Caillaux trial.

Mme Caillaux was paler now, her elegant embonpoint a bit reduced after the months in St Lazare. So much the better for her adroit advocate, Maître Labori, as he staged her in the dock. At every French trial of a woman for murder, the appeal is to the romantic susceptibilities of the public, with the jurors treated as typical males rather than as upholders of the law. It was certain that she would not go to the guillotine. The danger was that of a prison term. For there were nuances in this case that removed it from the category of the ordinary crime of passion. Henriette Caillaux had shot Calmette because he had been about to publish love letters. Yes, but they were not letters from her to him, or from her to any one. They were from Joseph Caillaux to her; the suspicion remained strong that they would have bared political scandals, and that she had fired to save his ministerial neck. This would never do. The motive of amorous jealousy was needed, one side or the other.

So the gossip that she had once repulsed Calmette as a lover was revived and fanned, a thing that was all the more deadly because it could only be implied in court. If the editor had sought to destroy her happiness as an act of personal vengeance, then he had been base and had deserved to be killed by her. Mortified by the equivocal details of her defence, she fainted one morning in the dock, to good effect. Another day Joseph Caillaux wept on the witness stand.

While this muddy whirlpool seethed, Austria-Hungary sent an ultimatum to Serbia with terms which could hardly be accepted by any nation, however small, and if accepted could not be fulfilled in the forty-eight hours specified. The Paris press admitted that this meant new warfare in the Balkans. Well, what about it? A war on an even smaller scale than the one between Italy and Turkey three years before. Was that a reason for reducing the space given to the Caillaux trial? Certainly not.

On the day after the ultimatum a band of a hundred students from the Latin Quarter, mostly South Slavs, marched to the Place de la Concorde and hooted the name of Austria. I watched them being dispersed by the police and felt that the incident was no joke. Yet not one important paper the next morning gave it as much as two inches of small type.

The Socialists of Europe were in full bay now. In Berlin the party declared officially: "Let the ears of tyrants everywhere hear our shout: 'We will not have war.' International fraternization for ever!" Similar defiance amounting to pledges came from every European capital, including Vienna and

Budapest. Jean Jaurès at the conference in Brussels publicly thanked his Teutonic 'comrades' in the name of the French people, and swore: "We shall continue to support them like brothers against the Attila-like campaign of the war-mongers." Almost as an afterthought, he added: "*I shall be true till death.*" Those who heard him say this did not guess that that day he was a prophet.

A great many persons, and I was among them, believed at this juncture that the Socialists would strike not merely against war, but against what was euphemistically being called 'protective mobilization' against the threat of war. A general strike of such magnitude raised fascinating possibilities. It might overturn all the leading governments in a unified coup and bring about the socialist millennium of which radicals had been dreaming. The most fiery of the leftist journalists in Paris, Gustave Hervé, editor of *La Guerre Sociale*, screamed for it openly, said that it was the only course worthy of Frenchmen. It would be as good as bloodless – naturally. For a fact, it was easier to imagine than war.

On 28 July, one month to the day from the deed of Sarajevo, two headlines shared the front pages. Mme Caillaux had been acquitted, and Austria-Hungary had declared war on Serbia. The former caused the greater excitement. There was bitter criticism of the verdict. Lawyers and witnesses who had figured in the trial were jostled as they left the Palais de Justice. Joseph Caillaux and his wife had to be escorted to their home by a strong bodyguard of police. By midnight the muttering in the cafés had swelled to a roar. Then the mob marched. Anti-Caillaux riots broke out along the Grands Boulevards, only to be sternly repressed. Opposite the Matin Building, I saw the crowds charged repeatedly by platoons of cavalry. Many persons were trampled under the horses' hoofs. Yet still the cry, "Down with Caillaux!" was raised by new manifestors. They resented the immunity of the deputy and ex-minister rather than demanded the life of the woman. Serious trouble was predicted for the next day.

But the next day the Caillaux affair was shelved with startling abruptness by both press and public. The international situation came into its own. Not as a menace of imminent war for France – Oh, nothing like that! Rather as a major 'incident', such as that of Algeciras, or that of Agadir, both of which had occurred within the past ten years. A thunderhead; not the storm itself, which surely would blow over. Yet the Paris crowds were feverish.

They gathered before the bulletin boards and milled about the sidewalks, like cattle that find a thunderhead disturbing, to say the least. Russia had already declared that she would not let Serbia be crushed. What then?

Poincaré and Viviani had learned of the ultimatum to Serbia the same night that they left St Petersburg. Its significance to them, at the centre of power, was of course clear. They cancelled their visits to the Scandinavian monarchs and sailed post-haste for France. The warship *Jean Bart*, aboard which they were, was accorded a presidential salute by a German cruiser in the North Sea. I was at the Gare du Nord to see them arrive. The solemn expression worn by Raymond Poincaré was a mask that sometimes slipped as he responded to cheers. He was a man of Lorraine, who in his youth had made a cult of the recovery of the lost provinces, had admired the fierce poet-nationalist Paul Déroulède. I followed Poincaré in a cab to the gates of the palace.

Then, as I was returning home I met, by coincidence again in a narrow street, a platoon of the heavy dragoons that I had seen during my first days in Paris. Once more the plumed helmets, the sabres, the glistening boots coming to the knees, the capes lined with scarlet fluttering behind them, the clanking of their accoutrement. The moustachioed faces were more eloquent than the face of the harassed Poincaré. They had been loftily histrionic a few months before, a little bored. Now they had the hope of *La Gloire* written all over them. These dragoons were professionals, and I imagine that they had been disappointed by Algeciras and Agadir.

Journalistic excitement mingled with my personal life in a way it is no longer possible to disentangle. I was in and out of the Café de la Rotonde at all hours and enjoyed being treated as a sort of oracle. Though cannon bellowed along the Danube and an Austrian army had struck at Belgrade, though Russia mobilized against Austria and the Kaiser proclaimed a state of siege in Germany, I said there would be no general war. The Socialists would prevent it. My friend Tom Hall, who shrank from events that might disrupt the artistic life, hoped I was right but began to talk of going back to New York. Other visitors grew pessimistic, restless. I paid no attention to them. It did not matter to me for the moment whether the girl Madeleine took cocaine. Actually, I think she was so beguiled by the patriotic chattering of many nationalities in the Quarter that it helped her to keep her promise to me. The last three days of July spun by on mounting wave after wave of drama.

Late on the evening of the 31st, I was in the *Brooklyn Eagle* office when a young Frenchman who made a living by selling tips to the English and American correspondents stuck his head through the doorway and said: "Go to the Café du Croissant. They have murdered Jaurès." He was gone before I could ask him a question. I thought it might be a hoax, but I lost no time in hurrying to the Café du Croissant. It was besieged by hundreds. I used my press card with the police and forced my way through. The body had been removed a few minutes earlier. I saw the blood of Jean Jaurès on the dark leather of a divan between two windows, on the marble top of a table to which he had been lifted, and in a pool formed by the steady dripping from table to floor.

This is what had happened. Jaurès had been conferring with the cabinet, in which though not a member he was a power. Viviani, the premier, was a former Socialist. The arguments set forth by Jaurès had been, naturally, in the interests of peace. Then the old lion of French socialism had gone to the office of *L'Humanité*, the party organ, which he edited, to give final orders and approve the next day's articles. Members of the staff often dined at the little Café du Croissant near by. That evening Jaurès went along with two of the editors, and they sat at their favourite table on the street side of the building. It was a hot, still night and all the windows were open. A hand coming from the street parted the limp curtains behind Jaurès, and a revolver was discharged twice. The victim toppled sideways, his head shattered. Although unable to speak, he had lived for a quarter of an hour.

The assassin was a narrow-chested student named Villain, who had been buffeted by the crowd. He had remained strangely calm and said later: "I resolved to kill the opponent of the three years' military service law. He was too harmful to France. I meant to shoot him at the door of his office, but was unable." The Socialists demonstrated in fury all night, and no one could tell what elements they were blaming for their leader's death. But in the morning Viviani took the shrewd step of issuing a declaration in which he eulogized Jaurès to the skies and said: "I bare my head at the grave of this Socialist who fought for noble things, and who in these difficult days supported the patriotic attitude of the government in its pursuit of peace."

Coming from the first minister, these words were well received. Crowds that sang the *Internationale* and shouted, "Down with war!" started to modify their proletarian fervour with shouts for *La Patrie*! Here and there a voice broke exultantly into the strains of the *Marseillaise*, proudest of national hymns, greatest of marching songs. Vengeance for Jaurès was somehow being transmuted into vengeance on foreign tyrants who had hated such as he. I knew then that the Socialists of France were not going to do anything that would seriously hamper the government. In a few hours I was still more sure of it. That day, Saturday, 1 August, Germany declared war on Russia. The news was followed almost immediately by the announcement of mobilization in France, to begin the next morning.

I left the office at dusk, and as I turned from the boulevard de la Madeleine into the rue Royale I saw a man affixing a white poster to a wall. I stepped up behind him and read, "*Mobilization Générale*", succeeded by the curt, clear terms of an order that called to the colours every man up to the age of forty-eight. A generation afterward that very poster was still to be seen in its original position, framed in bronze and under glass. It happened to have been chosen for preservation as a war relic from among the tens of thousands like it that went up that August afternoon on city walls, in municipal and other government buildings, and on every post office box throughout France. Its prompt availability showed that it had been printed hours, if not days, earlier as a precaution. The words I heard oftenest from those watching the posting were colloquial and pithy: "Ça y est!" which can be rendered in English as, "This is it!" They rang true. Mobilization meant war. France would never have faced so costly a disruption of her life unless she had known that war had become unavoidable.

I found the cafés of Montparnasse overflowing. A constant interchange of patrons went on between the Rotonde and the Dôme, which ordinarily did not occur. Groups met in the middle of the street and stood there arguing. The talk was not loud. I sought out my friends and took back my opinions of the evening before, but now no one wanted to believe me. Foreigners insisted that the citizens round about were calm enough. I answered that rather they were stunned, that for them this was a tranquil quarter to which the full significance of events had not yet penetrated; a tour of the Grands Boulevards would show a different attitude. It was agreed that a small party of us would go after supper to the other side of town.

Machefert was out with his Peggy. Tom Hall had with him a young French girl named Andrée, whom I had not seen before. We dined at one of our favourite places, the Maison Leduc on Raspail, where you sat at tables on the sidewalk blocked off from the traffic by shrubs in square wooden pots. A mild air stirred the leaves. Mme Leduc, a full-busted woman of thirty-five, beautifully coiffed, who always reminded me of the discreet mistress in a Paul Bourget novel, presided with unwonted gloom at the desk. Her husband, the chef, small and plump, appeared and joked with his guests. He was on the second day's call, he said, but as he was a cook and a good one he felt sure he would be put in a safe spot. I never saw him again.

My friends and I left at about nine o'clock. As we emerged from the Madeleine station of the Nord-Sud subway we were beset by newsboys with extras. The papers had been putting out special editions all day, but for the first time some of the headlines turned on the question of whether England would support France and Russia against the Teutonic combination. The *Entente* had been discussed in editorials, to be sure. But what was an *entente*? Nothing was down in black and white. I was not astonished to see those headlines. They counted for little in the streets as yet.

We turned onto the boulevards and encountered pandemonium. Men had swarmed down from all the outlying quarters, from Montmartre and Montsouris, from Passy and the Porte de Vincennes, from the fashionable environs of the Bois de Boulogne no less than from the slums of Belleville. They had formed impromptu processions and carried the flags of England and Russia along with the Tricolor. Not the faintest echo of the *Internationale* was to be heard. The *Marseillaise* came full-throated as the demonstrators passed between tight-packed masses. Persons of both sexes ran out of their shops to join them. I saw some waiters at the Café de la Paix leave their customers and place themselves at the end of one of the most ardent columns. The running fire of cheers included, "*Vive l'Angleterre!*" Parisians believed in their allies, though here and there on the pavement I heard the anxious mutter: "What will England do?"

At dawn on Sunday, 2 August, a compact little flock of aircraft rose from the aviation grounds near the Porte de Versailles and flew over Paris, headed east. Today they would seem fragile toys, biplanes as well as monoplanes, of which some could carry only one man. But their wings, glistening in the sunlight, were fabulous to those who rushed to the windows to see them pass. They flew low and swiftly. As the morning wore on, the soldiers of the line regiments poured out of the capital, company after company, many on foot, rifles over their shoulders and campaign kits on their backs, their faces, also, set toward the east. The red trousers surging in unison were like an endless rippling pennant. By nightfall the conscripts on the first day's call were going – men who had recently had military training and were therefore in condition to bear the early shocks of battle. Yes, the young went first. Few fathers of families left that Sunday, but many sons and many lovers.

They crowded the subway trains, the omnibuses, the trolley cars, the cabs, all the means of transportation leading to the Est, Nord and Austerlitz railroad stations, from which troop trains were being dispatched to the frontier every few minutes. They were dressed in their shabbiest suits, to be thrown away when they received their uniforms. Each man carried nothing but the small parcel of personal effects specified by the military regulations. Admirable order prevailed. Contrary to the predictions of enemy newspapers, the machinery of mobilization functioned like a stop-watch.

On the following day the early afternoon extras reported violations of both French and Belgian soil. *"Les Allemands ont Franchis la Frontière"* – I see the black type yet – "The Germans Have Crossed the Frontier". A few minutes after 5 p.m. the imperial ambassador, Schoen, demanded his passports and gave in exchange a formal declaration of war. It was an after-climax. Paris was already keyed to the high note of war, had known that the peace could not be saved. And then, the business of mobilization had been going on all day, dominated by the departure of artillery and the Red Cross.

The guns went eastward like a running tide. Always when the guns were passing, the atmosphere was bombastic and gay. I wondered, without finding an answer, why the artillerymen should take this war lightly, while the foot soldiers seemed austere and sad. There were roses in the mouths of the cannon, and behind the ears of the jaunty gunners. *"A Berlin!"* was chalked on the side of caisson after caisson. As one long procession of .75s thundered down the boulevard du Montparnasse and disappeared from view, I heard an American voice exclaim from the terrace of the Café du Dôme: "There's a thrill in this. But wait till they hear from the dead. There'll be a heavy vote from the dead." I glanced around to identify the speaker. He was the humourist Gelett Burgess, from my old San Francisco days.

Ambulances streamed by in columns, with lay nurses seated on the cross benches, and cases of lint, medicines and disinfectants piled high. Sisters of Mercy were leaving, too, for some reason invariably by train. I saw a group of young priests and monks, in cassocks and shovel hats, pass into the Montparnasse station. They were not going as chaplains, but to shoulder the rifle, to assume the blue coat and kepi of the common soldier. France did not exempt the clergy. For some years amity had not been the rule between Church and State. The rank of army chaplain had been abolished.

The fourth of August was the supreme day of doubt. The question, "What will happen if England does not march?" had become pre-eminent. Promises, honour – just so; these were only words, useless to France unless transmuted instantly into deeds. God alone knew what was happening on the frontier. German warships had shelled Algerian ports. The rumour of an ultimatum from London on Belgian neutrality made England seem less calculating. But suppose this were nothing but a bluff? Englishmen were button-holed on the streets and held personally responsible for the decision of the sole ally whose fleet could command the seas.

The city continued to answer the call to arms. The older reservists were going now. They came up from the workmen's quarters in droves – carpenters, bricklayers, masons and day labourers, carrying their small equipment in tool bags, in pillow slips. Groups of the very poorest tramped past me interminably in the Place de la Bastille, dressed in baggy corduroy trousers and blue shirts, and wearing the wooden shoes of the peasant. Except for their stern faces, they looked as they had looked on Bastille Day. Middle-aged men came, too, from easy bourgeois homes, from shops, from studios, from laboratories, from the stage. No one was exempted.

And so the night of 4 August fell. Powerful searchlights swept the sky, because of a canard that Zeppelins were approaching. A lone sentinel airplane circled above Napoleon's Tomb. For the first and last time during the crisis Paris went to bed sombrely. In the morning, the streets were a turmoil of roaring citizens. England had declared war on Germany. The party was as good as won. It would be over by Christmas. Comments such as these were tossed frenziedly from mouth to mouth. Women wept. The flag of England was cheered wherever seen. Little by little, the capital calmed down and became, by proclamation, an entrenched camp behind the firing lines.

That was Paris as I saw it on the eve of combat. For me, as for millions of others, no later experience could ever be so dramatic as the launching of the first of the century's great wars. Subsequent conflicts had been drearily expected. In 1914 the lightning broke from the blue, or we had the illusion that it did. What we did not know was that a libertarian period was dead beyond recall. It took the events of the next few weeks to make the truth clear to different men in different ways.

I WAS APPOINTED A WAR correspondent for the *Eagle* on the third day of mobilization. My luck in being on the spot drew this prize for me, whereas I probably would not have been chosen if I had been on the home staff of the paper. I became one of the youngest foreign correspondents in Paris, being not yet twenty-eight. Another man, not much older than me, was sent from Brooklyn and arrived a week or so later. Naboth Hedin ranked us both, but there was plenty of work in prospect for all three. It was agreed that I should concentrate on French sources of news, and the new man on English. Clearly I would be an independent agent most of the time.

As ever in war, a censorship clamped down upon the first rose-coloured reports from the front. There stirred an uneasy suspicion that victories had not been won on the Lorraine border. Then something authentic that lifted morale immeasurably came through. The Belgian army had had greatness offered to it and had not declined. The little country's high command must have been aware of the Schlieffen plan, which provided for a German assault on France by way of the Liège-Namur route, but it was tacitly accepted that Belgium would be unable to resist a violation of her territory. She was a strictly neutral state, guaranteed by all the leading powers, including Germany. The name of Schlieffen rang in Belgian ears as that of a sinister dreamer who had prepared a 'perfect' military plan which his government would think twice about using. However, if the worst occurred, there would be a gesture of resistance at the frontier, a throwing up of hands and bill of damages filed for settlement after the war.

Now the storm which had been gathering for a generation burst. The grey-green tide was at the gates of Liège. An ultimatum demanding a free passage was served, with the narrowest margin of time in which to answer. We must not be so credulous as to suppose that King Albert decided on the spur of the moment to be a hero. There had been secret conversations for five years with Paris and London. But it came as a staggering surprise to the officers in the field when they received orders from Brussels to fight to the last ditch.

Suddenly the Belgians were playing their part with a valour beyond all praise. Liège fired on the goose-stepping legions as they crossed the border, held up the grand march for the better part of a week. The outdated fortifications crumbled under the pounding of .420 millimetre Skoda siege guns, and the Germans went past, division after division of them, an endless horde, filling the poplar-shaded roads. They had trouble again, briefly, at Namur. They smashed Maubeuge, the first French fortress across their path. They ran over the English at Mons, surged onward to their one-sided victories at Le Cateau and Charleroi. But they were slightly behind schedule for Paris, and in other ways the Schlieffen plan had been thrown out of kelter. The entire pattern of Anglo-French resistance was reshaped by this. Because of it, we wrote the story in unanticipated words.

French mobilization, which had been at high pressure for the first few days, took on a more even tempo and lasted for three weeks. The loss of population in Paris was balanced by refugees drifting in from the east. The wounded were arriving also, and there began the spectacle of public military funerals from which Anglo-Saxon cities seem to shrink squeamishly at the outset of a war. In all the quarters, at all hours, coffins draped in the Tricolour went by, often with but a handful of mourners, sometimes followed by a host.

A recruiting office for the Foreign Legion had been opened at the Hôtel des Invalides. The rush was so great that the authorities decided to postpone actual enlistments until 21 August, when mobilization ended. In the interim separate nationalities formed their own groups to await the day. Naturally I was most concerned with the North Americans, headed by George Casmeze, a New York businessman who had lived in France for six years and whose headquarters was in a small office in the rue de Valois, behind the Palais Royal. Casmeze told me that he had several hundred volunteers, but the number that actually signed up on the 21st was 201. The first detachment of these, eighty-seven strong, rallied at the foot of the avenue de l'Opéra on the 25th, to march up to the Gare St Lazare and entrain. It was a news story for me, and I was there.

At the last minute, unobtrusively, with a nonchalance that managed to be haughty, the poet Alan Seeger took a place in the column. I had not even heard that he was back from London, a journey I was to discover he had made by way of Bruges, in the face of the advancing enemy. I moved over to where he was standing and said: "Seeger, for God's sake! The Legion –

you!" The merciless discipline that awaited him was in my mind. He gave me one of his remote, faint smiles. "France is worth defending," was all he said in reply. It was a sincere sentiment. He enlarged upon it in a letter he wrote later to a beloved woman. Not to have fought, as participation in the rhythm of the age, was inconceivable to this disciple of Byron.

THE DAY BEFORE, TOM HAD left for Le Havre, and I inherited his studio at 4 rue de la Grande Chaumière. The place consisted of two rooms, a small one with a skylight and a still smaller bedroom. It had been furnished by a previous tenant and had been sublet several times, the concierge acting as agent. Some modernist sculptor, who had lodged there, had abandoned a heavy block of stone which passed for a bust and which I promptly turned with its dubious face to the wall. As a dwelling it was colourless, really, the furnishings third-rate, and with only a single window on a court. To the girl Madeleine it seemed a heaven, and I installed her on her plea that she could not resist cocaine unless she were with me. I had yet to learn that such victims can almost never be saved.

The next week *taubes*, as the best of the primitive German airplanes were called, flew over Paris and dropped bombs. They caused much excitement, though the damage done was trivial. They came down so low you could distinguish the pilot's face. I observed more than one gendarme wrathfully firing his revolver at them; it was comical to say the least, but earned applause from the crowd.

Those planes were the heralds of calamity on the entire eastern front. In spite of the censor, journalists in Paris knew how badly the advance guards of the Allies had been beaten. The main French army under Joffre, as well as the English expeditionary force, were falling back steadily, but we could not judge what their prospects were for making a stand somewhere. Since the newspapers were bespattered with blank spaces where opinions that might have conveyed useful hints had been suppressed, politics on the ministerial level was the surest barometer. As August drew to an end, a brusque reshuffling of the cabinet said much to insiders.

Poincaré, echoed by premier Viviani, announced the need of a government of national defence in which all the important parties were represented. Most of the changes now seem of trivial import. But a face was missing from the combination, the blunt fighting countenance of Georges Clemenceau. He had long been an opponent of Poincaré. He edited a one-man newspaper called *L'Homme Libre*, and because it was more sternly censored than its rivals he had altered its name sarcastically to *L'Homme Enchainé* and managed to give the impression that the president had victimized him. Yet this political force, this undoubted patriot, Clemenceau, should have been in the government. The story ran that he had told Poincaré he would be premier or nothing.

The most meaningful new collaboration was that of two Socialists, Marcel Sembat and Jules Guesde. The former, head of the party since the assassination of Jaurès, broke precedent by becoming a member of a bourgeois government. Guesde was but a dissident Socialist, who had called Jaurès a traitor for setting the interests of internationalism above those of France. I asked myself whether Jean Jaurès, if he had lived, would have joined the coalition cabinet. He would have found it unavoidable, in my opinion. The socialist dream of a working-class strike against war in all countries had gone to smash, had been proven a sheer delusion. Everywhere the people had been led to believe that "the sacred soil of the Fatherland", et cetera, et cetera, had been basely attacked. Faith in the special favour of God had been established for every cause, with ridiculous ease. Sembat and Guesde had entered the cabinet for realistic motives. More power to them, I thought. From that day I began to cease to be a socialist.

No sooner had the ministry been made over than it was decided to change the seat of government. Bordeaux was chosen as the temporary capital. Poincaré departed on 2 September by special train with his entire official family, except the aged Bienvenu-Martin, minister of labour, who stayed as the government's representative. Private citizens at once concluded that Bordeaux was about the only safe spot in France. An exodus of huge proportions got underway.

I went as one of a group of American and English newspapermen to interview Bienvenu-Martin. He received us in the ministry without delay, and I felt that never before had I seen a statesman so morally crushed, so definitely off guard. His white-bearded face was livid. His eyes wandered. "Gentlemen, Paris is going to fall," he said, brushing aside preliminaries. "If you have women and children dependent on you, get them out of the city quickly to save them from becoming prisoners."

We were grateful for his advice, but the assertion that Paris would fall was the main point as far as we were concerned. No official had said anything like that before. "Will the censor let us cable your statement?" someone asked.

"No, no! Your women – send them away. I urge it upon you."

We persisted in holding him to military information. The former military governor of Paris had just been replaced by General Joseph Gallieni, a veteran of colonial wars. "What about Gallieni's preparations for the defence of Paris?"

"A mere gesture. How long do you suppose the garrison here can hold out against the enemy?"

"And Joffre's army? Surely it will give battle on the line of the River Marne!"

He threw up his hands. "Perhaps. But I am afraid the party is lost. Send your women and children to the country."

An interview of this sort is next to useless to a war correspondent. It cannot be written until long, long afterward. We retired, swearing under our breath.

Abruptly there were detonations. Houses on the northern and eastern outskirts of the city were being blown up, to clear the ground for the digging of trenches. There appeared to be no end to the motor trucks and wagons, loaded with barbed wire, iron palings, picks and shovels and other implements that rattled along the boulevards. It did not need much imagination to surmise that this material was to be used for Gallieni's hasty barricades. I took Bienvenu-Martin's pessimism more seriously. Paris, as he had said, was going to fall.

The following day I felt that no doubt of it remained. For in the morning some fifty Uhlan scouts, galloping ahead of the German First Army, reached the Meudon Woods. They were cut down, but the First Army was in the neighbourhood of Meaux, thirty miles away. We know now that the enemy was coming in a great arc, seven armies of them, pivoting roughly on Namur and Metz. Seven armies – a million men. What was to stop them?

In the afternoon the thunder of Kluck's big guns became audible from the northern, eastern and western gates of Paris. To satisfy myself that this was actually so, I made a hurried trip by subway to the Porte de Clignancourt. It took only a few seconds to convince me. There was no mistaking the sustained purring sound, the occasional soft thuds like blows dealt to a colossal punching bag suspended beyond the horizon. At the Porte Maillot,

I was told, the cannonading seemed louder. It was heard as far to the south as the Porte de Vincennes. Only the confusion of street noises prevented it from being distinguishable in the Place de l'Opéra, at the heart of the city.

On the morning of the fourth the *Eagle* ordered me to go to Bordeaux and report the activities of the French government. I hurried to the studio to pack a valise, which was all I could take with me except my portable typewriter. Madeleine was there. She had been behaving well, had not broken her promise so far as I could tell. It seemed heartless to desert her, but my assignment left me no choice. I carefully explained the situation and suggested that she go to her people in Rouen. The girl refused to do this. She was very tranquil about it, saying that she would look after the studio and that nothing would happen to her.

"Aren't you afraid of the Germans, in case they enter Paris?" I asked.

"No," she answered. "My father told me they got even to Rouen in the last war, and they didn't murder any women there."

"Occupation troops can stop short of killing and still do a lot of harm," I suggested drily.

"I think I'd know how to keep out of their way. But if not –." She shrugged. The stoicism of her ancestors who had seen many invasions spoke through her.

At seven that night I succeeded in getting away on a freight train composed of thirty coaches, all crowded to capacity by refugee peasants. I had the luck the following evening in Bordeaux to find a room in the home of a retired post-office employé. The hotels and lodging houses were all jammed full, with guests occupying sheetless mattresses in the foyers and corridors.

Installing the government had been a problem. The prefecture, a handsome building standing back from the street in its own garden, was turned over to President Poincaré and his entourage. Viviani obtained a suite in the municipal building. The General Military Staff had commandeered a hotel. The buildings of the University of Bordeaux had offered shelter to several departments, and to the press bureau. Education and Fine Arts took over a theatre. Jules Guesde, the Socialist minister without a portfolio, sat practically alone in a street with the evocative name of Esprit-des-Lois.

I discovered at once that Bienvenu-Martin's hysterical candour would not be paralleled here. No member of the government would see a foreign reporter. We were given information only at the press bureau, twice a day, and usually there was nothing beyond the reticent army communiqués which went all over the world by cable. Plenty of human-interest material was to be had from unofficial sources, and I sent off several articles of this nature. But I wanted something personal from a name that counted. Georges Clemenceau occurred to me. He, along with most of the other publishers of one-man newspapers, had moved to the temporary capital. Would he talk? It was worth trying. So I called at the small furnished flat he had rented off the Place d'Aquitaine and left a letter asking for an interview.

The response took a surprising form. A car driven by a military chauffeur stopped two days afterward at the house where I was living. An officer in uniform jumped off, rang the bell and stated loudly enough for me to overhear it in my room that he had come to "escort Monsieur Roberts to Monsieur Clemenceau". This gave me great prestige in the eyes of my landlord. How it was that Clemenceau, though not in office, could command a military car remained a mystery.

When I reached the flat, a maidservant let me into a stuffy parlour and asked me to wait. There was no sign of Clemenceau's personality about the makeshift premises. In France that sort of flat commonly has been equipped for rental as a place of assignation. Almost half an hour slipped by. Then portières at the farther end were parted, and Clemenceau came in alone. He was stoutly built, rather shorter than I had expected from his photographs, and moved with a slight balancing from one foot to the other that was more bear-like than feline. His head was impressively large, his eyes piercing under shaggy eyebrows, and the great downward-curving moustaches suggested the fangs of a sabre-toothed tiger. He had on a dark alpaca jacket, loose flannel trousers and carpet slippers, was wearing the famous grey cotton gloves but not the silk skullcap that so many interviewers have described.

I jumped up and said in French that I was much flattered to be received by him. Georges Clemenceau, I found, plumed himself on his English which he had perfected during a year or so of exile in the United States in the 1860s. He waved a hand and spoke, slowly, accurately. Without giving me a chance to raise the points I had intended, he asked me a series of questions regarding public opinion in America about the war, and especially the attitude of the Hearst press. I answered as best I could, and whenever I got an opportunity I put in a question of my own. Clemenceau adroitly evaded me every time. Instead he submitted me to an exhaustive interview, for what I was worth.

This went on for fifteen or twenty minutes. Worried at my lack of success, I finally expressed myself urgently.

"Monsieur Clemenceau," I said, "the readers of the *Brooklyn Daily Eagle* want your opinion on the chances of victory. If I cannot get that, my purpose in coming to see you will have fallen flat."

"Young man, you are too ambitious," he answered. "Why should I give you what I know for your newspaper? I prefer to publish it in my own."

I could not resist countering: "To judge by the blank spaces in *L'Homme Enchaîné* every morning where the censor has done his cutting, Monsieur Clemenceau, it does not seem that you are allowed to print much of importance."

He bridled and glared, as if about to destroy me with a swoop of his paw. Then suddenly he laughed. "You are right," he answered. "But before this war is over I print what I please – I say what I please – I do what I please."

A wonderful line for an article, had he not added genially: "Of course I withhold permission to quote what I have just said. The censor would not allow it to be cabled, but it would do neither of us any good if you tried to get it past him."

I gave him my word. He took me to the door, tapped me on the shoulder and growled, "Better luck next time, young man."

All the foreign correspondents, including myself, had regarded it as evasive that the official reports of 5 and 6 September said nothing about an assault on Paris. The faintly optimistic tinge of the language employed did not convince us. But on 7 September it became apparent that the German offensive had been involved in a far-flung battle with Joffre. No sense could be made out of the driblets of hope that were relayed to us, while the real news hung fire from the 7th to the 11th.

The great moment arrived at 10 p.m., 12 September, when the journalists gathered at the Faculté des Lettres of the University to receive the evening bulletin. No one who was present could ever forget the scene in the dimly lighted corridor as Commandant de Thomasson stepped out of his office, placed his back against the door and commenced to read in a voice that trembled with emotion. Before he had finished the first paragraph, a triumphant roar went up. He must have anticipated this, but he did his best to remain impersonal. The repeating clapping and shouts of excitement, however, brought tears to his eyes. He continued: "From the beginning of this action, the German right wing [Kluck's army] found itself obliged to fall back before the menace of envelopment of which it was the object. . . . By violent and repeated attacks, the Germans have attempted to break our centre, but have failed to do so. Our success on the plateaus to the north of Sezanne have permitted us, in our turn, to assume the offensive. During the course of the past night, the enemy has abandoned the fight on the front comprised between the march of Saint-Gond and the district of Sommesous. . . . The general situation has been completely transformed during the last few days. Not only have our troops stopped the advance of the Germans, but the enemy is retreating before us at almost all points."

The government announced that it would not return to Paris immediately. This was the prudent stand to take, for it was still uncertain whether the German threat to the capital might not be renewed. All the same, it was agreed by an exchange of telegrams with Hedin that I should go back. Paris was the centre for most of the stories that would interest American readers. The international news agencies would cover Bordeaux. I left two days after the termination of the Battle of the Marne, and on arrival I went straight to the office, where I exchanged notes with Hedin and wrote an article.

My first and burning ambition was to visit the battlefields, but I was told that the chances were not good. The military authorities had refused all such requests by foreign correspondents. A new hopefulness about a quick ending of the war prevailed. It was thought that the enemy might soon be pushed out of France and across the Rhine, and the generals felt that journalists would simply be a nuisance. The romances of current history could await the telling until Christmas. True, Kitchener in England had said that the war would last for two years or longer, but that particular week he was regarded as a pessimist and killjoy.

I took a taxicab in the afternoon to the rue de la Grande Chaumière. The concierge gave me a noisy welcome and handed me a package of letters from New York. Her expression was a little odd, as if there were something she hesitated to say, but I attached no importance to it and ran upstairs. On the chance that the girl might be in, I shouted gaily at the door, "Madeleine, I'm here!" There was no answer. I turned the key in the lock and entered.

Madeleine was lolling on the couch, her lips bloodless, her eyes prenaturally bright and a perfectly idiotic look on her face. She swung her right hand in a half-circle, grinned and mumbled incomprehensible words. She was in an advanced state of stupefaction from cocaine. I set down my baggage and stared at her. She went on mumbling, and from occasional tag-ends of phrases that I caught it appeared that she imagined herself to be in some elysian field where there were flowers as large as cabbages, and that she was deriving great satisfaction from them. I walked about the studio, noting its dirt and disorder. Soiled dishes and pots behind a screen contained scraps of food, but clearly none of them had been touched for days. There was a broken egg on the floor. Anger made my temples pound and knotted my stomach. "She went on a debauch while the armies were fighting outside Paris. What a hell of a time to choose!" I said to myself. I refused even to glance at her for many minutes. When I did, I found that she had lost consciousness.

I left her where she was, made a round of the cafés, talked with acquaintances and eventually had supper by myself. On my return I found Madeleine still insensible, and I went to bed. The constriction that had spoiled the enjoyment of eating or drinking allowed me only to sleep in snatches. As soon as it was light I got up and stepped into the main room. The girl had not changed her position on the couch, but she had recovered consciousness and her whole face was wet with tears. She lifted her arms vaguely, perhaps to the Magdalene for whom she had been named, and said: "All is finished for me. I deserve it."

That gesture – and the tears – undid the knot of snakes in my belly. I said quietly: "Get up, Madeleine, and make some coffee. You want to hear what I did in Bordeaux, don't you?"

"Then you have forgiven me?"

"It's not a question of forgiveness. I believe you could not help yourself."

"But you will chase me away?"

"Not at once, anyhow," I answered, with more carelessness than I felt.

A reprieve was enough for that city sparrow. Though her physical system remained violently upset for hours, her spirits revived and she drove herself to perform domestic duties, chattering the while. I did not pin her down as to how she had got money for cocaine, or how much of the drug she had taken. Probably she had used the money I had given her and had starved herself. At least, as a look around the place convinced me, she had not sold any of my belongings. I decided that she was an incurable addict. The needs of my work and my peace of mind required that she live elsewhere, and presently

I found her a room in a street called, as if in mockery, the rue de la Gaîté. She accepted the move in so docile a manner that my heart was wrenched. But I forced myself to be hard. The plan of buying her a meal whenever I ran into her hungry at the café was the only way I felt I could help her. I was not the reformer type. I would not wrestle against hopeless odds for her soul.

THE TRUE SITUATION ON THE Aisne took hold of the general consciousness. This was what ended an epoch. The grand assault that had been repulsed at the Marne was but a version of war as the world had known it for centuries, and if it had been followed by a campaign of manoeuvre and pitched battles a decision might have been had in a matter of weeks. But the deadlock of trenches from the North Sea to Alsace was something new and appalling. Kitchener had been right. It would last for years. I perceived that my own youth had been stopped short, also. The green time was over.

CHAPTER 10 › **World War I**

THE ACTUAL DETONATION OF WAR HAD BEEN THE most dramatic event of my life, nor was it ever to be surpassed on that score. The period that now followed was a special phase of existence, a chaos that is vivid to me in the round, while the details are dislocated, episodic. I had few assignments to go to the front, but I covered effects upon the civilian life of France and was involved in various strange side issues. I did not keep a diary, or save the printed record of my work, except sporadically. A consecutive narrative is, as a result, impossible. But let us see how much I can recall that is worth recalling.

One of the first trips I made after the armies had gone into the deadlock of trench warfare was a hurried one to London. Its object was to compare the English and French reactions to the crisis. I had never been in England before and welcomed the thrill of seeing it under unique conditions. The Channel crossing from Dieppe to Folkstone was calm, and the run on the boat train unrevealing, since they were made at night. When I reached Victoria Station, I stepped out into a darkened yet surprisingly busy street. This was a contrast with Paris, where also the lights were dimmed but where people usually crept indoors by 8 p.m. There was no curfew compelling Parisians to do so; they had acquired the habit after weeks of other forms of self-repression.

Boarding a Piccadilly bus, with but the vaguest idea of where it would take me, I rode to the Circus, got off and received the same impression as at Victoria of an active nightlife flourishing in the dark. A jostling mass of human beings crowded into the theatres, hotels and restaurants, or surged out to be swallowed up almost immediately by the gloom. It struck me how many young men there were among them. England had not yet introduced compulsory military service. The country was at war, yes, but a war beyond its borders. I became aware of recruiting sergeants who buttonholed passers-by, an activity unknown in France.

I pushed on from Piccadilly to Leicester Square, turned through a maze of streets to the northwest and found myself in Soho. A restaurant with a French name attracted me. As a tribute to bohemian atmosphere, I checked in for the night at a hotel on Greek Street, which proved to be a needlessly dingy spot. The morning was leaden grey, a mere prelude to the experience with London weather that was about to befall me. After doing a little sightseeing and shopping, I engaged a room on Coram Street and settled down to writing early impressions for my newspaper. I had planned to go to a theatre, but a rather heavy snow began to fall and I turned in. When I awoke, it was to face the blackest pea-soup fog that I had ever conceived in my wildest imaginings.

The room was filled by a grey murk which became yellowish when I turned on the electric light. Outdoors it was so dark at eight o'clock that I could not see the pavement below me, much less the opposite side of the street. The obstruction was dense, unshifting, as if the waters of a morass had reared up at night and hung arrested within a yard of my face. The canopy above was equally impenetrable. To right and left, at what seemed remote points, a pale formless glow indicated street lamps.

My feeling was one of lively curiosity. How was a stranger to function? I asked myself. I had made no arrangements with the landlady for breakfast and would have to go looking for it. I had noticed a small restaurant two corners away and knew which direction to take. My topcoat buttoned to my chin, I set out. There was slush on the sidewalks, the result of the snow the day before. But the temperature was mild, as is generally the case in a fog. Breathing the pea-soup was not so difficult as I had thought it might be. It is no exaggeration to say that I had to feel my way along, touching the railings of the front yards to prevent myself from striking off at a tangent. If I had met a person moving carelessly, we should have bumped into each other. There was nobody, and presently I arrived at the restaurant, a pool of yellow behind its misted plate-glass front.

Inside the fume was considerably more fluid than it had been in my room, mingled as it was with the steam from beverages and food. The idea of drinking tea in the morning has never appealed to me, so I ordered coffee and was served a terrible brew along with oatmeal porridge and kippered herrings, a type of breakfast favoured in cheap surroundings in England. I made the best of it. Several other customers were at the tables, and their talk held me. Except for an occasional remark they ignored the fog, but against its sinister background they harped on the war in bewildered terms:

"Aren't the French and Russians able to handle the Germans on land, while England whips them on the sea?"

"Does England need more than a million men in the field?"

"Is it really a bloke's duty to enlist?"

"*He* says it is," muttered a hollow-chested fellow, jerking his head toward the rear wall.

I had not looked in that direction since coming in. Now I did so and saw the famous Kitchener poster spread across half the width of the room. The stern countenance of the secretary of state for war, Lord Kitchener of Khartoum, scowled with the eyes focussed upon you, the face barred by the enormous moustache like a pair of horns, the right hand raised and the index finger pointing. There was no body, only the head and hand. The slogan in large type ran: "Your Country Needs YOU."

The restaurant had no allure, though my companions seemed to intend to linger there. I decided on the risky adventure of exploring the featureless byways. Walking slowly and memorizing the crossings, I advanced until I came to a wide street the name of which I do not know to this day. I slipped past a few fumbling pedestrians who spoke no word. Then I was halted by an extraordinary sound that drew closer and closer. It resembled the barking of asthmatic dogs, irregular, harsh, and presently I identified the tramp of feet. The source baffled me. When it was directly opposite, I edged into the street and pushed up against a straggling column. Its business astounded me. Here were sandwich men with boards upon their chests and backs, marching in the fog and coughing. No one could have read what they were advertising, but presumably they had an engagement which had not been cancelled, and they had gone out to earn the shilling, or at the most one-and-sixpence, a day which their work commanded in London at the time.

The pitiful and grotesque encounter caused me suddenly to fear that I would lose myself in some nether hell. I returned to my room, and except for lunch and supper at the neighbourhood restaurant I stayed indoors. The weather cleared a bit in the afternoon. Murk still hung in the air at dawn, but it was not sufficiently opaque to cause trouble and my normal acquaintance with London began. I visited the British Museum and the National Gallery, then headed for Fleet Street, matrix of journalism in the English tongue. Architecturally it is not an imposing centre, as everyone familiar with it knows. Such are its associations, however, that a member of the calling cannot see it unmoved.

I made a few calls on editors and correspondents I had been told in Paris to see. The one passing friendship I struck up that day was with a young chap who reviewed books. Interested to learn that I was in London for the first time, he invited me to go with him to the Café Royal. The large, high, almost square room with its painted ceiling and marble-topped tables did not look so Parisian as it was reputed to be. I was yet to know certain Antwerp resorts for which a liking grew on me. They were what the Café Royal more closely resembled. But the point mattered little. The atmosphere of the Café Royal was still that of the 'yellow nineties', in a mortal phase, doomed to evaporate very quickly as the army reached out and took the younger habitués. I saw languid men and women, consciously dressed as bohemians, drinking absinthe and other exotic beverages, the girls smoking cigarettes with their escorts, a defiant novelty for those days.

I thought the place had much charm, and certainly the talk surpassed in literary sophistication any that I heard elsewhere in London. There was a nostalgic sadness about it, as about all good things that must die. I should have enjoyed haunting the Café Royal, and I did return at least twice. Newspaper appointments, however, kept me busy. Among these was a visit to the War Office, not to interview but to listen to that stupendous oracle, Kitchener.

The London correspondent of the *Eagle* got me invited as one of some thirty foreign reporters that the field marshal, serving as secretary of state, received on a sleety afternoon. We filed into a rather small office and sat in a semicircle in front of Kitchener's desk. His expression was the most overpowering that I have ever seen on a human face. His eyes were of a cold, deadly blue, like glass or polished steel, the skin a bronzed red, the moustache a strengthening adjunct of the unsmiling mouth and salient chin. The recruiting poster had fallen short of the original.

If anyone imagines that the effect was histrionic, or that produced by a statue, he is mistaken. Kitchener was formidably alive, and he conveyed a sense of professional ability. It would have taken a brave man to cross him. I do not recall his exact words. They were necessarily conventional. The telling of military secrets that would have made news formed no part of his talk. He said that victory over the Central Powers could be won; characteristically he did not boast that it would be. The war required a great effort, which the British Empire was ready to exert. He hoped that the United States and other neutral countries would appraise realistically the problems that were arising and shifting every day. That was all. This soldier was a prime extrovert, obviously, but therein lay the source of his vigour. It would be a poor understatement to say that he had impressed me.

I took a keen interest, naturally enough, in the Foreign Legion and especially in that group of volunteers which had rallied the previous August at the rue de Valois and filed up the avenue de l'Opéra on its way to the Gare St Lazare to go to Rouen for training, my friend the poet Alan Seeger among them. I learned that the group had stayed in Rouen for only one week and had then been transferred to Toulouse, where it had been incorporated into the new Second Regiment of the Legion. At the beginning of October, the regiment was ordered to Epernay, behind the battle line of the Aisne, and by the end of the month it was in the trenches.

I missed Seeger on his various leaves in Paris, for he went straight to a woman he loved and appeared to scorn the cafés of his peacetime memories. He remained for me the outstanding North American wearing a French uniform, and I heard vivid accounts of him. I had wondered how he would endure the rigours of active service, the companionship of the average desperados who enlisted in the Foreign Legion. Seeger was arrogant, individualistic, a poet of the Renaissance born out of due time, contemptuous of whether he had popular approval. Yet this man embraced the role for which Fate had cast him and made a legendary soldier.

Unlike the contemporary young English poets, nearly all of whom were pacifists at heart but enlisted out of a sense of duty, Alan Seeger thought war was glorious, a manifestation of the old high romance. The notion that a waste of creative talent was involved seemed paltry to him. He speaks in one of his best sonnets of his "three idols – Love and Arms and Song". He writes early from the front to his mother: "Had I the choice I would be nowhere else in the world than where I am. Even had I the chance to be liberated, I would not take it." He notes in his fragmentary diary on the eve of an attack: "I have been waiting for this moment for more than a year. It will be the greatest moment of my life. I shall take good care to live up to it."

AND WHAT WAS THE PHYSICAL background of this proud enthusiasm? I saw the trenches often enough to conceive what it must have meant to await in them an opportunity for glory. It is not a subject upon which I like to dwell, so the impressions that have lasted from but one visit will have to suffice. The bureau of the French Ministry of War which then co-operated with the foreign press allowed only conducted tours of sections of the firing line. Parties were limited in number, and no newspaper could expect to be represented every time. When its turn came, it could send any man it pleased. The chief correspondent preferred to go himself, in the generally illusory hope that he would run into a major assault and get the sort of story that would build his reputation. Juniors would be given a chance now and then, on the theory that the experience would make them more valuable to the paper. I am convinced that the authorities chose for these visits the areas they believed would be relatively calm. I was given an assignment without warning during a spell of cold, rainy weather in the first winter of the war. Newspapermen going up to the front did not as yet wear uniforms. Revolvers were prohibited. I put on my heaviest overcoat and carried a small handbag.

Propaganda was the object of the Bureau de la Presse. The hope was that the hellish conditions under which the line of the Aisne was being defended would be told, and the newspapers favoured had been picked accordingly. Most of them were North American, because we were rated a sentimental lot who could be moved by horror stories to sympathy for France. There was a fair representation of South American papers, but only a few English. The latter were in the war already and their readers knew what the allied troops were suffering. Every trip of journalists to the front was a move to get the Americas to enter the war.

We left the train at a flag stop, the name of which had been erased, somewhere to the southeast of Reims, not far, I estimated, from Vitry-le-

François. The guns on both sides were booming sporadically. Columns of rubbish and smoke dotted the horizon at a distance of no more than a mile. Fixed landmarks were gone. Presently we came to a ditch which connected, more or less at right angles, with an occupied trench. The officers serving as guides strung us out in a single file and took us 'underground', as they called it. But the ditch was only about five feet deep, and we walked in a crouch, lowering our heads, for protection. We had been given tin helmets such as the soldiers wore against shrapnel, and I for one felt that a German observer with a telescope could scarcely fail to note the irregular emergence of the bobbing line of demispheres.

Perhaps the ceaseless, dreary rain and the mist blotted out our movements at the distance. But there simply must be some clear spells, even in the winter climate of Flanders. Water dripped in a cold mask from the rim of my helmet, and I admitted to myself that I was frightened. In addition to a clanking of metal accoutrements, we heard a muttering as of whispered conversations as we drew closer. Then we turned a corner and edged behind a row of standing men wearing greatcoats. Word to expect us must have been sent in advance. The soldiers slewed their heads around, their expressions marked by curiosity at this break in the monotony, and no signs of rancour at our comparative comfort compared with the filth that begrimed them. Mud was oozing above the level of their boots. There did not seem to be a dry spot anywhere. The very shelters that had been scraped out in the walls of the trench were soaked, spongy and crumbling. Poisoning the air, a vile odour of human detritus permeated everything.

A captain passed along our file, dispensing information in clipped tones. Immediately the soldiers started to talk louder, but he waved them down. "No sense in encouraging the Boches," he said. "Hand-grenade throwers may be creeping out there." He insisted, however, that it was a quiet sector. "No raid for weeks. The guns, pah! They're kept going just for effect. Until someday – you know!"

We were with part of a regiment of conscripts from a department due west of Marseilles, swarthy fellows who looked utterly out of place in that autumn drizzle. I asked a sergeant named Duval a series of the questions that might have been expected, and I got answers that really told me nothing. Things might be worse, he said. Only one casualty in that trench so far, the work of a sniper in a fog. It was going to be tough when the order to advance came. Couldn't be long now. The dirty Prussians must be booted clear out of France.

The one point I noted for inclusion in an article was the persistence of the term 'Prussian', a legacy from the 1870 war. The enemy were all Prussians, or else Boches as a contemptuous nickname, to the men of 1914. 'Germans' would have been thought bookish, or absurdly formal, and the rural levies would not have known what a Bavarian or a Wuertemberger was.

The officer at the head of our party rather hurried us away from this first halt. We must get an idea of the whole defensive system, he declared. The trenches were not in a straight line, but set at slight angles to one another, connected by narrow passageways. It was a riddle whether each was not more dreary than its predecessor. I, at least, received the impression that it was. The pace of our inspection perversely slowed down, and we had barely finished with the third trench when a noise like a thunderclap literally deafened us for the moment. The ground shook under our feet. Smoke rose in a gust, and the pebbles and dust intermingled in it began to shower down upon us.

"My God, a direct hit on the line!" shouted our chief officer. "Right where we came from. Let's go see."

We happened to be in one of the corridors, and so we broke easily into clear territory behind the trenches. Soldiers came running from several directions. If the Germans had been prepared for what had occurred and had charged at that spot, there could have been a major disaster. Groans and cries of anguish could be heard as we centred on that first trench we had visited. Instead of having fallen in, it had been forced apart, back and front, and gutted with emphasis on the middle section. A shell of no great calibre had dropped into it with chance accuracy, and meeting with no resistance had not exploded until the miry bottom was reached. Machine guns from close to the two ends had been torn loose and lay on their sides. So far as the men who had held the position were concerned, the only word applicable was shambles. Seventeen had been killed outright, or mortally wounded. Twice as many had suffered less serious hurt, including being struck senseless by the mere shock.

I saw Sergeant Duval plastered in a slouch against the front wall, his shoulder blades driven into the packed earth. His dead face was uninjured, but his whole chest had been torn off; blood pulsed in jets from it. Hands and feet had been ripped from bodies. Entrails were running wild in the mud. Gobbets of human flesh bespattered the survivors. The acrid stench of the explosive mingled with the saline reek of blood.

The narrowness of my personal escape was an obvious reflection. Ten minutes earlier, and that shell would have killed most of my party. It was not directed against us; it was aimed at a line on the map. But what a story it would have made in the press of the world! "Journalists massacred in enemy coup!" or some such thing. Showing how little the Germans realized what they had done, there was no stir, no shouting beyond No Man's Land in the direction from which the missile had come. The picture stayed with me as the most monstruous I was to see at the front. It was a group of men with jangling nerves who reported back in Paris that evening. I did not even get a byline on the account I wrote.

To balance this bloody episode and a few others that distantly approached it, the life of the capital had little to offer except the fact of being there, ready at the heart of wartime Europe where anything might start. It was possible among the politicians to engage in a sort of watchful intrigue. A hint, correctly understood, could result in an article of opinion which might seem harmless to the censor. If a view did not work out, why it remained harmless. If it did, one gained credit as a prophet.

France was being ruled by members of a Chamber of Deputies and by a president who had been elected when there was peace. Under the constitution of the Third Republic, all real power rested with the premier of the day, by reason of his control of the Chamber. But with eleven parties represented, it was easy to form a new combination and bring him down. Raymond Poincaré, a strong man, had seized the opportunity given him by war to exert an influence it had never been intended that he should have. He had got the ministry under his thumb, the premier, René Viviani, an orator, being particularly amenable. But this state of affairs had lasted only a matter of weeks. Poincaré had been forced to recast his cabinet to bring in certain influential men, and his own authority weakened. France was soon back at the game of a manoeuvring for power by the parliamentary leaders.

Aristide Briand, who had emerged from the utmost radicalism, had formed a government the following year by the old methods, but Georges Clemenceau, the 'Tiger', had refused to accept a portfolio and thereby had denied it prestige. It was not admitted officially, of course, that he had been approached, but it was an open secret that he could have had almost any department he chose to name.

It looked now as if he were on the point of achieving his boast by the sheer force of personality. But the juggling continued for longer than I had thought it would. I managed to smuggle out an article in which I told of the founding of an Action Nationale composed of fifty-five deputies and senators. Its leadership was distinctly tigerish. "This fact alone gives the movement enormous significance," I wrote. "Clemenceau has come back. Clemenceau has determined to overthrow Briand." The *Eagle* published it with my signature, under the headline:

"Crisis in France – Briand Tottering – Drift to Dictator".

I was queried by the Bureau de la Presse, which ended by overlooking my indiscretion. I had left the country when at last the veteran seized the reins, created a new morale, and earned the affectionate title 'Père la Victoire' given him by the people.

LIFE IN THE BOHEMIAN QUARTERS of Paris ran its course through the long, sad years of war. The young men were all in the army, and to that extent the girls were desolate. But many soldiers whose homes were far away took their leave in Paris, and it was to the Latin Quarter, Montparnasse and Montmartre that they preferred to go. The rumpled uniforms of horizon-blue swarmed the cafés. Because they very often had no other source of revenue, the girls flocked about the newcomers. The soldiers were willing to pay for wine and the girls, if little else. A traffic flourished that was nothing but a brand of prostitution, though prettied up with talk about it being a patriotic duty to make love with men from the firing line.

There were a few cases, of course, like my own, of unattached civilians legitimately employed in Paris. The sentimental grisettes favoured them, because they had a certain degree of stability. To some men, it was an invitation to orgy. I did know of liaisons that had been started before the war and that lasted to its finish. Meanwhile I corresponded regularly with that Katharine Hickey to whom I had temporarily said goodbye with a kiss in New York.

The atmosphere at the Café de la Rotonde had been more artistic in the past, and the time would come when publicity made it one of the flash tourist resorts of Paris. But that war period was the one in which the Rotonde developed a unique personality. It was related to the national drama with a curious intensity, and even if you did not ask its frequenters a single direct question it served as a clearing-house of news. A prerequisite, to be sure, was that you must carry an all-over mental chart of your own, and the gossip of the soldiers would tell the rest.

Thus, it was at the Rotonde that I learned not only that my friend Alan Seeger had fallen in action, but where it had occurred. About the middle of July 1916, three haggard men, obviously foreigners, appeared in uniform. They implied with muttered generalities and shrugs of the shoulders that they were fresh from the trenches, where the slaughter had been awful. Where was that? someone asked. They shook their heads and answered that it was against army regulations for a soldier on leave to tell where he had just been serving. But there was hand-to-hand fighting such as is seldom seen.

"We lost comrades who have drunk with us in this very café," said a Greek. "For instance, a queer American who certainly died well."

"In what way was he queer?"

"Imagine, when asked what he was in civilian life, he just replied, 'I am a poet.'"

"Did you laugh at him?"

"One did not laugh so easily at that fellow. He was cool and proud. For a while he was unpopular, and a committee was sent to advise him to get himself transferred to another company. He pointed out that he never changed his course because he was threatened or disliked. 'My reason for being here is to serve France,' he said. 'For me, the men who sent you do not exist.' There was a great deal of respect for him after that."

I pricked up my ears and moved closer. It was Alan Seeger's characteristics that had emerged from the talk. He had been expected in Paris on the 4 July, granted special leave to take part in ceremonies at the Washington and Lafayette monument and read a poem. But he had not come. I knew that the Second Battalion of the First Regiment of the Foreign Legion, to which he was attached, was on duty on the line of the Somme, rumoured to be the scene of a bloody offensive.

"If he fell at Belloy-en-Santerre it would not astonish me," I murmured.

"A good guess," answered the Greek soldier drily.

That, indeed, had been the spot where Seeger died in a charge on the 4 July. I think he had had an intuition that he would not live through the war. The feeling runs in every phrase of his beautiful poem "A Rendezvous with Death":

> God knows 'twere better to be deep
> Pillowed in silk and scented down,
> Where Love throbs out in blissful sleep,
> Pulse nigh to pulse, and breath to breath.
> Where hushed awakenings are dear . . .
> But I've a rendezvous with Death
> At midnight in some flaming town.
> When Spring trips north again this year,
> And I to my pledged word am true,
> I shall not fail that rendezvous.

His body was buried, along with those of dozens of his fellows, in a common grave close to the centre of the action. After the war his father tried to identify the remains, but was not successful. The French government placed a memorial in Paris to the foreign volunteers who had given their lives, with Alan featured as the symbolic figure. A tree dedicated to him was planted in Washington Square, and a plaque attached to Madame Branchard's 'House of Genius' opposite, where he had once had a room. I was present at those ceremonies. How many remember Alan Seeger now, I wonder?

THE LATTER HALF OF 1916 was a period when, for those who were at all on the inside of events, the United States were moving closer and closer to active participation in the war. One of the vital issues was the German submarine campaign against commercial shipping, and much rancour was caused by the attitude of supposedly neutral Spain. The feeling grew that that country's government was winking at the re-fuelling of both surface raiders and undersea craft in Spanish waters. A spy ring which collected information from all over Europe reputedly had its headquarters in Barcelona. Suddenly I was ordered by my newspaper to make a hurried round trip south of the Pyrenees to observe the situation at first hand. It was not imagined that I could solve the mystery, but I was to see certain persons acting as correspondents, who apparently did not dare to use the telegraph or mails to tell what they might know in making detailed reports. I left Bordeaux by train, crossed the border at Irun and went to Madrid. First impressions of the country were fascinating to me. Like most people who love France, I responded to Spain as being more exotic, if sterner, as a home of the Latin spirit. The capital, on its high plateau, had a chilly, disagreeable climate. Its art museums, of course, delighted me, for they were among the best in Europe.

The government, headed by the Count Romanones, proved to be the most formal and secretive with which I had as yet tried to establish relations as a correspondent. After failing several times to see Romanones, or even his *chef de cabinet*, I used this as the text of a story which made a small hit. Any premier who secluded himself from the foreign press, I argued, must have much to hide. By what stroke of luck I managed to get this past the censorship I do not know. It went by ordinary mail. Fearing that the Madrid police would expel me from Spain when copies of the printed article were received, but hoping that I would be ignored if I had left the capital, I moved on to Barcelona. This turned out to be a wise course. I certainly was kept under official observation in semi-autonomous Catalonia, but that was all. Barcelona charmed me. I took a room in a flat on the Calle Mendizábal, within a short walk of the Ramblas, and shared briefly the masked hysteria of this 'neutral' port in a continent at war.

The men to whom I had been recommended made no secret of their suspicion (doubtless their virtual knowledge) that petrol was being supplied offshore to German buyers. But they had absolutely no proof to this effect. Regarding espionage, they shrugged their shoulders. "Until you bring a spy to trial, you can't be sure about him," a spokesman said. "But I'll show you one I don't trust." He showed me several, as a matter of fact, including a woman I had seen on the Grand Boulevards in Paris before the war – Mata Hari.

If I had penetrated to any inner pro-German circles in Spain, it probably would have been at the cost of my life. Observation at first hand of the current tolerance of the enemy sufficed, particularly as the time allowed me was very short. At the end of a week in Barcelona, I was summoned by wire to come back and receive a new assignment. Hedin told me in Paris that I had been transferred to Brooklyn as an assistant on the foreign editor's staff.

A voyage to the United States was a ticklish adventure, for German submarines were active in the Atlantic. The torpedoing of the *Lusitania* in May 1915 was a recent memory. I saw no hostile craft, though the erratic course sailed by my ship in the Bay of Biscay, as she drew free of the mouth of the Gironde, convinced me that she was dodging a U-boat.

CHAPTER 11 ❧ *Ainslee's* and Its Legend

THE WAR STILL HAD A YEAR TO RUN when I received an offer that changed the course of my life. I had sold a couple of short stories to *Ainslee's* magazine, a periodical cheap in format and price, but which had a certain literary prestige. The editor, Robert Rudd Whiting, wrote me to come in to see him, and on my arrival asked me without preamble whether I would replace him temporarily. He had decided to seek a commission in the army. His standing with his publishers was evidently so good that he had been allowed to appoint a successor, but it would have to be someone willing to turn the job back to him when the war was over. Why Whiting chose me was never quite clear. We had not been personal friends, nor had I had experience on that type of fiction magazine. I suppose my years in France had seemed impressive, and young men who had been exempted from military service were hard to find at the time. The United States had just entered hostilities.

There had grown up in me, by the time I returned from France at thirty, an irritation with the anonymity of daily journalism. Besides, I wanted fame, to be an influence in the profession, more than I wanted money, though I held the trustful belief that the former was always rewarded, more or less in proportion, with the latter. I had heard about geniuses starving in garrets, but felt that their plight must be due to failure to get their names before the public.

I was delighted at the magazine offer, for I thought it a promotion in the publishing game. Though I ranked as an assistant foreign editor at the *Brooklyn Daily Eagle*, I had found the status only nominal, and I nursed

Figure 17. Roberts in 1917. MS353.6.1.

a sort of grudge against the management for having recalled me from Paris. The city editor growled a bit at my resigning. He said it was folly to leave a national newspaper in wartime, but I would not listen to him. Nothing is to be gained in suspense by postponing an almost immediate development. Whiting got the Spanish flu after a few weeks at training camp and died. I sat in at what proved to be a long and interesting spell, having been allowed to inherit his place.

Ainslee's had a prestige that was unique for a monthly fiction magazine printed on cheap paper and sold at 20 cents a copy. It was one of the large number of titles issued by Street & Smith, a firm that specialized in detective and Western thrillers, some of them as periodicals, others as 'dime novels'. A decision to experiment along more sophisticated lines was reached in the late 1890s, and a new magazine was called after a business associate, one Mr Ainslee, who soon vanished. If it could be said to have had a policy at the beginning, this was merely to be clever. A succession of editors chanced to contribute viewpoints that gave it a certain colour, based upon a romantic, slightly unconventional appeal to women. Of major importance, however, was the fact that *Ainslee's* could boast that it had discovered O. Henry.

The critics were at the time building up a cult of the short story as an art form, and their bright, chosen star in the United States, on a scale that the present generation can scarcely realize, was O. Henry. The magazine public, then as now, favoured short fiction, and it was certainly true that the ingenious stories of this author with their sentiment and their trick endings were good for circulation. The cult as such may have meant little to readers, but *Ainslee's* flourished by proclaiming it. And it was *Ainslee's* that had introduced O. Henry to New York by accepting a series of stories from him and getting him to adopt the city as his home.

His real name was William Sidney Porter. He was born in North Carolina, but spent most of his youth in Texas, worked on newspapers and edited a small weekly magazine appropriately called the *Rolling Stone*. He took a job in a bank, became involved in a shortage of the accounts which has never been clearly explained and was sentenced to prison. The episode wounded his spirit and turned him into a man of mystery. Upon his release, he tried his hand at short stories, signing them with a name concocted in New Orleans from a list of guests at a Mardi Gras function. At first, briefly, it was Oliver Henry.

New York was the beloved Bagdad-on-the-Subway to him. He lived his decade of success there almost furtively, moving from one obscure lodging house to another, quailing at the fear that he might be recognized as the man who had been in the same jail and at the same time as Al Jennings the bandit. He accepted the friendship of very few, and these were devoted to him. Publishers increased his rates by twenty-five to one, but he had only the faintest idea how the money went. He scattered it among the down-and-out. He drank in sharp bouts and he gambled. O. Henry had been dead (at forty-three) for eight years when I became editor of *Ainslee's*. I had had a single glimpse of him many years earlier, but we had not exchanged words. Now here I was with the assignment, so to speak, of giving a modern twist to the legend that the fame of the master storyteller and of my magazine were romantically interlocked.

The period was one of low prices. *Ainslee's* ordinarily paid a cent a word, though this could be as much as doubled in special cases, at the editor's discretion. Authors with names could not be asked to accept such a poor reward, yet would occasionally send us a tale that had been rejected by several of the big publications. I never bought blind for the sake of the name alone, but did accept some borderline bargains so as to keep alive the impression that we had a notable standing in the fiction field.

A number of old contributors were steadies who could be depended upon to repeat themselves satisfactorily. My main object, naturally, was to catch young writers of talent on their way up, encourage them and try to hold them for a reasonably long spell. I had enough success in this to make my years at *Ainslee's* fascinating to me. I did not find any best-sellers in prose as salient as O. Henry himself, but the list of competitors with a future was long. The poetry published won far more critical attention than that in most magazines of the sort, if we may judge from the extent to which it was reprinted. We also offered book and dramatic reviews, occasional essays and a series on the great women of history. The author whom it flatters me most to have helped along the path to fame was Edna St Vincent Millay. Poems by her appeared in nineteen consecutive issues, and she also did fiction under a nom-de-plume. But I shall reserve her for a separate chapter.

Fruitful at the time, but strange and baffling in the long run, was my editorial relationship with June Willard. The name was unknown to me when I received, from an address in southern France, a remarkable short story entitled "The Riposte". It was about a dancer who avenges herself upon an inconstant lover by sending him an imperious message to come to her apartment, then committing suicide while he is on the way. He is found there by the police and knows no way to clear himself of a charge of murder. They tell him finally that the woman had notified the police of her intention to kill herself, with the comment that they could scarcely arrive until after her lover had had the "bad half hour" he deserved.

The story was written with a dramatic tension, a beauty of style, a vivid characterization that were far out of the ordinary. I made June Willard an offer, and was astonished to learn from her reply that "The Riposte" was her second story and the first she had had accepted. I subsequently bought several shorts and a novelette from her. All were up to her original standard. Readers sent in a flood of enthusiastic letters, and when that happens an editor can be pretty sure that he has touched a vein of gold. Yet after I left *Ainslee's*, I never again saw her name in print. If she used another signature the fact escaped me, against the probabilities. I could have sworn she was a predestined star. Why did she flash, only to fade?

Figure 18. Olga Petrova, one of Roberts's lifelong friends. MS353.6.8.

Olga Petrova was a well-known actress, both of the stage and the screen, who proved her versatility with plots. A one-act sketch by her drew more letters of admiration than any other feature printed in *Ainslee's* by me.

I used a number of her stories. We formed a personal friendship which has lasted to the day I write these words. Other contributors must wait to enter the narrative until I have done with the O. Henry theme.

THE PHOTOGRAPHER WILLIAM M. VANDER WEYDE told me one day during my second winter at *Ainslee's* that O. Henry had had a weakness for posing for his portrait. In his usual haphazard fashion, however, he often failed to return for the prints and soon forgot all about them. Vander Weyde made several portraits which the author liked and some of which are well known. But there had been a number of other sittings. The subject had lost interest in the results of these, and the plates had been filed away.

There was a fresh wave of enthusiasm for O. Henry the year Vander Weyde spoke to me. Autographs, original manuscripts and first editions were fetching high prices in the auction rooms, and magazines were eager to print new material concerning him. The photographer showed me two portraits which he had dug out of his files, and which were the only copies ever made from the plates. A certain periodical had bought the rights from him, but had wanted some personal reminiscences to accompany the pictures. O. Henry's only daughter, Margaret, had been asked to write the article. She was the wife of Oscar Cesare, the cartoonist.

"Margaret was glad of the opportunity," said Vander Weyde. "But she took it for granted that it was to be a task of pure sentiment. The magazine sent her a cheque for sixty dollars the other day and – what do you think? – she's hurt and offended. She absolutely refuses to accept the money, because she feels that that would amount to commercializing her father's memory."

"There's nothing to prevent her from returning the cheque," I remarked.

"Oh yes, there is! She did return it, but the magazine took the stand that it preferred to pay for value received. The editor sent the cheque back to her."

"It's a situation," I said. "What is she going to do about it?"

"I'm coming to that," chuckled Vander Weyde, who loved to build up dramatic suspense. "She won't spend the money on herself. She has a poor opinion of organized charity, so she won't give it away through regular channels. But she's taken that cheque to the bank and got the cash for it in one-dollar bills. She's turned the bills over to me, with instructions to go out some night and give them away – a dollar at a time – to bums in Madison Square."

I saw the point instantly. Some of O. Henry's most poignant stories were written about the derelicts who sleep on park benches. His favourite setting for such tales had been Madison Square. The price of his daughter's memoir was to be divided among representatives of the tragic crew which once had touched his heartstrings.

"It's justice – and poetry," I said.

"Exactly," replied Vander Weyde. "And think what a thrill there will be in playing Santa Claus to sixty of those poor beggars. Think of the effect upon them when I say, 'This money comes to you from O. Henry!' Do you want to come along?" It will be perceived that William M. Vander Weyde was a man of almost boyish enthusiasm. He shared Margaret Cesare's sentiment to the full, and he conveyed the spirit of the proposed adventure to me.

Of course I wanted to go along. We talked it over and decided that a few other persons should be invited. First there was William Johnston, the novelist, who as Sunday Editor of the *New York World* had published a long series of O. Henry's early tales. Johnston was allowed to bring a *World* reporter – Frank Sullivan, later a successful humourist – and Mrs Vander Weyde joined the party.

The night of 19 December was chosen, largely because we thought it would be nice to distribute the dollar bills a few days in advance of Christmas. If I remember rightly, William Johnston recalled the fact that "The Gift of the Magi" had been the last of the 132 storiettes that O. Henry wrote for the *World*. But the irony of fate was at work. The 19th of December proved to be one of the coldest days that New York City had known for years. The thermometer was around zero at nightfall. We thought this was a pity from the standpoint of our own comfort, but that the dole would be all the more of a windfall for the tramps. Not once did it occur to us to postpone the party.

We had gathered at Vander Weyde's studio at 8 East Fifteenth Street and had noted the blurring of the windowpanes under an iron frost. At ten o'clock we resolved to start. A cruel breeze tore at our faces as we walked toward Fifth Avenue. It was out of the question to complete the journey on foot, so we took a cab to Madison Square. In the innocence of our hearts, we got out near the Seward statue and ploughed forward in search of park-bench derelicts.

There was not a soul to be found in the whole square. So bitter was the weather that if a bum had been foolish enough to try to loaf there he would have frozen to death before long. A dry snow lay upon the benches and pathways. It squeaked electrically under our feet. The wind howled among the trees with Arctic malice. We looked at one another and laughed, astonished at ourselves that we had not foreseen this anti-climax.

"O. Henry's ghost is probably laughing at us right now," said Vander Weyde. "We here with sixty dollars to give away – and no takers!"

"If he were here," remarked Johnston, his teeth chattering, "he would say, 'Come on over to Mouquin's.' Or else, 'I'll best you a game of pool and bet you five dollars you miss your first shot.'"

Frank Sullivan then reminded us that Madison Square had lost its vogue, anyway, as a hangout for the breadline brigade. Bryant Park, behind the Public Library, had become the favoured resort. The trend of life in New York was uptown. We admitted the truth of this and took a taxi to Bryant Park, bluffing mightily in the hope that we would find a way to save our faces. We were secretly sure that there would be no tramps abroad – in any park. Nor were they. We discovered a policeman, however, at the corner of Forty-First Street and Sixth Avenue, whacking his chest with his arms in an attempt to keep warm. Vander Weyde leaned out of the cab and gravely enquired after the habitués of the benches.

The officer observed with some profanity that it was no night to be looking for drifters. Were we crazy? And, if not, what did we want with them?

"We're trying to give some money away as Christmas presents," said Vander Weyde.

"Soft-headed do-gooders, eh?" retorted the cop, rolling the words with an Irish brogue. "Well, if you're really hunting for bums, why don't you go to the flophouses downtown? That's where they'd be in zero weather."

We held a hasty conference to decide whether this course would be in harmony with Mrs Cesare's wishes, or whether we should wait for a warmer evening so that we might hold to the Madison Square idea. It seemed to us that the derelicts in flophouses would be O. Henry derelicts all the same. If the cold had driven them to cover, why should we quibble? So we asked the policeman to direct us.

"The cheapest flops are on East Twenty-Third Street," he said. "You's likely thinking they should be on the Bowery, but that ain't true any longer. Try East Twenty-Third, between Second and First Avenues."

We rode to the block mentioned, and were at once convinced by its squalid appearance that it must be the haunt of the abandoned. An elevated railroad ran up First Avenue and swung along this block before it turned into Second Avenue. The dirty houses were made to seem more repulsive by the bedlam created by the trains.

On the south side of the street we saw a twenty-five-cent hotel bearing the incongruous name of the Olive Tree Inn. We entered it without ceremony and found ourselves in a musty lobby where perhaps a dozen men were sitting. They were dressed in the shabbiest of clothes, but they did not give the impression of being hopelessly down and out. For one thing, they did not look hungry. I assumed that they were workmen who had fallen on hard times. The fact that they could pay twenty-five cents for a bed, when so many houses sold shelter at fifteen cents or even ten, was an indication that they were still clinging to some of the decencies of life.

Our party of two women and four men stirred an immediate interest. The lodgers huddled down in their chairs and stuck their heads forward. We walked straight to the desk, where Vander Weyde asked the clerk whether there was any objection to our giving away dollar bills.

The clerk plainly took us for misguided members of a charity organization. "If it's a handout – all right," he said curtly, "but I can't let you annoy my guests by conducting any investigation here."

We reassured him and advanced upon the men. Vander Weyde presented a seedy-looking old fellow with a dollar bill, saying: "This is a gift to you from O. Henry, with the season's greetings."

"It's a what – from who?" stammered the other, gaping.

The statement was repeated. "Of course you've heard of O. Henry, the great writer?" added Vander Weyde.

We failed to make out the mumbled reply, because all the other men had left their seats and were crowding about us. They preserved a certain dignity, neither begging openly for money nor cringing for sympathy, but showing a natural curiosity in what we were doing. Each of them was handed a dollar bill.

"O. Henry wrote stories about the sort of life you lead down here. Do any of you happen to have read his books?" asked Vander Weyde hopefully.

The men exchanged glances. "I don't know what you're talking about," said one of them at last – a man with a week's growth of beard but who carried himself too erectly to be a bum. "If there's no string on this cash, I'm damn grateful. I sure need it. But I never heard of Mr Henry."

The others joined in a chorus of approval. Their oft-repeated thanks and their evident hope that this would increase the gift became embarrassing. We beat our retreat.

"These were not typical derelicts," said Johnston. "Let's try a real low-down place – a dime shelter."

Up the street a bit we noted a building called the Washington House. A red lantern above the doorway had the sign "10¢" painted on the glass in huge figures. Shivering human forms were crawling through the entrance at that moment, and we caught a glimpse of foul smoke beyond them. It was a horrible-seeming dive, and we concluded to take a shot at it.

The lobby in this case was a big, murky room, with a pot-bellied iron stove in the centre around which nearly forty men were jammed. Their clothing steamed and stank. Here was poverty of the most desperate sort. No one could doubt that these lodgers for the night were the sort that never worked, that lived as casually and as wretchedly as the alley cats that feed from garbage cans. In fine weather they surely would be found sleeping on park benches.

They greeted our arrival with a certain dumb hostility. No doubt they thought that we were slummers who had come to treat ourselves to a morbid thrill at their expense. At any rate, there was a wild-beast glare of resentment in their eyes. We again pushed our way to the night clerk's desk and explained our errand. The fellow looked us over superciliously.

"You can throw your money around for all I care," he said. "But you'd better watch out. If this gang sees real dollar bills you're likely to be mobbed."

Vander Weyde reacted to this warning by producing what remained of the roll and holding it in his left hand, in full view. His voice shook a little, however, as he spoke to the astonished derelicts.

"There was once a writer named O. Henry," he announced. "Some of his best stories described the problems of down-and-outers, of men who were getting a raw deal from life. And tonight it happens that his daughter is sending a Christmas present to a few of you boys, in his name. It's not charity. You don't have to prove that you are deserving cases. First come, first served, and I only hope there'll be enough to go round."

"He handed a dollar bill to the nearest man. The latter took it and held it close to his eyes, as though he feared it might be counterfeit.

"It's perfectly good money," said Vander Weyde. "But I wish you'd tell me one thing. Have you ever heard of O. Henry?"

The other shook his head slowly. He was too dazed to utter a word.

Vander Weyde then walked quickly around the circle and pressed bills into the outstretched hands. A wave of excitement spread rapidly. The men were suddenly convinced they were getting something for nothing, and a whole dollar loomed in their eyes as a fantastic sum. They commenced to babble and whine, calling down blessings on our heads in one breath and begging for extra alms in the next. Some of them claimed brazenly that they had been overlooked and succeeded, I feel sure, in getting away with it as repeaters. The tender-hearted Van der Weyde was quite unable to say "No" to them.

But he was tenacious on one point. After the last dollar had been given away, he insisting on lining up the beneficiaries and passed from man to man, addressing them separately.

"Do you know who O. Henry was?" he asked over and over again, until it became monotonous.

The replies varied in form. Many of them were attempts at hedging, because the speaker feared he would get it wrong if he denied acquaintance with an obviously eminent character. But the upshot was the same in all cases. None of these representatives of the submerged half of society knew O. Henry from the man in the moon. The most articulate of the crowd declared that he had been a Tammany politician.

If it had gone on much longer, I believe we'd have been forced to seek relief in hysterical laughter. But abruptly Vander Weyde quit and led the way to the street. "What an irony!" he remarked, as we stood shivering and trying to flag a cruising taxi.

"Take it that it is in itself a typical O. Henry story," I said.

"He would have thought it great stuff," William Johnston muttered. "He would have used it as material for his next yarn – but he'd have directed his satire against us, and not against the bums."

We decided by unanimous vote that Johnston was right. Then Vander Weyde mused aloud. In death as well as in life, O. Henry had contributed to his legend. On a Wednesday evening in early June 1910, he had gone with Gilman Hall and William Griffith, two editor friends, to bowl at an alley on University Place. As usual, they played for half-dollars, with at times a doubling of the stakes. O. Henry's vagueness about money was such that he soon had not the slightest idea about his winnings or losses. It was easy for his companions to persuade him that he was far behind, but they dropped silver into the pocket of his coat when his back was turned. Eventually his hand fell upon this cash, and pleased as a child he spun the fifty-cent pieces and the quarters down the alley as tips to the attendants.

Near midnight he complained that he was feeling more tired than he should be. The doctors had told him that he must not drink or smoke. What nonsense! It would take the fun out of life. He returned alone to his room at the Hotel Caledonia and was not seen alive again by Hall and Griffith. He collapsed three nights afterward of acute cirrhosis of the liver.

When asked his name at Polyclinic Hospital, he replied: "Call me Dennis; my name will be Dennis in the morning." He died early in the morning, 5 June, and as a result of his whimsy the body was sent under the name of Dennis to an obscure undertaker. His friends had to search for longer than two hours, going from mortuary parlour to mortuary parlour, before they identified the remains of O. Henry. The day of his funeral at the Little Church Around the Corner, a wedding party arrived late and passed his coffin at the gate. O. Henry's friends stood aside. They bore him in at last over the confetti and rice with which the pathway had become sprinkled. It had all run true to form.

OTHER DEAR FRIENDS – ALL contributors to *Ainslie's* – get briefer mentions. Solita Solano had lived in the Philippines and drew much of her inspiration from the unique commingling of the Hispanic spirit with that of the Orient which she found there. My only editorial grievance with her was that, as the years passed, she wrote less and less. Her literary talent was sufficient to have made her a very successful author. But she preferred living life's subtleties to writing about them, and with her it is the memory of sympathetic friendship that I treasure most keenly. No one understands me better than Solita.

Salomón de la Selva was one of the first authors to come in to see me, after I took the post of editor at *Ainslie's*. He was a Nicaraguan, twenty-four years old, a remarkable young man in several ways. His features were rather Anglo-Saxon than Latin, his hair light-coloured. This was no doubt explained by the fact that one of his grandmothers had been an Englishwoman, but he said he also had Indian blood, which did not show at all. He was bilingual, without even an accent in English, and he wrote poetry bearing no traces grammatically of being the work of a foreigner. It was good verse, very much to my taste. If I remember rightly, he had contributed to the magazine under

Figure 19. Solita Solano, one of Roberts's lifelong friends. MS353.6.8.

R.R. Whiting. Anyway, I was glad to accept a number of pieces from him.

De la Selva had taught romance languages at Williams College and lectured at Columbia University. He already had a book in the press, *Tropical Town and Other Poems*. The publisher's blurb said that in 1910, on the death of his father, the Nicaraguan Congress adopted him as a ward of the nation. He waved this aside in talking to me, but excessive modesty was not one of his failings. He told me that Edna St Vincent Millay, Stephen Vincent Benét, and he were the three young poets who would be important in the United States in that generation. The two first-mentioned were beginners at the time; they certainly lived up to his prophecy. I find it difficult to account for his own failure to figure in any large way. He did not, so far as I know, even issue a second volume in English.

He greatly admired his countryman Rubén Darío, one of the finest Latin American poets of the period, and he was familiar with French as well as Hispanic literature. Locally, de la Selva regarded himself as the poet of pan-Americanism. It took foresight to adopt ardently this political doctrine, which was thought visionary at the time. De la Selva was full of Catholic sentiment rather than mysticism, and he liked to portray himself as a sinner fallen under the spell of the old pagan gods.

He produced sonnets with the utmost fluency. At dinner one night I

Figure 20. Salomón de la Selva being sworn into the British Army in New York on 18 July 1918. Photograph from the *New York Herald* (19 July 1918).

heard him reel off, on a challenge, an unrhymed sonnet in iambic pentameter that somehow rang with the traditional sound effects.

Salomón startled his friends in 1918 by enlisting as a private in the British Army. He said he could not let the war pass without paying a tribute to the memory of his English grandmother. But he was probably influenced more by Rupert Brooke, Alan Seeger, Wilfred Owen and other soldier poets of his generation. Luckier than those three, he did not fall. He trained in Canada. Then, under date of 14 September, he wrote me from camp at Felixstowe, Suffolk, as follows: "They would not let me join the Guards because I am not an English citizen. At least that is the excuse they gave. For that same reason they barred me from joining air service or the tanks. The Lancs [Loyal North Lancashire Regiment] are good fighters, anyway, and I am not kicking. By November I trust to be *in it* at last!" November, however, was the month of the Armistice, and Salomón was soon back among us.

Probably the chief woman in his life, during his kaleidoscopic New York years, was Jeanne Robert Foster. Beautiful and a good poet herself, she worked on the staff of the *Review of Reviews*, was a friend of John Butler Yeats and went often to his famous salon at the Maison Petitpas. When the old sage died, rather suddenly, no member of his family was in the United States, and his many admirers who volunteered to conduct the funeral wondered where they should bury him. The large public cemeteries seemed all too cold for the beloved J.B.Y. Mrs Foster solved the problem by offering a lot in the private burial ground of her family, a short distance up the Hudson River. The spirit of the Celtic Twilight hovered over that widely attended funeral.

George Sterling, author of *A Wine of Wizardry* and other books, only visited New York occasionally. He enjoyed his standing as laureate of San Francisco's bohemians, and he professed to believe that nowhere but in that city could true bohemianism be found in the United States. Recognition by New York editors, however, was important to his ego, and he seldom let longer than a year pass without coming to renew his contacts. His poetry is largely forgotten today, I fear, for although consistently graceful it was lacking in real feeling or depth.

Sterling was a fellow of much charm, popular among men as well as women. He pursued pleasure in the classic spirit and liked to be thought a kind of reincarnation of Dionysus or Pan. That, rather than the romantic shiftlessness of the *vie de bohème,* coloured his eloquence and was marked on his handsome face. One day he showed me a little bottle containing, he said, a painless, swift and deadly poison. Probably it was cyanide of potassium. If ever he were seriously ill, or plunged into a melancholia he could not control, he swore that he would swallow a dose. I did not believe him, but that is exactly the path he took in the Bohemian Club, San Francisco, about eight years after I went on *Ainslee's*. The blue phial was found empty in his room. His estranged wife had done the same thing a few years earlier. His last telephone call was to B. Virginia Lee, whom he was helping to revive the *Overland Monthly*. She wrote of him: "He filled his cup and sipped it beautifully. Then, when the wine of life had lost its savour, not when he tasted the dregs, then only did he toss the cup away."

I have never known a man who belonged more definitely to an age before the one we lived and moved in than did Richard Le Gallienne, author of *The Quest of the Golden Girls*, and many other books. They had called him 'the Golden Boy' in the 1890s, the days of the *Yellow Book*, and that by temperament was what he remained. His very appearance – tall, slender and dreamy – transmitted the aura at its best, with a touch of Ernest Dowson's melancholy and none of Oscar Wilde's coarseness. A common remark about him in London was that he looked as if he had walked out of a Cinquecento painting. He was more authentically the bohemian than Sterling, and a good deal of the hedonist too.

Le Gallienne had been for some years a voluntary exile, a survivor of a movement which was only a name in his new home. He said he enjoyed New York life, bizarre though it must have seemed to him. Within the range of the possibilities, he was a habitué of cafés just as if he had been in Europe. He had minor importance as a poet. One could detect overtones and echoes from Swinburne and other stars of his young years. His gift ran strongest to the fairy tale for adults and to the essay, forms for which I could seldom make a place in *Ainslee's*.

An event of my years on *Ainslee's* was my marriage in December 1917 to Katharine Hickey. I have written of my friendship with her, formed at the Petitpas's *table d'hôte* under the eye of that genial sage, John Butler Yeats. Our union would have occurred more logically in 1913, when we met. But I had been eager then for my first visit to Paris, and she had not tried to turn me from it. Katharine seemed a curiously fatalistic woman, in her cultivated, non-intellectual way. She wrote to me regularly while I was abroad. I had not

Figure 21. Katherine Amelia Hickey in 1912 around the time Roberts met her. Their short-lived marriage began in December 1917. MS353.6.2.

been faithful to her in Paris, and she appeared to know it; but she received me back with a smiling, equable affection. So we drifted insensibly into a decision to marry. The mayor of Atlantic City performed the ceremony.

I had no suspicion that Katharine would prove to be a dramatic – or should I say melodramatic? – wife. She had represented calm to me. Almost at once, however, I discovered that a deadly physical fear of childbirth haunted her. This amounted to a mania, and at the slightest hint of a pregnancy she stopped at nothing to abort it. I felt no special urge at the time to meet the responsibilities of raising a family. Yet her abnormal frenzies wounded me, and when I came to think about it I did want a daughter. Our marriage limped along for four years and ended in divorce. By that time my tenancy of *Ainslee's* had wound up too. The publishers had decided that they wanted a certain woman as editor.

CHAPTER 12 Edna St Vincent Millay

A MYTH IS CERTAIN TO GROW AROUND THE elusive personality of Edna St Vincent Millay, the greatest woman poet since Sappho. There will be many biographies of her, and it will not be easy for the authors to arrive at the full truth. Those whose lives touched hers in special ways ought to record their memories before it is too late.

I knew her best between 1918 and 1921, the three years that were undoubtedly the most bizarre in my experience of New York. The war had disturbed the ways of the city, though up till the Armistice and for a few months afterward the confusion seemed to be superficial. Recent movements had been affected, as well as old habits. The new wave of bohemianism centred in Greenwich Village, where a Latin Quarter developed rapidly, at first along romantic lines but soon veering to a wild eccentricity. Edna St Vincent Millay was not a bohemian, though for a while she enjoyed living as one. She was not an archetype of the Jazz Age, though she wrote the best lyrics it produced. She was a completely free soul, who would have lived as she chose in any epoch – with adaptive colouration.

I first heard of her in 1912, in connection with Mitchell Kennerley's *Lyric Year* contest. Her "Renascence" failed to win one of the three prizes in spite of the backing of the editor, Ferdinand Earle, who tried to sway the judges to rank it first. After publication, it was praised by the critics as being the finest poem in the volume. I agreed with this opinion. Later, when the talk about the piece led to a book by her under the same title, the youthful lyrics had even greater charm for me than "Renascence" itself. I heard no more of her work for a long time. She had not won the immediate success she deserved.

It was strange that the 'dime novel' firm of Street & Smith should have been the medium through which an editorial relationship of value to me, and to her, was made. Her poetry was actually above the heads of the average reader of *Ainslee's*, but I did not let that deter me. My predecessors had used verse to fill the space left blank when a story ended near the top of a page. They had not exercised much judgement in their selections. The publishers were still more indifferent. They cared not a rap what was inserted to garnish the blank spaces. Such being the case, I had resolved to indulge my personal bent and try to make the poetry in *Ainslee's* among the best printed in the United States. I wanted to discover new poets of talent, as well as give those already known another magazine in which they would be glad to appear in advance of book publication.

I have said nothing so far about the editorial offices in the Street & Smith building. We occupied a row of private rooms on the sixth floor of the Seventh Avenue, or western, side. Large rolls of paper generally stood in the corridor with a narrow lane between them. This overflow from the stockroom added to the mercantile air of the shop, but many a good author threaded his way to *Ainslee's* door, and we joked about the paper columns and said they were picturesque. The view from my window was drab enough, a wilderness of decayed brick and brownstone houses, and the flat roof of a convent where nuns rusty as crows came out to sun themselves.

One morning in September 1918, Edna St Vincent Millay's name was phoned to me from the desk and the word given that she should be sent in. I had written asking her to call, and had received a note marked by elegant, quaint expressions saying that she would. I had been struck by the handwriting, vertical and open, with very tall initials and heavy terminal strokes. Of her appearance, I did not have the least idea. Presently I looked up and saw a slim, blonde girl with sea-green eyes, finespun reddish hair and remarkably small hands. Pretty would have been a poor term to apply to her. She was vivid and had much charm, with a touch of Celtic wonder. The floral comparison that occurred to me was that of a tiger lily.

She sat down and I led her on to talk about poetry. Exactly what literary ideas passed between us I have forgotten. But I gathered that she was appearing in only a few magazines and was willing to become a contributor to *Ainslee's* at our poor rate of fifty cents a line. Even her most generous publisher at the time, Harriet Monroe of *Poetry*, could not pay much more. Edna spoke as if the money involved hardly mattered. She was astonished that an editor whose main concern was fiction should be hospitable to verse, and when I sketched for her the Street & Smith background and explained that the attitude was uniquely my own she clapped her hands with pleasure.

"I hope you have brought some manuscripts," I said after a while. She produced just one, which I thought was a small allowance. But that poem was her exquisite "Daphne":

Why do you follow me?
Any moment I can be
Nothing but a laurel tree.

I murmured that of course I would accept it, and she must send me a large selection. She promised to do so. When she left I had the feeling that the room had been emptied of a sprite-like presence, a being given to old-fashioned mannerisms, yet that all this was but the mask worn by a passionately creative mind.

A week or so later I telephoned and asked her to dine with me. Where did we go? Who knows? To Mouquin's on Sixth Avenue maybe, or the Lafayette on University Place, or one of the many downtown French *table d'hôte* restaurants that were still unpretentious and favoured by bohemians. Wherever it was, we were to go there again and to the rest in turn. The blight of prohibition merely threatened then, and with a bottle of good wine between us we could not suppose it to be serious. After dinner I saw Edna home to a flat in the ancient brick house at 25 Charlton Street, was invited in, and met her sister Norma.

The family consisted of parents who were divorced and three daughters, of

Figure 22. Edna St Vincent Millay. Photograph by Herman Mishkin. Edna St Vincent Millay Papers (15.10, "Mishkin portrait of Millay"). Courtesy of Archives and Special Collections Library, Vassar College.

whom Edna (I never called her Vincent, as most of her friends did) was the oldest. All that I knew about the Millay antecedents was that Maine was their home state and their descent principally Irish. Edna in her flickering way of talking about herself had told me that no place meant so much to her as the seashore at Camden, Maine, where she had been brought up. Her mother was expected to come to New York soon. Her younger sister Kathleen was away, I believe in school. But here was Norma, the middle sister, who wanted to go on the stage and meanwhile was working in an airplane factory.

I remember Norma as the taller and more Irish-looking of the two. She was blonde, comely, friendly, smiling, with no particular aura of magic, and in Edna's company manifestly the one who would follow rather than lead. I had been thinking of the poet as fragile and unearthly; suddenly I perceived that she was strong. The girls felt they must move, for although Charlton was a picturesque street in the oldest part of Greenwich Village and much to Edna's taste, the flat would be unsuitable for the whole family. More space at a lower rent was needed. That was the subject discussed during the first minutes I was there that evening, and the planning was entirely in Edna's hands.

"Daphne" appeared in the next issue of *Ainslee's* and was reprinted by several newspapers. The additional poems I had asked to see had been coming in steadily, so eventually nineteen consecutive numbers of the magazine contained poems by Edna which were widely clipped for verse columns ranging from those in *Current Opinion* and the Sunday edition of the *New York Herald-Tribune* to many a provincial journal. The circumstance last-mentioned, rather than the original publication in *Ainslee's*, helped the growth of her fame. The exchange editors had sound judgement. My nineteen titles were the pick of the shorter lyrics that went into her *Second April* and *A Few Figs from Thistles*. They included "Elegy Before Death", "Departure", "Inland", "Alms", "Exiled" and "Song of a Second April"; also two or three sonnets, but not of her most famous.

Fifty cents a line as pay for imperishable verse would have been scarcely any help in solving her financial problems. So when she hinted that she would like to attempt writing fiction, I gave her every encouragement. As early as her fourth letter to me, postmarked 9 January 1919, she refers to a short story from which she had "cut out the things that troubled me, and now I find that I quite like it. . . . This story is twice as long as I told you – it's just about six thousand words. I hope it's not too long. I never have any idea how long anything is – or how broad or how high – until I sort of take a tape-measure to it."

We agreed that she should use the pseudonym Nancy Boyd for fiction, and under that name seven short stories and a novelette appeared during 1919 and 1920. All of her published work of the year 1919 was in *Ainslee's*, except for two poems in Harriet Monroe's *Poetry*. It amused me whenever the chance arose to run an Edna St Vincent Millay lyric in the blank left at the bottom of the last page of a Nancy Boyd tale. Also, the irony is worth noting that while I had paid her four dollars and fifty cents for the magazine rights to "Daphne", I was able to send her a cheque for four hundred dollars for her novelette, *The Seventh Stair*. Tacitly we both admitted that fiction with her was pot-boiling, but she was far too gifted to fail to do it readably.

The shift from Charlton Street had taken place in December, or perhaps the first week of January 1919. The new Millay home was a ground-floor flat at 449 West Nineteenth Street, in the colourless, rundown block between Ninth and Tenth Avenues. It was an incongruous setting for the family, but that signified little. Strong personalities create their own atmosphere, and this did not apply only to the poet. I now met her mother, who was very much of a personality. Mrs Cora Buzzell Millay was not beautiful, and she looked workworn, gnarled. After the separation from her husband, she had gone out as a practical nurse to support the household. But she had made time from the beginning to teach her daughters to love literature and music. She wrote poetry herself, and she had encouraged the child Edna to write. Her conversation was pithy and the ruggedness of her character salient. A sense of regard pulsed unexpectedly between us, and whenever she had occasion to drop me a line her words were warm. At Nineteenth Street I got to know Kathleen, too, a pretty brunette but decidedly the weakest one of the family.

THE WINTER IN QUESTION SAW the ending of World War I. False Armistice and real Armistice had been wildly celebrated in the streets of New York. The peace conference had gathered at Versailles. I cannot recall, however, that Edna showed a concern with war or international politics, except to vow that both repelled her. She liked to hear my peacetime experiences in

Europe, never those as war correspondent. Love, poetry and the theatre were the three subjects she preferred to discuss with me. I believe she thought me a barbarian on certain other matters; notably music, of which I have no critical appreciation. But let us hold to the three, in reverse order.

The theatre was the influence that most positively drew Edna St Vincent Millay into the bohemian life of Greenwich Village. She had concluded, even before I met her, that making a living at writing would be terribly difficult, and she had chosen the stage as a promising vocation. Unlike her sister Norma, who saw herself as a professional actress, Edna wanted to act in order to be free to write. Everyone knows that she had had remarkable success at Vassar appearing in her own gay and fanciful sketches, so it was natural that she should enter the ambit of the Provincetown Players, who produced in a basement on MacDougal Street just off Washington Square South and whose artistic standards were high. Edna acted for them without pay, because it gave her pleasure and as a stepping stone. The wide contacts resulted in an effervescent social life for her.

I have nothing to tell about that particular bohemia. I could have joined in it, but I would not because I was jealous of its influence over Edna. I went, of course, to the plays she had written or in which she appeared. Some of the other members of the group were and remained superficial acquaintances of mine. There were bohemias of writers and painters in which I did mix, without seeking to bring them and Edna together. I took her once to a Kit Kat ball, the annual costume affair of a club of illustrators, and I think that was the only time we were ever together in a large gathering. I was enamoured of such communion as she gave me, and more deeply than she guessed or probably cared I wanted it to be an exchange between us only.

Her conception of stage drama at that time was a mixture of romance and irony. The delicate, the whimsical, the bejewelled, glittered in the best scenes she composed, as in her letters and much of her talk. Her one-act play *Aria da Capo*, which she directed for the Provincetown Players at the end of 1919 with Norma in the role of Columbine, was a perfect example of the attitude. Critics, though not all of them, took it as a mere fantasy. Indeed Columbine and Pierrot have the most lines, and they prattle gracefully. The scene is a stage with Colthurnus directing. Presently he dismisses the pair and summons Thyrsis and Corydon. They play at a game of owning land and build a wall as a boundary, work up a quarrel about it and kill each other. Columbine and Pierrot are called back. They cry out at sight of the corpses. But Colthurnus says:

> ... Pull down the tablecloth
> On the other side, and hide them from the house
> And play the farce! The audience will forget.

The mimes obey and continue their persiflage as if nothing had happened. *Aria da Capo* reveals itself as a subtle stroke at the pity of war.

Earlier that year she had appeared in the Theatre Guild's production of *The Bonds of Interest*, by the Spanish dramatist Jacinto Benavente, at the old Garrick on West Thirty-Fifth Street. This was almost a professional engagement, for the Theatre Guild then had a complicated system of salaries in proportion to the receipts at the box office. She portrayed a minor role with charm, and I can still see her slender figure with sloping shoulders and hair of fiery gold, still hear her clearly modulated voice. But when the next play was cast she was not given a part and, according to Floyd Dell, she "cried like a heartbroken child". I never knew her to shed a tear myself.

The truth was that Edna had not been born to be an actress. She perceived this, and fortunately for English poetry she ceased pouring out her energies in the direction of the stage. Her liking for it continued unabated. She dwelt upon Elizabethan methods and even speculated about the possibility of recapturing the spirit of mediaeval comedies. I gave her a sketch of the interior of a Shakespearean theatre, which enchanted her.

We talked a good deal about poetry. One of her first statements was that it was impossible for a poet not to be influenced by the work of those he venerated as artistic ancestors – that this was in fact desirable, for it assured a continuity and development of the general stream of poetry. I knew that she did not mean actual imitation, but rather an absorption of the spirit and methods of an admired predecessor. That she could say such a thing, however, proved her essential modesty and love of truth. Most poets like to believe that their work is fashioned from original clay.

Naturally, I asked her what influences she recognized in her own case. Leaving aside the demigods, she answered that one of the most important had been A.E. Housman, author of *A Shropshire Lad*, and that another had been Tennyson. The former for his emotional attitude and spare poignancy of expression; the latter for narrative power and technical innovations. I thought it curious that she should rank Housman so high. The kinship was plain, particularly as to directness and a mingling of the stoic and epicurean philosophies. Both writers could compress a whole theme into a short lyric in ballad metre, or a song. But their merits did not have the balance expected between master and disciple. Edna was the better poet, and I repeat it was singular to hear her credit Housman with having moulded her. No doubt she felt young.

"If we were able to turn back the calendar for him, you could give lessons to that Cambridge recluse," I said.

She replied severely that A.E. Housman was a true poet, and I must not be blasphemous.

Tennyson's influence had more far-reaching aspects. The generation of Edna's childhood loved him. The critics had not then started to becloud that vast Victorian fame, which rested upon fine gifts and must again emerge. She was soaked in the *Idylls of the King*, and who could deny their effectiveness as stories. She had written some frankly Tennysonian lyrics; witness her "Elaine". But I was puzzled by her regarding the late laureate as a technical innovator. The body of his work had been composed in traditional measures. He had experimented, to be sure, as in the following: "Ilion, Ilion, dréamy Ilion, píllared Ilion, hóly Ilion, / Cíty of Ilion, whén wilt thóu be mélody bórn?" But this was academic toying, and not a practicable enlarging of the scope of English rhythms. Edna herself would have been the last to adopt it.

"Surely the innovator of the period in lyric verse has been Swinburne rather than Tennyson," I said. "Many of Swinburne's poems are in new metres, many employ new rhyming schemes, others distil fresh values from words. The language is richer in effects because of him. Its old Germanic limitations have been broadened. All later poets, except those who have purposely held aloof, have learned something from Swinburne."

Edna gave me a quizzical look, the light from her sea-green eyes seeming to make the freckles across her nose like a tiger lily's spots, her mouth elfin. She told me to read favourite stanzas of mine. I began:

I hid my heart in a nest of roses,
Out of the sun's way, hidden apart;
In a softer bed than the soft white snow's is,
Under the roses I hid my heart.

"That is but sound," said Edna.

"Do you deny the images?" I asked.

"No, but they are for the sake of the sound."

It was the start of a long argument between us. I maintained that Swinburne was an impassioned and musical improviser, whose gift, as George Meredith had said, was to be "fired on the instant to deliver himself orally", and who wrote it down superbly. His thought content was positive though general, the details subservient to the singing. Sheer lyricism resulted, and the best examples of it were the most brilliant in the English language. But Edna would not have it so. She extolled certain lines, then grew impatient with what followed. This might be innovation for me, not for her, she declared – and I could have my Swinburne. The debt she recognized was to Tennyson. The day came when I realized that she saw Swinburne as nothing but a musician in words and very much the inferior of, say, Chopin. I, who was indifferent to instrumental music, delighted in him. The test held good with others. I have never known a music lover who cared for Swinburne, and vice versa. The poet himself, incidentally, would leave the room at the first threat of a piano or violin being played.

Edna had studied Old English and greatly admired Chaucer; she had read the *Morte d'Arthur* of Mallory and delved into still earlier Saxon romances. The lasting nature of this interest is apparent from the subject she chose for her opera, *The King's Henchman*, with Deems Taylor in 1927. She had an excellent knowledge of French, but I do not recall her praising highly any of the poets of that language. Baudelaire is one of my favourites, and I should not have forgotten if she had shown a special enthusiasm for him. Yet there would be a time when she would make masterly translations from Baudelaire.

Toward contemporary American poets who were any good at all she had a generous attitude and praised them beyond their worth. She appeared to have a comradely feeling of being in the same struggle for recognition and of wanting to give them all the credit possible. She praised the wonderful versatility of Salomón de la Selva, and this was just. He tossed coloured balloons borrowed from a dozen masters, but his ability to do so perfectly and then to write poems that were beautiful and original marked him for a literary success which only his concentration upon pan-American problems prevented him from winning. When last I heard of him, he was on the staff of the University of Mexico.

Edna lauded Arthur Davison Ficke's work, and although a strong personal sympathy existed there, Ficke's talent was in fact of a high order. She admired Stephen Vincent Benét, Witter Bynner and Ralph Hodgson. I mention only those of whom I remember her speaking. Louise Bogan and Elinor Wylie were to come later.

A free verse school had started, with Amy Lowell as chief exponent in the United States. Edna's attitude toward it was lenient, much more so than mine. She held that all sincere experiments should be read with sympathy. Who could say no to that? When she added that some masterpieces had neither metre nor rhyme and quoted examples, I saw that she demanded rhythm and a certain intensity of diction. Naturally I agreed that *The Song of Solomon* was the purest poetry, but denied that it established a case for the discords produced by the freaks of our day. She smiled cryptically and said that we could not tell what the freaks might discover. She was writing a little *vers libre* herself. And what *vers libre*! It is impossible to overpraise the lovely poem in *Second April* which begins:

> To what purpose, April, do you return again?
> Beauty is not enough.
> You can no longer quiet me with the redness
> Of little leaves opening stickily.
> I know what I know.

In his memoir of her published in the *Nation* after her death, Edmund Wilson remarks pleasantly of the early period that she had "no real market for her poems; she sold a lyric only now and then to the highbrow *Dial* on the one hand, or to the trashy *Ainslee's* on the other". Then Frank Crowninshield, the editor of *Vanity Fair*, took her up. His magazine could afford to pay decent prices, and he was as generous as possible. He arranged for 'Nancy Boyd' prose, too – in the form of satirical dialogues and sketches. The combination permitted him to make her a regular allowance, on which she planned her first visit to Europe. By 1921 her name had disappeared from *Ainslee's*, rightly and inevitably. *Vanity Fair* had the privilege of launching her as a success with a public that counted.

Edna and I talked about love, but not so much as about poetry. It will be useless for the annotators and the biographical essayists to seek to bowdlerize her legend, as already there has been some tendency to do. She was a genius, and the world will insist upon knowing her personality to its core. To suppose that amorous liberty was an idea she was content to take out in words would be as foolish as to believe the same thing about Byron. Edna loved where she pleased in her youth, and she loved often.

She would – very rarely – get pedantic on the subject of woman's right to sex freedom, associating it with the broad feminist doctrine that was then in the air. This could scarcely have been otherwise, for one of her first heroines had been Inez Milholland, the women's suffrage leader. I have no information regarding Miss Milholland's private life, but do know that many of the young suffragists were total libertarians in practice as well as principle. Their error was not to confine the claim to their own type as exceptional human beings, a point which reasonable persons endorsed then and would endorse now. The feminist nonsense lay in preaching the necessity of freedoms to the great mass of domestic women whose natures rejected them.

Edna was supremely exceptional, and that is what matters. I had known her for a short while when she told me that there was only one man she loved, that he had a wife and children, and probably would never love her. This, of course, was Arthur Davison Ficke, whom I did not identify until later. With an ebullience that was not so light as it seemed, Edna found solace. The conduct was masculine, though not the style. She has expressed it forthrightly in many a poem.

I shall mention her friendship with the artist Pieter Mijer, because his name has been mysteriously left out of the material printed since her death in 1950, while one reference to him in a published letter from her to me was averred editorially to apply to another man. Pieter Mijer was from Java, of Dutch descent though his olive-brown complexion and shining black hair suggested that he had Malay blood in him. Young and handsome in an exotic way, his pose of dreamy indifference to women was doubtless an added attraction. He had a studio on West Tenth Street, on the second floor of a small brownstone house in the best tradition of old New York. The place was crowded with bibelots. Pieter Mijer specialized in making designs for batik, a Javanese decorative art which involves waxing those parts of a textile which are to remain blank and then plunging the whole into a tank of dye; only the pattern takes the colour. Batik frocks, scarves and curtains were the rage in 1919.

Edna made no pretence of hiding from me her fancy for Pieter. She called him "exciting", and "clever" and "sweet", and as good as said that it would be foolish to allow such qualities to go to waste until she should be weary of them. More than once when she bade me *au revoir*, she would add airily that she was going on to Pieter's. This was disconcerting, to say the least. But no man friend challenged Edna's moods or acts in those days, unless he were prepared to quarrel with her. I, for one, took her temperament exactly as I found it and preached no sermons.

The friendship with Mijer lasted for several months, perhaps until she sailed for France early in 1921. After that I heard no more about it. Let it stand as an illustration. I shall not comment on hints in memoirs I have read by men who confess they were in love with her. But I freely admit that I was. It was something other than the great love of my life, though worshipful in quality. The fact of having an affair with a genius bewitched me, and I was grateful to her. There came an occasion when she had said she would spend the whole of the evening at my place and then abruptly remembered an earlier appointment. The faint resentment with which the latter was foregone decided me to sue no more, though we remained close friends.

CHAPTER 13 ❧ The *American Parade*

MY NEXT SERIOUS EDITORSHIP CAME FROM A MOST unexpected quarter. The type of magazine for women that Richard Duffy and Robert Whiting had shaped, and that I had carried forward, had aroused more interest in publishing circles than I had supposed. To my surprise, Harper & Brothers sent for me and said they were inclined to experiment with a monthly on cheap paper, in which clever fiction would be the trump card. The policy should be somewhat like that of *Ainslee's*, a little less daring, perhaps, but realistically modern. Did I want to have a try at it as editor? Of course I wanted. The firm was one of the oldest and most dignified in New York. It usually had a major success or two on its spring and autumn lists of books. The periodicals that bore its imprint included the famous *Harper's Monthly*. A branching out along the line suggested would be an innovation that was assured in advance of publicity.

The new magazine was named *Brief Stories*. I started with a good deal of enthusiasm to build it up from scratch, depending at first largely upon talent with which I already had connections. But it was an ill-starred venture, and so I shall not linger over it. The machinery at Harper's was keyed to selling by subscription. This changeling, as I fancy it was regarded by the circulation department, was strictly a newsstand product. *Ainslee's* had been profitable, but it had never commanded a big public. Besides, *Brief Stories* was offering rivalry to *The Smart Set*, more sophisticated, edited by the well-advertised H.L. Mencken and George Jean Nathan, and growing fast. *Brief Stories* lasted for about a year, and then was quietly killed by Harper

& Brothers. It had printed a certain amount of good work, but had made no valuable discoveries as writers. In the history of publishing it was a dud.

I passed on to various editorial jobs of a temporary sort. Then, as a result of social contacts and chance assignments, I got drawn into the bizarre field of motion picture journalism, which had recently bounced to a financial height. I do not intend to dwell on this phase. From one point of view, it was just a lark to me. At other times, I saw it as a perilous deviation from the path of my ambition. But it can scarcely be ignored. Theatrical producers, mostly Jewish and with a large sprinkling of press agents of all races, had started the cinema in New York, calling it an industry out of a vague respect for the art of the stage. Hollywood was comparatively new as the scene of manufacture. A feeling spread that heavy publicity in the east of the country was required to maintain interest, and at the same time the so-called 'fan' magazine caught on as a purveyor of gossip about the players and the general glamour of the business. Public spectacles and parties for insiders had begun before I left *Ainslee's*. These grew more and more lavish every year. A return to New York on the manufacturing end took place when the studio of United Artists was built on Long Island, and it could then be boasted that the activity stretched from coast to coast. Why the 'motion picture industry' should function in a 'studio', instead of a factory, was an anomaly never explained. The appeal, at all events, was real enough. That was the day of the famous pioneers, of Mary Pickford and Douglas Fairbanks, of Charlie Chaplin in comedy, of Rudolph Valentino as every girl's ideal lover, of the Gish sisters, Norma Talmadge, Olga Petrova, Adolphe Menjou, and of many stars who were temporary recruits from the legitimate stage.

Movie parties, as we lightly termed them, were given in honour of some star, or to celebrate the opening of a picture that featured several luminaries. Everyone who could contribute publicity was invited. The do would be held at one of the more fashionable hotels, or at a studio, if a producer were behind it. Souvenir gifts were distributed. Expensive brandies and whiskys, champagne and other wines, made an inexhaustible showing – and that during the worst of the crazy era of US Prohibition. A few small, exclusive, and extravagant affairs occurred in the private homes of the stars themselves.

There was a thrill in appraising these fabulous, well-advertised people, the very tones of whose voices remained unknown unless you met them face-to-face. The silent cinema, remember, still prevailed. You did not demand

Figure 23. Roberts, Antonio Moreno (1887–1967) and admirers. A publicity photograph taken during Roberts's stint working on movie magazines. A star of the silent movies, Moreno played opposite actresses such as Greta Garbo and Clara Bow. MS353.6.7.

much of them on the critical side, but as a matter of fact some were distinctly cerebral. Witness Petrova. In addition to her, I became close friends only with Norma Talmadge, who laid no claim to being a highbrow, but had a quiet charm almost domestic in character. She gave me a book or two inscribed "To Adolphe from Norma", which made them collectors' items to the fans, and which I still have.

I was soon reviewing pictures for general magazines, writing interviews to order for the cinema press, and making plenty of money at it. Inevitably, I found myself taking this or that editorial post until I swear I had no standing except as a caterer to the latest hysterics in entertainment. Strangely enough, I was not lured to Hollywood, which might well have involved me beyond redemption. Nor did I attempt, save casually and unsuccessfully, to invent plots for the movies, or to dream of talking pictures when experiments with the new form started. I did, however, write sensational detective fiction on the side. With interruptions for travel, this wasteful period of my working life lasted for some five years.

In the middle 1920s my discontent inspired what was, for me, the act of a plunger. I resolved that I would be a publisher on my own. A bid for mass circulation was out of the question, since I did not have the capital to promote it. I would issue a quarterly, cloth-bound, like a book, to sell for a dollar a copy. In short, a magazine for the elite, charged with the appeal of the exotic as I had learned it editorially, or thought I had learned it. A sale of five hundred copies would pay expenses and the rest would be profit. That was how the *American Parade* came to be. It proved that I was no businessman. But it contained some good things, which the years have stamped for oblivion. It meant much to me.

The first number was dated January 1926. It ran to 224 pages and contained twenty-nine items, including articles, fiction, poems, full-page drawings and departments. Most of the contributors were moderately well known, a few were youngsters I believed to be talented. In all cases I had persuaded them to gamble on the future of the quarterly, or at least to show good will. Instead of cheques, they received certificates entitling them to payment from profits, if any, that the number earned.

Old Gamaliel Bradford, the New England novelist, led the procession with a short story. It was not a noteworthy story, but of prestige value as coming from his generation. The novices did better, though their best was still below the horizon. Authors of articles came close to stressing the rhythm at which I aimed, as may be judged by such titles as "This Wicked New York" and "The Boston Political Circus". There were poems by my friends George Sterling, Richard Le Gallienne and others, of course. I had written the chief feature myself about Woodrow Wilson and the Mexican Revolution.

That first number of the *American Parade* did not sell rapidly, though it eventually went out of print and showed a small profit. It was well reviewed, which encouraged contributors to gamble with superior unsold material, and even to write specially for me. The second number, dated April, was perhaps the best of the series, both as to contents and in the manner of a printing job. The fiction was particularly good, with original characterization and plot, and the lucidity we regarded as being in the spirit of the 1920s. There was a story of novelette length, called "An Idyll of the Province" by

Orrick Johns and pungent shorts by Eleanor Ramos and Louise Townsend Nicholl. The Prohibition folly was fiercely raked by Ethel Watts Mumford, who denied that women had wanted it and had been chiefly responsible for getting the law passed. Race prejudice was treated to some smooth comments, as in Nunnally Johnson's Southern tale "The Black Menace" and Poultney Bigelow's article "My Friend the Jew".

A falling-off in quality is evident in the third number, no doubt because manuscripts on a royalty basis were becoming scarce. The most arresting contribution was probably "Mencken, the Foe of Beauty", by William Salisbury, and of course I was accused of having published it as a challenge to the famous 'H.L.M.' with whom I was in a sense competing. But I had covered myself by printing an editorial in which I explained why, or how, mine was "a magazine without a policy". "The *American Parade* obviously seeks to celebrate the life and arts of our times," I wrote. "But our approach is not didactic. We have no pet moral theory that would cause us either to suppress certain phases of a subject or idealize others. We are realists, and it is in that sense that we have no policy. Our writers are free to express their views, so long as their personalities are not flagrantly antipathetic to the personality of the magazine. The article on Mencken finds a place because Mr Salisbury has set forth logically and pungently his own opinion of Mencken."

Figure 24. The cover of one of the four issues of *American Parade*, the journal founded and edited by Roberts in 1926.

I made a great effort to get first-rate stuff for the fourth number, maybe realizing that it would be the last, as proved to be the case. Even so, I had to fill space with a one-act play by myself and two articles under pseudonyms, in addition to several items in the departments. I was satisfied for the rest. Eleanor Ramos gave me the finest short story of hers I had read so far, "The Red Waltz". It was about a blind musician who had escaped from Sing Sing and had gone directly to a cabaret, where he was known, and they would let him use the piano before the police came for him.

The star article in that last number of the *American Parade* was by Adolphe de Castro, concerning the life and mysterious death of the Californian satirist Ambrose Bierce. Vastly admired by many of his contemporaries, Bierce seems a rather outmoded figure today. He waged a ceaseless feud with San Francisco newspaper publishers who failed to appreciate him. In his old age, he went off to take part in the Mexican revolution, joining Pancho Villa in the Huerta period, and shortly afterward disappearing.

De Castro revealed, for me, that Villa had had Bierce shot for criticizing him. Other persons affirmed that it had been Bierce's sardonic way of committing suicide. Anyway, the article caused talk. And that was the last of the *American Parade*. I may have shown originality as an editor, but as a businessman I had been an amateur. Collecting my small bag of subscribers had been like shooting at quail with a cannon.

A ragged and on the whole unrewarding spell of working for any publisher who would hire me ensued. I was with Hearst on his *International*, with Macfadden's and Brewster's and other firms that were ready to issue a magazine on any subject that had a momentary vogue. Macfadden's was undoubtedly the most freakish. The old man Bernarr had begun as a health faddist and brought a certain devotion to promoting the monthly *Physical Culture*, which he had started years before. He had recently been branching out in every direction, and with unpredictable financial success. His *True Story* had attained a huge circulation, so he had followed it with other 'confession' periodicals that all earned more money than *Physical Culture*. He had crime story magazines, and even a monthly entitled *Ghost Stories*.

I had billets on several of his ventures, though not, thank God, on *Physical Culture* or the *True Story* type. I have no intention whatsoever of lingering over my editorial sins at that juncture, in defence of which I plead disillusionment. They went so far that, apart from two little collections of verse issued, one (*Pierrot Wounded*) in 1919 and the other (*Pan and Peacocks*) in 1928, the first book that bore my name was not by me at all. I had devised a mystery plot for a friend and contributor to the *Parade*, Pauline Brooks Crawford: I gave her only a synopsis and she had produced a carelessly written novel. A publisher was found for it, and she submitted the manuscript as being by her, with a credit to me. She was told that she had no name in the profession, while I had. Unless the book could appear under my name alone, the publisher would not go ahead with it. I actually agreed to this as a service to her. The title was *The Haunting Hand*.

But I had many non-journalistic activities, many hobbies, and my private life was full of interest. I travelled widely, often staying away from New York so long that I half believed I had abandoned it. There were moods when I wished I had become an art critic, or a naturalist with emphasis on birds, or a breeder of pedigree cats, instead of a writer. Fancies, all of them, pursued with a degree of intensity from which the vital orientation was as yet missing. An element of supreme importance, which had little to do with career, was the influence of women and love. Let us commence with this. It is time that I should speak intimately of my relationship with Eleanor Ramos.

IN MAY 1921, SHORTLY AFTER I left *Ainslee's*, I was invited by Louise Rice, a former contributor, to a luncheon for people of the calling. I have forgotten the restaurant's name; it was a French *table d'hôte* far downtown. I greeted a number of old friends, and then found myself being introduced to a tall girl. I noted that her eyes were grey-green and that she had the most virile red hair I had ever seen. The hair luxuriated under her hat and looped down on either side as if it could not be controlled. The nose was slightly aquiline, the cheekbones strong, mouth and chin beautiful. Her name reached me as Mrs Eleanor Ramos, but she corrected this almost carelessly, in a soaring voice, to Miss. It was her way of telling that she and her husband were separated.

I do not recall much of what was said at that luncheon. It appeared that the girl was writing, but had not yet had anything accepted. She also wanted to join the staff of some magazine, for the sake of experience and the salary. Louise Rice knew of a prospect with a cheap fiction monthly for women. Perhaps literary advice from me would be helpful. It was odd, I mused with one part of my mind, that Eleanor Ramos should be trying to get into the desk end of 'the game', as we called it, just as I had stepped aside. With the other part, I dwelt upon her charm, making small talk the while.

As it turned out, she was promised the assistant editorial post. There remained the chance to act as critic of her work. I had seen her once more on the street, with Louise, in passing, and I learned a few things about her. She lived in Brooklyn, was an Irish American, born Haviland, and had married a Spaniard very young. There was one small daughter before he returned to Europe. She assured me, her tone high-pitched and gay, that she would send a manuscript, but it had not come. Her personality was unique, and the memory of it grew on me from day to day. Urged on by an intuition that would not be stilled, I telephoned her and asked her to have dinner with me. She accepted for the next evening, 4 June. We were to meet at a Greenwich Village restaurant run by a Mrs Pickett.

I heard her step on the bare boards of the corridor leading from the street before I opened the door for her. I had felt sure it was hers: a firm step with a hurrying run and lift to it, the heels rapping evenly. I got a vivid impression of her wide, smiling mouth, with teeth like rows of kernels on an ear of corn, of her imperious red hair looped on either side of her face, below her hat. Actually, we did not exchange a greeting in words, but we stared intently at each other.

Seated at a little corner table, we made up for it by chatting with vivacity. She had brought a rather wordy script in an old briefcase, but she would not let me look at it. "Not now," she pleaded. "It's part of a novel, which you'll probably hate as much as I do." I did not press her. We talked instead about our interests, searching for the tastes we shared, about ourselves in short. She loved poetry and cats as much as I did. By that strange contradiction, however, that had occurred already between women and myself, she clearly had a passion for music and I had not. She brushed the difference aside. Experiences I had had in France beguiled her, though she was lukewarm to anything connected with the war. Louise Rice must have described me to her as a ladies' man, for Eleanor lightly called me one in querying me about my motion picture friends. I did not reject the term. I parried, saying that of course I valued the companionship of women. Just flirting was juvenile. Only being in love mattered.

"What is being in love?" she asked.

I can quote my reply almost word for word, having used the ideas in it before.

"Being in love is being absorbed in the other person," I said, "not necessarily for a lifetime or any set period, but for as long as the mutual attraction lasts. There should be no heavy tragedy in love, no jealousy and no cruelty. The one who loves longest should be ashamed to put a blot upon the beauty that has been by torturing the other."

"You see it in an absolutely perfect way," she answered, her eyes impenetrable.

I was still living with my wife, but for peace had rented a studio room at 8 East Fifteenth Street, where I kept most of my books and did my writing. It was a comfortable spot, in a building with no elevator, but only two storeys up. I had furnished it myself, featuring curios that I had collected on my travels. Sharing it was Grisette, my current treasure among cats, a blue-grey Angora with golden eyes, given to me by Olga Petrova.

A silence had fallen between Eleanor and myself. Suddenly I reached into my breast pocket and drew out a portfolio. "Oh!" I said. "This may interest you. The most demanding beauty of them all has given me her photograph. Want to see it?"

Eleanor took the snapshot from me coolly, and the next moment I was rewarded by a cry of delight. "What a lovely, lovely cat!" she exclaimed. I sketched Grisette's pedigree and then drifted from that to a few words about the studio room, where she waited. "I'd like you to see herself," I said. "May I take you there, after dinner?" Eleanor flashed an unhesitating smile at me. "That would be nice," she answered. "I want so much to stroke her."

We walked through a tangle of Greenwich Village streets, crossed Washington Square and turned up Fifth Avenue, my hand tightening on her arm. At the house, she whispered in a little dry voice, "You had better go first." I remember acutely how I fumbled as I unlocked the door and showed her into the studio. I pressed the button of an electric light, and a little naively, nervously, I called at once for Grisette. The cat did not come, because a stranger was there, but settled herself contentedly when I picked her up and crossed the room to show her to Eleanor.

Grisette's lavender forepaws hung guilelessly below her cloudy ruff. She moved her head responsively as the girl caressed her with ecstatic touches. "She's making friends more easily than with most people," I said, pleased. But I restored the now gently purring beauty to the cushion where she had been sleeping. I swung ardently back to Eleanor. The next moment we were in each other's arms, and nothing else mattered.

A few days later, she wrote that she believed "deeply and superstitiously in our good luck with each other", and diverged to add: "Last night I dreamed of Grisette. I thought she had a monocle in her eye. Perhaps she is our mascotte. . . . I would like so much to know if you truly like me – if you like me

Figure 25. Eleanor Ramos, probably in 1922, photographed by William Vander Weyde. MS353.6.8.

extremely. Some very little things make me almost certain that you do. I wonder if you believe that I love you. It is a thing that one never can be sure about, of course. That is the danger of loving too much: one begins to want to be sure, and then the joy goes away from the whole thing. So with you I will not think of the question, and we will love each other as long as possible and then be good friends. It would be charming if the thing turned out so that we were always good friends. I think we shall have a happy summer together, don't you. . . . I have the idea that we shall affect each other's lives in some subtle way."

I kept every line that Eleanor ever wrote me. Not one of my letters to her has been preserved, so far as I know. I would wish to offer them all side by side with hers for the sake of truth, though I was by no means her equal in finding the passionate word. The thought that some critic may condemn me for printing her letters, on the grounds that I regard them as a tribute to myself leaves me contemptuously indifferent. They are a tribute to her, to her capacity for emotion and her gift for expressing it. I love Eleanor. I loved her more and more, and I still love her now that I am an old man. But it was a calamitous insincere pose on my part to have said that first evening that love should be kept pleasant and kind, no matter what. Worse, I sought to prove that heresy sound. Men often pay too much honour to an unworthy love. I committed an uncommon error; I treated the birth of a great love as if it were a light one.

Toward the end of that July, a new note appeared in her letters. Her heart pained her, and she was forced to rest. At the same time she grew ambitious about her writing, which I had praised, and developed an ironical mood: "I am afraid that I am getting to like you a degree too much. How can one avoid a thing like that? Being a scientist in love, you may know. . . . The way I felt last evening has been the cause of all the silly things I have done in my life.... All the time I was with you, I wanted to be perfectly horrid, but with you, somehow, it wasn't possible. And so you have triumphed over the mood."

Not long after, I received a note that shocked me: "My poor little jazz brother is dead. He was operated on too late for intestinal obstruction. We feel dreadful, because we did not know how he suffered." I had not met any member of her family as yet, and she had barely mentioned this young brother. The way she took the tragedy was proud and strong. I wrote, distressed for her, and she answered: "Death at seventeen is somehow beautiful. So many mourning young creatures, and my brother so beautiful and arrogant-looking. My mother is sick and my sister continuously crying. But I am secretly exulting that he is free from their defective love."

A day or two after the funeral she came to see me. She had had her wonderful hair cut, bobbed as the term was, and although I was startled, even saddened, I had to admit that the new glamour justified itself. She now had the appearance of a tall Florentine page, such as the Renaissance masters would have painted. I held her to me in a timorous sort of way, thinking of her as in mourning for her brother. She embraced me with undisguised emotion, speaking in a tone I found memorable: "Our love is a thing of this life and this world. The dead have no part of it."

The manuscript which Eleanor had left with me would have made a long novel if carried out as planned. There was no artistic reason why it should not be, for her style was singularly lucid. But it is very difficult for a new writer to get recognition for a novel. One of Eleanor's currents of interest could be followed out for its own sake, and I advised her to make a novelette out of it under the title of *The Exotic*. She had been working on this, and we discussed it further. The logical place to which it could be submitted was the Mencken and Nathan *Smart Set*.

The point that Eleanor should have had a brilliant career in authorship can be made quickly. She got part of *The Exotic* into shape as a novelette without any help from me. It was rejected by Mencken, but on her making changes that he suggested, it was bought. She wrote several stories that were well received by the co-editors of *The Smart Set*. She and I tried our hand at doing one together and were successful.

Letters passed between us on personal subjects for the rest of 1921. She wrote me twenty-nine from 5 June to Christmas Day, with no really false note struck in any of them. But during the next two years, and forever thereafter, the total was only twenty – some of them very short. The year 1922 started gently enough, no more than that; for some intuition of harm had lodged in her subconscious. On 7 February, she complained, "Have been furiously unhappy today, but am taking it out in writing; have reached page 200." Her reference was to the unpublished part of *The Exotic*, which she was enlarging and recasting in novel form.

Over a month later, she scribbled from my place on East Fifteenth Street, to which I had given her a key: "I have been working here since four o'clock. I had an uncontrollable desire to do some work on my novel, and since the desire was a virtuous one I sneaked out of the office and came down here. Could work until midnight, the way I feel now, but suppose you will be coming here to do the same thing." Apart from little notes, there was nothing more in 1922. Nothing! I cannot account for that. What I do know is that my own psychic condition was deteriorating. I was unfaithful to her a couple of times without any rational excuse. I had held back from getting her involved in my motion picture acquaintances and their parties. Her suspicions were aroused, no doubt, in the wrong direction. A longing to see Paris again, which grew in me as a mania, proved still more disastrous.

I wanted Eleanor to make the trip with me, but was not in a financial position at the moment to assume all of the responsibilities. She was doing well at her job as assistant editor of the fiction magazine for women, and she said she hated to lose it. I advised her to hang on, while she completed the novel, and then join me. The months dragged on in desperate uncertainty. She finally agreed with me, or said she did. Let the rest be told in a series of communications I got from her in Paris. She wrote the following under date of 25 February 1923: "I've been so very unhappy since you left. I went right home from the boat. . . . Never mind my pessimism, dear; I'll surely come. I didn't think I would be so awfully unhappy so soon. I did think I would miss you as the days went by, but couldn't imagine this feeling of utter desolation at the bare thought that it was impossible to hear your voice, see you, for months." And on 5 March: "Dear, I'm awfully tired and unhappy. Haven't made a plan lately. Things will just have to take their course. . . . Why must I always love men who are quite impossible in some essential point? You are even more impossible about some things than the Spanish one. Well, as far as I am concerned, you will lose me as surely as he."

On receiving this letter, I should have gone straight back to New York. I was insane not to do so. It was a last chance, and at that I might have been too late. Her next letter, dated 2 April, showed that the chance had worn thin indeed, though I did not fully realize it:

Figure 26. Roberts in 1922, photographed by William Vander Weyde. MS353.6.1.

> I should have written you long ago, but I hated to do it. Now I'm taking my courage in my hands; besides, I'm not quite as sore as I was before. I went to some of the balls they've been giving lately, with R's friend, Ted Bourland. . . . Ted is a very nice boy, plays the piano wonderfully and draws very interestingly; good family and all that sort of thing. I thought he'd be a good person to play around with moderately. At the Newspaper Women's Ball, we met a party including G—— H——, who tried desperately to vamp Ted. . . . He thought she was an awful cow, to quote his words, and rather laughed at her eye-rolling technique. Consequently, she became rather nasty to me and spilled the sweet news that you had been infatuated with her, taken her to dinner several times; that she could have taken you away from me, had she succumbed to your passion for her, etc., etc. She seemed to be awfully proud of this fact.
>
> Well, it was your affair – but for heaven's sake why didn't you finish the job and not give her the chance to be so conceited and scornful? It was sweet the way Ted disposed of her, and she tried very hard with him. You know, I believe what she said, because I remember the way you once looked at her as she came down the stairs. Well, I just hate this whole thing, and certainly shan't go to Paris. I thought you were a little harder than that. And she is so vulgar and conceited, and looks so darned willing to go to bed with a man at a moment's notice. I'm just disgusted. I laughed the matter off gaily and said.
>
> "Oh, I do think you make an impression on him. He's very fond of women, G——."
>
> I suppose you think I'm hard. Well, why not? One always suffers for not being so. You should have made me come with you to Paris. Now I'll probably marry this Ted, give up my job, or do something equally insane. After all, I want only love; a firm, hard love. . . . Dearest, I don't hate you. I can't.

I had barely absorbed this when a notice dated 19 April – her birthday incidentally – called me to the office of the Guaranty Trust Company to be given a cablegram. It read: "IMPOSSIBLE – MARRIED GO-GETTER – ELEANOR". Finally, on 17 May, Eleanor had this to say to me, in a letter from which whole paragraphs had been erased, blotted out with ink:

> I understand you so imperfectly that it is difficult to guess your mood over this parting of our ways. And yet I'm sure you'd like to hear from me, once in a while. You have been so sweet to me that I want to do just as you like about it. With my usual inferiority sense, I can't imagine that you have been so awfully cut up. If you are truly the cynic you make yourself out to be, you aren't. But then, I think grave doubts may be held against your cynicism! Away from you, my dear, I have a clearer idea of your true character; you are a creature of conflict, of contradictions; but, over all, you are a true idealist. Is that a horrid accusation, I wonder? I like it, but don't think you do. I only don't like that you don't understand yourself. . . .
>
> As a matter of fact, it wasn't the G—— thing that decided the question. I was just getting tired; I think I'll always get tired of everyone. . . . Probably my work will suffer; but after I'm thirty I'll get serious.

To my honest indignation, Eleanor's novel was rejected by the publishers, though the margin was narrow in some cases. Even Mencken could not tip the balance for her. I do not know what she did with the manuscript. Destroyed it, I fear, as she had threatened at least once that she would. She turned her fine talent to the writing of stories for the cheap women's magazines. Her life with her husband became disordered. He drank a great deal, and I have reason to think that they were soon unhappy together.

When I returned to New York, however, in 1925, I got her collaboration on my plan for founding the *American Parade*. She even showed a certain enthusiasm for that gamble with fate. If it had been a success, it might well have had the effect of re-arousing her literary ambition. I had hoped for much in connection with her. All remained sterile. The last letter I ever received from her, dated toward the end of May 1927, fits but remotely into the pattern of this chapter. It was about the breeding of long-haired cats.

CHAPTER 14 ⟩ The Lure of Travel

THE WRETCHED EARLY MONTHS OF 1923 HAVING BEEN lived through, somehow, I looked for forgetfulness in travel. I had proposed to write a book, a novel. It moved slowly, and the first draft I wrung out of my inner consciousness did not prove satisfactory. There was small reason why it should, for my restlessness caused me to do more travelling than writing. I have always found travel to be a lure for its own sake and an anodyne in days of trouble.

On that and succeeding voyages, I saw a good deal of western Europe. I shall not be fettered by chronology, but shall give a selection of memories as they come back to me. A second trip to London was inevitable in 1923, under conditions superior to those that had prevailed during the war. I wanted to meet editors, for one thing, and to talk to literary agents. So I went and must have transacted a certain amount of business, which I have wholly forgotten. I spent hours in the British Museum, the National Portrait Gallery and the Zoological Gardens in Regent's Park. I recall nothing about everyday events. One experience, however, is clearly mirrored, and why it should have been that one instead of another, who can tell!

I started out on a Sunday afternoon to identify some houses where the poet Algernon Charles Swinburne had lived. The first was number 7 Chester Street, his supposed birthplace. The house, which was in good repair after more than a hundred years, was somewhat Italianesque with its narrow iron balconies. The reality of its connection with the poet impressed me only vaguely, a feeling which extended to the whole block. Doubtless I was influenced by my knowledge that Swinburne had been born in Chester

Street by accident, his mother having been on a flying visit to London from the Isle of Wight.

After wandering here and there on my pilgrimage, I took a bus to Putney where I easily found The Pines, number 2 Putney Hill, the house where Swinburne spent his last thirty years in semi-seclusion and where he died on 10 April 1909. It was tenanted, but seemingly closed for the day. I had to content myself with peering through the ivy-covered gate at a house of the suburban villa type, and with exploring a side street where a wall masked the back garden upon which Swinburne's study windows opened. I stole leaves from the ivy and such of the shrubbery as I could reach. I loitered about the place, both front and rear, until I must have appeared a suspicious character plotting some more serious mischief.

The reason for my loitering was a vivid and swiftly augmenting sense of the contact which this house gave me with Swinburne. I felt his presence, and it was scarcely that of a shade. A memorial plaque in blue-and-white enamel told that he and Theodore Watts-Dunton, the guardian of his old age, had both been gone for a quarter of a century. But their day had become like yesterday to me. I cared little about Watts-Dunton. It was Swinburne I could almost see looking out of this window and then that one, or standing in the porch at the top of the short flight of steps.

"It will not be well to stretch this mood much further," I said to myself. "The danger is, that it will give way to the obvious present and grow ridiculous. I shall walk to Putney Heath, as Swinburne used to do."

Edmund Gosse, T. Earle Welby, Coulson Kernahan and others have written in their accounts of the poet that it was his habit to leave The Pines at a rather late hour every morning, ascend Putney Hill until he came to the Heath, strike across the latter, and come circling back, solitary, to his lunch at the sober Watts-Dunton board. He who in his youth had been a famous bibber, permitted himself but one break in the regime. There was a pub he passed on the way, and he always stopped there, going or coming, for a single drink, some say of beer and some of Burgundy.

As I mounted the steep road called Putney Hill, I swear I was acutely conscious not of being accompanied by Swinburne, but of watching him with an inner eye as he followed the same route long ago. I perceived the frail body and sloping shoulders, the large head, the odd, hurrying gait. He was not in front of me. Rather, he was treading exactly where I trod.

The mental picture of him, however, was that of a man seen from behind.

At the entrance to the Heath, I found the public house and immediately recognized it. It was a low, detached building with a bar and a side room to the right for tables. A broad road ran past it, cutting the Heath in two. To the left was an expanse of rolling common. I began to speculate. "When Swinburne left the pub," I thought, "he would not have taken the road, because the traffic would have annoyed him. He certainly would have chosen the common, where there are footpaths and an occasional bench on which to rest."

I, too, wandered across the common, and presently my attention was quite definitely seized by a gnarled old tree under which a bench stood. No one could have persuaded me that Swinburne had not sat there often. I was sure of it. I sank down onto the bench. The trunk of the tree behind me was spattered with the carved initials of vain, sentimental, and idle mortals. The back of the bench was similarly decorated. The idea forced itself upon me that some memento of Swinburne would be found among these records. I rejected the preposterous thought. He would not have behaved like a schoolboy or a city clerk on an outing. From one point of view he was too dignified, and from another too humourless, to add his initials to such an array in a public place. I said this to myself with a great deal of positiveness.

My adventure so far had been of dubious psychic significance, and I should hesitate to write about it were it not for the extraordinary thing that now happened. An argument developed in my mind, which I clearly remember and which was phrased in the first person. It ran: "I would not, of course, have carved the tree or the back of the bench. Premeditation would have entered into that. But sitting here, bored, as I often was, I scratched with my penknife upon the seat between my parted legs. It was done half-consciously."

As these soundless words shaped themselves, I again had the illusion of being in the precise spot that Swinburne had once occupied. The very posing of my body seemed to be identical. My own legs were parted. I looked down and saw, cut into the wood of the bench, the initials "A.C.S.". The first two letters were fairly deeply graven. The double curve of the S had offered difficulties. The line wavered and was thin in spots, but it was an indubitable S. If you care to argue that some other person with those initials may have been responsible, you are at liberty to do so. In the circumstances, I cannot question that they were carved by Algernon Charles Swinburne.

I took a rubbing of my discovery and returned at twilight to the north bank of the Thames. My feeling about the afternoon's events was void of credulity. I was not even astonished, really, but baffled by the enigma which poses itself in every experience of the kind. Had I been in communication with the disembodied ego of Swinburne? Or had I, by going with a receptive attitude to the house where he had lived longest and latest, thrown my mind open to a flood of telepathic suggestions from survivors who had known him in the flesh? There was no answer.

WHILE WORKING TO ESTABLISH THE *American Parade*, which was a quarterly, I had leisure enough to indulge a desire to know better the countries of the Caribbean region and the cities of the United States, particularly those of the South. The War of Secession in the 1860s had long been a special study of mine. I soon had visited every state of the old Confederacy. I went several times by train or bus to Richmond, Charleston and other centres of outstanding interest. The expanding of my travel longings backward to take in Caribbean countries was natural enough. I had left Jamaica for New York at eighteen without having seen any of the adjacent islands. There had been only one trip home, a hurried affair for the purpose of helping to settle a small legacy to the family.

Through Naboth Hedin, who had been my chief in Paris at the time war broke out, I met the American manager of the Swedish Line. The latter was organizing winter cruises to all parts of the world, which are still being run successfully. He said that he had a cruise director and lecturer aboard each ship, but that he thought it a good bet to try out an author from the region as an extra on the *Kungsholm,* which was about to leave on a long tour of the West Indies. I was invited to be that man. A winter cruise can be little more than a social riot, with emphasis on drinking and dancing, given variety by conducted trips ashore. That was the general plan of entertainment for the company of the several hundred on the *Kungsholm*. But for the voyager like myself who really wanted to broaden his knowledge of the region there were endless opportunities. The cruise director, Eugene C. Van Wyk, a South African, was a genial and observant mixer who gave me many leads regarding who and what to see, and who has remained my close friend to this day. We visited Barbados first, if I remember correctly, then Trinidad, Venezuela, Curaçao, Panama, Jamaica, Haiti, and one or two islands in the Leewards and Bahamas.

Havana was not on that schedule, but it did not matter, for I had already adopted the city as the place to go whenever I felt bored. Two things drew me toward Havana before I landed there and judged for myself. One was that it obviously was the sophisticated capital of the Caribbean; the second, repeated to the point of monotony, that visually and by the freedom of its customs, it was the Paris of America. I landed in 1928 and perceived that the claim had some justice, at least in part. A resemblance to Paris did exist. The evidence was both physical and temperamental. Happily – for individuality is always more pleasing than imitation – the ancient streets and houses of Havana were pure Creole in style. They owed their charm to wrought iron balconies, massive carved doors and the tiled patios glimpsed beyond the doorways. But wherever the city had been improved for reasons of decoration, you got an effect of the spaciousness of Parisian avenues and a wealth of monuments characteristic of *la ville lumière*. It is somewhat astonishing to recall now that the open-air cafés, which struck a more definite note, did not get started until two summers later. I liked Havana so much that it became a habit to go there. I have been in and out of Cuba eighteen times, once for almost two months and on some other occasions for mere weekend dashes from Florida.

The island appealed to my temperament for reasons that it is hard to define exactly. I was interested also by what appeared to me the obvious fact that here was the representative Caribbean country, the one which the Dominican Republic and Puerto Rico took as a model without perhaps realizing it, the one to which English Jamaica will conform more and more by the force of destiny. Havana is the natural capital of the Caribbean, bearing some exterior resemblance to Barcelona, a little to Seville, none at all to Madrid. The pompous *hispanidad* of Mexico City and Lima was not attempted here. This is a tropical seaport, pungent with the aromas of tobacco, sugar and rum, its tempo set long ago by African slave labour. But Havana avoided the shabbiness of the English insular towns, the pioneer roughness of the North American. It built for beauty rather than utilitarianism, and indulged in luxury, in spaciousness, in decoration. A character was achieved with which the West Indian of any ancestry can feel sympathetic.

I found the cult of national liberty nurtured with ardour. Monuments to the heroes were tremendous for a small country, including the equestrian statues of Generals Máximo Gómez and Antonio Maceo, with supporting groups. Martí was portrayed as the civilian, his austere features repeated in marble busts at many turns. Certain streets were monuments in themselves, notably the Prado, which from the waterfront to the Parque Central is a raised promenade of mottled, reddish marble shadowed thickly with laurels and flanked by driveways.

Rumba dancing and the cockfight, gambling, and that fastest of games, *jai-alai*: these were omnipresent. Cubans, however, had never cared for the bullring, which they associated with the arrogance and cruelty of Spain. They were ebullient in their liking for western things. Better than any other Latins of the hemisphere, it seemed to me, they got along with North Americans. It was natural therefore that I should come to feel strongly about doing a book with a Cuban historical background.

I soon concluded that Havana was less a new Paris in appearance than a cross between Seville and Barcelona, with marked borrowings from Montparnasse. The lower Prado, from the harbour to the Parque Central, had originally been very like Las Ramblas, of Barcelona. It had been reconstructed opulently and had become a tree-shaded raised walk of gleaming, many-coloured marble slabs, with its low walls guarded by bronze lions. The new open-air cafés flourished on the upper Prado, fronting the Capitol and skirting the Plaza de la Fraternidad. Morro Castle on its high bluff beyond the bay was visible from several angles.

It was manifest that the public relations and the economic interests of Cuba were bound up closely with the United States. The island indeed could properly be considered an unofficial protectorate. How could it have been otherwise? Washington had intervened in 1898 against Spain and turned the struggling War of Independence, which José Martí had launched, into a clear-cut victory. The question in that age of blatant imperialism had simply been whether the North Americans would not regard Cuba as having been automatically annexed. That they should gradually set up a free republic was held to be a rare triumph of democracy. The retention of a naval base at Guantánamo was not in the least resented.

Cubans on the capitalist and middle-class levels had accepted the system with enthusiasm. The whole community benefited, on the surface anyway, from the general prosperity that resulted. It was known that most politi-

Figure 27. Roberts in Havana with Conrado Massaguer to his left, Paul Milton to his right. MS353.6.7.

cians, including some of the presidents, had been crooked financially, but people brushed that aside as an unescapable evil in politics. Years and years were to pass before a serious reaction took place. The citizens of Havana when I first met them were frankly pro-American, while nurturing a form of escapism by developing manners that were a mixture of those of Paris and any typical Hispanic capital.

I made numerous friends among writers and artists at the various rendezvous of the sidewalks. One was pretty sure to see there such interesting figures as Dr Ramón Grau, later president of the Republic; Conrado W. Massaguer, the brilliant caricaturist whom the Machado regime was to exile to New York, after his success in publishing three magazines of his own;

the painter Armando Maribona, a lightning-fast satirist with his pencil and a poet in his conversation; Abela, the merciless cartoonist of the *Diario de la Marina*, with his suave, disarming smile; Antonio Gattorno and López Méndez, painters; and a clever radical journalist who, perhaps prophetically, always insisted on signing his full name of José Antonio Fernández de Castro. I was most intimate among these with Massaguer and Maribona. Massaguer was then publishing a magazine of his own, called *Social*, to which I contributed. My work began to be discussed, and by the time I had made half a dozen trips I was somewhat of an insider.

A PASSION FOR THE SPANISH DANCE was one of the artistic rewards which I owed to travel. That type of dancing had no popular hold in Jamaica. Consequently I saw it first as a young man in New York and San Francisco, mostly as acts by second-rate performers in vaudeville theatres. The brilliant, regular tempo, the overtones vital and clear, appealed strongly to me. I sensed a true art form, and I hunted for finer and finer manifestations of it. I enjoyed Carmencita at Hammerstein's Victoria, New York. She had a certain fame, and for a long period she was my idea of what a female Spanish dancer should be. But no devoted following, even for her popularized version, existed among North Americans. I was slow in catching on to the fact that I would have done better at the entertainments given by Cuban and Mexican exiles. In Mexico itself I did see some creditable acts at the Cafe Gambrinus, Guaymas. In the winter of 1912–13 I was charmed by the Spanish musical show, *La Tierra de la Alegría*. The scope broadened for me in France, up till the time when World War I sent performers in every category flitting home.

One evening during my second Parisian residence, in 1923, I dropped into a variety house on the Grands Boulevards, attracted by the top billing of La Argentinita and her company. The name was unfamiliar, but a few minutes after the curtain rose I knew that I was watching a supreme artist. Apart from the note of genius reflected by face and figure to the point of physical beauty being secondary, the difference from Carmencita and others lay in the rendering of regional and gypsy measures without a trace of the false flourishes which outsiders expect in a Spanish dance. Here were gestures still more vigorous, but sparing and classical in their verity. This woman opened a *flamenco* number with the terrible long cry, the controlled expression of a demoniacal melancholy.

I was so fascinated by La Argentinita that I followed her from theatre to theatre in Paris for four weeks. After the Grands Boulevards, she played half-weeks. I saw her, therefore, seven times. She repeated the same bill, and I did not weary of it: an Aragonese *jota*, a dance from the Spanish suite by Granados, a *zapateado* evoked by the bullfight; also several *fandanguillos* or gypsy dances, including that tuneful one, my favourite, poignant with Moorish sadness, the *fandanguillo de Almería*.

The botanical gardens of Paris, which includes a large zoo, is called the Jardin des Plantes. While strolling there, I had noticed the sounds of hammer and chisel ringing loudly, and audible at an extraordinary distance. I traced this to a short, burly fellow who looked like an artisan, stationed in front of the cages housing the great cats. He was working on a block of diorite, the hardest of all stones, jet black, and was carving a panther directly from life. I learned that he was the Spanish sculptor Mateo Hernández, who specialized in animals. His method was something at which to marvel, for he was no impressionist. He reproduced his model with telling realism, and I doubt if any other sculptor has achieved this in diorite without first moulding his subject in clay.

After I had watched Hernández more than once, I felt free to sit beside him at the Café de la Rotonde and compliment him on his technique. His answers were those of a man who found truth with his hands and had no theories about it. Since our topic was art and he was a Spaniard, I alluded naturally enough to La Argentinita and sang her praises. His rough, dark face lighted up in a flash.

"What!" he exclaimed. "You, a North American, really appreciate her! And you come with a fresh view. Tell me the qualities you chiefly admire."

I replied to the best of my critical ability, which was not expert at the time. But it gratified Hernández. This man who dismissed his own work awkwardly became eloquent about the meaning of La Argentinita's art. He said that she was the soul of her country. He quoted Jacinto Benavente, the celebrated playwright, who had pronounced: "To think that many great men, in their crazy vanity, should believe that they signify more to Spain than does La Argentinita!"

It appeared that she was born in Buenos Aires, of Spanish parents called López. Her given name was Encarnación. She had been taken to Seville at the age of four, had immediately been set to practise the dance and had made her first professional appearance at twelve. In three years she had been acknowledged as a star.

"You see, it was God-given – the talent and the rage to study as God intended," Hernández said. "You certainly must want to meet her and write her story. It can be arranged."

"You are able to do that?" I was joyful, yet a little taken aback at the sudden opportunity.

"Of course. I pay tribute to her whenever she comes to Paris, and she allows me to introduce others in the arts. How lucky that you spoke to me today. This is her last week here."

Hernández took me the next afternoon to an old-fashioned hotel on the Boulevard des Italiens. Its fittings had a lush elegance, faded now. It probably never had been patronized by society, but by stage people and foreigners. One could imagine Alexandre Dumas the younger climbing its stairs with camellias for his latest star, the Goncourt brothers taking notes there for their journal. Furniture and *objets d'art* overcrowded the rooms, and against this background the Spanish dancer looked inevitable, seated on a divan beside a balcony facing the boulevard. She was about twenty-five.

I found La Argentinita a more seductive woman off the stage than on it, doubtless because she was now according a personal response. Her complexion was of an even golden-brown; her hair black, and her eyes almost so. Her mouth was full and soft, but a slightly aquiline nose gave hauteur to her face. The vibrancy of her movements contrasted oddly with her steady gaze. I looked back hard as we talked, showing my admiration yet bridling my words.

This was in the tradition. A Spanish dancer of the first order does not recognize the members of the audience as individuals, never communicates across the footlights save as an artist. She does expect to be worshipped as a female sublimated by her art. Anything less would be an affront to her primitive ego. A man who reaches her presence is assumed to be motivated in part by sex, since any man who loves the dance must regard it as tremendous good fortune if he can arouse the interest of a star. Woe betide the admirer, however, who ventures beyond homage at the beginning. It is her privilege to give a sign, if she chooses, a thing that would scarcely occur once in a hundred times.

I asked La Argentinita if her work was understood as well in America as in Europe. She replied that probably it was not, as yet, because those were young countries that ran after new and simple ideas, but there was enough emulation among the girls – yes, and the boys, too – to make her feel that the coming generation would repossess the true dance forms. Like all Latins, she meant by America the whole hemisphere, with an implied claim that the Spanish part of it was the one that mattered most. I pressed a distinction, and enquired whether the United States was appreciative.

"I have not been there," she said. "One thing is certain. There will never be great performers of the Spanish dance among North Americans."

"Why not?"

She gave me an answer that I have always remembered: the ruthless passion in her eyes, as well as her words. "Because the parents hold that a child must have a happy childhood, and get some book learning first. We say that a dance student begins almost as soon as she can walk. She must live the life of a slave."

"For how long?"

"Till she is an artist. And, even then – with me, if there has been time for books, or love, or no matter what else, it has been extra time."

The interview amounted to little more than that, for exotic retainers with demands upon her attention flitted in and out of the room. A stout maid clothed in black cotton to her heels came and whispered hoarsely in her ear, reminding her of an appointment with the hairdresser. Two or three Spaniards, who looked like bullfighters, thin-faced, wearing an inch of side-whiskers, bowed from the doorway one after the other and lingered briefly, rolling cigarettes. A messenger delivered a great bunch of red roses.

Hernández and I said *au revoir* and went back to the Café de la Rotonde. I spoke enthusiastically to him of the dancer, but I was not prepared for the terms of the report which he at once made to some sculptor friends of his at the café. "I have just taken Monsieur Roberts to meet La Argentinita, and he was stricken with emotion (*il était tout émotionné*)," Hernández cried in his thick French. It turned out that I did not see her again, or hear directly about her, for the next seven years.

AS ONE OF MY LAST jobs in the periodical game, I had become a feature editor of the Macfadden Publications, with the monthly *Dance Magazine* as my special charge. Editing the latter was regarded by my employers as a sort of side-issue for a hobbyist. I was given an assistant who attended to the details of make-up, comprising as it did a lavish use of pictures. He was Paul R. Milton, a son of the eminent theatrical director Robert Milton.

It chanced that young Milton had lived in Spain and was as much of a zealot for the Spanish dance as I was. He had seen La Argentinita and was impassioned over her. For some years there had been another performer, older and well known in the United States, who appeared under the stage name of La Argentina because she, too, had been born in that South American republic. She was grounded in the Hispanic art, but had pretentious ideas about raising it above the folk level. Admirable in her way, she seemed to both Milton and me to have sacrificed a certain colour and soundness by abandoning tradition for a self-devised medium. We much preferred La Argentinita, who, as I say, had come after her in point of time and indicated this by using the diminutive form of the name – 'the little one from Argentina', so to speak. The North American public did not appreciate the distinction.

In 1930 a New York producer called Lew Leslie announced that he had engaged La Argentinita for his *International Revue*, a long hodge-podge of a show that included novelties of a varied and indiscriminate sort. It badly needed cutting, and on the opening night it dragged itself out to all hours. Spotted, without judgement, as a music-hall turn, the great Spanish dancer did not make her appearance until half-past eleven, and the result was a fiasco. The bored audience had already started to go home. It was not being deliberately rude; but a fair number of New York first-nighters live in the suburbs, and they simply had to catch their trains. A few toughs in the second balcony took a false cue from this action and hooted. La Argentinita conducted herself with restraint. She did not walk off the stage, but rendered her two numbers a little coldly. The next day the newspaper critics were almost unanimous in reporting that she had been a flop, and in convicting themselves of total ignorance of the art she represented. La Argentinita at once withdrew from the cast of the *International Revue*.

Paul Milton and I were furious. I am happy to recall that we lost no time in scheming romantically that we would do our personal best to induce some promoter to star her in a concert. We went to see her feverish Spanish manager, whose name I have forgotten, and found that the idea was shared by a number of other people. We were placed on an informal committee pledged to work for La Argentinita's fame in New York, and we played a considerable part in the developments that ensued.

Fortunately, the next issue of the *Dance Magazine* was just about to go to press. I wrote an article for it, in which I jibed at the critics with studied sarcasm. I picked out for scorn their most nonsensical comments, as, for instance, the remark by Robert Garland of the *Telegram* that "the idol of Spain is a middle-aged female who puts her best foot forward only to be laughed at", and the analysis by Burns Mantle of the *Daily News*, of the charm of Spanish dancing: "A little stamping from old Grenada, perhaps, or it may be Andalusia . . . the tattoo of the heels, the slight frown indicating temperament, or passion, or something." My article 'carried a bite' as we used to say, and its prompt appearance was effective.

Meanwhile, I had Milton keep in touch with the manager. One day the latter asked me to call, and the three of us had a curious talk. The Spaniard, a grave young fellow, innocent of North American reactions, announced calmly: "La Argentinita has not yet made up her mind about this concert. I tell her that such a tribute by admirers is flattering to her dignity. She agrees to that, but says her luck has been bad here and wonders whether it should be tempted. She has cabled Mejías. His opinion will decide her."

"Mejías!" I repeated, baffled for the moment.

"Yes, the famous *matador*. She is in love with him."

The name registered then. Mejías was the current hero among Spanish bullfighters. He was not precisely literate, and no doubt was a firm believer in luck. "Oh, yes!" I answered diplomatically. "He will approve without fail."

"You get that impression! Good, good!" the other said. "Now I shall take you in to speak with her. I warned you in case you might have felt like crossing her about Mejías. But you relieve me."

I delighted in meeting her again, particularly as she remembered the first occasion in Paris and paid me compliments. Her mixed attitude toward events in New York was interesting, being partly realistic and partly that of an injured and superstitious queen. She said to me, for example: "The average North American audience has not been trained to enjoy the Spanish dance. It is not astonishing, in the special circumstances, that I was slighted. When I appear again, the public will have been forewarned that they are to see a wholly foreign and uncompromising dancer. I hope I can convince them that the art is worthy of their support."

But the next minute she was telling me that she had consulted a colleague as to whether the time was auspicious, or whether it should be some other year. I replied solemnly that I had had a dream in which I had heard her asking that very question of a Spaniard whom I did not know, and that his view was favourable. Her face lighted up. I must have guessed correctly about Mejías's decision, because her backers were notified the following day that she was prepared to go ahead. The date for her concert was set for Sunday, 23 March, at the Ethel Barrymore Theatre.

The episode, however, was fated to have a sensational aspect, apart from the genius of the star. It was to make theatrical history. A group called the Lord's Day Alliance, which was subject to spasms of righteousness in seeking to enforce a dead-letter statute forbidding Sunday performances, chose that very week to get into action. There were two dance concerts scheduled for the twenty-third, the promoters of which were warned by the Alliance not to proceed. In one case, the backers quit cold. La Argentinita's management argued feebly with the frightened lessee of the Ethel Barrymore Theatre, but saw no real way of resisting.

Then William A. Brady, a producer with a reputation, who owned the Playhouse Theatre, offered the use of his stage to the Spanish dance company, and swore he would fight the thing through to a finish. Somehow, La Argentinita saw nothing but good luck in this. The enthusiasts who had been helping her, including myself, went to the Playhouse that Sunday in a mood of keen excitement. Brady, a bald-headed, oldish Irishman, stepped before the curtain and made a fiery speech. He challenged not only the police but the mayor and the governor of the state to stop the show and arrest him. "It will be no fake arrest, either, for I'll go with them and spend the night in jail," he cried. "Things have reached a sorry pass in this great city when there can be interference with an entertainment of high artistic standard. Yet the same dancer, if employed right around the corner in one of the big production houses which are at this moment going full blast, would be allowed to do her stuff unmolested." He closed his speech by inviting the policemen present to meet him at the back door. None of them budged. Mayor James J. Walker's administration being far from a puritanical one, the issue of Sunday concerts was settled for good. Brady took a seat in the audience, and the curtain went up.

La Argentinita gave a beautiful and memorable performance. I feel that she can never have surpassed it, before or afterward. There were the regional measures I had so enjoyed in Paris: of Andalusia, Valencia, Aragon and Old Castile. In her *tango de Cádiz*, she demonstrated that the tango was originally a Spanish dance, of rather simple pattern and slow time. The South Americans speeded it up, to create the version that was going around the world at that period. La Argentinita's *gaucho*, on the other hand, was a true dance of the pampas. She was lavish with gypsy *alegrías*, especially as encores. She showed too that to some acts she could bring a fine and biting humour.

The victory that evening lay in the frenzied applause with which every single number was greeted. Sincere dance lovers of various nationalities had come to see her, and it was not just a matter of their cheering her in a spirit of fair play to make up for what had happened at Lew Leslie's *première*. Also, a more subtle type of newspaper critic attended, and the notices the next day were comprehending and fervid. La Argentinita gave several other successful concerts on that visit. She had been established in New York, and she returned several times for engagements. Once she was a guest star of the Ballet Theatre at the Metropolitan Opera. She died in 1945 at the comparatively early age of forty-seven. The reader is perhaps thinking I shall now tell that my devotion was rewarded by a tempestuous love affair. But this was not on the cards. La Argentinita and Mejías were companion stars in a profound Hispanic sense. She remained for me a dear friend, and the perfect exponent of her art. I dedicated to her my novel *The Pomegranate*, which has a Spanish dancer for heroine, by no means a portrait of the *bailarina* herself. And I wrote the following poem, which comes closer to being drawn from life:

Villanelle of a Spanish Dancer

Heat that is fused to flesh for my despair,
Spark from the flint that is the soil of Spain,
Her art has stripped the body of beauty bare.

She dances to the mad guitars, aware
That in her rapture is a core of pain –
Heat that is fused to flesh for my despair.

The hoofs of goats upon a rocky stair
Beat in her castanets a fierce refrain.
Her art has stripped the body of beauty bare.

A poppy glows like blood upon her hair,
And her wet mouth is as a fiery stain –
Heat that is fused to flesh for my despair.

Lust on those lips, but in her eyes a prayer!
Of a vast ecstasy her soul is fain.
Her art has stripped the body of beauty bare.

Though I should die for her, she would not care.
She is so young she loves to flaunt disdain.
Heat that is fused to flesh for my despair,
Her art has stripped the body of beauty bare.

CHAPTER 15 ⁂ **Freelance**

WHEN THE DEBTS AND OTHER problems of the *American Parade* had been liquidated, I did intensive writing of every description. Editorial links persisted to some extent, as for example the connection with Macfadden's *Dance Magazine*, which gave me a chance to defend the fame of La Argentinita. But fiction stories and articles took up most of my energy. These included political commentary on issues growing out of the war, travel pieces and a large number of book reviews. Publishers associated me with certain subjects, particularly espionage because of the studies I had done of the trial and execution of Mata Hari. I had observed her both in Paris and Barcelona, and she had become a dramatic international figure. There was a time when practically every spy book that came out was sent to me for review by one or other of the big New York newspapers.

I was, in short, a busy freelance, to use our favourite term for it, and I rather liked the status. It seemed to guarantee me independence. Yet under the surface I had my doubts about it. I had reached my early forties and was allowing myself to drift along without rising above the level of hack work. My carelessness over book rights has been mentioned. Not only had I permitted a woman writer to sign my name to a mystery novel I had merely plotted, but another such volume had been knocked together from some casual fiction of mine, and I had let it appear in return for a single advance royalty cheque. What was the matter with me? I felt that some sort of destiny was involved with my work as a West Indian author, and it was time that I should do something about it. Little by little, I came to a decision resembling in inspiration other moves both of my past and my future. This one was to have important results.

I decided that I would go to live in Paris and create there for myself a background more congenial than that of New York. Some magazine assignments would still flow in my direction, and I could build up new contacts abroad. Subjects that strongly interested me could be pursued with a broader scope. I should be able to think more clear-headedly in the planning of a literary future. Europe had superior facilities in the way of research libraries and museums. No doubt I should want to write a serious book, though as yet I had no specific theme for one.

History, of course, beguiled and fascinated me in a general sense. I toyed with the possibility of historical novels rather than formal history. But there were other subjects: a cosmopolitan's survey of global politics, or nature, or art. My enthusiasm over the last-named was urgent just then. I did not imagine myself to be a potential painter, for I had no talent whatsoever as a draughtsman, and the shapeless abstract school of the moment moved me to scorn. But I could very easily have become an art critic. My mind vacillated; that at least is clear. The trip itself was governed by what seemed to be illusions. It was supposed to place me definitely in Paris, and it turned out to be one of the shortest stays I ever made there.

I sailed early in 1931 on a drab one-class ship called the *Westernland* that landed me in Plymouth. Naturally I paid a visit to London, where nothing of consequence relating to my work materialized. On the urging of the travel agent, I had booked a return ticket and wondered why I did it. He had persuaded me that the reduction in price was considerable, and that it would always be simple to dispose of the ticket. The next stage was an indirect journey to Paris by way of Antwerp. There were art shrines in Belgium I wanted to see, notably the house of Felicien Rops in Namur. I had recently discovered Rops and much admired him, a feeling that has grown in me. He was a late nineteenth-century etcher and engraver, with a Fleming's liking for robust female forms, a cousin in black-and-white of Peter Paul Rubens, but touched by a satanism of which Rubens was innocent. The museum at Namur, which had been the artist's home for most of his lifetime, did full justice to him. I also lingered at Liège and Reims, though I was already familiar with what the Germans had spared of them, and at

Moret-sur-Loing with its architectural remnants of the Renaissance. They reawoke in me memories of how I had first become interested in such things.

My boyhood in Jamaica was passed among people who had little realization of art. I remember being told that Raphael was the greatest of painters, an opinion undoubtedly due to his Madonnas and infant Christs and the general sweetness of his style. There was irony in the fact that the then recent Pre-Raphaelite school was also esteemed, though even its name formed no part of the critical baggage of my mother and her women friends. To them Watts and Holman Hunt were spiritual. I feel sure that they did not extend similar merit to Dante Gabriel Rossetti with his 'Blessed Damozels' and so forth.

My father's views were broader. He had commended Velázquez to me and said that in sculpture Michelangelo was the one giant since the Greeks. But my father would have been the first to deny that he understood the subject very well. Nothing but a few prints were available at Berry Hill anyway. No original masterpieces were to be seen in the island. The best paintings at the Institute of Jamaica, Kingston, were there predominantly on account of their local historical interest.

On first reaching New York, I had of course gone as a dutiful sightseer to the Metropolitan and other museums of art. Their lavish exhibits bewildered me, yet I came upon some discoveries for myself. I found that there was a man named Rembrandt and another called Frans Hals who had a great deal to say to me. Raphael took on a syrupy consistency alongside them, though I am far from rejecting the genius of the Italian. Several Spaniards were masters, including Ribera and Goya, as well as Velázquez. The Pre-Raphaelites were finer than I had supposed – not, however, for the reasons that moved my mother. There also was an admirable French school called the Impressionists: Manet, Monet, Renoir and Degas captivated me.

Haphazard judgements, all of them, until I had begun to meet illustrators at the offices of the *National Sunday Magazine*, frequented their studios and took part in the talk at Petitpas's. I had rapidly grown to be a lover of pictorial art. I accepted the traditions as they then stood. On the eve of the rise of futuristic art, or term it what you will, the tastes I developed caused me to condemn that drift, then and afterward, as barbarism, infantilism or charlatanry.

Robert Henri was the acknowledged leader of young painters who were in revolt against the despotism of the National Academy of Design concerning what works should be exhibited. None of them were as yet futuristic and some never became so. Others in the group were John Sloan, George Luks, William J. Glackens, Everett Shinn and Ernest Lawson. Sloan was a regular at Petitpas's, and the rest often dropped in. Most made their livings from magazines and newspapers. It was a day when the serious side of every illustrator's career was painting, my conservative friends Franklin Booth, Charles Sarka, C.B. Falls and T. Victor Hall along with the rest. Of these four, only Booth won a reputation among the elite.

The names in the two preceding paragraphs are for the record. This is not a book on art, though mention of my comradeships among artists must have a place in it. I confess that on my trips to Paris, I was staggered by some of the confusions I encountered. There was the French-Catalan sculptor Aristide Maillol, who had mistakenly begun his career as a painter. I saw in his studio powerful figures of an early Greek classical style, affected by the semi-Orientalism of Egypt, figures intended to stand in the open air under a Mediterranean sun. Nothing could be more lucidly representational. Yet Maillol praised Picasso to me, while saying of Negro art: "Those who attempt it here are making a foolish mistake. This is the country of Ronsard, of La Fontaine and of Racine. Where is the connection with Negro sculpture?" Then he averred of the landscapes and apples of Paul Cézanne that they excelled the work of any other living Frenchman. For me Cézanne is at the exact borderline between post-impressionism and nonsense. I cannot trace the course of Maillol's critical judgement. I can but say that his own nude created for the monument to Cézanne is far greater art than its inspirer ever succeeded in getting onto canvas.

On the trip to Paris in 1931, I took a room and bath close to the Panthéon, not far from the Sorbonne and the cafés of the Boulevard St Michel. The atmosphere was *rive gauche* in a degree that had not been the case with my earlier haunts in Montparnasse, and I liked it better. I dawdled for nearly a month, happy that there was really no obligation to work. I was then surprised at the office of the *Brooklyn Daily Eagle* with the news that friends of mine from New York, a married couple named Farquhar, were living in the rue de l'Arcade, behind the Madeleine, and I went to see them.[1] The man

---

[1] It will be understood why names, places and dates concerned with the episode that follows have been deliberately masked by me to some extent.

was of American birth, had fought in the war, had been badly wounded and pensioned. The woman was an Italian, named Giulia, a charming little creature with much zest for life. They had one son, then about eight years old. The husband, Donald, drank too heavily to be a rational companion the greater part of the time. Giulia and I had drifted together in occasional indiscretions, which we called love without insistence that the divine word was really the one to use. But when we met again in Paris, a strong attachment sprang up between us. Whatever else should or should not be said, the atmosphere for it was right and we were sincere in what we did.

There were endless places for us to see, dream-roads to the past to traverse, theatres and cafés to enjoy together. Donald seldom came with us. He was steadily growing physically unfit for any effort. Giulia and I fell into the way of planning for the future as if he were out of the picture, always a rash attitude – no matter how sincere – in such circumstances. She concluded and I eagerly agreed that the one essential link was a child of our own. The mere thought that that might occur moved me to poignant emotion. I had needed a daughter for years now, ever since the refusal of my wife had been the chief cause of the break-up of our marriage. The initiative taken by Giulia seemed wonderful to me. I began to love her for it. I did not doubt for a moment that it was a girl we would have.

Anyhow, we removed all the minor obstacles. That Donald might prove to be the actual as well as the nominal father could be eliminated. Giulia assured me that he was on the verge of impotence, yet susceptible of finding the bare possibility of another child flattering. Should I be ashamed of this version of the cuckoo's nest? I do not deny the deception involved, but Giulia was more than willing and I am unable to feel very guilty.

We knew before long that she was pregnant. I wished then, poetizing the thought of prenatal influences, that we could make a trip to Italy together. Far from this shaping favourably, Giulia's stay in Europe was cut short by news received concerning Donald's family. The child would be born in New York. How well I remember the misty spring day when I rode to the Gare St Lazare to help put the party on the boat train for Le Havre.

I had resumed writing, and at the same time had embarked upon new and fruitful research. The project of working on a nonfiction book with the scene laid in the West Indies had been confirmed in my mind. Furthermore, it must be primarily of Jamaican significance. A biography would be best. I asked myself which personage born in Jamaica, or closely associated with the island, had most powerfully shaped its history and also had had a lasting effect upon the story of the region and the world at large? The answer, excitingly enough, was Henry Morgan, the buccaneer. I sent a précis of the subject to publishers in New York and received favourable replies, a definite offer of a contract from one of them. This was enough for me. The illusion of Paris as my home dissipated like morning mist. I sailed from Antwerp, using the return booking on the *Pennland* which I had made so fortuitously in Southampton a few months before.

Reunion with Giulia and the prospective birth of our child had much to do with my happy acceptance of the shape of things. If I had believed, however, that I could be close to her in person at the crisis I was mistaken. The Farquhars had moved to a house in New Jersey connected with one of the military establishments, and that is where a little girl was duly born. I gave her the pet name of Nell, a variation of a formal name that has long been in my family. My grandmother on the paternal side was called Nell for short, and I leave it to the reader to appraise the possibilities. Her full baptismal name could have been Helen or Ellen, or it could have been Eleanor. Giulia never warmed to my speaking of the girl as Nell, even when some years later I dedicated a book to her under that name. But I like it, and it will serve meaningfully to identify her in these pages.

I was not urgent at the beginning with Giulia as to our future together. Perhaps I was wrong. Perhaps it was another case in my life which Eleanor Ramos would have ruled was one demanding immediate firmness. But I was on the trail of a book, and this is as good a point as any at which to tell that shortly after the research period ended I asked Giulia to divorce Donald and marry me. She answered that she would not be able to live with herself if she left her invalid husband while he still needed her. And that was that. She meant what she said.

The itinerary which I had sketched out called for a tour of the Greater Antilles, starting naturally with Jamaica, then visits to several of the small islands and important continental places centring about the Isthmus of Panama. I sailed on a United Fruit Company ship, and put up at the Cardiff House, Duke Street, Kingston, an address that later was to play a role in political developments.

I finished my biography of Morgan in 1932 and it was published the following year in both the United States and Britain. Later there was a French edition. The book was given a friendly reception by the critics. There remained no doubt in my mind that, so far as authorship was concerned, my work from then on would have a serious bearing on history. I wrote and attached to the biography a short appendix, which I called "Self-Government in Jamaica". If I were composing this today, I would make additions and revise the whole approach, to establish some relevance with Henry Morgan's career. But I give it unchanged as an early document in my own political development.

Self-Government in Jamaica

Jamaica today is a Crown Colony, which means that it is administered by the British king and Parliament, through the Colonial Office in London. The governor is appointed without consulting the wishes of the people of the Island. His powers are little short of dictatorial. He presides over a Legislative Council consisting of fourteen members elected by popular vote – one for each parish – and a government bloc of equal strength, made up of heads of executive departments and a certain number of 'nominated members', chosen arbitrarily by himself. In the event of a tie between official and local policies, he casts the deciding vote. Money bills are to some extent exempt from this. But in general the governor embodies the remarkable principle of self-government reduced to a simulacrum, by the device of combining the functions of chief executive and speaker of a packed deliberative body.

That any country should tolerate such a state of affairs is astonishing. It becomes the more astonishing when we recall that Jamaica has been a political entity under the same flag since 1655, and that for more than two hundred years it administered its own affairs under a constitution, with a governor general as the sole important link with the British realm. Add that the constitution was voluntarily surrendered in the year 1865, and the case of Jamaica becomes of unique interest among communities stemming from the Anglo-Saxon root.

The dominant planter class of early Jamaican history did not easily win the rights and privileges of self-government. Samuel Long, William Beeston and others resisted vigorously the attempt of Charles II to reduce the Island to vassalage and the paying of tribute. Long, in particular, was eloquent in phrasing the absolute refusal of free settlers to be governed by a clique in London which could not be familiar with their problems. The amiable monarch conceded the power of making laws, but persisted in asking for a permanent revenue to the Crown. This point was bitterly contested until the year 1729, when the Jamaican Legislature agreed to a grant of eight thousand pounds per annum, with the proviso that the total amount was to be spent in the colony. In consideration of this act, the following Royal proclamation was issued: "All such laws and statutes as have been at any time esteemed, introduced, used, accepted, or received as laws of this island, shall, and are hereby declared to be, and continue laws of this his Majesty's island of Jamaica for ever."

It would have been difficult, indeed, for any English government to repudiate so sweeping a recognition of the country's right to shape its own destiny. Nor was this attempted. The local Council and Assembly frequently angered the central authority by the extreme independence of their behaviour. But Jamaica remained free until, as the result of a combination of circumstances in the nineteenth century, the representatives of that same planter class which had demanded and maintained political liberty, most abjectly yielded it and petitioned to be governed by the Crown.

The primary cause was the abolition of Negro slavery in 1838. The planters had opposed emancipation with an aggressiveness that amounted almost to rebellion. They proceeded to deal ineptly with the accomplished fact. Discontent spread among the freed slaves, and in 1865 culminated in an uprising of the latter. It was savagely suppressed. The leaders, including an eccentric and but slightly guilty coloured politician named George William Gordon, were executed wholesale. The governor, Edward John Eyre, a man of the Puritan type who would have enjoyed being with Cromwell in Ireland, was chiefly responsible for the blundering violence with which the crisis was handled. He was soon recalled to England to give an accounting, and the investigation of his acts became a *cause célèbre* which dragged on for years. With liberal opinion ranged against him, he was nevertheless whitewashed and the costs of his defence paid by the House of Commons.

But in 1865, promptly after the quelling of the Negro revolt, and while martial law was still in force, Governor Eyre had called the Jamaica legislature together and told it that the existing form of constitution should be abolished. The planters voted obligingly: "It shall be lawful for Her Majesty the Queen [Victoria] to create and constitute a Government in this island, in such form and with such power as to Her Majesty shall seem fit, and from time to time to alter and amend such Government."

Eyre then informed the abdicating elected persons: "In releasing you from further attendance upon your legislative duties, I cannot lose sight of the probability that you may never be called upon to exercise these duties again, under the existing form of constitution, and that this general sacrifice has been consummated by yourselves from an earnest and sincere desire, regardless of all personal considerations, to benefit the colony. On behalf of the colony and of the many interests associated with it, I return you the thanks which are so justly your due. History will record the heroic act, and I trust that history will show from the ameliorated state of the country, and a renewed prosperity, that your noble self-devotion has not been in vain."

W.J. Gardner, the historian, remarks ironically: "Never, perhaps, in the history of the world, were patriots less appreciated. Men and women went about the common business of life as usual, apparently unimpressed by the greatness of the sacrifices which had been made." The truth was, that the legislators of 1865 abandoned their powers, asked for and got a Crown Colony, because they doubted their ability to control the huge Negro population. They thought in the terms of a Jamaica owned by the white minority, and for ever to be so preserved. The Civil War in the United States had just ended. It was believed in the Island that the millions of slaves liberated in the former Confederate States would run wild and plunge North America into anarchy. The planter class of Jamaica wanted the strong hand of England to protect it from the bogey of a similar disaster.

No democratic public opinion existed in 1865 to restrain the planters. The lower orders of society were quite inarticulate. The several generations which have come to maturity since then have shown an almost unparalleled indifference to their country's destiny. Culturally and politically, the people of Jamaica have been dormant. They have developed a natural individualism, because that is a gift of God to all human entities; but it has had almost no public expression. Jamaicans have worn the veneer of a superimposed northern attitude of thought unsuited to children of the tropics, and have allowed their land to be ruled as a Crown Colony far beyond the moment in history when the right to complete self-government should have been re-asserted.

CHAPTER 16 ⟫ **The Author at Fifty**

FIFTY IS ACCEPTED AS A NEAT FRONTIER BETWEEN the middle and final periods of a man's life. In my case it was much more than that. I was fifty on 15 October 1936, but the emphasis here is on the year of my half-century rather than any particular date. As early as March a ripening of various impulses was taking place within me. Obstacles of duty, habit and expediency appeared to shift aside of their own accord.

My mother, who had reached her eighties, died in a nursing home in Brooklyn. We had not been close, for I had found her views on religion and life lugubrious. As sometimes happens with old people, her thought mellowed toward the end, and she wondered aloud whether she had not been too rigid. We at last understood each other better, of that I am sure. One of her requests surprised me, coming from so conventional a person. She wanted her body to be cremated and the ashes cast into the ocean far from land.

I had been planning to take a trip after she was gone and had decided it would be to some Caribbean country I had never before visited. The same day that I bought my ticket, the crematorium sent me a metal canister about large enough to hold a pound of tobacco. The contents rattled, when shaken, like small pebbles and sand, with none of the smoothness suggested by the word 'ashes'. A handful or two of grit constitutes all that is retrieved from the furnace. Ashes is but a traditional name for it. I was not so morbid as to open the canister, but put it in a suitcase and later on a shelf of the clothes-closet in my cabin aboard the *Coamo*, bound for San Juan, Puerto Rico.

The constellations of my Jamaican boyhood reappeared in the changing sky, the Southern Cross showing above the horizon as we passed east of the Bahamas. Porpoises rolled ahead of the ship's bows, and flyingfish broke the surface to glide and fall back like little silver toys. The air grew bland. I thought a good deal on that voyage. Since the outbreak of the war in 1914 my activities had been mercurial, as I have shown, and I was not happy about the results. I had left journalism for magazine editing in 1918, and magazine editing for the writing of books in 1930. I had married and been divorced, without having had the daughter for whom I had longed. I had then known a great love and by treating it as mere passion had lost it, a reversal of the usual folly which mistakes passion for love; the scar I carried was ineradicable, like a knot in a tree's trunk. It was true I now had a daughter but with difficulties attached. I had pursued so many interests – history, international politics, poetry, chess, art, the Spanish dance, travel – that I feared I had dissipated my force and would accomplish nothing lasting. Searching those moonstone years for urges that had been deep and constant, I realized that there had been only one: the desire to know and do more about my native Caribbean region, and especially to help in giving Jamaica a voice in the world. True, the matter had dropped out of my mind for longish periods; but I had always veered back to it, as I was in fact doing on the present journey.

Some four years earlier, when I sought a theme for my first serious prose work, I had decided to write about the Jamaican who had most influenced regional history, while winning at least a degree of cosmopolitan fame. I had written my biography of Henry Morgan with its rather irrelevant appendix to a seventeenth-century chronicle, stating that self-government for the island was overdue. A *New York Times*' critic had mocked lightly at this last, thereby giving publicity to the notion. I had contributed an article to *Current History*, a New York magazine, in which I repeated my argument and expanded it to take in other British West Indian territories. For the time being, I supposed that I would go no further. But aboard the *Coamo* I felt more and more strongly that I had a role to play. The time appeared to be ripe, politically. Edward VIII had come to the throne of Great Britain in January. I did not admire him, but I speculated that his vague liberalism, in combination with the insularity of the premier, Stanley Baldwin, might soften the attitude of the Colonial Office. This was to prove a factor of no consequence whatsoever. More to the point, there was a weak governor in Jamaica, Sir Edward Denham, who paid little heed to the problems of unemployment, low wages and hard times generally, and who appeared to think that the apathy of the public was an unalterable state of affairs.

The day before we reached San Juan was Easter Sunday. A Protestant Episcopal service was held in the main saloon. I stood by the door to hear it. Then, as one of the beautiful hymns of the season started, I slipped away to my cabin, took the tin canister on deck and threw it at large off the Mona Passage. A romantic grave for my mother, who preferred everything English, at a latitude where the packets from the West Indies used to swing northeast.

My acquaintance from Greenwich Village literary circles when he had been studying at Columbia University, the poet Luis Muñoz Marín, was a figure in Puerto Rico politics, as his father had been. Muñoz preached independence then. I had looked forward to seeing him, but he was absent from San Juan during my short stay. His wife, Muna Lee, a North American from Mississippi, also a friend and a poet from the old days, asked me to dinner. She suggested that I address joint classes at the University of Puerto Rico, and seizing the opportunity I announced that I would talk on political conditions in the British West Indies.

This speech was the first that I had made on the subject. I sketched the history of government under the English, with its many anomalies ranging from the old, limited constitutions which still obtained in Barbados and the Bahamas, to the Crown Colony system accepted by Jamaica after the Morant Bay Rebellion of 1865 and its slight modification in the direction of democracy nineteen years later. The present attitude in the islands, I said, was apathetic, yet I believed that national sentiment could be aroused. Probably there would be long resistance by conservative elements. I quoted my friend Herbert George de Lisser, editor of the *Daily Gleaner*, Kingston, who had told me a couple of years before that political change would occur only over his dead body. While I could not picture him falling on any barricade, I imagined that he and others like him would fight with words, and they ought to be put to the test.

The Puerto Rican students in the audience were politely interested and asked questions. Obviously they thought British West Indians very backward. Such had been the justified opinion of Latin Americans since the days of Simón Bolívar. It did not disconcert me. I had launched an idea, and this served to clarify my own thinking. Puerto Rico itself had no

Figure 28. Muna Lee in 1930.
Courtesy of Jonathan Cohen.

great reason to be proud of its political situation. It elected a legislature of two houses, but the governor was appointed from Washington, and so were three important lesser officials, as well as federal judges. One party worked for admission of the island as a state of the United States, and another for more autonomy under the existing system. There was ardent nationalist leadership, too, ranging from that of traditional patriots like young Muñoz Marín to the fascism of Pedro Albizu Campos who drilled a few score blackshirts against the armed revolt that he said must come.

Muna Lee arranged trips into the interior for me, to the Luquillo forest park of which the salient feature was El Yunque Peak, to the Treasure Island camps near Cidra, and several other places. Puerto Rico reminded me of Jamaica, but the scenery was on a subdued scale. The mountains were less bold and high, and except in the forest reserves had been pretty well stripped of their trees. A dense and rising population farmed most of the land that was not planted to sugar cane. This struck a European note, reinforced by the fact that about three-quarters of the inhabitants were white. But there were more hands than jobs to be done. People sat idly in the dappled shade under fruit trees, their manner curiously light-hearted seeing they were so poor in everything but children.

The appearance of the towns was Spanish colonial, as yet unaffected by modernistic architecture. I stayed in San Juan at a hotel on the old Plaza de Armas, centre of the small insular capital's public life, where gossips collected about the doorways of the City Hall or gesticulated on the park benches, and orators spoke to the crowds. I took pleasure in standing at the northwest corner of the Plaza and looking up the slope of narrow San José, its roadway in turmoil like an ants' nest as pedestrians spilled over from the sidewalks. Behind it was the street called Del Cristo, mainly given over to bordellos. Puerto Rico as a whole might not have been awake to the course in history it desired to follow, but it had a definite personality. My clearest impression was of the boys and girls at the University, their alert faces, their strong preference for the Spanish of their ancestors rather than the English of their rulers; and in contrast the sense of happy-go-lucky waiting on the part of the countryfolk.

ON MY RETURN TO NEW YORK a magazine ordered from me a long series of articles unconnected with politics. This freed me from financial worries, and I gave all the time I could spare to the question of Jamaica. I realized that I must look for support among the thousands of the islanders living in Harlem. I had few acquaintances in that Negro centre. I had paid little attention to the recent activities there of Marcus Garvey, a Jamaican by birth but a man who had agitated along international racial lines. What had I to do with his dreams of a black African empire? A Jamaican expatriate named A.M. Wendell Malliet, a well-read man of mixed blood connected with the *Amsterdam News*, was known to me by reputation. He was said to have a strong pro-British bias. However, as the only démarche that could be made immediately, I wrote for an appointment and went to see Malliet. I remarked a buried note of hysteria in his combative manner. He appeared suspicious of my motives, but warmed presently to the suggestion that I try out the responsiveness of our compatriots in exile.

He got me invited to address the British Jamaicans Benevolent Association, an old and respectable society concerned with welfare work. I read a prepared speech. The audience consisted mostly of practical people, who wore nostalgic expressions when I referred to the far-off island home, showed a certain incredulity at the thought that direct British rule could ever be shaken, but applauded warmly. A few among them took my words to heart. They called a special meeting at the office of an influential coloured physician, and on that occasion I proposed that we take action.

Sympathizers materialized as it seemed to me from nowhere: men in the learned professions, merchants and women of liberal tendencies. Several more conferences were held. It was decided to form an organization. I wanted to call it the Jamaica Self-Government League, and I remember with some amusement that Malliet and others so feared to offend the Colonial Office by the use of the term 'self-government' in the name that we compromised on the Jamaica Progressive League. Our aims were unaffected, as may be judged by my preamble to the declaration then adopted, as follows: "Firmly believing that any people that has seen its generations come and go on the same soil for centuries is, in fact, a nation, we pledge ourselves to work for the attainment of self-government for Jamaica, so that the country may take its rightful place as a member of the British Commonwealth of Nations."

The league was created at a public meeting on 1 September 1936, when members were enrolled and officers elected. I was made president. Malliet, to our surprise, refused the nomination as secretary and dropped out of the picture. Unfriendly critics said that he was an agent of the British Consulate General, paid to observe Jamaican activities in Harlem. If so, he had already learned enough to file his report on us. The Reverend Ethelred Brown, a Unitarian minister, was elected secretary, and brought unflagging zeal to the post. Wilfred A. Domingo, an importer of tropical foodstuffs, at times a journalist, became a director. So did Jaime O'Meally, a former teacher who had established himself as a Spanish translator and had made a good collection of books on constitutional problems. Brown and Domingo were Negroes, O'Meally a light mixed-blood with a Hindu mother.

We now campaigned in the manner common to all agitators. We rented halls and staged mass gatherings. We lectured on such subjects as libertarian struggles everywhere, the history of government in Jamaica, the abuses of the Crown Colony system, and the right of the people to conduct their own affairs. We adopted resolutions, which were sent to the proper authorities in London and Jamaica. We published pamphlets.[2] The meetings were held in Harlem, because we wanted the support of the masses, and most of the Jamaicans we could reach had gravitated, being coloured, to Harlem. Nevertheless, a handful of white islanders came.

It looked like an uphill job of educational propaganda which might some day earn for the league the credit of having pioneered. How could we know that the inertia not merely of Jamaica, but of the whole British West Indies, was on the point of being ended by cumulative forces that had long been masked! I did maintain that ideas of the sort we were scattering could not

---

2 *Self-Government for Jamaica*, by W. Adolphe Roberts, 1936; second printing, 1937. *Injustices in the Civil Service of Jamaica*, by Ethelred Brown, 1937. *Onward Jamaica!* by the Board of Directors of the League, 1937. *Why We Demand Self-Government*, by Jaime O'Meally, 1938.

fail to win supporters. A truism, the importance of which depended upon how quickly it proved itself, and upon how many responded.

On 20 February 1937, *Public Opinion*, a liberal weekly, was started in Kingston by O.T. Fairclough, to provide a literary organ in a community which did not have one, a medium for the exchange of opinions. The appearance of this paper was fortuitous and not inspired by the Jamaica Progressive League, but it published articles by members of our organization and was destined to have a potent influence. Less than a month after the weekly was launched, Ken Hill of the *Daily Gleaner*'s editorial staff wrote as a man troubled about the league, in a signed column he conducted: "Is it not a disgrace that we at home have not a similar movement to represent the needs of the majority of our people?" He announced that he would be active in trying to bring this about. But the role of the National Reform Association, sponsored by Ken Hill and others, was brief. It was too confused to face the real issue. Autonomy was not demanded. Only the desirability of improving the form of government found mention in its plan. It held, I believe, just one big public meeting.

I made up my mind to go to Jamaica late in 1937, for a speaking tour, uninvited, and unheralded except by letters to a few individuals from the league in New York. I was met at the dock by a very mixed group. The agent of a civic association was determined to present me that same evening at the regular monthly meeting of his society in a suburb of Kingston. I consented and was taken to a private home where a porch served as platform and the audience sat on camp chairs amid blossoming shrubs. The chairman, a Jewish creole who had adopted an ultra-British name, was the elected legislator from the parish. He beamed at me, but after he had introduced me to the gathering in vague terms and I began to speak, he tapped his chin with a bony forefinger, his expression that of a man who had not expected to hear fairy stories. His path and mine did not cross again.

Two nights later, I was on a programme just ahead of the mayor of Kingston. He seized on my subject as a text and made some explosive impromptu remarks about the need for greater self-government. Word of this went the rounds. Indeed, I had no cause to complain that the idea or my advocacy of it lacked publicity. For the ink to flow, it was enough that I should be making public addresses. De Lisser wrote in the *Gleaner*: "We wish to be fair to any proposition brought forward, realizing as we do that an intelligent conservatism cannot possibly mean the eternal maintenance of any *status quo*. But an intelligent conservatism will hardly allow one to support some tremendously radical deviation from an existing Constitution, and an ignoring of all the intermediate stages which may be a means of general political education."

And what was the local model of the Crown Colony system, described by the editor of the *Gleaner* as resting upon a constitution? I thought the term a mockery. The system was a remarkable device, by means of which the opinions of elected persons were heard but need not be heeded. The governor was appointed by the Colonial Office, and his legislature consisted of heads of department nearly all birds of passage, residents nominated by himself, and fourteen members chosen under a franchise severely limited on a property basis both for voters and candidates. The official side of the House had a majority of one. In addition, the governor presided as speaker, yet had an original as well as a casting vote; if threatened with defeat in spite of all that, he could declare any measure to be of 'paramount importance' and compel its adoption.

It was my view that a system of the kind could justifiably be cancelled without delay. As for my friend de Lisser, he had in his precocious, ebullient youth written with some scorn of the Crown Colony, but had found that it afforded him a stage on which he could shine. His was the keenest journalistic mind of his day in Jamaica, and his gifts won for him the power that he loved, and the rewards of power. It was easier for him to be effective in a torpid society than would have been the case if he had agitated for liberty. This explains his attitude, which was not wholly insincere; he had persuaded himself that it was of benefit to the people. Herbert de Lisser's lead was followed by conservatives and the well-to-do, though they squirmed a bit at his sparkling and rather theatrical manner.

A handful of persons had been interested, even before my arrival, in forming a branch of the Jamaica Progressive League. They staged a large public meeting which I addressed, and members were enrolled. I told them that it was undesirable, if not impracticable, for a nationalist movement to be permanently directed from abroad. They must regard their organization as the nucleus of a political party, the activities of which should soon take precedence over anything we could do in New York.

I went out into the country after that and spoke to village gatherings.

Sympathizers lent their cars and often chauffeured, as I do not drive. We would leave Kingston shortly after nightfall, dash some twenty or twenty-five miles across the alluvial plain between dense groves of bananas, or fields of sugar cane, then swing up one of the roads leading to the mountains. The ascent was often at precipitous angles, through gorges, around hairpin turns and along the banks of tumbling rivers. In half an hour the temperature changed from the humid warmth of the tropics at sea level to the coolness of altitudes above two thousand feet where mist formed in the valleys. One shared the road with primitive wayfarers – teams of humped zebu bullocks, drays drawn by donkeys, long files of barefooted peasants carrying their burdens on their heads. Many half-remembered patterns of my boyhood came to life amazingly for me. On nights when the moon was full, the details were almost as clearly etched as in sunlight.

I once reached the township of Linstead during a fog so soft it was like a fine rain. The slightest inclemency of the weather after dusk is feared by tropical countrypeople, who wrap their throats and chests against fevers they think they will inhale, and stuff the chinks in their dwellings. Yet the old schoolhouse with the sagging floor had attracted a fair crowd. The speakers ahead of me talked in conservative terms, extolling the ancient bond with Britain and advocating a "reasonable measure" of progress.

When my turn came, I gave them stronger meat. I recall jibing at the nominated members in the legislature, those Jamaicans or transplanted Britishers who accepted seats on that advisory body to vote for the governor's policies and were especially useful to him when the elected minority felt disposed to give him advice he did not relish. Questions were asked from the floor. Only one was mordant, and it interested me. An oldish lean fellow, Arnold Lecesne, descendant of French refugees from the slave insurrection in Saint-Domingue, inquired why I stopped short at preaching self-government within the Empire. As he saw it, Jamaica should be a republic. I had found an extremist. He always had been one, but the general stirring of national consciousness brought him out.

Later I spoke in the town hall at Port Maria on the north coast. I was presented this time with a flourish. The elected member for the parish introduced me. He was smooth-tongued, a political type which you encounter in all countries and of every shade of complexion. This one was a mulatto. He promised me in rotund asides to bring my ideas before the Legislative

Council, as he would doubtless have promised anything that seemed to strike a popular note at the moment. He did not keep his word. The fact was unimportant, really. I considered the Port Maria meeting a turning point, because of a quickened tempo of response I observed in the audience and because of phrases that fell from other lips than mine: "This a wakening" . . . "Wholehearted support" . . . "Let us use the means at our disposal."

Meanwhile, I was seriously misunderstood in middle-class, property-owning circles. Most of the men I had known in my youth avoided me, trying to make up their minds, I suppose, whether I was plotting a revolution. I had not signed the visitors' book at King's House, which would have been the conventional thing for a man who knew he would be in the limelight to do. It had been deliberate on my part, because I thought it possible I might decide to attack Governor Denham in my speeches. To my surprise, a plainclothes intelligence agent called on me one night and suggested I should repair the omission.

"Why?" I asked.

"Well, His Excellency might want to discuss things with you. If you haven't signed the book he won't just invite you to call. An order from him that you come to King's House might cause people to wonder."

I said it would have to be an order, but Denham did not summon me. Shortly afterward, in broad daylight, I observed the same detective lounging at a street corner and watching me. I asked him to have a drink with me at a nearby bar. He accepted, a puzzled expression on his face, and we talked about the weather.

I could spend only five weeks in Jamaica. Before I left I privately visited some influential persons whose views were known to be liberal. Thus I met Norman Washington Manley. The others had expressed an evasive sympathy. Manley listened with thin-lipped close attention. He was the leader of the Jamaica bar, a King's Counsel. The corporations employed him as a barrister, yet he had many poor clients and had won sensational murder cases. He administered a trust fund for social rehabilitation, given by the banana business at his suggestion and called Jamaica Welfare. Physically he was an ascetic who looked the part. Stomach trouble had led him to give up smoking and drinking and to go on a diet which consisted almost exclusively of fruit. His health fully restored, his physique wiry, he remained gaunt to

Figure 29. Norman Manley in the 1930s. Courtesy of the *Gleaner*.

the point of being cadaverous. He looked like certain high-caste Asiatics of the Aryan race, though the exotic strain in him was African.

Manley summed up his reaction to my argument by saying that self-government necessarily would become an issue in Jamaica someday, but that it was premature to try to raise it now. If a political movement to that end started nonetheless, I asked, would he support it? He replied that he would. I pressed him: Would he be active in its leadership? Would he, for instance, allow a popular party to run him for the legislature? He shook his head. Apart from his legal practice, his interests were almost wholly philanthropic, he answered firmly. He had no wish to enter politics.

The circle of young people that had formed about *Public Opinion*, the new weekly, encouraged me with more understanding and ardour than any other group. There may only have been a round dozen of them, but they were articulate. Let me recall a few: Ken Hill, Latin in appearance, dreaming out loud, never quite sure whether he was a journalist, a politician or a labour reformer; round-faced Frank Hill, Ken's brother, passionately writing a play, *The Upheaval*, about the very events through which he moved, and making a success of the production; Dick Hart, small and clever, like a pertinacious terrier with a brain; Elsie Benjamin, with a flair for the theatre, a slender dynamic brown girl who has remained my friend to this day; H.P. Jacobs, a critical-minded, tenacious Yorkshireman with a thin, high-pitched voice, completely naturalized as a Jamaican; O.T. Fairclough, black as midnight, who had lived in Haiti, and who made a cult of King Christophe.

The *Public Opinion* group and the officers of the local branch of the Jamaica Progressive League were responsible for staging me a mass meeting at the Ward Theatre, municipally owned and the traditional place for rallying the citizens of Kingston. This meeting was set for a few days before Christmas, which would ordinarily have been an unfavourable time for presenting a serious subject. But we got a large audience. I spoke for longer than an hour, giving the historical background and winding up with realistic arguments for self-government. A movement, support for which was real though small and scattered, and including persons attached to various economic theories, came into existence that evening. It was a long step from agitation under the United States flag in Harlem.

Personally, the author at fifty was consciously putting into effect the maxim of Benjamin Disraeli: "A literary man who is a man of action is a two-edged weapon."

CHAPTER 17 ❧ **1939**

THE PUBLISHERS OF MY BIOGRAPHY of Henry Morgan had run into financial difficulties, and the original American edition had earned no money for me except the advance royalty. I had had to make new connections. The Bobbs-Merrill Company, of Indianapolis and New York, signed me up to do a life of Raphael Semmes, commander of the Confederate raider *Alabama*, our choice being influenced by the distant resemblance that the deeds of Semmes had borne to those of Morgan. The Southerner had made one colourful fighting voyage through the Caribbean and had put prisoners of war ashore in Jamaica. He and the *de facto* nation that he had served came within the scope of my historical interests. I had done some research on Semmes in Kingston, helped by his grandson, Father O.M. Semmes, a priest there. A few chapters of the book had been written. It was now necessary to complete it quickly. To do that I would have to go to the Southern states, especially to New Orleans, where there were important archives, and to Mobile, Alabama, where Semmes had passed his later years.

The Jamaica Progressive League could function during my absences, which I foresaw would be frequent for one reason or another. Domingo as vice-president and Brown as secretary were both energetic men. So I went to New Orleans in February 1938, this being my first visit to that city since I had passed through it on my way to California thirty-one years before. The part that New Orleans would soon be playing in my life was unsuspected by me. I took rooms on Esplanade Avenue not far from the Levée, on the more

Latin side of the old French Quarter, or Vieux Carré. To my joy, I found that the type of progress which had destroyed the charm of the New York I had once loved had done no great damage as yet in New Orleans. True, it appeared that I had come during an era's last and twilight phase, but at least I got a taste of the life that Lafcadio Hearn and George W. Cable had described, and against a practically unaltered background.

Superficially, the Vieux Carré was down-at-the-heels, indolent, a place where lodgings in picturesque houses of Franco-Spanish architecture were cheap and food in bohemian restaurants cost very little. Antoine's on St Louis Street was an exception, for it was one of the dozen finest eating places in the world and decidedly expensive. Tourists in numbers were to be seen only at the Mardi Gras season. Pat O'Brien's was the sole tourist bar. Tearooms and gift 'shoppes', transplanted with poor taste from the hinterland, were as yet few and inconspicuous.

I knew from the literature on Louisiana that the Vieux Carré had a small, well-to-do Creole aristocracy, but I penetrated no inner circles on that visit. I sought out only newspaper men and people who could give me information about Semmes. The deadline for delivering my manuscript was close, and I worked hard. I ate in, except for dining once a week at some new restaurant until I exhausted my list and then started the circuit again. Their names were evocative: Tujague's, Turci's and Maylie's, leisurely and good *tables d'hôte*, where no one would have been so barbarous as to eat without drinking the red wine of the house; Galatoire's, La Louisiane, Broussard's and Arnaud's, more pretentious places with *à la carte* service as well as *table d'hôte*; and Antoine's itself. Madame Begué's, noted a generation earlier for its Sunday morning breakfasts that lasted half the day, was struggling to keep alive now Madame was gone, and I went there once before it perished. At Maylie's a wisteria vine had clambered years ago to the ceiling from a boxed space in the middle of the floor. A hole through the roof had been cut for it. The stem thickened to the size of a small tree-trunk, and blossoms rioted both inside and outside the building. At Broussard's there was a creditable marble statue of Napoleon in the patio.

Antoine's marvellous cuisine will not be described here, but the old-fashioned atmosphere of the dining rooms is worth a word. There was no bar, for the proprietor believed that intelligent drinking was done at a table; no music, because it was held to spoil conversation. The rooms were lighted and heated from gas chandeliers and quaint gas lamps on the walls. Framed pictures with an association appeal were everywhere. Subdued, romantic patterns of nineteenth-century wallpaper added a gentle touch. In a hundred years the restaurant had been managed only by the founder, his son and grandson.

I made a trip of a few days to Mobile. How threadbare in an agreeable way, how somnolent a hybrid the city then was, with traces at the centre from its Latin period when it had been French and after that Spanish, a broader circle of Dixie mansions going to dust, and nondescript suburbs. I identified the last home of Semmes on Government Street, an empty and crumbling house shadowed from the street by tall trees. I saw at the public library the sword of honour which English admirers had presented to the brilliant sea-raider. A florist with whom I chatted got out his battered Ford and took me to the Catholic cemetery, where Semmes had been buried during a tempest, his coffin lowered into a grave half filled with water symbolic of his stormy life. Dr Toulmin Gaines, grand-stepson of Semmes, received me in his office, leaned back, his fingertips joined, and murmured childhood reminiscences of the hero.

Research into a not-too-distant past produces fascinating details easily enough. But Dr Gaines horrified me by remarking that a relative had hauled several trunks full of papers from the attic of the Government Street house and burned them in the yard, without investigation, just to get rid of a dead man's rubbish. Such crimes are commoner than I supposed at the time. The doctor shrugged and said he agreed it was an awful thing to have done. "Yet if everybody saved everything," he added philosophically, "the hunt for facts would be less enthralling, wouldn't it?"

A journey to Baton Rouge also rewarded me. I had made good progress with the biography when news from Jamaica began to take a startling character. There had been labour disturbances the year before in several of the smaller British Caribbean islands, but I had thought them trivial. Suddenly my own country was shaken by strikes of some magnitude, accompanied by a far-reaching unrest that seemed to be non-political. The main incident had occurred at Frome sugar plantation, where living conditions were deplorable and wages low. The police had handled it clumsily and there had been bloodshed. Enraged field hands in other places refused to work. Dock labourers followed suit, and there was rioting in Kingston. It was the more astonishing since unions capable of directing strikes did not exist. The local government always had opposed unionism.

The name of Alexander Bustamante emerged. I had heard of him as a usurer who wrote illiterate letters to the newspapers. Now he had proclaimed himself a labour leader and was having great success with the crowd. His violence and his reckless statements soon landed him in prison. But Norman W. Manley hastened to the aid of arrested strikers, and to Bustamante's defence: by making himself responsible to the governor for the agitator's future conduct he got him released. Then Manley toured the scenes of excitement throughout the island and talked reason to the peasantry. Calm was being slowly restored. Bustamante announced the forming of an omnibus union of the unskilled, to be called after himself.

At a distance I found these events highly suggestive. That the philanthropist and liberal thinker Manley should have offered his legal services to correct injustice was in character. He could no more have expected than I had that the pattern of discontent would assume this shape. What then about a political movement to mould the situation knowledgably? I regarded it as logical that he must already have perceived that it was necessary for Jamaica to manage its own affairs.

The next happening was the death of Governor Sir Edward Denham, following an emergency operation. The malicious said that he had been killed by stomach ulcers aggravated by too much whisky and worry over Frome, but one of the doctors who attended him told me afterward that Denham had had an ordinary intestinal obstruction and had stubbornly postponed the use of the knife until it was too late. He left orders that he was to be buried at sea, which in the state of popular feeling gave the no doubt false impression that he scorned to lie in Jamaican soil. Hoodlums pelted his coffin with offal as it passed down King Street to the warship that carried it beyond Port Royal. Naturally I was tempted to go at once to Jamaica. However, I had my book to consider, and it was important that I should do some strategic planning with the members of the league in New York. So I finished the book, to which I gave the title of *Semmes of the Alabama*, forwarded the manuscript by airmail and then followed it north.

Developments moved rapidly indeed. The British Colonial Office named as the new governor of Jamaica Sir Arthur Richards, a man with a reputation for toughness in Malaya, North Borneo and the Fiji Islands. He appeared to us to have been chosen expressly to put down our stirring national movement and to crush labour unionism. Soon a royal commission under the chairmanship of Walter Guinness, Lord Moyne, was dispatched from England to the West Indies to investigate conditions and hear complaints. I felt that it was an opportunity for the Jamaica Progressive League to go on record officially, and I urged that our secretary, the Reverend Ethelred Brown, should be sent to Kingston to state our demands to the commission. We passed the hat to raise funds and got him off in a hurry.

Propaganda in Harlem was intensified at public meetings held at short intervals, and by means of printed matter. We circulated a few issues of a mimeographed magazine. I quote from an article which I contributed to it:

> Jamaica, tomorrow, must be political-minded. She must support an energetic Nationalist Party and use the present limited franchise to elect persons who actually represent the aspirations of the country . . . Jamaica, tomorrow, must have a system of education which gives her a true perspective on her position in the Western World. If the Government persists in ignoring the realities of our tropical background and imposing an English curriculum, Jamaica must find a way to compel a change. We must write the history of the Island for the first time in simple and accurate terms, emphasizing the roles of the men whose lives were spent in building our future nation, as against the English rulers who came and went without leaving any part of their hearts with us. . . . There must be social justice in Jamaica, tomorrow. The scandal of underpaid labor . . . must come to an end. Health and housing conditions, excessive taxation of the poor, inequitable customs duties, property restrictions on the franchise: these things cry out for reform. No Crown Colony regime brought about by the Colonial Office in London will ever understand our problems. Only we ourselves can change Jamaica for the better. To do it, we must think as a people and obtain recognition as a nation. It is not an impossible dream.

Virtually overlapping the above words came the speeches at a mass meeting held in Kingston on 18 September. It is true of every vital movement that various men act simultaneously, swung by the same tide. Manley addressed the mass meeting, and so did his close friend Sir Stafford Cripps, a leader of the intelligentsia among British Labourites who happened to be in the island. The Jamaican proclaimed the need for a party to advocate self-government. Cripps gave his blessing to the idea in terms which the local official and propertied elements found frighteningly radical.

The People's National Party (PNP) was thereupon launched, engulfing Ken Hill's National Reform Association. Its programme called for responsible autonomy – eventually. With my approval, the Kingston branch of the Jamaica Progressive League affiliated itself with the party, but refused to be absorbed into it and reserved the right to demand immediate Dominion status. The chairman of the party was none other than Manley, he who had told me that he cared mainly for philanthropy and had no wish to enter politics. I knew him to be a socialist, and Cripps' support of him emphasized the point. Could a socialist be wholeheartedly for a national movement? I asked myself.

I concluded that my next book must have as its central object the placing of Jamaica in proper perspective as a unit of its region and of the Americas. If I were to write a history of Jamaica alone, I almost certainly would not be able to get it published in the United States, for the small island would seem undeserving of a full-dress treatment. Jamaica had been quiescent too long. Nor would such a presentation really suit my purpose. A background had to be portrayed, with my country emerging from it.

It came to me that I must write the history of the entire Caribbean, from the discovery by Christopher Columbus up to the present day. Nothing of the sort had yet been done. There were studies only of this or that European power's colonizing efforts in the region, and annals too of most of the separate units. The task was to show what had been occurring at every important juncture in all parts of the Caribbean, and to analyse the results. That I would tell Jamaica's story with a special emphasis was probable. But there is a degree of bias in all readable history; the other kind consists of mere chronology. I took the idea to my publishers. It pleased them, and they gave me a contract. I had a fair general knowledge of my subject, had read widely in it. But I no sooner started to delve into the obscurer records than I perceived it would take me the better part of two years to produce a book. I had no intention meanwhile of slackening my political work. It was going to be hard.

The Irish struggle, then a recent memory, had lessons for us, though I was aware that its success had been largely due to the homogeneity of the Irish people, to the unifying power of their religious faith, an ancient literature and a long record of resistance to tyranny. These factors were weak with us, could scarcely be said to exist in some respects. But there was much to be learned from the technique of any revolution that has evoked the heroic virtues, and I stressed the Irish example at several meetings held before Christmas.

One Sunday I took Eileen Curran to speak in Harlem. She had served her cause at home and in New York, had helped patriots with a price on their heads to escape, had pulled strings in enterprises of gun-running and the circulating of secret mail. Quietly she stood before an audience of hundreds in a YMCA hall, told how she had worked and how it might be necessary for Jamaicans to do similar things. It was strong meat for most of her hearers. The league had always taught that peaceful means should suffice, but Eileen Curran did well to show that there could be no guarantee against bloodshed initiated by violent men on either side.

The West India Reference Library at the Institute of Jamaica contained, as I have already said, one of the finest collections of books and documents in the world relating to its field, particularly the activities of the English in the early days. I felt that I could at least begin my history with that library as a source. Return to Jamaica was essential if I was to play a part in the developments there. So on 28 December 1938 I sailed for Kingston on the *Quirigua*, of the United Fruit Company line.

W.A. Domingo had preceded me by arrangement, this serious enthusiast having resolved to jeopardize his business by leaving it to run itself while he campaigned for self-government. He had proved himself a much better stump speaker than me, and his aid would be invaluable. We were both prepared to spend a long time on the island. One of our concerns was to see to it that the People's National Party did not relax into a welfare, reform organization, as advance word about it indicated might be the case. We wanted a frankly autonomist party with an aggressive programme, and we believed that the PNP, as it was called for short, could be stimulated into becoming one.

THE YEAR 1939, OR AT least the first eight months of it, was the outstanding period of my connection with Jamaica's struggle for a new regime. I landed in Kingston on New Year's Day and found myself regarded as one of the three principal leaders. There will be some to dispute this, to say that various civic reformers and inheritors of Marcus Garvey's back-to-Africa mirage had more supporters than me. But the record is clear. Alexander Bustamante as head of the inchoate labour agitation, Norman W. Manley as chairman of the People's National Party, and I with the league that sought total autonomy were the men who commanded active vanguards. We might later be pushed aside as individuals, but the advance of the things for which we stood could not be halted. Programmes conceived in a milder atmosphere scarcely counted now and must wither on the branch, while conservative thought that detested change of any kind was disorganized. Publicity would be wider than before, for a new daily newspaper, the *Standard*, had been established, and it was being conducted in a sensational way. Its imported English editor, F.J. Makin, was as shallow as a saucer, but his journalistic technique was colourful.

I lodged for a few weeks at 98 Duke Street, a guest house. The succession of meetings held at my initiative or to which I was asked as a speaker unrolled at a swifter tempo than when I had been last in the island. The object was less to awaken the audience – for that had occurred among the elements that would ordinarily turn out in the city – but to give direction to its interest. Manley and his lieutenants appeared on the platform at my meetings, and I went to his. Bustamante held rallies mainly to enlist union members, but now and then his bizarre figure would loom up among the nationalists. The play of personalities became more and more emphatic.

I recall the first big gathering. It was staged at the old Metropolitan Hall, as a welcome to me. Manley delivered a lucid address. He said that the PNP had put organization ahead of an immediate demand for self-government, but he was certain that the larger aim would develop in his party. He was glad, however, that the league had gone on record "in a naked and uncompromising form". Also, he avowed frankly that he had not originated the idea of Jamaica as a nation. Still less had he originated the call for self-government. The year before, when I had visited his chambers, he had not seen the possibilities. But he, Manley, had travelled in his own mind a long way in twelve months, and he felt he had travelled with the country and not away from it.

This was typical of Manley at that time. He would go on to make the same admission publicly more than once. A generous candour toward friends seemed second nature with him. He well knew besides that he could offer an enormous contribution, against which the claim of having been the first to speak out would seem a mere vanity. It is impossible to appreciate what came of the movement without a true view of Norman Washington Manley.

He was born and brought up in the country parish of Manchester, where I too had passed my boyhood. His father had a small farming property, and even so was about the most prosperous of a widely scattered family. Among the cousins, first and second, of Norman's generation were Edna Swithenbank, born in England, whom he was to marry, and Alexander Bustamante, the labour agitator whom he was first to help and then to oppose in politics. Anecdotes of Manley's youth show that he was clearly the genius of his circle. His successes culminated in his entering Jesus College, Oxford University, as a Rhodes scholar. He had decided to read for the bar. This was shortly before the outbreak of World War I.

A story ran that colour discrimination against Manley had prevented him being commissioned as an officer, that as a result he hated the English and wanted by way of vengeance to humiliate them in Jamaica. It is false. He enlisted in the artillery, served for three years in France and Belgium, and received the military medal. He disliked the Tory point of view, was fairly contemptuous of the monarchical idea, but thought well of most British institutions, especially the Labour Party. To me it seemed energizing that patriotic Jamaicans should be anti-English until they achieved their aims. Manley took no such stand. He looked from the start to England for comprehension, and to liberal opinion there for help. I attached more importance to arousing pan-American sympathy.

After the war Manley completed his studies at Oxford, returned to Jamaica in 1922, and rapidly became a legal star. His method of pleading was ingenious as well as learned, and shot through with social idealism where and when that was pertinent. His courtroom technique delighted professionals, but his type of oratory could not be called popular. The crowd respected him as a thinker above the common level, a remote man, a sage.

At Drumblair, his home on the outskirts of Kingston, he and Mrs Manley, a charming woman and a gifted sculptress mostly in wood, had long been entertaining an intellectual group and half the interesting persons who visited Jamaica. Now, on his few free evenings, political partisans swarmed to the house, to suggest plans or merely to discuss their hopes. I was there often. Manley's private conversation had a distinct eloquence, fed by his wide reading. He could do justice to honest heresies with a singularly sweet smile, and the next moment pour acid upon hypocrisies.

What did I find, however, that this man almost overwhelmed by his law work had committed himself to doing! Three or four times every week he left Kingston after office hours and spoke at meetings in the small towns, returning the same night though it meant on occasions a round-trip journey of a hundred miles. He was building the People's National Party at the grass roots. A country-wide, democratic party was an absolutely new idea to the Jamaican peasant. It could be made real only by a torrent of words explaining the issues in simple language, incessantly repeated. An adequate hall was seldom to be had. Little schoolhouses and market sheds were used; sometimes the meetings were held in the open.

Domingo and I went out with Manley frequently and supported him along broad lines. I closely studied him in action. He was extremely fluent, could talk for ten minutes or an hour with equal readiness, always made his points plain and never lapsed into demagoguery. You felt that he knew he must educate, rather than appeal for a decision as if to a jury. Yet his barrister's manner would emerge in spite of him; he would sway lightly on his heels, grasping the lapels of his coat, his face impassive as he uttered words without heat. Afterward you seldom remembered any of his phrases, but were clear about his programme. Everywhere he left the seeds of an organization behind him. I do not think that he moved the people to ardour at that juncture. But they were aware of his prestige and were flattered that he should be bringing a message to them.

Manley's approach impressed me as bound to be formidably effective in the long run. I could not even think of emulating it, for I did not have his local connections, his flying wedge of auxiliary speakers with cars at their disposal, or his probable ability to finance the vast effort. Many of my best talks with him occurred on our drives to and from country meetings. His type of socialism disturbed me a little, though he stopped short then of preaching that the party should be socialist. On the question of national independence I was more radical than he was, on the other matters less so. Manley wanted labour unionism to be firmly established and allied, as I understood him, with the self-government movement. He also wanted universal suffrage without a literacy test.

Now the declaration of the Jamaica Progressive League, framed by me,

Figure 30. The flag of the Jamaica Progressive League flying in a Jamaican village, c. 1939. MS353.6.10.

had specially advocated "the right of labour unions to function legally", and also the unelaborated principle of "universal suffrage". We had not meant unions to be tied in with political activities, and I now feared that if they should be they might become the dominant factor. As for the vote, it had not struck me, or I think any of us in New York, that it could be given to illiterates. New York State did not give it to them. I regarded registration as the test. If a man or woman could not read a simple passage in English and sign his name, it seemed nonsensical to register him. Let him acquire the necessary knowledge and come back next time; the privilege of the ballot ought to work as an incentive and so reduce the high percentage of illiteracy in Jamaica. I expressed these views to Manley as we navigated the hairpin turns of the Junction Road across the mountains. He smiled and answered that if I reflected I would see that pure justice was on his side. The arguments appeared at the time to be academic, and I let them pass. We could debate them when or if we had a hand in writing Jamaica's new constitution.

The physical aspects of Manley as an early campaigner that dwell with me are his hair bushing backward from a high forehead, the fact that even in the hottest weather he was never seen without a waistcoat, the leanness and vitality of his frame, and his tirelessness. It was not for nothing that he had been a champion runner at school, had done the 100-yards dash in ten seconds flat, a record which stood for forty-one years. He was still half-vegetarian and preferred apples to sandwiches.

THE OTHER LEADER, ALEXANDER BUSTAMANTE, offered the sharpest of contrasts. His real name was William Alexander Clarke. He said that while living in Spain and serving in the Spanish Foreign Legion he had conceived an admiration for one Bustamante, a labour politician, and had decided to call himself after him. This was of a piece with some other stories he told about himself. It is doubtful that he ever was in Spain. He averred that in Panama he had been a section manager of a streetcar system, whereas he had been only a conductor; that he had been in the secret police of the Cuban dictator Machado, whereas he had been no more than a special policeman for a few weeks, a sort of watchman distinguished from civilians by a band around his arm. The last-mentioned detail I established from the rolls while on a visit to Havana. Bustamante claimed to have been a dietician at a New York hospital; actually, he had been an orderly.

It is certain that he spent many years away from Jamaica as an adventurer, that he made a little cash in New York, reputedly on the stock market, came home and set up as a money-lender. Following the upheaval in Frome, he sprang from his usurer's office to proclaim himself, at the foot of Queen Victoria's statue, the voice of awakened labour. When I heard of it I felt that a man of his calling could scarcely last as a popular champion. Hundreds must have hated him for the harshness with which he had collected debts at compound interest. But his words had fired the crowd. He showed physical courage during the strikes he instigated. A helpful touch of martyrdom was added by his brief term in jail.

I first saw him in 1939 from the balcony of my guest house on Duke Street. His tall, gangling figure with interesting, salient features and unkempt hair, strode at the head of an impromptu march of extremely ragged citizens. More than half of these were women. One beldame pranced just behind Bustamante, leaping at intervals clear of the ground and crossing her ankles in the air like a grotesque ballet dancer. All joined in the chorus of a song: "*We will follow, follow Bustamante, / We will follow Bustamante till we die.*"

I perceived that the man was impervious to the ridicule of the few, so long as he had the many at his heels. The value to him of this capacity was not to be underrated. I had noted it in some others abroad, from politicians to publishers. Invariably it had made them rich.

Marches of the kind I watched were being held spasmodically by Bustamante, to keep up labour morale, as he understood the term. But the strike situation was relatively quiet for the moment, and the leader did not always know what to do with himself. His headquarters was a narrow wooden house of two stories further down Duke Street. He would come out hatless in blazing sunshine and shamble in the roadway, where he was more conspicuous than he would have been on a sidewalk. I stopped on two or three occasions and exchanged views with him.

Bustamante's schooling had been fragmentary, to say the least of it. His English was odd. In spite of Spain, Panama and Cuba, his knowledge of the Spanish language consisted of a minimum of garbled phrases. He had little comprehension of labour unionism, and not much more of nationalism, upon which indeed he usually poured scorn. Professing loyalty to the British Crown in one breath, he would in the next curse everybody who had money or authority. His suspicious gimlet-eyes would narrow as he discussed Manley. Once he accused him absurdly of having no real sympathy with black people. "And which of us is the darker," he ended, "me or Cousin Norman?" I laughed in Bustamante's face as I agreed that he was not the darker of the two, but I was aware that I was laughing at a dangerous fellow.

Other early memories of him are connected with his car. The masses were already making sacrifices for him such as the starving Irish had made for Daniel O'Connell. A fund subscribed penny by penny bought Bustamante a seven-passenger Buick. Whenever he drew up on the streets an eager group collected, whipping out rags and kerchiefs from tattered clothing to rub off every speck of dust on the car. The Chief, as they called him, had to beg them to cease this overzealous attention, for they were ruining the lacquer.

He drove himself, but generally had his secretary, Gladys Longbridge, beside him. At important crossings, she would bend over and whisper to him. Word spread that he had no sense of direction, that without her to tell him what turn to take he would lose his way. It was but a pose which appeared to humanize him for the crowd, though why uncertainty as to his road should have been found attractive in a leader it is hard to say. He was a consummate actor and knew instinctively what would be effective with a simple people.

One evening I was going on foot to a political rally. The famous Buick glided up behind and Bustamante offered me a lift, a 'drop' as it is called in Jamaica talk. He was alone for a wonder. I told him my destination, and he said in a distrait way that he thought he could find the place. We talked about other things. A few blocks from the hall he stopped by a sidewalk, leaned out and addressed a ragged black girl about twelve years old.

"Can you direct me, my dear?" he asked softly. "I want to get to – "

The child gave him one look and started to blubber: "Mr Busta, Mr Busta, don't tell me it is you!"

He patted her on the head. "Yes, of course, my dear," he murmured, and repeated his question.

She managed to stammer the information. By this time there were fully a score of bemused witnesses. Bustamante drove on smiling, waving salutes.

On another occasion I was crossing the island by bus. In the public square at Claremont, where we halted, I was astonished to see Bustamante standing by himself, his head thrown back, and staring at the sun or seeming to stare at it. Awed and silent observers were gathered about him in a ring. I leaned out and caught his attention. He promptly came over and said, pitching his voice so that it would carry to all parts of the square:

"You wonder what I am doing, eh? When the troubles of the people torment my mind, I look up at the sun."

I served as the excuse for his showman's claptrap, which was frenziedly applauded.

His platform manner was very different. Then he would pour out a cataract of words, passionate and incoherent, empty of reasoning. It did not matter much what he said, outside of the sweeping promises with which the speech was larded. That he could talk so resonantly and so long moved his followers to rapture. The raving voice certainly had magnetism. A considerable percentage of the ignorant accepted him as an unconquerable being, whose bombast and truculence had a mystic meaning.

However, Bustamante had no gift for organization. His interlocking unions were a jumble of crafts workers, the unskilled, and even domestic servants. Dues were collected, often at the rate of a few pennies a week, but no provision was made for either sick benefits or strike pay. All powers reposed in the leader, who chose his officers and did not have to make a financial accounting. As for establishing a network of branches throughout the island, Bustamante did not have the least notion of how to do that. He said at the time that he had no political aims, yet his dictatorial urges were manifest. In the words of his theme song, he expected men to rise and "follow, follow" him until they died.

There were one or two weak little unions which had been trying to function before Bustamante's advent. These looked to the PNP. But Manley did not then regard his party as a sponsor of individual unions. He assumed that all labour organizations would work together, at least temporarily behind Bustamante. On the other hand, the party would constitute the political movement, entitled to support by every union. This pattern struck me as being the logical outcome of events. Where, in the circumstances, could I and my group expect to figure?

I had faith that our drive to arouse national consciousness must win a following capable of becoming a majority within the PNP and forcing the latter to take a more positive stand. A good many lower-middle-class people supported me on this, and when I explained the idea at meetings volunteers seldom failed to speak up. A marked readiness to catch fire existed among the young, but the number that could be enlisted in a practical sense was limited. Since we did not favour violence, there was no immediate action that could be asked of them. I urged them to study the island's past, to think and discuss so as to make a patriotic elite of themselves.

Late in February, Bustamante precipitated a crisis by ordering a general strike. His union membership had grown to about fifty thousand. Some trades had not been organized even partially, and others had balked at giving him allegiance. The attempt, therefore, was bound to fail. Bustamante did not understand that a general strike is a revolution, and that its leader must be prepared in the event of success to take over the government. Workers on banana plantations and longshoremen who loaded fruit formed the sole considerable element that responded to Bustamante's call, but as much of Jamaica's revenue from abroad was derived from bananas the chaos in the ports caused consternation.

Governor Sir Arthur Richards struck back hard. He used his sweeping powers to declare a state of emergency, warned the militia to hold itself ready, and announced that law-breaking would be sternly handled. The only statesman in the situation was Manley. His extra-political prestige and his integrity gave him the governor's ear, while the services he had rendered labour in the past made it impossible for even the erratic Bustamante to refuse to treat with him. Manley obtained assurances from King's House that if the strike were immediately called off, bygones would be bygones; otherwise Bustamante would be arrested.

Uncertainty lasted for a day and a half, while conferences to which I was not invited were held. The streets filled ominously with demonstrators, not all of whom were members of Bustamante's unions but seemed equally ready to do whatever he wanted. Late the second evening PNP leaders decided to send a committee of three to try to influence the chief agitator. I do not know why Manley did not go himself, but I imagine it was felt that the sight of him entering the labour headquarters might touch off disorder.

Significantly enough, Domingo and I were asked to go, the league having expressed no views about the strike. The third man was a Negro barrister named Erasmus Campbell, an elected member of the Legislative Council. A car would make us conspicuous, so we walked through the dark streets, were questioned by a guard at the side gate of Bustamante's place and allowed to proceed. We climbed a back stairway in the yard to the second-storey room where we were expected. It was then after midnight.

An electric globe surrounded by fluttering moths dangled above the bare table behind which Bustamante sat, glowering. We spoke at once, to prevent him from taking the offensive. It would help neither the cause of labour nor that of political self-determination for the abortive strike to continue, we told him. The compromise arranged by Manley with the governor was reasonable. All the popular leaders must appear at a mass meeting the following afternoon and enunciate a programme of unified action in behalf of the working classes. Bustamante must read a prepared address, accepting the authority in labour disputes of a Trades Union Council of which he would be a member and on which the government would not be represented. He must tell his men to go back to work at once.

Bustamante no longer looked the picturesque charlatan. His expression was tense, fanatical. Suddenly he proved to me that a man's eyes really can blaze. He crouched as if he were about to leap upon us across the table. "I am beaten this time and I will have to give in," he snarled, then broke into vituperation against all who had opposed him, cried that he alone controlled the masses and if ever he were crossed again there would be a terror. For the moment, he gave the impression that he was insane. "I can cause Jamaica to run with blood," he shouted.

Domingo said: "Mr Bustamante, you do wrong even to think of violence in this country. There is no necessity for it, and if it got out of hand it would be punished by massacres of our people." A malevolent stare was the only answer. "We shall inform Mr Manley of your promise about the strike and the Trades Union Council," said Campbell. Bustamante gave a scarcely perceptible nod, and we went out.

The audience of ten thousand that gathered the next day, a Sunday, at the old Race Course was thought to be the largest that Kingston had ever known. It included some middle-class persons but not enough to prevent it from being inflammable. The judge's box, a wooden cabin on tall stilts, was the rostrum, crowded with political and labour personalities who took turns at the loudspeaker. Domingo was chairman. I sat right beside Bustamante.

The labour leader held an approved text, but behaved as if he were totally incapable of such uninspired formality as reading it aloud. He stumbled through the first paragraph, then went off at a tangent, embroidering the theme with garbled rhetoric. The typed pages slipped from his hands. Someone picked them up and returned them to him, whispering that he must keep his word. Bustamante went through the motions of making another attempt but found it useless. Brandishing the manuscript, he explained his difficulty to the crowd, asked whether preventing him from speaking from the heart would serve any good purpose. A tremendous roar of adulation upheld him. He gave his usual emotional performance, telling in his own words why he had cancelled the strike – and was allowed to get away with it. The newspapers printed the prepared address, be it said.

A number of sober speeches were made. The proceedings, however, were controlled by Bustamante. It had been agreed that he was to name the members of the Trades Union Council, or Advisory Board as he called it. In startling contrast with his manner of the night before, he had compliments for everyone. Domingo, Campbell and I were all appointed members, along with N.N. Nethersole, the vice-chairman of the People's National Party; H.P. Jacobs, editor of *Public Opinion*; and others. Manley was to be legal adviser to the unions. The endorsement of the public was unnecessary, but Bustamante did not fail to ask for a showing of hands. He got almost unanimous approval as he announced each name. There were optimists who believed that the labour movement had been lastingly put on a sane basis at that meeting. I doubted it myself, and I did not prove to be wrong.

APART FROM RESEARCH IN THE archives at the institute, I had made no progress with my history of the Caribbean. I decided that I must take lodgings where political friends could not reach me too easily, and I ended up by renting a furnished house at Gordon Town in the hills, about nine miles from Kingston. It was a lovely place named Rawcliffe, built against a hill-

Figure 31. Rawcliffe, in Gordon Town, the house Roberts rented in 1939. MS353.6.10.

side, with fruit trees and a large garden, watered by its own piping system from the Hope River below.

The rent in those days of moderate prices was eleven pounds a month, or less than forty-five US dollars, the pound sterling being at about four US dollars. If I had wanted to buy, I could have had Rawcliffe for twelve hundred pounds. The only disadvantage was the location in a deep bowl, whereas from nearby hilltops there were splendid views of Kingston and the sea. A rickety automobile serving as a bus would call and take a passenger for a shilling to Papine, three miles away, connecting point with the municipal transportation system. Of course, people who had cars thought nothing of driving out for a talk. But I turned the semi-isolation to account and wrote the important first six chapters of my book in a couple of months. It was plain by then, as I knew it would be, that I would need access to a much larger library.

In April the People's National Party held a convention. Delegates from all over the island reduced their aspirations to sober language. It was dramatic because unique in local history. The demand would still have been for something less than complete self-government if Domingo and I had not fought for this principle on the floor. Support flocked to us, persuading Manley, who having once taken the advanced standpoint adhered to it firmly. Naturally this seemed to me the most valuable outcome of the convention.

Bustamante lost little time in demonstrating his hopeless instability. He flouted several decisions of the Trades Union Council, then withdrew his representatives and it collapsed. A new council was formed of unions friendly to the PNP. I was asked to serve on it, but declined, stating that trades union experts were required rather than persons like myself who were pledged to a political programme. I still thought that parties and unions might work separately in Jamaica. The mountebank labour chief, meanwhile, led a large delegation of his members to a PNP meeting one night, obtained the floor and declared that they had come to join as a proof of solidarity with the political patriots. A few days later Bustamante turned in the membership cards which had been rather naively issued, and made the grotesque statement that he had found the party too radical. I often saw Manley pale and tense with anger at his cousin's tricks during that period. He told me more than once that Bustamante was evil, that he hated to keep a promise, that in Manley's opinion he would never grow up ethically to the point where he could be trusted to hold a consistent line. Yet we both respected his ability to win strikes and thus to improve conditions for the unskilled.

A rumour spread that the report of the Royal Commission under Lord Moyne would be hastened and a modification of Jamaica's status recommended. From the Legislative Council came an anachronism. The elected members formed themselves into a committee headed by J.A.G. Smith, their *de facto* leader and the shrewdest among them, and prepared a plan for submission to Westminster. The proposal was a virtual return to the regime of 1865 with its irresponsible executive branch, appointed upper house, and lower house elected under a limited franchise.

We had fun setting up the so-called Smith Constitution as a straw man, ridiculing it and tearing it to pieces. Three years before, the public would have been flattered to see Jamaica restored to the standing of such ancient and minute commonwealths as Barbados and Bermuda. Now there was no one so simple-minded as to miss the point that there had been progress in democratic ideas since 1865 and that a new form of government should at least be new. The PNP and the league jointly drafted their own proposals, introduced an embryo of responsibility, and warned that without these the constitution would be unacceptable even as an experiment. Manley insisted upon adult suffrage and got his way.

Governor Richards had been by no means blind to my activities. I was told by several persons close to him that he had thought seriously of deporting me. He had the right to do so, for I had been since 1921 a naturalized citizen of the United States. But the world was libertarian in such matters in 1939, and there can be no doubt that if I had been expelled from the country of my birth for advocating self-government I would have been given a friendly press abroad. This probably was a factor with Richards, who wanted the Jamaica movement pooh-poohed. He sent for a copy of my biography of Semmes, and is reported to have commented that I seemed an intelligent political thinker with whom there was no reason to interfere as yet. Not a word about my citizenship was said officially.

It is proper, however, that I should make clear my attitude on this point. I felt myself unalterably a Jamaican, and if Jamaican nationality had been a recognized legal fact I would never have given it up for any other. That I had been born a British subject was a lesser consideration, because I had not asked for the status and did not concede it the right of precedence over the impulses of my true ancestry. General Jan Smuts, a native of the Cape Colony, had taken a similar stand in the Boer War; Éamon de Valera, born in New York City, had declared for embattled Ireland. The cases are not exactly parallel, but they serve to illustrate what I mean.

I had found it difficult during World War I to travel as a British subject working for a North American newspaper, so I took out American 'first papers' and later completed the process. I knew that this obligated me to serve the United States loyally, even against Britain, if international differences should arise. It did not, I believed, debar me morally from advising a course of action opposing Britain in the land of my birth. I might be charged someday with filibustering, but in that event I would be in good company historically. United States citizenship proved a source of strength for me with young Jamaican nationalists. It convinced them that, at all events, I was playing no sort of masked British game.

There came a lull in island politics and labour agitation, but not in world affairs. There was a connection between these circumstances. War was looming closer. I had written a series of articles for the Jamaica *Standard* in which I had called a second global struggle inevitable. Acting now on

Figure 32. Roberts in Chicago, 28 October 1939. Photographer A.S. Knobble. MS353.6.1.

my own prediction, so as to avoid trouble in booking a berth, I sailed late in August on a Norwegian freighter for New Orleans. My plan was to go on to Washington and complete my history of the Caribbean.

I heard the non-aggression pact between Germany and Russia announced over the radio while I was in the Gulf of Mexico. On Royal Street, New Orleans, on 1 September, I bought an extra which screamed "Hitler Opens War: Nazis Bomb Polish Cities". England and France formally took sides against the Führer two days afterward. It was my opinion that little or nothing more could be done for our self-government cause until the strife in Europe ended. I assumed that Governor Richards would not allow me to land in Jamaica now unless the Colonial Office should come out in favour of a new and liberal constitution, a step that seemed most unlikely. I supposed that a Defence of a Realm Act, perhaps martial law, would be used to muzzle both the PNP and the labour unions.

But unexpected fruit ripen upon the tree of war. Manley offered, indeed, to suspend all polemical activities, and Bustamante beat his breast proclaiming that victory for the Empire's arms had become his sole concern. Richards let matters ride. The truce was short-lived. Inactivity bored Bustamante, and after he had called some strikes that hampered a shipping already restricted by German submarines, he was interned. Manley felt that the problem was one of conflict with the arbitrary Crown Colony system. He resumed action with his party, and as its influence tended to calm the unions, Richards did not object. Personally I foresaw that my absence must last for many months. I acknowledged the necessity as a writer. For the international situation had greatly increased the importance of my book, both in my publishers' eyes and in my own.

CHAPTER 18 ❧ The Act of Havana

MY LIFE IN WASHINGTON FOR THE BETTER PART of a year may be dismissed briefly. It would have been interesting to mix with journalists and politicians at this crucial time when the United States government became more and more friendly to the western democracies, while crank lobbies strove to foster isolationist sentiment. But my task left me no leisure. The Library of Congress and the admirable specialized collection at the Pan American Union Building contained the material I needed. Half of each day was spent in research and half in writing. I do not remember it as drudgery, but rather as the most intensive, fascinating work I have ever done.

I completed *The Caribbean: The Story of Our Sea of Destiny* in the summer of 1940. My publishers rushed it through the press. In the last chapter I had made a prediction that, as a measure against the greed of Hitler, and particularly for the defence of the Panama Canal, the United States would acquire naval and air bases in European colonies in the West Indies. I mentioned Jamaica, the Bahamas, Antigua, St Lucia and Trinidad, as well as some others not so accurately picked. Within a few days of the issuing of my book on 3 September 1940, the deal between Franklin D. Roosevelt and Winston Churchill for overage destroyers in exchange for ninety-nine-year leases of bases was announced. This helped to focus attention on my history, which newspapers all over the United States reviewed in flattering terms. A State Department official told me that he had commended the book to every embassy and consulate in the Americas.

Meanwhile, I had gone once more to New Orleans for a holiday. France,

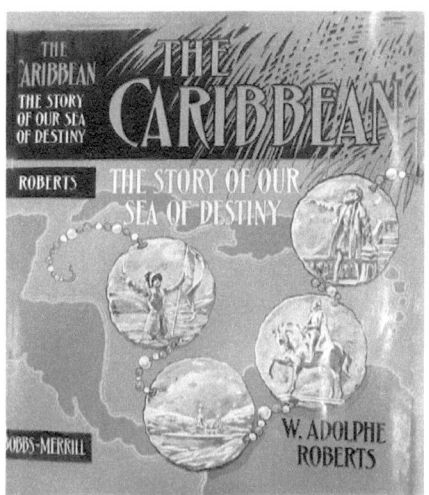

Figure 33. The cover of *The Caribbean: The Story of Our Sea of Destiny* (1940).

Belgium and Holland had fallen. The Battle of Britain was raging. Roosevelt had stiffened his pan-American defensive policy by calling a conference at Panama of the foreign ministers of all the American republics. The decision was to resist any military move threatening the New World which might develop out of the war in Europe. By July the situation had become still more serious. England was reeling under the German air attacks, and if she were crushed it was possible that Hitler might announce that he had thereby acquired all the European territories overseas by right of conquest.

In these circumstances, Roosevelt summoned a second conference of foreign ministers, to meet at Havana and decide upon a specific course of intervention to prevent the Nazis from taking a foot of territory in the Western Hemisphere. The transfer by any means of a colony from any one European power to another was not to be tolerated. A plan of joint action was sought, to be applied at once if Britain went under. Naturally the interested belligerent governments were not invited to take part in a discussion of how their own autopsies might have to be conducted. It would have been logical, however, for them to send observers to Havana. They did nothing of the kind. The legislatures of the bewildered colonies made no move to be heard. Local political organizations appeared to have been struck dumb, and this included even the People's National Party of Jamaica.

I thought it vital that our right to self-determination should be placed before the conference at Havana. W.A. Domingo thought so too. A letter I wrote to him from New Orleans, proposing that the Jamaica Progressive League send an unofficial delegate, crossed one from him. He informed me that the West Indies National Council, a group he had organized in New York to watch over the wartime concerns of all the British Caribbean territories, was working on an appeal. I promptly wrote a memorandum which I urged Domingo to have the league adopt and place in the hands of all the foreign ministers. Both his project and mine were carried out. A West Indian lawyer, Hope R. Stevens, went to the Cuban capital as the representative of the league and the council.

I shall give the whole text of my memorandum, for the effect produced by it is an episode of unwritten history:

> The Jamaica Progressive League, expressing the political aspirations of the people of Jamaica, and taking cognisance of the effect of international affairs upon European colonies in the Caribbean area, respectfully present this declaration for your sympathetic consideration.
>
> In behalf of the Jamaican people, we claim the protection afforded by the Monroe Doctrine as enunciated in 1823 and definitively interpreted by Congressional Resolution in June, 1940. We claim also the right of self-determination recognized by many American statesmen and especially by President U.S. Grant in his message to Congress December 6, 1869, on the question of European colonies in the Western Hemisphere, when he said: "When the present relation of colonies ceases, they are to become independent powers, exercising the right of choice and of self-control in the determination of their future condition and relations with other powers."
>
> Jamaica has been a British colony since 1655. It has never sought to detach itself from the British Empire, and does not now seek to do so. Local nationalist sentiment has been most strongly manifested in the legitimate aspiration of the Jamaica Progressive League, and other political organizations, to attain Dominion status within the framework of the British Commonwealth of Nations. This legitimate political aspiration was expressed in the memorandum filed with the West India Royal Commission at Kingston, Jamaica, November, 1938, and also embodied in other literature hereto attached. But if, as a result of the present war, through agencies beyond the control of Jamaica, it should appear that British rule in the Island will cease, we go on record as demanding that the Jamaican people be consulted regarding its future political allegiances.
>
> We are unalterably opposed to any plan that would transfer Jamaica from one sovereignty to another, even though the new sovereignty be Western, or which would place the Island under a trusteeship of any sort, without negotiation with Jamaican leaders and a plebiscite to determine the wishes of the electorate.
>
> The status of an independent nation is the only status that could automatically follow the demise of British imperial authority. It is equally unacceptable to the Jamaican people that the Island should be bequeathed like a chattel to new rulers, or appropriated by a neighbour on the latter's terms. Neither the dead

hand of foreign political control nor an arbitrary power should be permitted to dictate the future of any American democracy.

Jamaica is a national entity in the Western world. Because it has been bound to Europe by governmental ties, a fortuitous economic dependence on Europe has prevailed. But in the future, and especially if British rule should cease, the interests of Jamaica will be identical with those of the countries in the Pan-American Union. We recognize that it would be morally obligatory on Jamaica to aid in every possible way in the defence of the Caribbean Sea and the Panama Canal. The Island has no armed forces. Its aid, therefore, might take the form of conceding naval and airplane bases to some strong American power.

Honour and the democratic ideal dictate, however, that the use of Jamaican soil for purposes of pan-American security is a matter which should be arranged by, and with, one of the following responsible parties:

1. The existing British Empire, of which Jamaica is a part.
2. An independent Jamaica.
3. Any unit with which Jamaica may have voluntarily joined her fortunes.

Under the old order, the Jamaican people has been subject to a Crown Colony system which, we sincerely believe, was on the point of giving way to local self-government. We shall not be contented under any new order that may emerge from the present war, to be less than free citizens in our native land.

The United States inevitably took the lead at the Havana conference. Cordell Hull, secretary of state, said that if the American republics found it necessary to occupy any colony, such action would not imply annexation. A trusteeship would be set up. A commission, consisting of a member from each one of three nearby republics, would administer until the future of the colony in question could be decided by the general pan-American body. If it proved safe, when the war ended, to restore the territory to its original sovereign, this would be done. Otherwise, independence was to be granted when the capacity for self-government was evident. The old-fashioned terms resembled the mandates created by the Treaty of Versailles after World War I. There were no guarantees that the inhabitants of an occupied colony would be consulted as to the form of administration. No time limit was placed upon the government by commission.

This was the type of policy which the Jamaica Progressive League's memorandum challenged. A copy was given to every delegate at Havana, and to members of the ambassadorial staffs. They acknowledged its receipt, but did nothing about it – with one exception. Dr Leopoldo Melo, foreign minister of Argentina, became interested in both the memorandum and the West Indies National Council's appeal. He used them to support proposals in conference with US assistant secretary of state A.A. Berle Jr, which greatly liberalized the pan-American attitude toward the colonies.

Melo obtained an agreement that an organic law must be adopted after consultation with the people in whatever manner possible. The resulting administration would in the first instance be limited to three years, and if it became necessary to extend it a renewal for ten years would be the maximum. Only the unlikely circumstance of the war being still in progress could then postpone a decision between restoration and independence. These provisos were written into the Act of Havana.

Reporting to his government, Melo cabled: "As to tutelage, it must be remembered that this is an institution for incompetents and that it would wound the sentiments of certain units as cultured as, for example, Jamaica; all the populations of America are not in the state of backwardness of French Guiana." Later he declared: "Pan-Americanism now includes the principle of self-determination, sustained by the Argentine delegation and accepted with enthusiasm by the inhabitants of those regions of America which have not yet rounded out the cycle of democratic organization. Outstanding among those inhabitants is the people of Jamaica, who in a considered document by the Progressive League, after recording the country's past as a British colony, addressed the following message to the delegates: . . ." He proceeded to quote the league's memorandum from the words, "The status of an independent nation" to the end. The safeguards granted were extremely valuable as a precedent, even though at the time the question proved to be academic, for Britain did not fall. The bases for destroyers compact was made. The United States enlarged its Caribbean interests by acquiring footholds in Jamaica and six other territories. Local autonomy remained a prize to be wrested from Downing Street or not at all.

I cannot say whether Governor Richards resented the fact that Jamaicans had gone over the heads of the Crown Colony regime and filed a plea at Havana. It is at least certain that his personal attitude was harsh that year. He denounced in a speech the leaders of the self-government movement as "political quacks" and "fireside financiers" who had "an itch to rule". Early in 1941 Manley asked W.A. Domingo to come from New York and work as a paid organizer for the PNP. Domingo had been exchanging letters with a friend in Kingston, an obscure person, to whom he incautiously expressed opinions about English colonial methods. Referring to this correspondence, he wrote me just before he sailed: "Letters from me to everybody else in Jamaica were opened [censored] while those to him were invariably unopened. It looked as if they had set a trap and were waiting to catch me. That is my real fear. I may have written something carelessly long ago (though I can't think of any) and it might be held against me. Still, regardless of everything, I am determined to go. Let them do their worst." He had in mind the well-known practice under a censorship of encouraging a 'dangerous' correspondence until the writer has thoroughly committed himself. The envelopes are steamed, the contents photographed and replaced intact, the flap resealed.

When Domingo's ship reached Port Royal, he was arrested on board by order of the governor and interned in the concentration camp. This action was announced as a preventive measure. There were no public hearings, but after considerable delay it leaked out that Domingo was charged – on the strength of his letters to his Kingston friend – with intent to hamper the war effort by stirring up labour troubles at the US naval base and promoting ill-feeling generally between whites and blacks. I have said enough about this moderate Negro, whose nationalism had never been founded on racial feeling, that he stood strangely accused. It proved to be the governor's pleasure to detain him for twenty months.

CUT OFF INDEFINITELY NOW FROM Jamaican affairs, I adopted New Orleans as the place to live, and the result was several books that I might not otherwise have written. The first one was a natural outgrowth from *The Caribbean*. I had come upon much interesting material about the colonizing efforts of France in the islands and on the Gulf Coast, which had never been correlated for English readers. So I wrote a brief history entitled *The French in the West Indies*. It aspired only to be an introduction to the subject. The general public paid little attention to it. But it got into the reference libraries. Of all my books it has been the most quoted by lecturers and by other writers.

I also produced in New Orleans a factual yet romantic study, *Lake Pontchartrain*, a view of the city through its backdoor approaches, instead of its frontage on the Mississippi; and a trilogy of historical novels: *Royal Street*, *Brave Mardi Gras* and *Creole Dusk*. I mention the books in order to be done with them. The spell that New Orleans and the remnants of its exotic civilization cast upon me is what matters here. The French settlements in lower Louisiana early took on the aspects of a Caribbean plantation colony, luxurious and gay, respectful of religion but not dominated by it. That financial orgy, the Mississippi Bubble, was based upon Louisiana and sowed the seeds of a wild gambling spirit. The capital, New Orleans, grew up aspiring to elegance. After the Seven Years' War, France ceded the colony to Spain, to compensate the latter for losses elsewhere. A unique amalgam resulted. The Spaniards largely rebuilt the city and put a subtle Andalusian stamp upon it, but spiritually they yielded to French influence.

Then the slave revolution in Saint-Domingue caused a great influx of fugitive planters, some of whom brought not only family portraits and furniture but serving retinues of Negroes devoted to voodooism. The aura of the islands spread once more at the mouth of the Mississippi. It was not long before Napoleon recovered Louisiana and sold it to the United States. Anglo-Saxon adventurers then flocked down, leading to the division between the French city and new American district south of Canal Street which marked the character of New Orleans throughout the nineteenth century and well into the twentieth. The Creoles entrenched themselves in their Vieux Carré. They were the elite, responsible for the glittering cult of the duel that prevailed till the War of Secession, for the development of carnival, and a passion for grand opera such as few communities outside Italy have known.

The Creoles were not sternly exclusive. They intermarried freely enough with newcomers who accepted their ways, but turned up their noses at anyone who sought to 'Americanise' them. The War of Secession ruined the Creoles. Yet even in their disintegration they struck the pleasure-loving, libertarian note which their neighbours of the other race adopted. New Orleans remains different among the cities of the United States. For how long, who can tell?

I felt regret that I had not migrated there when I left Jamaica as a boy, or at least had not discovered it much sooner. It seemed to me that I should have been happier, perhaps more successful, if my journalistic experience had been obtained against a background I should have understood better than I understood New York. Such notions are sheer dreamstuff, to be sure. A radical deviation from what I did do would have altered the trend of my life. Anyway, there I was in my fifties exploring New Orleans with greater interest than had been aroused in me by any other place in North

The Act of Havana ⁍ 307

Figure 34. Looking down St Ann Street from Royal Street, New Orleans, c. 1940. This photograph was the basis for the cover of Roberts's novel *Royal Street*. MS353.6.11.

America. I had rented as a home a small old house on Dumaine Street. It was of two stories, but each consisted of only one room. I wrote *The French in the West Indies* there.

Several blocks of nearby Royal Street, starting at Canal, were largely given over to antique shops, a sort of museum in sections crowded with furniture and *objets d'art* from mansions deserted, most of them, in my own youth. The debris was ornate. Fortunately, the destruction of buildings had ceased. For the whole Vieux Carré had been declared by law a state monument, under the control of a commission which passed on proposed structural changes. Dwellings had in many cases been turned to business uses without damage to the architectural effect. It was still possible to visit rooms in Exchange Alley and elsewhere that had been the academies of famous fencing masters a hundred years before.

From the standpoint of regional literature, the moment was one of decline. Up until 1900 books of considerable interest had been published in French, ranging from history to novels and poetry. There had been some creditable work by coloured Creoles, mostly in the field of *belles lettres*. French-language newspapers had persisted long into the present century. To uphold the tradition, nothing survived but the Athénée Louisiannais, a scholarly society with its organ, *Comptes Rendus*, and its prizes for the best essays in French on a specified theme.

But there had been a concurrent activity in English, and this was not dead. The successors of Hearn and Cable owed something to the Gallic atmosphere. They belonged to a New Orleans school whose patterns differed subtly from those of writers elsewhere in the United States. Lyle Saxon was the outstanding figure around 1940. Though from upstate Louisiana and speaking little or no French, he loved the old city on its crescent-shape curve of the Mississippi and described it well. He lived between a room in the St Charles Hotel, refurnished with antiquarian touches, and a lovely house in the Vieux Carré which movie money for his biography of Jean Lafitte, the pirate, enabled him to buy.

Saxon, who never married, was a generous host. He was an aesthete and conversationalist who liked to be surrounded by people. His rather soft face belied the pungent quality of his wit. He had come to be regarded as a sort of 'Mr New Orleans', whom distinguished visitors must not fail to meet. The reverse of the picture was his unpatronizing feeling for Negroes, rare among Southerners. His novel *Children of Strangers*, which deals with a mixed-blood community, has notable charm. He had begun as a reporter and still wrote his impressions of each year's carnival for the *Times-Picayune*. It was a typical attachment. Nearly all the New Orleans writers in my time had come up by way of the newspapers.

There were libraries and fine collections of relics of the old culture, in the Cabildo and elsewhere. But the living word is better. I learned a good deal at the meetings of the Athénée, which generally took place in the Presbytère, one of the two Franco-Spanish governmental buildings that flanked the Cathedral. Only French was used at the Athénée. Its president, André Lafargue, a small, tense man with birdlike features, took as a personal responsibility the dictum of the founders in 1876, that if the language were not perpetuated there would "no longer be any Creoles". Ties with the Institut de France were maintained, and brilliant lecturers often came from France.

I did not ignore the other side of New Orleans, which had a gracious social centre, very Southern in atmosphere, in the so-called Garden District, and otherwise was cosmopolitan after the fashion of a great port. Indeed, some of its rowdier aspects overflowed into the Vieux Carré. Decatur Street, the former Levée on the riverfront, with its sailors' bars and restaurants, was anything but Creole. Bordellos stood on Dauphine, Burgundy and several of the crosswise streets, a residue of 'Storyville', the enormous red-light district that was broken up in World War I.

As for gambling, it was everywhere, a fantastic network of racetrack bookmaking, of card and dice parlours, of illicit roulette wheels, hidden in backyard rooms or even behind street fronts on the drawn blinds of which the shadows of addicts moved like magic-lantern puppets. Gambling has never had the least attraction for me. Bawdry and barroom carousing were sometimes amusing to observe. The favourite New Orleans sport of 'fishin' and crabbin'' had a certain allure, though I had not thought of myself as a prospective angler. Here the labyrinth of hundreds of miles of bayous about the city, the brooding swamp oaks hung with Spanish moss, the channels dense with blue water hyacinths, offered a bizarre setting. The practice was to leave by motorboat at about two o'clock in the morning and work one's way toward the Gulf. The best catches were likely to be made at dawn.

It stood to reason that New Orleans was a seafood town. Dozens of little places vied with the celebrated restaurants in serving a good *bouillabaisse*, as well as oysters, soft-shell crabs and many sorts of fried fish. Coffee blended with chicory was drunk at meals and between meals, day and night. The old French Market had coffee-stalls of repute. There were counters that enticed you to halt on the sidewalk for a quick *demi-tasse*. Coffee was the first thing offered a visitor in all homes, and in some offices. Rio de Janeiro is said to have an even greater devotion to this beverage than New Orleans, but I dispute the claim.

One evening I attended a routine session of the Athénée Louisiannais. When it broke up, André Lafargue called to me from the chair. I turned back and he introduced me to two Creole girls of the purest type, their skins of camellia pallor, their hair black. They both had married names which struck me as not being sufficiently colourful to suit them. But Lafargue explained that they had been born Constance and Yvonne le Mercier-du Quesnay. In *The French in the West Indies*, I had mentioned their family, which after the slave revolution in Saint-Domingue had emigrated first to Jamaica, and had then divided. One branch had settled in New Orleans, its most eminent early member having been the Abbé Guillaume du Quesnay, whose bones lay in the crypt of the Cathedral. It appeared that the girls before me, their unmarried sister and their mother, had seen my book, and on hearing from Lafargue that I was in New Orleans, had said that they wanted to meet me.

Thus began one of the most delightful friendships of my life. I dedicated my *Royal Street* to the le Mercier-du Quesnay ladies. Why did I not remain in their city, where I was happy enough? This poses a timeless issue, and it takes precedence over one's social contentment. The effort to build a nation is comparable to that of the creative impulse in art. The artist thinks it important to write a certain book, paint a certain picture, or compose a certain piece of music for its own sake. It is also his answer to the lukewarm who argue that a people may be satisfied under a colonial regime and might have to pay an unjustifiable price for liberty. The nationalist forecasts a new adult voice in the world, able perhaps to contribute something of beauty or of wisdom. This is an end which he must serve. He does not accept the calm, pedestrian pace of custom. He helps to make history.

CHAPTER 19 ❧ The Shaping of a Nation

LETTERS FROM JAMAICA KEPT ME INFORMED OF DEVELOPMENTS there. These did not seem, at long distance, to have much import during the darkest of the war years. The PNP had in 1940 declared itself to be socialist, a move with which I had no personal sympathy and which I thought a psychological error since an agricultural tropical country like Jamaica was not keyed to socialism. But all such issues were academic, I told my friends, until the political future of the whole world was decided. I failed to count on the war itself proving a solvent where Britain and self-government for colonies was concerned.

Journeys to New York and Washington interrupted my New Orleans life in 1941, 1942 and 1943. The reasons were literary work on the one side, and on the other the activities of the still energetic Progressive League. An overnight trip from New York to Boston was made for the purpose of addressing a group of Jamaicans who had been moved to emulate the Harlem organization. It led to my meeting Dr Eric Williams, the future chief minister of Trinidad. The slight young man, as he then was, with a round, very boyish face, stepped up after I had done speaking and introduced himself to me. He had come to the Boston affair from Howard University, Washington, where he had the post of assistant professor of social and political science. This was the start of an exchange of ideas pursued at intervals whenever I visited Washington. Williams was one of the organizers of a conference on the economic future of the Caribbean held by Howard in the summer of 1943. I was invited to take part. Among the other speakers was Captain

John Huggins, head of the British Colonies Supply Mission in the United States, very shortly to be knighted and appointed to replace Richards as governor of Jamaica. A wooden figure, this Huggins, who dispensed platitudes from a manuscript and handled all queries by barking: "I am afraid I cannot answer that question."

A few weeks before, the Colonial Office had announced that a constitution with adult suffrage would be granted Jamaica, "to meet the desires of the people and to put an end to controversy". It would go into effect after the taking of a census, and other preliminaries. This had astonished me to the point of wondering at first whether there were not some catch in it. But I recall that I was quite optimistic at Howard about the constitution. It offered an executive committee of ten, five to be chosen by an elected lower house and five by the governor. I felt that this was enough of a start for full autonomy to grow out of it. Nothing really creative was said on this subject by delegates to the conference. I find it more interesting that the possibility of federation of the British West Indies was brought up for discussion, and that I made the following statement: "I believe that [eventually] there will be two federations, one in the west consisting of Jamaica, the Bahamas and British Honduras, with Kingston as its capital; and one in the eastern Caribbean consisting of Trinidad, nearby islands and British Guiana, with Port of Spain as its capital." We shall see what came of 1943's hopes and prophecies.

In our frequent chats Eric Williams did not once say, as I remember, that he might enter politics. He had accepted a strategic job on the staff of the newly formed Anglo-American Caribbean Commission. Committed to historical and social research, and touched by racial indignation, Williams appeared to me to be a pedantic type. He lacked eloquence in public speaking. I did not think of him as a leader, but as a tireless worker who would amass ammunition for use by spokesmen dispassionately chosen by himself. It is not always possible to foretell the direction in which a fermenting talent will expand.

The year 1944 was a period of suspense. It would have been manifestly impolitic for me, a United States citizen, to go to Jamaica and participate in time of war in the elections that were set for December. The news that reached me by mail was puzzling. Bustamante, when he and his fellow internees had been freed, had at once proclaimed the existence of a political party headed by himself and had nominated a ticket of thirty-two for the House of Representatives. He called it the Jamaica Labour Party (JLP). At a certain rally a faint murmur arose over the calibre of one of his candidates. Busta shouted in reply that if he told his followers to vote even for a yellow dog they must do so. This had caused no bristling of revolt.

There was another impromptu party, the Democratic, which backed the interests of the large landowners and merchants and seemed likely to be a failure. Only the PNP was a solid political organization, built up since 1938, with district branches in every parish. On the face of things, it should win, especially as the majority of its nominees were well-known men. At mass meetings, however, the crowds were frenziedly cheering Bustamante for promising the impossible, such as jobs for everybody and the doubling of wages. Election returns anywhere can seldom have been as startling as these proved to be. Yet a minimum of analysis was sufficient to explain them. The PNP had been routed, having elected but five men of whom Manley was not one. He had been beaten in Eastern St Andrew by a bush therapist. Bustamante was in, with a miscellaneous group of twenty-six, though a couple of them passed as independents. He was slated to be chief minister.

The franchise under the Crown Colony had been limited to fewer than twenty thousand Jamaicans. Suddenly over seven hundred had gone to the polls to vote for the first time. The majority imagined, I must assume, that an elected person would have the power to do anything that he had promised, so they cast their ballots for the side that had promised most. On the emotional plane, a budding nationalism had been chilled by the PNP's turn toward socialist, that is to say international, ideas. The Labour Party had probably given the impression of being the more Jamaican of the two. I was greatly disappointed at the outcome, for I saw the campaign methods of Bustamante as charlatanry.

A few weeks afterward, on 5 February 1945, I asked for a British visa good for travel to Jamaica. Strict wartime regulations were in force, and it did not surprise me that I was questioned about my political views. The war, however, was drawing to an end, and I anticipated no trouble. I said that my visit was for the purpose of seeing how the new constitution worked. The passport official in New York nodded and replied that he would have to get clearance from Jamaica. A cryptic silence prevailed for a month. I then received the following note from the British passport control office:

"We regret to inform you that the Government of Jamaica is unable to accede to your request at the present time."

A visa had been refused me because the new Executive Council of my native land had declared that it did not wish me to have one. The matter had been put before the Council by the governor, Sir John Huggins, despite his power to deal with it on his own initiative. Plainly, he had consulted the chief minister, and on learning from Bustamante that the latter wanted me barred, the governor had made it part of the order of business of the embryo cabinet. This was the start of a *cause célèbre* that had reverberations outside the island. It came before the Jamaica legislature, and the details can be read in the pages of *Hansard*.

I shall briefly retrace the outstanding points. But first let me deny the charge often made, that I have nursed a special venom against Bustamante for shutting me out of Jamaica. On the contrary. He provided me with vast local publicity, which was useful to me in view of the fact that I had been absent during the war. I had always been critical of Bustamante; my fresh distaste, if any, was caused by the foolish terms in which he attacked but could not harm me. From April to July the case was furiously argued in the Jamaica press, with the PNP organ, *Public Opinion*, naturally taking the lead in my favour. A request by the Executive of the PNP that the denial of a landing visa be reconsidered was formally turned down. This in the face of an assertion by H.G. de Lisser, published in the *Gleaner* before the whole controversy started, that he was "not aware of any power that can prevent a distinguished naturalized American citizen" from "visiting or residing in a British Colony with whose affairs, according to Mr Winston Churchill, the United States of America will in the future have a great deal to do".

On 24 July (incidentally the birthday of Simón Bolívar and a libertarian fiesta throughout the Americas, though I do not think that any of our island politicians remembered that) a resolution by Florizel A. Glasspole, PNP member for Eastern Kingston, was brought up for debate. It asked the House of Representatives to place on record its disapproval of the decision of the Executive Council. If carried, the resolution would have been a vote of no confidence in the government. A mere gesture, since the PNP was in a pitiful minority. But no better forum existed for saying things wise and otherwise.

The opening phase of the discussion concerned my nationality. Glasspole had described me as a Jamaican, and several JLP members sought to establish that I was nothing of the sort. The legalistic quibbling wasted a lot of time. Neither side won. The Speaker ended by declaring that the question of whether I was a Jamaican, or a non-Jamaican, would be "ruled out as being irrelevant". None of the members was sufficiently acute to make the point that, as the country was not independent, the word 'Jamaican' had no standing in establishing citizenship, but did have the clear meaning that I had been born here.

Getting around to motives, Frank Pixley said that the government had "no intention of allowing persons to come from abroad to affiliate themselves with any Socialist group".

"Communist," amended the chief minister. His curse word was shrugged aside.

Someone suggested that, in view of my work for self-government, it was only logical that I should be interested in seeing the progress that was being made. Dwarfish Isaac Barrant quipped, "Write and tell him." This was greeted with hearty merriment by the majority. The debate failed to rise to a level which would justify further quotations. On division, three votes were cast for and twenty-two against. There were seven absentees.

The following year, 1946, the war having ended, I flew from Cuba and appeared without warning at the Palisadoes Airport on 19 July. I was working on a travel book about the West Indies, which would take note of new conditions growing out of the war and would be entitled *Lands of the Inner Sea*. Passport regulations had been changed. The airline had not required that I show a visa for Jamaica. But I wondered what sort of reception I would be given. It turned out that the government had long expected that I would come. The polite immigration officer was ready with a formula. I could land as a tourist, he said, with permission to remain for six months. But he warned me not to make political speeches, because the police might think my ideas subversive and report me to higher authorities. Various security rules were still in force, and under them an alien could be deported. I thanked him, smiling, for giving me such valuable information, and he smiled back.

Newspaper interviews and a round of social calls began at once. Public rallies and a dinner at the Myrtle Bank Hotel were staged to welcome me. I made a good many speeches which assuredly could not have been called non-political. My approach was to announce that I was a tourist, and then to

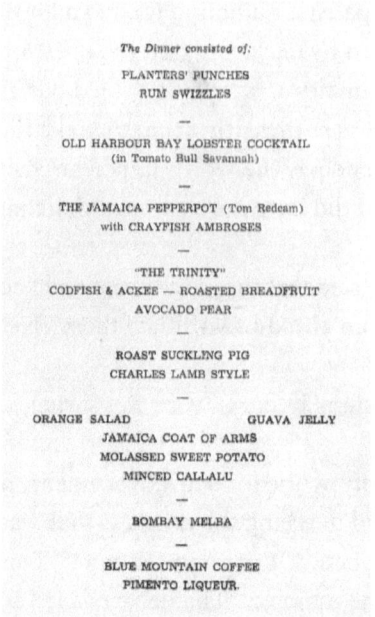

Figure 35. Menu from the dinner held at the Myrtle Bank Hotel on Wednesday 7 August 1946 to celebrate Roberts's return to Jamaica. MS353.10.1.8.

appraise conditions in terms of mock innocence. At times I dispensed with the irony. It would have suited me to have the government cap my tour with an arrest and more publicity. But they let me alone. Policemen on duty at my meetings went out of their way to be friendly.

The affair at Myrtle Bank was perhaps the high-water mark of my political prominence in Jamaica. It would be an error of emphasis to ignore that. Dr Ivan Lloyd, ranking PNP member in the House of Representatives, acted as chairman. The speakers were Norman Manley, N.N. Nethersole, W.A. Domingo and W.G. McFarlane, in the names of the two branches of our self-government movement; the moderate Philip Sherlock, for general culture; T.E. Sealy, editor of the *Gleaner*, for journalism; and Hugh Paget, for the newly formed Jamaica Historical Society.

Manley discussed my work in some detail. He said generously that to me, when we met in 1937, he owed his first serious and deliberate consideration of the subject of a national outlook and life for Jamaica, and his first and most lasting inspiration about it. He had carried the idea forward and pleaded for a federation of all the British West Indies. Not a week passed, he said, without bringing him evidence that the peoples of the other islands were looking to Jamaica to build the foundations for a future of the sort. This caused me to prick up my ears. It was more significant than I realized at the moment. Paget and Sherlock dwelt upon what they called my other love: history. They stressed the point that I had shown with objectivity in my books the importance of the relationship between West Indian history and West Indian geography.

My response in that atmosphere of friendship and praise is not remembered by me as having been particularly effective. But I did take the opportunity to develop an aspect for which Manley and Paget had provided me with the text. Jamaica, I agreed, might be in a federation someday: I had admitted as much at Howard University. First things first, however. It was more important now to understand our affinity with the people of the whole region, so that we might be guided in setting up free institutions. Jamaicans were Caribbean by temperament, a fact nothing could alter. In the long run we would react more like Cubans than like Englishmen or West Africans. We must study the experience of our neighbours, from whom in the past colonial prejudices had largely separated us.

Manley and I had several private talks at his home. Defeat a year and a half before had only served to stiffen him as a thinker and founder. One got from him the conviction that his fine intelligence was being brought into full play. But I did not have the chance on that visit to observe him in party action. The demands of my book allowed me barely three weeks in Jamaica. I went to stay with friends, the Grants, for a few days at Lucea, a sleepy little port I have always loved. The set of impressions which began to form served me well, as will be seen presently. On 10 August I left by plane for Puerto Rico, the Lesser Antilles and Trinidad. Returning to the United States, I made stops in the Dominican Republic and Haiti, and again in Cuba. It was my intention to go back to Jamaica as soon as possible, and to arrange my work so that I could live there. Except for hurried round trips, I was not able to carry this out until 1949. For I had decided to write a historical novel about the Cuban War of Independence, as I had promised myself for years that I would do.

In 1948 Manley took me to a meeting or two of the PNP Executive, held in the ramshackle former headquarters of Marcus Garvey on Slipe Road. The place bore the name, ludicrous in the tropics, of Edelweiss Park. A leftist air prevailed. The salutes with clenched fists and the incessant use of 'comrade' as a greeting did not appear to me to come naturally from Creoles. But I found that the party was extremely well-organized from this centre. Its branches in the parishes far outnumbered those of the JLP.

There was no doubt in my mind that Manley would prove a statesman in office. I hoped that his party would win the next elections, and I promised to aid it. I started to carry out the pledge by urging the Jamaica Progressive League of New York again to raise funds for the PNP. The league prepared the way for mass meetings, which Manley was asked to fly to New

York to address. He went up on several occasions and met with great success.

At a session of the Jamaica Historical society which I addressed, I was elected an honorary member. The president of the society, my boyhood friend Sir Noel Livingston, was a conservative man who had warily left unanswered the letter I wrote him at the beginning of the self-government movement asking for his support. I had a glimpse of the embryo from which the University College of the West Indies was growing rapidly. The land at Mona used during the war as a camp for Maltese and Gibraltar refugees had been turned over to the organizers. Some of the rough wooden buildings were still serviceable, and skeleton classes were being held in them. Subject No. 1 was medicine. Philip Sherlock, named as vice-principal, acted as my guide. He asked whether I would help by giving lectures on history in advance of the staffing of a regular history department. I answered that I would. But not until the following year. Another stay at Lucea, this time for nine days, crystallized certain mental pictures. And then I was gone from Jamaica once more.

I BEGAN WRITING MY NOVEL *The Single Star*, in New Orleans, in August 1948. The title was taken from a pledge by José Martí, the Apostle: "The day will come when we shall place, on the strongest fort [Morro Castle, Havana] of our country, the flag of the single star." Next to Simón Bolívar, Martí struck me as being the most impressive of the leaders who had worked to free their countries from Spanish rule in the Americas. The son of a sergeant, he was not the aristocrat and not the victor on battlefields that Bolívar had been. He was more the man of letters, who knew how to be a supreme animator. The impetus he had given the revolution did not falter when he fell at Dos Ríos.

The scene of the early chapters was to be laid in Jamaica, where a young man of the planter class adopts the cause of the sister island. His home is near Lucea, the little north-coast port I had visited recently and which had been a haven for blockade runners during the War of Independence. I needed no further local colour for these chapters and they were quickly written in New Orleans. The main theatre of action, however, would be the eastern half of Cuba. Observations on the spot were necessary, and toward the end of November 1948, I started on a deliberately slow journey to Oriente Province.

Bus travel is the best way of getting the feel of a countryside. It is not merely a matter of being close to the landscape. People come and go under your eyes. I took a through ticket on a bus that ran down the *carretera central* from Havana to Santiago de Cuba. The service was as comfortable as on any Greyhound express in the United States, a thing which could not be said about most of the lines north and south of that central highway.

The tactics imposed by geography on two revolutions could be grasped after you left Sancti Spiritus. Across open, level country at the narrow waist of the island, the Spaniards had built the row of blockhouses from sea to sea which they called *la trocha*. It was an effective frontier at first. The Cubans broke it in the War of Independence, but the heaviest fighting consistently took place to the east of it. The land sloped in a broader and broader sweep the farther eastward you got until you skirted the towering mountains where all important Cuban uprisings had incubated. Sugar cane and tobacco, with endless royal palms interspersed, gave the lowlands their visual character. On the heights it was the starry blossoms and red berries of coffee against a setting of noble hardwood trees. The lushness in the sense of fertility seemed greater than that of Jamaica, though not so deeply tropical.

I made Santiago my centre, an interesting town the old neighbourhoods of which I affectionately explored, and then turned to the surrounding terrain. I was not looking only for battlefields. Relics of colonial activities and manners are plentiful close to Santiago. It was the first port established by the Spaniards, the first capital of Cuba. Hernán Cortés sailed from there to the conquest of Mexico. Traces of social links with Jamaica in the days of long ago are still to be found.

There was an active historical society in Santiago, and through the kindness of some of its members I was taken to out-of-town sites. I retraced the route followed by the US expeditionary force, supported by Cubans, from the Daiquirí and Siboney beaches to San Juan Hill in 1898. From a vantage point on a cliff I got a bird's-eye view of the coast down which the Spanish fleet had run westward in its suicidal attempt to escape from the harbour. A rough triangle of metal still wallowed in the surf offshore, part of the skeleton of the *Almirante Oquendo*. I stood under the 'Peace Tree' where the Armistice had been signed.

The resulting impressions were used fully in *The Single Star*. But, as I have said, other aspects of Cuba's past drew me. I enjoyed a visit to El Olimpo, an abandoned coffee estate at an altitude above two thousand feet near the Gran Piedra, a massive geological oddity of a peak the sides of which are scored by horizontal grooves. The ruins of El Olimpo closely resembled similar works of the kind to be seen in Jamaica's Blue Mountains. And why not? In both cases the builders were French refugees from the slave revolution in Saint-Domingue. No one in the West Indies cultivated coffee more successfully than they. A far larger group fled to eastern Cuba than to Jamaica, but those who failed to establish powerful connections, notably by marriage, were expelled ten or twelve years later when Napoleon overthrew the Bourbon Spanish monarchy and placed his brother Joseph on the throne in Madrid.

My Santiago friends pointed out with a measure of embarrassment that the French plantation roads were much superior to those built by the Cuban colonists. I noticed for myself that the roadsides and the environs of the ruined houses were dotted with trees of vivid foliage, or blossoms, not native to the province – poincianas and bougainvilleas in many hues, flame-of-the-forest and others. The bush was throttling the older trees, yet the seeds had spread. "Those French planted for colour wherever they went. They brought exotics with them," I was told. I recalled that the name of the poinciana came from a governor of the smaller French West Indies, the Sieur de Poincy, and bougainvillea was derived from the navigator de Bougainville, who made a voyage to the Pacific Ocean and returned to fight under de Grasse against Rodney in the Battle of the Saintes.

Santiago likes its tinge of French manners. But its great pride is as the mother of patriot leaders. Though José Martí was born in Havana, he died near Santiago and is buried in its chief cemetery. Practically all the rest, from Céspedes to Maceo, were from the eastern city or close to it. Máximo Gómez, the commander-in-chief, was from the Dominican Republic; he undoubtedly felt more at home in Oriente than in Havana, the life and intrigues of which were irritating to the non-politically minded old man.

I was back in Havana around Christmas. On New Year's Eve, the dying year being 1948, I left the little hotel in the Calle Industria to which I had taken a fancy and went to stroll on the Prado. I thought I would take a look at several cafés, and which one it happened to be at midnight would not matter. But gradually a mood of melancholy, even grief, took possession of me. I lost all taste for the prospect of merrymaking in cafés. Disaster seemed to

Figure 36. Drawing of Roberts collecting his Orden Nacional de Mérito: Carlos Manuel de Céspedes in Havana in 1950, by Conrado Massaguer in the newspaper *El Mundo*. [Newspaper cutting], Bobbs-Merrill mss., Box 149. Courtesy of the Lilly Library, Indiana University, Bloomington, Indiana.

threaten someone dear to me, though I had no idea whatsoever who that might be. Pain was as if struggling to make itself felt through covering scar tissue. Yet it did not become actual pain. It was sorrow. I gave up long before ten o'clock, and went home to bed.

A few days later in New Orleans I found several letters awaiting me. One was from a mutual friend of Eleanor Ramos and of me. She told me that Eleanor had died of a clot of blood to the heart, at the very hour that I had been walking on the Prado. I stiffened and stared at the wall for several minutes, seeing nothing, feeling as if I had been pinched heavily above the heart. It was not a shock from which one rallied normally; it remained fixed for an indefinite time. The experience is given bluntly. I had not before had the sensation of telepathic contact with her, that being what I must regard it as having been, or with anyone else at the moment of death for that matter.

I had got precisely the material I had gone to find in Cuba. So I worked intensively on *The Single Star* and completed it in May 1949. It appeared a few months later. An English edition followed. It was a source of deep satisfaction to me that the Cuban government, under President Carlos Prío, thought it sufficiently important to bracket it with my history, *The Caribbean*, and give me the Orden Nacional de Mérito: Carlos Manuel de Céspedes for the two books. This medal, which I received in 1950, is the highest decoration ever awarded by Cuba to a foreigner.

MY PLAN AFTER THE WRITING of *The Single Star* was to live in Jamaica, but I was not quite ready to move there bag and baggage. I paid a preliminary visit in the summer of 1949, to start the series of lectures I had promised the University College of the West Indies to deliver. As it turned out, they lasted for the better part of three years, but this is perhaps the juncture at which to sketch the whole enterprise. The first talk outside Kingston was at Highgate, St Mary, and thereafter I ranged from Spanish Town, Mandeville and Montego Bay to some of the small inland places, such as Balaclava and Chapelton, which seldom heard a lecture on a subject as grave as history.

The experience cheered me. I felt sure that fifteen years earlier an audience could have been attracted only in the larger towns, and out of curiosity at best. But the self-government movement had been doing its work of fermentation. The people wanted to know the history of their country and of the Americas generally. The old primers in the Jamaican schools had not given it to them, and they flocked as if to a theatre. Crowds of from two to three hundred were not uncommon. Questions at the finish were eagerly pressed.

At times the far backwoods proved naive, but wholesomely so. There was a village schoolroom in St Elizabeth, not on my schedule, to which the teacher came to fetch me one afternoon from the town where I was to speak in the evening. He wanted me to tell his mainly adult class about what he called the Morant War. Labourers came in from the fields, carrying machetes, their ragged clothes stained with red earth. They grew indignant over the heavy reprisals on the peasantry and the hanging of George William Gordon after his illegal court martial. Had the soldiers been punished? one man asked. Was there still a chance of justice being done? another demanded. Nothing I could say satisfied them that it was a bit late to think of penalties for the errors of eighty-five years before. They had just learned all the details for the first time, and it seemed proper to them to be angry.

I often talked about the careers of Toussaint L'Ouverture, Simón Bolívar and José Martí, as the regional liberators of most significance to us. The name of Toussaint was, I found, familiar to some ordinary Jamaicans, that of Bolívar to a very few, while Martí was utterly unknown. Their personalities and the stories of their deeds, however, invariably won response. All three are discussed and quoted today. I flatter myself with having been responsible for that. Bolívar especially is seen in his true light as one of the great men of history. The fact that he lived here for seven months as a political refugee and wrote here his prophetic and celebrated "Jamaica Letter" appeals to local sentiment. Lectures on two and three successive nights at the same town were given now and then, and return engagements were arranged. The series served its purpose, due to the initiative of the Extra-Mural Department of the University College.

I was even sent to the Cayman Islands by plane, and that decidedly was a breaking of new ground. The interest there did not derive from Jamaica's nationalist awakening, an issue which had scarcely touched the Caymanians. They were suspicious, anyway, of pressure by the big island. Their own history did not contain much drama upon which to dwell. But the founding of the University had appealed to their imagination, and they turned out at two meetings that packed their only hall.

I asked some members of the Vestry whether it would not be a logical political development for the Cayman Islands to become a Jamaican parish. Their spokesman answered that such a solution would be distasteful to them. What then? Independence? He supposed that that would not be allowed. Let the Caymans remain a dependency, neither one thing nor the other, he said. I should have been glad to visit the Turks Islands for comparison, but the University College failed to give me that assignment.

The offbeat locality where I spoke on history with the most pleasure was Balaclava. Perhaps this was because the deepest roots of my Jamaican ancestry were there. On the paternal side, my great-grandfather, George Roberts, had come from South Wales early in the nineteenth century and settled on the high slopes of the spur called Don Figuerero's Mountains. It was wild country then. The old Spaniard, Figuerero, had not been identified; the English pioneers committed the error common among them of linking 'Don' with this family name.

My great-grandfather married Ruth Angell and acquired through her the property Lookout, some three miles to the south of Balaclava and just within the border of Manchester. Their son John, my grandfather, was born there. He married Eleanor Lind, whose mother, Margaret Scott, came of a family so long in the island that traces of its origins had been lost. My father, too, was born at Lookout, but was taken as a child to the southern part of Manchester, where I grew up. My mother, Josephine Napier, was born in central Manchester of British parents.

I had many distant cousins in Balaclava and places nearby. Lookout, near St Paul, a one-storey pre-greathouse dwelling believed to have been built in 1720, was still occupied by family connections. I had visited it, but had never passed a night there. The idea of sleeping at Lookout tempted me, for the house had the name of being haunted. My grandmother Eleanor had complained that she was disturbed by poltergeists. She had sent for an Anglican priest to exorcise them with the appropriate ritual, and as she believed in the efficacy of this it had proved to be so – for her. Others had not been immune.

The supernatural leaves me incredulous. Yet I must say that I had no sooner blown out the oil lamp in my dead grandmother's bedroom than a weird racket started, including the sound of my shoes being dragged across the floor and tossed into corners. It was a clear moonlit night. When at last I tumbled out of bed, I saw a vague creature of some sort leap to the windowsill and into the coffee piece beyond. My hosts said it was a cat. If so, it must have been a Siamese, for only this breed is given to the noisy juggling of objects. My two shoes were as widely separated as they could well be in that room. I shut the window and went back to bed. Nothing else happened. I left the ghost story out of my talks at the Balaclava schoolhouse. But somehow the memory of it tinged the zest with which I sought to arouse in my hearers a feeling for the long-linked annals of the past.

FOLLOWING THE FIRST SERIES OF lectures I gave for the University College of the West Indies, I went to New York for six weeks, the impression strong in me that this would be a farewell visit. I had no real reason to think that professional interests would not bring me back from time to time. But I have never lived in New York since, and if I should return today it would be like travelling to the scene of a former existence. There is a strangeness about the experience. All told, I spent a little more than thirty years in New York, and I had taken for granted that it was my home, a mighty city, a city in which to glory. Yet when I left by train for Washington and Miami on 26 September 1949, I threw a final glance at landmarks and was not grieved. It was as though I had long forecast subconsciously the end to which fate had been working.

Curious, too, because coincidental in its way, was the fact that the juncture at which I may be said to have broken with New York was marked for my family by the rise to prominence of my sister Ethel's son, Richard H. Rovere. Dick, as we call him, had been for several years a busy journalist in the field of clever, analytical writing for weeklies such as the *New Yorker*. He was steadier than I had been, had not dissipated his energies in the pursuit of

The Shaping of a Nation ≫ 325

Figure 37. Roberts in Washington Square in front of the statue of Garibaldi, late 1940s. Photograph in private collection.

adventure for its own sake, had married and had children early. In the late 1940s he started to publish books. The first was *Howe and Hummell* (1947), a glittering study of a pair of shady criminal lawyers of the recent past. This has been followed – to anticipate the fruit of a decade – by *The General and the President* (MacArthur and Truman) (1951) done in collaboration with

Arthur M. Schlesinger Jr; *Affairs of State: The Eisenhower Years* (1956); *Senator Joe McCarthy* (1959); and *The American Establishment and Other Reports, Opinions, and Speculations* (1962). He is a nephew to be proud of.

I flew on to Havana from Miami and stayed there for three weeks, regarding the visit as one that I would often repeat, as in fact I was to do. I arrived in Kingston on 24 October 1949. A couple of weeks later, I took a flat on Hope Road, and toward the end of January received my books and other belongings which had been in storage in the United States. Jamaica's second general elections under the constitution were about to be held. I had to decide whether I would actively take part in them, for the campaign was well underway. An enquiry confirmed the suspicions I had previously had about the Bustamante administration. It was humiliating to the country, a government by bunglers with dubious motives, as far as I was concerned. My natural impulse was to throw in with the PNP, whose leaders were my friends. But what did I find when I examined the current functioning of the party? The socialism it had embraced in 1940 had grown to be, at least superficially, a revealed religion. The clenched-fist salutes which had irked me in 1948 had multiplied to the point of seeming an exhibitionist mania. I found the rank and file to be chiefly trades unionists and district politicians. Devotees of the old ideal of an independent Jamaica were rare among them.

Certain persons – a larger number than I have ever admitted publicly – came to ask me whether I would back a new party based on the principles of the Jamaica Progressive League. This could not be just shrugged aside, and I gave serious thought to it. Nothing, however, was clearer than that such a party would have no chance to win the elections. Organization and funds were lacking. If relatively successful, it would draw most of its support from the PNP and help Bustamante to victory. An appalling prospect. For I definitely preferred the PNP to the JLP, and I did not believe that Manley in power would be an extremist and try to suppress free enterprise in an agrarian country like ours. Furthermore, I had promised to be on his side.

I perceived that I would cut an insincere figure in a socialist campaign. So I would remain silent, but soothe the rising doubts of the Progressive League in New York and tell it to go on collecting money to aid Manley. The latter and his lieutenants, by the way, noticeably refrained from urging me to appear on their platforms. In contrast with the early days when they welcomed any patriotic expression, they had become cautious, perhaps on the grounds that I might utter some social heresy, perhaps fearing that in a post-war atmosphere their opponents might make an issue of my United States citizenship. I felt it to be a pity that my friend and associate, W.A. Domingo, was not in Jamaica to exert an influence at that time. He had suffered morally to the verge of a nervous breakdown while held in the internment camp, and as soon as possible after his release he had gone back to New York. He should have been one of the PNP members of the House of Representatives. The JLP again carried the elections, though by a much reduced majority. Manley personally ousted the bush doctor in Eastern St Andrew, and his party won four other seats of the six in the metropolitan area. The parishes, with a few exceptions, showed a strong drift toward the PNP.

I went to see Manley at Drumblair the next day. On the whole his mood was philosophical. He said, however, that he could not understand why the PNP had lost. I suggested that socialism had been the factor that had scared away the margin needed for victory. The people had become sceptical about the ability of Bustamante to keep his extravagant promises, but those among them who owned land now harboured the negative feeling that what they had might be taken away from them, or taxed heavily, to support a co-operative state. The one attitude was as foolish as the other extreme; both were typical of the masses. A straight nationalist programme would have been better understood and would probably have triumphed.

Manley mused over this and said he did not agree with me. Anyway, the temperate socialism that he professed would not be an obstacle the next time. I reminded him that the PNP had a leftist wing that threatened to grow more and more radical. He looked grave. Either on that occasion or a little before the elections I asked him why the leftists should not be expelled from the party. He bridled against the thought, arguing that every man in a political organization had the right to his opinions. Norman Manley was unquestionably an honest libertarian, but he was forced before very long to modify his stand. Indeed, the political event of 1952 was the purge of leftist elements in the PNP. It cannot be doubted that Manley took the step reluctantly, as he had said would be the case. From a careful, protracted investigation begun in 1951 there emerged proof that the radicals had had relations with Communist circles in Europe, and that money presumably to be spent for propaganda purposes had been sent to Jamaica. Ken Hill, then a member of the House of Representatives, Richard Hart and others were officially driven from the party.

My sole connection with the matter was to study the proceedings, so that I could advise the Jamaica Progressive League of New York. I wrote the latter that if the evidence against the leftists was strong and they were whitewashed nonetheless, I reserved the right to propose a new attitude toward political action here, and that I should feel obliged to counsel the league to cease collecting funds for the PNP. Fortunately it did not prove necessary for me to do anything suggesting hostility toward my old friends.

The form assumed by the awakening of Jamaica had been imperfectly foreseen by most of us. It had been expected that the English would long resist self-government, and such a course on their part would have served to develop our national consciousness. The half-way constitution had been a fruit of World War II, a gift instead of a victory. The general run of our people were unaware that global conditions had favoured them. They joyfully accepted the gift and slipped easily into playing the lesser game of strikes and elections. Even the interest in history, which I found on my lecture tours, stemmed more from a wish to understand how the island had come as far as it had than from eagerness to know the evidence pointing toward independence.

We did not have, in short, the tightly knit nation that a period marked by sacrifices might have brought into being. We had only an inchoate public opinion leaning in that direction. An effort to enlighten and shape it was worthwhile, with factional issues ignored. I concluded that my future work lay along those lines. I would not resume British citizenship and seek office. It was later than ever for me to lead a new party; the answer plainly must be 'no'. History, local culture and the story of liberty were already my themes, and I must make the most of them.

About this time I began to use the term 'nationalist liberalism', which I felt got at the heart of what we had meant in New York when we founded the Jamaica Progressive League in 1936. A movement for full self-government necessarily would be nationalist. Liberalism was not to be taken in the sense of any of the nineteenth-century liberal parties, but associated with freedom of choice and a generosity of outlook deriving from the key word – 'liberty'. Our stand had been that the future Jamaica would be against coercion, that it would be democratic; in truth, if not in name at the beginning, it would be republican. Within the framework of the British Commonwealth, that would mean dominion status. The welfare state, socialist or otherwise, could evolve here; but we were not building a nation for the sake of social welfare. Man does not live by bread alone. From this view certain old-fashioned axioms recurred naturally:

- Freedom is a supreme end, and it is not to be judged by the goodness or badness of the particular system it seeks to repudiate.
- Self-government ranks ahead of good government.
- There is a sustaining and guiding strength in national consciousness. Until it appears, a people is not adult.
- "Let us found a fatherland at all costs, and all the rest will be bearable." – Simón Bolívar.

To be sure, these are emotional sentiments, but they are not emptily romantic. The unity to which a people aspires can never be real until divergences from the mood of the old rulers sharpen into profound emotions.

I had written nationalist liberalism into the very theme of my novel, *The Single Star*, without employing the phrase itself. At home I now set forth the doctrine in impersonal speeches and articles, with illustrations from history. But a current issue, which challenged it and had to be bluntly tested by it, had risen above the horizon. The last thing that Domingo, our associates of the league in New York and I had intended was that Jamaica should sink part of its identity by surrendering its individual sovereignty in a union of former colonies. A closer tie with other Caribbean lands, including free Cuba and Haiti, a loose confederation, or league, attracted us. But Jamaica as a country with its own flag and unhampered in forming its own personality we emphatically designed to create.

So it was a shock when, in 1947, the British Colonial Office had called a conference at Montego Bay and had proposed a federation of the West Indies which both Jamaican parties supported. It did not seem to matter to the London politicians that the other islands were less advanced toward autonomy than we were, that they suffered from overpopulation and unemployment, and that nearly all of them were as small as parishes and too distant from Jamaica for normal everyday intercourse.

I thought for a while that nothing could come of the project, especially as the Bahamas refused even to send a delegate while British Guiana and

British Honduras dropped out after the preliminary talks. Norman Manley, however, made himself its chief advocate, next to the Colonial Office itself, and his prestige counted. By 1953 a union of ten islands alone had been agreed upon, a constitutional structure drafted.

CHAPTER 20 › Full Circle

I CONTINUED MY LECTURES FOR the University College of the West Indies during several years after my return to Jamaica in 1949, with diminishing frequency as the permanent staff of that institution grew. There was much else in the field of history to occupy me. It is generally assumed that an honorary member will be inactive, but I threw myself into the work of the Jamaica Historical Society, became the editor of its publications, and was elected president three times. Excursions were conducted to important sites throughout the island. I interested myself in plans for restoring some of them and marking others with plaques, notably at Port Royal, scene of the first Jamaican drama that had gripped me as an author, the biography of Sir Henry Morgan.

Belief in the potency of Simón Bolívar's acts and thought as a stimulus to national consciousness here caused me to join in the founding of the Bolivarian Society of Jamaica on the 24 July 1952. I was made president, held the office for seven years, retired briefly and was re-elected. We celebrated four anniversaries connected with the Liberator: his birthday and the day of his death, the date of his arrival in Jamaica as a political refugee in 1815 – the year of Waterloo – and the date of his masterly "Jamaica Letter" which is regarded as one of the three key documents of his leadership. I was instrumental in getting a prominent site in Kingston named Bolívar Place. A plaque was affixed on the house at Tower and Princess Streets, where a Spanish-inspired attempt had been made to assassinate the Liberator. A mahogany tree was planted to his memory in a public park. A bust, offered by the Venezuelan government, was projected for the near future.

Figure 38. Celebration at the foundation of the Bolivarian Society of Jamaica at 79 Constant Spring Road on 24 July 1952. MS353.6.9.

The Gleaner Company started the Pioneer Press and got into the paperback business with Jamaican titles. Miss Una Marson was the first editor. I succeeded her in 1953. A best-seller appeared on an early list. It was S.A.G. Taylor's *The Capture of Jamaica*, which ran to over twelve thousand copies, a figure that would be profitable in any country, and that was relatively enormous when we consider how small the local book-buying public is. The subject was the conquest and settling of the island by Cromwellian forces in the 1650s, told in the form of a novel with strict adherence to the facts of history. This success was undoubtedly due to the theme. The buyer could tell at a glance what to expect, and it was something he wanted to know. Just how had Jamaica been captured? Taylor's lively style did not disappoint. He contributed too to *The Capitals of Jamaica*, and wrote *Pages from Our Past*.

Also on an early list was *Orange Valley and Other Poems*, the collected work of Tom Redcam, the late laureate, including his admirable historical drama of Christopher Columbus. But this was art, rather than exciting narrative, and it sold only moderately. The Pioneer Press then published *Tales of Old Jamaica*, by Clinton V. Black, and *Sir Henry Morgan* and *Six Great Jamaicans*, by me. All three found favour with the public. Black's 'tales' were legendary in part, but were based upon truth, such as the 'white witch' Annie

Palmer of Rose Hall, and the gaudy career of Constantia Phillips, known in the middle of the eighteenth century as Jamaica's 'Mistress of the Revels'.

A few Pioneer Press books of divided historical interest should be mentioned. *A Literature in the Making*, by J.E. Clare McFarlane, consists of brief lives of Jamaican authors, mainly the poets. *Your Health in the Caribbean*, by Dr W.E. McCulloch, is what its name implies. *Bird-Watching in Jamaica*, by May Jeffrey-Smith, is especially rich in the folklore of natural history. Patrons seemed aware that historical material of the sort featured by Pioneer Press was probably not attainable in any other format. The distribution of books, however, was never placed on a fully efficient basis, and the venture slowly perished.

I remained keenly interested in the work of the Institute of Jamaica, the leading cultural body established in 1879, and which bears many curious resemblances to the British Museum as to traditions and methods. I was awarded its Musgrave Gold Medal in 1955, becoming one of four ever to have received this honour. The same year I was appointed a member of the board of governors of the institute, and I was elected chairman in 1960.

Meanwhile, what was the share, as an adviser if nothing else, that I might be supposed to have had in the decisive shaping of Jamaica's autonomy? The answer is: I had very little, if any, locally. But I played a role in the opposition to the federation of Jamaica with Trinidad and the small islands. Throughout the early period of defeat for his party, Manley continued to keep in touch with me, at first by mail and after my return to the island by means of frequent talks. We discussed all problems as they arose. I do not recall his ever saying that he had been converted away from one of his theories, but he listened and he took notes.

The constitutional position was improved during the 1950s by various British orders in council, leading up to the complete home rule that went into effect in 1959. A truly responsible cabinet system was proclaimed, and the appointed governor became a figurehead. Early in 1955 the third general elections were held, and the PNP won with eighteen seats against twelve in the House of Representatives. The campaign had shown that the red in the party's socialist ideals had been watered down. This and the good impression caused by the purge of leftist members three years before had cleared the way for a victory long overdue. Its success was reaffirmed by a still larger majority in 1959.

The post of chief minister, later premier, went to Norman Manley, of course. He gave the country its first competent, dignified and patriotic administration under self-government, even if its main objective was the welfare state of British socialism. But I am unable to say what decisions on policy were reached behind the scenes, or how. Manley, preoccupied in office – one might well say grown arrogant – saved his candour for his inner party circles. A lawyer who has attained political authority often reacts markedly in that fashion. Manley no longer conferred with veterans of the general fight for independence – at least, not with many of them. Once more it was made clear that there is faint friendship, and little room, at the top. I was one of those who ceased promptly after 1955 to be invited to Manley's home, Drumblair, for the purpose of exchanging ideas, though he was always ready to pay a compliment in public to my record.

He moved without hesitation from a merely doctrinaire to a pontifical attitude. At a cocktail party following a ceremony in 1957, Manley, Douglas Judah and I got into a discussion. Judah remarked that Jamaica was perhaps getting self-government too easily for its own good, to which Manley retorted that self-government was not coming as a gift, but because of our sense of responsibility and the readiness we had shown. I answered, using one of my favoured theories, that it would be better if it had been the result of a victory, that it was good for a country to have displayed the heroic virtues in a struggle for self-government. Manley then made this astonishing statement: "Ireland engaged in such a struggle, and yet now she has so backward a government that she has gained nothing."

"True, one hears that there is clerical domination, a censorship of ideas, a sort of Catholic puritanism, and so forth," I said. "But it is inconceivable that there should be no rewards. There must be pride in the nationhood that has been won. The present state of affairs should be regarded as a reaction, from which the Irish people will rally."

Manley, however, would not listen to this line of argument. He repeated, "Ireland has gained *nothing*." He only succeeded in making me want to go to Ireland and judge for myself.

MY LATEST NATIONALIST ACTIVITY WAS in 1961, when I opposed the West Indies Federation of which Jamaica briefly formed a part. The self-government movement started by myself and others in New York, in 1936, had made it clear in a declaration that our aim was the recognition of nationhood for Jamaica. The possibility of a union of all West Indian English-speaking lands had been mentioned among us, but we had rejected it as visionary. The early political factions that sprang up shortly afterward inside the island followed much the same line. They either began with the conviction or took it as a matter of course, that their mission was to work out Jamaica's individual destiny.

The idea of Federation was brought into the picture some ten years later. It was inspired largely by the Colonial Office itself, backed by various English interests as well as by certain Jamaican and regional leaders. A feeble structure came into actual existence. Norman Manley supported it, but refused to give up his Jamaican premiership to run for a seat in the Federal elections. The latter course probably would have made him the first premier of the Federation. That office fell to Grantley Adams of Barbados.

Following various complicated manoeuvres, the final act of union was tentatively set for 31 May 1962. Then Manley suddenly exercised a reserved power and ordered a referendum to be held locally in September 1961, to decide whether the island should proceed as planned or secede from the Federation. There is little doubt in my mind that he was sincere in making this gesture on the grounds of democracy, but also that he believed the vote would be heavily in the affirmative because that was what he favoured, and that he was now ready to move over to Federal politics. I could have told him that history shows few wins of referendums by governments when the terms set forth were similar to those he used.

Napoleon III was especially fond of holding what he called plebiscites. But his method was to act first, and ask for approval afterward. Thus, he struck down the Second Republic in France by means of a *coup d'état*, while he was still president; later, he announced the restoration of the Empire. After both crises, he informed the electorate and solicited its endorsement. Large majorities for him were rolled up – twice in a single year – and on a third occasion he did it again. If he had put on the ballot, "Shall I overturn the Republic?" he would have been as good as asking for defeat. The crowd thinks it safer to be on the side of an established winner, but if asked to choose between two courses it tends to gratify a sense of power by vetoing the wishes of the government. Had Manley taken the stand that the Federation was fact, and were the people glad about it – yes or no? – he might well have got a 'yes'. Personally I was relieved that it was to be a wide-open referendum, because I wanted the answer to be 'no' and I was willing to work for that.

A representative of Bustamante's Labour Party approached me and asked me to speak on their side, in opposition. I answered that I would not support Bustamante directly, but if anyone wished to arrange radio time for me as an independent it would not matter to me who paid for it. This was what was finally agreed upon. Seven fifteen-minute periods were engaged and I spoke without censorship of any description. I never mentioned either Bustamante or Manley by name. Contrary to what was being said by the other side, I pointed out in my radio talks that Federation would mean increased taxation to meet the cost of grants-in-aid to the small islands and other special expenses. It would, in short, be cheaper to go it alone than to remain part of the combine. When the ballots were counted, it transpired that in a total vote of 468,335, a majority of 35,535 had favoured secession.

Manley showed small capacity as a leader in this referendum campaign. He had never been much of a nationalist by conviction or temperament, but rather a mild socialist. He had made himself Jamaica's chief advocate of Federation which presumably he held firmly would be to the advantage of the largest possible number of citizens in the region. But he was dealing with a people that had been stirred emotionally by the prospect of nationhood, and he failed to lead it into accepting an alternative. He at least took his defeat with good grace and promptly set about implementing Jamaica for independence.

The reactions of the other English-speaking West Indian islands was interesting. Dr Eric Williams, whom I had known in Washington, had unexpectedly won the premiership in Trinidad two or three years before. He now declared that his country also would secede, and that he had only been waiting to learn the result of the Jamaican plebiscite, win or lose, to publish the fact. I regard the sincerity of this as being a little in question in view of the timing. The small islands, including Barbados, are seeking at the time of writing to merge their governmental problems with a federation of their own. Whatever the outcome may be in the eastern Caribbean, Jamaica is well out of it.

ALONG WITH A PUBLIC RECORD, touched upon here in an episodic, somewhat fragmentary way, I had a private life during the years that followed my return to live in Jamaica in 1949, which brought the story to full circle. I published my last book abroad, *Jamaica: The Portrait of an Island*, in 1955. It was the only one that dealt solely with my native land, and so may be said to have rounded out my earliest ambitions as a writer. I also paid several lingering visits to Manchester Parish, refreshing my boyhood memories. I broadened these by exploration in various quarters. Nor did I fail to find new interests as a student of history, and precious emotions as a man.

The most distinguished greathouse in the neighbourhood of Berry Hill, where I was raised, was the crumbling structure called Marlborough. For part of the distance, the two places had a common border on opposite sides of a parochial road. Both had once grown coffee. They had become cattle pens in a haphazard way. But Marlborough was the more famous. It was by far the larger in acreage, and there had been a time when one of its activities had been the breeding of race horses. Rich men had built the house in the eighteenth century, and big money had been connected with it till my lifetime. An early owner named Boucher, a French refugee from the slave insurrection in Haiti, Saint-Domingue, had refused to recognize the abolition of slavery in Jamaica, and when forced by militia to comply, he had shot himself. His tomb in a garden near the house was regarded as a sinister spot.

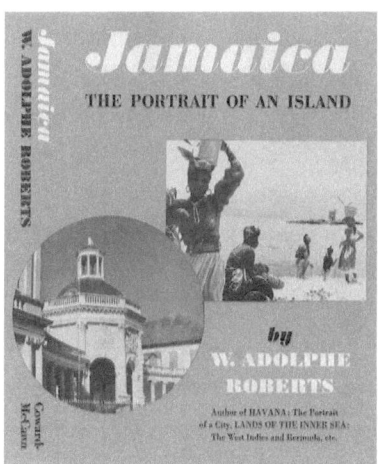

Figure 39. Cover of Roberts's last major publication, *Jamaica: The Portrait of an Island* (1955).

The highly eccentric Hall family lived at Marlborough when I was very young. The grandmother was an Irishwoman who had married three times. Her eldest son, Charles Hall, and his brother, had both been sent to Oxford, completing the course with what distinction, or lack of it, I do not know. On returning to Jamaica, they set about drinking themselves to death and made a quick job of it. There was a third child, a girl, through whom the title to the property descended. Mrs Hall's second husband was one

Lushington, a name he adopted in place of Lopez. They had a son, a doctor. The grandmother finally married an Irish adventurer called Barry, and it is as Mrs Barry that I remember her. Words fail me to recreate her legend, which was in every sense bizarre – probably to an undeserved extent, if the facts were justly weighed. She soon found Barry unbearable and bought a wayside shop for him in the lowlands twenty miles distant. This worked as long as it was needed. According to my father, she rushed to the front door when she saw him riding up one day and greeted him with hilarity: "Glad to see you. I've great news. Old Barry is dead!"

Marlborough suffered long years of neglect. The boom in bauxite eventually made it possible to sell most of the land at a good price. The house and adjoining grounds, however, were wisely retained, and much interest in it began to be shown by the Jamaica Historical Society and other national bodies. Several tenants rented it for brief periods, and the possibilities of restoration were discussed. In the early 1950s the visiting painter Hector Whistler lived there. He sketched hasty murals on the whitewashed walls at the ground level and encouraged interested parties to come and see the general effect. I was one of a group of Historical Society members that drove there on a Sunday morning. As a former neighbour, I was happy to see it again, but that was merely the start of the visit.

As I stepped on to a back verandah, I noted a number of people leaning over the rail and observing the prospect of rolling pastures and woodlands. Among them was a striking-looking young woman with prematurely grey hair and a most sweet expression, to whom I was presented. Each of us at once realized who the other must be, though we had never met before. Her name was given as Mrs Ferland. I knew that Dr Lushington's eldest daughter had married a North American during the war. This must be she, Barbara, a child of the place at one remove. Why, this was a granddaughter of Mrs Barry.

I had a singular, poignant feeling of relationship with her. We were not blood relations, even remotely. Nor had she been born at Marlborough. Yet the geographical nearness of our ancestors helped to make her seem like family. She was not less than a cousin to me, so readily did we understand each other, and there was no rule to say that a man should not fall in love with a cousin, as I began to do that very day. She was to be my last love.

Barbara Ferland lived with her parents in Kingston, fairly close to my address. I used to walk to see her of an evening, several times a week, and we sat on the verandah exchanging ideas with a certain tender ardour. She was interested in everything I had done and eager to know more about my latest activities. She wrote good poetry. Better still, she appreciated the finest things in the language, and was fascinated by the personalities of those who had written them. Of all the memories I resurrected for her, I think she was most moved by my accounts of Edna St Vincent Millay and of the circle that gathered in New York about old John Butler Yeats, the painter.

Her father was in failing health and her mother none too strong. She had had one child from her marriage, a son, Mark, then a robust boy of about six. A divorce from Ferland was pending, and more than one young man had hopes regarding her. I write this as dispassionately as it is in me to be. If I had pressed her to marry me, as I longed to do, I might have succeeded. But I was well on in my sixties, while she belonged to a much younger generation. I had begun to feel the evidence of advancing age, and other symptoms threatened. It would have been unfair to saddle her with an old man. On the economic side, I had never made an investment; I did not even have an insurance policy. My life of individualist adventure had been no preparation for a Jamaican marriage. My own Nell was a factor in the puzzle. Though thwarted of my dream of having the child grow up with me as her acknowledged father, I still dreamed of winning her. Would I be justified in asking Barbara to accept the care of her, if difficulties were cleared from the way? Hardly. Yet, as between Barbara and Giulia, it was Barbara that I loved and wanted.

Figure 40. Barbara Ferland, in the early 1950s; she was Roberts's last love. MS353.6.8.

A relationship tinged with melancholy on my side established itself. Presently, Barbara's father died, followed in a year or two by her mother. She was working for the Kingston office of the British Council, and naturally enough she began to talk of moving to England to live. I had no alternative to offer her. Her plans, however, developed more slowly than I deserved, and I did not lose her companionship until 1960. A year later, I visited her in London.

I HAD HAD THE GROWING feeling that my memories of Europe would be incomplete unless I went there at least once more. I had had in the past only a glimpse of Italy, had never so much as stayed overnight in Rome. I now bought a ticket on the Italian cruise ship *Venezuela*, of the Grimaldi Line, which would take me directly from Jamaica to Naples. There would be short stops at several other West Indian islands, at La Guayra, the port of Caracas, at the Canary Islands and Madeira, at points in Portugal and Spain, and at Genoa. I should be afloat for twelve and a half days, one of the longest sea-trips I had ever made.

I did not go ashore at most of the ports in the West Indies, because I had seen these islands before and the present calls were very brief, some of them at night. Grenada was an exception. We had the better part of an afternoon in its beautiful harbour of St George's, and I drove among the rolling hills behind the town. I could not prevent the amused reflection that this little jewel of a place, area 133 square miles, had been rated as a full partner of Jamaica in the proposed Federation.

The leisurely run northeastward across the Atlantic worked the old charm, relaxing and soothing my nerves. I found the *Venezuela* an unusually comfortable ship. Most of the passengers were Latins, and they gave me the feel of European life. We passed through the Straits of Gibraltar after dark, cheating me of a spectacle to which I had looked forward. But the Bay of Naples made up for it. I went on deck early in the morning, just as the sun was fairly up, and there confronted me the classic silhouette shown on a hundred postcards. The peak of Vesuvius loomed inland, and scattered from its foot to the borders of the city proper were white houses and endless gardens. To the left were the islands of Capri and Ischia. The bay across which we moved was glowing in the sunshine as it acquired its hue of unearthly azure. The wonders of Pompeii were close by. An uncle of my father had spent a good part of his life on Capri, as a painter. A female relative of the same period had written a novel in Sicily, under the nom-de-plume of Linda Mazini. I had dreamed of visiting all those places, but not yet. I was in a hurry to reach Rome, and to Rome I went by train that same afternoon.

Climbing the Spanish Steps, associated with the death of Keats, I chose a large *pensione* at the level of the Trinita dei Monti, near an entrance to the Borghese Gardens. Naturally enough, I began my sightseeing with the great Borghese Museum. I soon discovered that the spot which exercised an unequalled magnetism was the Pantheon. It is a pagan temple preserved in its entirety, the best in good condition in all Italy, having been stripped only of bronze decorations from the ceiling and marble exterior facings. Fortunately, one of the Emperor Constantine's first acts as a Christian had been to turn it into a church.

There is nothing of extraordinary beauty about the Pantheon. Nor does it now contain any notable works of art. It is a round temple with a portico behind sixteen Corinthian columns, an obelisk in the square in front of it. The stupendous dome is pierced at its summit by the typical Greek orifice. The general atmosphere of the building and its narrow surrounding streets is perfect. Rome contains many surprises of this character. The ancient capital of the world is like a broken mosaic. Districts have survived from imperial days, a small proportion of the whole it should be said. Patched in, filling what would have been the gaps, and with borders that can be traced, are the districts of every succeeding age. I do not suppose the average tourist cares much about the Pantheon, which is severe and weather-stained. Myself, I could take rooms in one of the buildings facing it, and muse away the rest of my life there.

IN LONDON, I FOUND BARBARA being tenaciously wooed by an Englishman whose business was commercial radio. I learned soon after I left that she had married him. The climax for that voyage came in the person of my daughter, Nell. I saw her in New York, for the first time since she was a baby.

Her mother, Giulia, was away in hospital, but a first-born brother had charge of the household. He received me amiably, without giving a sign that he understood the relationship, except that he would not allow Nell to go out alone with me. The child herself seemed happy, even excited, about getting to know me, for that was what our meeting amounted to. She answered leading questions in a reticent way, however. I could not very well ask her bluntly whether she had been told who I was in her life, for that might have been called a

Figure 41. "Nell", Roberts's daughter, c. 1950. MS353.6.2.

Figure 42. The area of the Mandeville churchyard where Roberts's ashes are buried, unmarked. Photograph by Peter Hulme, January 2014.

move in a plot to kidnap her. The brother certainly was aware, and I suspect that she had done some shrewd guessing.

Nell, at sixteen, was a handsome brunette, not a *petite* type like her mother, but promising to be shapely and tall. She was intellectually alert. Beyond that, I was utterly unable to think anything illuminating about her. I saw her with illusioned eyes, as being younger than she was, as the little girl who should have grown up beside me. There were several visits, and since then she has corresponded regularly with me. A true feeling concerning her is only now assuming shape in me. From New York I flew to New Orleans, to greet old friends. Jamaica followed. Almost immediately afterwards, the anti-Federation campaign served to draw together the ends of the circle of my public life. If more is yet to be told by me, it will first have to be lived.

Annotations

Note: Details of Roberts's writings, referred to in these annotations by title and date, can be found in the bibliographical note at the end of the introduction (xxvii–xxxii). References to his papers in the National Library of Jamaica take the form MS353.0.0.0.

Title page
These Many Years: This title comes from the *King James Bible* (Luke 15:29): "And he answering said to his father, Lo, these many years do I serve thee, neither transgressed I at any time thy commandment." Given the absence of any sign of religious faith in the autobiography, the title may best be taken as referring to Roberts's actual father.

Chapter 1. Tropical Boyhood

p. 3
where I was born: As Walter Adolf Roberts, a spelling he used until the outbreak of World War I when the Germanic Adolf became the French Adolph, and then Adolphe.

p. 4
Manchester: See the map of Jamaica (figure 1, p. 2). Manchester is south-central, west of Kingston. The parish was regarded, as least by the journalists who wrote the survey, as the most prosperous parish in the island in 1890. See *The Land We Live In: Jamaica in 1890*, ed. Brian L. Moore and Michele A. Johnson (Kingston: Social History Project, Department of History, University of the West Indies, 2000), 93.

Berry Hill: The house at Berry Hill has fallen on hard times, though the surrounding area is still much as Roberts describes it.

their main peak: Blue Mountain Peak, still 7,402 feet high.

p. 5
Ethel and Ivy: Ethel Josephine Roberts (1888–1981) married Louis Halworth Rovere. Their son, Richard Halworth Rovere (1915–1979), became a well-known writer and journalist (see p. 324). Ivy R.F. Roberts (1889–1985) married John Wesley Steele. Their son, Robert W. Steele (1918–2005), corresponded extensively with his uncle. Roberts seems to have remained close to both his sisters, though they appear only fleetingly in these pages.

p. 7
wholly to my father: Adolphus Sigismund Roberts (1853–1927). Roberts Senior had been educated at Ockbrook School in Derbyshire, England.

p. 8
to please her: Roberts's parents were married on 22 October 1886.
George Downer: The Reverend George William Downer (1837–1912) was rector of the Kingston Parish Church from 1873 to 1908.

p. 10
H. Rider Haggard: Haggard (1856–1925) was the pre-eminent novelist of Empire and these were all very recent novels: *King Solomon's Mines* (1885), *Allan Quatermain* (1887), *She* (1887), *Nada the Lily* (1892).
mythical country: Over eight hundred pages of Roberts's childhood writing survive, including a 350-page novel written when he was eight years old, evidence of precocious ability and testament to his father's skills as an educator.
"Why Are the Churches Not Better Attended?": Roberts Senior's essay was published in the *Gleaner* on 22 December 1900. (References to Kingston's newspaper are regularized in these notes as *Gleaner*, though it was previously known at various times as the *Jamaica Gleaner*, the *Kingston Gleaner* and the *Daily Gleaner*.)

p. 13
Moravian Church: The oldest Protestant church, with a long missionary tradition.
an illegitimate child: A.S. Roberts had at least one other, whose birth he announced to his son in a letter (MS353.2.1.1, 25 January 1925) full of deeply racist sentiments.

p. 14
my mother: Josephine Fanny Roberts, née Napier (1854–1936).
Bishop Charles Douet: The Right Reverend Charles Frederick Douet (1839–1905), a Jamaican, was assistant bishop of Jamaica under Enos Nuttall (see note to p. 32) from 1888 until Douet's death.

p. 15
Greco-Turkish War: A short (thirty-day) war fought between the Kingdom of Greece and the Ottoman Empire over the status of Crete.

p. 16

Cuban War of Independence: Fought between 1895 and 1898. A previous war of independence (1868–1878) had ended with many Cubans taking refuge in Jamaica, some of whom stayed permanently.

José Martí: Martí (1853–1895) twice visited Jamaica during Roberts's childhood. On the first occasion, in October 1892, he was photographed by a Cuban photographer who had settled in Jamaica, Juan Bautista Valdés Acosta. Roberts would later write about this visit in "La historia de un retrato" (1941).

Valeriano Weyler: Don Valeriano Weyler y Nicolau (1838–1930) was a Spanish general who was appointed governor of Cuba in 1896. He was reviled in the US press – and given his nickname of "Butcher" – for his policy of *reconcentración* which led to thousands of civilian deaths in Cuba in 1897. He later served three times as minister of war in Spanish governments.

guardacostas: coastguard.

Máximo Gómez: Born in the Dominican Republic, Gómez (1836–1905) left the Spanish army to become its scourge in wars of independence. He travelled with Martí to Cuba and led the military wing of the Cuban struggle between 1895 and 1898.

Dutch uncle: A term for a person who issues frank and severe comments and criticism to educate or admonish someone.

armoured cruiser *Maine*: All the names and places in this paragraph became famous during the summer of 1898. The sinking of the *Maine* – still unexplained but probably an accident – was blamed on Spain in the United States and is usually seen as the trigger to the conflict between the two countries.

Theodore Roosevelt: Roosevelt (1858–1919) had resigned his position as assistant secretary to the navy in order to volunteer and went to Cuba as second in command of the First US Volunteer Cavalry Regiment, better known as the Rough Riders. He became vice-president on the basis of his exploits in Cuba and then the twenty-sixth president of the United States (1901–1909) when Thomas McKinley was assassinated, and was comfortably re-elected in 1904. He appears in Roberts's novel *The Single Star* (1949), leading the Rough Riders in Cuba in 1898 (see p. 318). And see p. 56 for Roberts's encounter with him in the flesh.

Sampson and Schley: Rear Admiral William T. Sampson (1840–1902) and Rear Admiral Winfield Scott Schley (1839–1911) fell out over who should take credit for the destruction of the Spanish fleet outside Santiago harbour in May 1898.

'Fighting Joe' Wheeler: A feisty ex-Confederate general, Wheeler (1836–1906) volunteered to fight in Cuba.

Calixto García: (1839–1898). The Cuban general in charge of the military campaign in the eastern part of the island. Battles were fought between US and Spanish troops at **El Caney** and **San Juan Hill** before the surrender of **Santiago** brought the short war to a close.

Spanish ship: This would have been the *Leonora*, interned in Kingston harbour for the duration of the war.

p. 17

Boer War: The Second Boer War (1899–1902) ended with the conversion of the Boer republics into British colonies, which would later form part of the Union of South Africa. The British fought directly against the Transvaal and the Orange Free State, defeating their forces first in open warfare and then in a long and bitter guerrilla campaign, despite suffering heavy losses due to both disease and combat. The controversial policy of civilian internment in concentration camps took a heavy toll on non-combatants, leading to a significant erosion of support for the war in Britain and its colonies. As a twelve-year-old, Roberts eventually took the side of the underdog, the names and deeds of the Boer heroes engraved on his memory. The Boers were protecting against the British the land and minerals they had wrested from native peoples. One might therefore say that Roberts and his father were creoles sympathizing with a creole perspective on another continent. There is some irony, perhaps, in that Swinburne – Roberts's favourite poet – was at his most jingoistic in his support of the British and excoriation of the Boers in 1899.

Cecil Rhodes: (1853–1902). Larger-than-life English-born South African businessman, mining magnate, politician and enthusiast for the expansion of the British Empire.

Paul Kruger: (1825–1904). State president of the South African Republic (Transvaal) and the face of Boer resistance against the British during the Second Boer War.

Fred Selous: Frederick Courteney Selous (1851–1917), British explorer and hunter, famous for his exploits in South-East Africa. He was supposedly the inspiration for Rider Haggard's character Allan Quatermain.

Tchaka: Now more commonly known as Shaka (c. 1787–c. 1828), the most influential of the Zulu kings.

Lobengula: Lobengula Khumalo (1845–1894), the second and last king of the Ndebele people.

p. 18

David Lloyd George: Lloyd George (1863–1945), who would later be a Liberal prime minister, made his national reputation through his vehement opposition to the Second Boer War.

Roberts: Field Marshal Frederick Sleigh Roberts, later 1st Earl Roberts (1832–1914), was one of the most successful British army commanders of modern times. He served in the Indian rebellion, the expedition to Abyssinia, and the Second Anglo-Afghan War, before leading British forces to success in the Second Boer War.

After relieving Kimberley he defeated Piet Cronjé at the Battle of Paardeberg in February 1900 and the remaining Boer forces at three further battles in quick succession before being succeeded in command in December 1900 by Lord Kitchener and fêted on his return to England.

Kitchener: Herbert Kitchener, Lord Kitchener of Khartoum (1850–1916). Given his title after securing control of the Sudan by winning the Battle of Omdurman in 1898, Kitchener also fought in the Boer War and commanded the army in India. In 1914 he became secretary of state for war and organized the largest volunteer army that Britain had ever seen. He was killed in 1916 when the warship taking him to negotiations in Russia was sunk by a German mine. See p. 190 for Roberts's encounter with him in the flesh.

de Wet: Christiaan Rudolf de Wet (1854–1922), Boer rebel leader and politician, regarded as the most formidable of the guerrilla campaigners during the Second Boer War.

p. 19

Macaulay's *Essays*: Thomas Babington Macaulay (1800–1859). His political and historical writing is known for its confident emphasis on a progressive model of British history. The three volumes of his *Critical and Historical Essays* (1841) were widely read and hugely influential.

Chapter 2. Journalism in Kingston

p. 21

Swinburne: Algernon Charles Swinburne (1837–1909) was one of the most innovative of nineteenth-century poets, and decadent in theme if not in behaviour. Roberts owned all his poetry and many books about him.

Clara Maude Garrett: Born and brought up in Jamaica, close to Mandeville, Garrett (1880–1958) left the island in 1908 when she married Frederick Miller in San Francisco (with Roberts present), though they soon separated. From 1938 she lived in Etna, New Hampshire, writing poems which were published in Jamaican and Canadian newspapers. No collection ever appeared. There are eighty-four items in the Roberts/Garrett correspondence in Roberts's papers (MS353.2.1.3–6), indicative of a long and deep friendship.

p. 23

William Pringle Livingstone: Livingstone (1865–1950) had come to Jamaica in 1889 and recently published *Black Jamaica: A Study in Evolution* (1899). He would go on to write several other books, mostly about missionary activity, as well as the work which later took him with Roberts to the United States, *The Race Conflict: A Study of Conditions in America* (1911).

p. 24

Thomas Henry MacDermot: MacDermot (1870–1933) was a Jamaican poet, novelist, and editor of the *Jamaica Times* for over twenty years. Publishing under the name Tom Redcam, he worked to promote Jamaican literature, starting a weekly short story contest in the *Jamaica Times* in 1899, and founding the All Jamaica Library in 1903, a series of novellas and short stories written by Jamaicans about Jamaica which were reasonably priced to encourage local readers.

Walter Durie: Walter Randolph Durie (1876–1933) was a Yorkshireman who came to Jamaica in 1897 and founded the *Jamaica Times*, which he ran with Basil Parks.

p. 25

a stick and a half: The reference is to a composing stick used in setting type. One would hold about thirteen lines.

Headquarters House: Now usually known as Hibbert House, on Duke Street, currently the head office of the Jamaica National Heritage Trust.

p. 26

Sydney Olivier: Sydney Haldane Olivier, 1st Baron Olivier (1859–1943), was a British civil servant, a Fabian and a member of the Labour Party. He had held posts in British Honduras and the Leeward Islands before in 1897 becoming secretary to the West Indian Royal Commission. Despite causing a stir through his opposition to the Boer War, Olivier was posted as colonial secretary in Jamaica in 1900, three times becoming acting governor before returning as governor after the 1907 earthquake. His governmental reforms proved popular. He went back to England in 1913 and, after a short retirement, was appointed secretary of state for India in 1924 in the first Labour government. He was noted for several books on colonial matters, including *White Capital and Coloured Labour* (1906) and *Jamaica, the Blessed Island* (1936).

Sir Augustus Hemming: (1841–1907). A British politician, who acted as governor of a number of colonies, including British Guiana (1896–1898) and Jamaica (1898–1904). He was a keen but hardly outstanding cricketer, scoring fifty-six runs and taking six wickets during his first-class career with the Marylebone Cricket Club.

Alexander Dixon: Born in Kingston, Dixon (1852–1917) was a businessman and local politician who became the first black member of the national legislature, where he was known as fearless and outspoken. With Solomon Alexander Gilbert ("Sandy") Cox (1871–1922), he was one of the founders in 1909 of the National Club, a precursor of a sort to Roberts's much later organization, the Jamaica Progressive League (on which, see p. 270).

p. 28

special article on the fishermen: "The Kingston Fisherman" was followed by many similar sketches for the *Gleaner*, which were eventually formalized into two sequences, "People of Note" and "Island Sketches." This is where Roberts learned his trade.

Getting about Kingston: On Kingston in this period, see *"Squalid Kingston" 1890–1920: How the Poor Lived, Moved and Had Their Being*, ed. Brian L. Moore and Michele A. Johnson (Kingston: Social History Project, Department of History, University of the West Indies, 2000).

p. 31

the Jamaica Club: The all-male Jamaica Club closed in 1998 after 126 years of existence.

Athenaeum: The Kingston Athenaeum was founded in 1899. As well as acting as a meeting place, it sponsored lectures and ran a subscription library. It was dissolved in 1948.

Institute of Jamaica: Established in 1879 by the then governor of Jamaica, Sir Anthony Musgrave, the Institute of Jamaica is still the island's premier cultural institution, with overall responsibility for Jamaica's main museums and its national art gallery. What since 1979 has been the National Library of Jamaica, next door to the institute, was originally the West India Reference Library, part of the Institute of Jamaica.

Stephen Chalmers: Born in Scotland, Chalmers (1880–1935) became an active member of the Robert Louis Stevenson Memorial Society of Saranac Lake (New York), produced many volumes about Stevenson, contributed to pulp magazines, and wrote mysteries, historical novels, poetry and science fiction. He died in California.

Herbert George de Lisser: One of the most prominent Jamaican journalists and authors of the twentieth century, de Lisser (1878–1944) was even more precocious than Roberts, working on the *Gleaner* and the *Jamaica Times* as a teenager before becoming editor of the *Gleaner* when he was twenty-six years old, a position he occupied until his death. He wrote many works of fiction and nonfiction, of which the best remembered are probably *Jane: A Story of Jamaica* (1913), significant for being the first West Indian novel with a black central character, and *The White Witch of Rosehall* (1929). He also worked for the Jamaican sugar industry, was general secretary of the Jamaica Imperial Association, honorary president of the Jamaica Press Association, and chairman of the West Indian section of the Empire Press Union. He would be one of Roberts's *Six Great Jamaicans* (1952).

Walter Parker: (1877–1914). A brilliant journalist, regarded by his peers as having worked himself into an early grave.

Gerald Hamilton: (1877–?). He later wrote for the *Panama City Star and Herald*.

p. 32

Frank Cundall: Born in London, Cundall (1858–1937) became secretary and librarian of the Institute of Jamaica in 1890. Prior to his appointment he had written *Reminiscences of the Colonial and Indian Exhibition* (1886) and *The Landscape and Pastoral Painters of Holland* (1891). During his tenure at the Institute of Jamaica his focus was on historical research and the development of the West India Reference Library and the Art Gallery. Cundall used his extensive connections overseas to build up the institute's collection. His own publications include *The Story of the Life of Columbus and the Discovery of Jamaica* (1894), *Historic Jamaica* (1915), *The Life of Enos Nuttall, Archbishop of the West Indies* (1922), *The Aborigines of Jamaica* (1934) and *A History of Printing in Jamaica from 1717 to 1834* (1935).

Enos Nuttall: A Lancastrian, Nuttall (1842–1916) went to Jamaica in 1862 as an unordained missionary of the Methodist Church. He was ordained a priest in the Anglican Church in 1866, was consecrated bishop of Jamaica in 1880, and became primate or archbishop in 1897. He is another of Roberts's *Six Great Jamaicans* (1952).

p. 33

Alexander Bedward: Bedward (1859–1930) was a Revivalist preacher and the founder of Bedwardism. After spending some time in Panama, he returned to Jamaica and was baptized by a local Baptist preacher. He became leader not merely of a Revival branch but of a new movement, the Bedwardites, with affiliated groups all over Jamaica and in Panama. In 1880 he started to gather large groups of followers by conducting mass healing services. He identified himself with Paul Bogle, the Baptist leader of the Morant Bay Rebellion. Bedward was arrested for sedition in 1895 but sent to a mental asylum. On release he continued his role as a Revival healer and preacher. At its height – in the years following Roberts's interview with him – the movement gathered about thirty thousand followers whom he led into Garveyism by finding the charismatic metaphor: Bedward and Garvey were as Aaron and Moses, one the high priest, the other the prophet, both leading the children of Israel out of exile. Later Bedward proclaimed that he was a reincarnation of Jesus Christ and that, like Elijah, he would ascend into heaven in a flaming chariot. He then expected to rain down fire on those that did not follow him, thereby destroying the whole world. In 1921 he and eight hundred followers marched into Kingston "to do battle with his enemies". Bedward was arrested and sent to a mental asylum for the second time, where he remained to the end of his life. Roberts's article appeared in the *Leader* on 16 January 1904.

p. 36

Robert C. Guy: One of Jamaica's most distinguished newspaper editors, Guy (1862–

1916) was notorious on the island during the Boer War for having branded the commander-in-chief of the British forces in the Transvaal, Sir Redvers Buller, a "colossal failure". He returned to Scotland a year before his death.

p. 37

Ian Maclaren: This was the pseudonym of Reverend John Watson (1850–1907), a Scottish author and theologian. His stories of rural Scottish life, *Beside the Bonnie Brier Bush* (1894), achieved extraordinary popularity, selling more than three-quarters of a million copies, and were followed by other similar collections. He also published several volumes of sermons under his own name.

p. 38

King's House: The governor's mansion, destroyed in the 1907 earthquake.
as Kipling says somewhere: In his poem "The Stranger" (1908):

> The Stranger within my gate,
> He may be true or kind,
> But he does not talk my talk –
> I cannot feel his mind.
> I see the face and the eyes and the mouth,
> But not the soul behind.

p. 39

the action of my latest serial: The *Leader* ran from 2 January 1904 to 29 July 1904. There was no obvious sign of deterioration when Roberts was in charge. His fictional serials during those seven months included "The Mystery of the Ruby", "Besieged: A Tale of the Maroons", "Treasure Seekers: A Tale of the West Indies" and "Somala: The Maroon". G.A. Henty and Rider Haggard were the dominant influences.

Chapter 3. Baltimore and Northward

p. 42

Baltimore *Sun*: Started in 1837, so a well-established newspaper. It is still running.

p. 43

Druid Hill Park: 745-acre park in the northwest of Baltimore, home also to the Maryland Zoo.

p. 45

James E. Martine: James Edgar Martine (1850–1925), known as "Farmer Jim", had the last laugh, serving as US senator for New Jersey from 1911 to 1917. Roberts met him again in 1912 (see p. 130).

p. 47

Brooklyn Bridge: Completed in 1883, it spans the East River, connecting Manhattan and Brooklyn.

Park Row building: At 391 feet it was at this time, and for four more years, the tallest office building in the world. It now consists almost entirely of residential units. The **St Paul Building** and **New York World Building** were demolished in 1958 and 1955 respectively. The **Battery** is the southern tip of Manhattan island. **Trinity Church** was built in 1846 at the intersection of Broadway and Wall Street. The **Bowery** is the southeast section of Manhattan; in the early twentieth century it was one of its poorest areas. **City Hall** was completed in 1812 and is still an impressive landmark.

masquerading as a post office: Commonly referred to as "Mullett's Monstrosity", after its architect, Alfred B. Mullett, the building was demolished in 1939.

Astor House: Once the most famous hotel in New York, part of it was demolished in 1913, the rest in 1926.

p. 48

newspaper buildings: The New York Times Building still stands at 41 Park Row, now part of Pace University.

Bannerman Company: On the 500 block of Broadway. The company had also purchased a huge stock of Spanish weapons after the 1898 Spanish-American War.

Grace Church: A Gothic Revival landmark designed by James Renwick Jr and completed in 1846.

Union Square: Marking the union of what were once the island's chief thoroughfares, Broadway and Bowery Road (now Fourth Avenue).

Flatiron Building: Still considered one of the groundbreaking skyscrapers, completed in 1902.

p. 49

a youthful poem of mine: "Jamaica", which has never been reprinted.

p. 50

printed in the Sunday magazines: It was only after his return to New York in 1909 that Roberts's pieces began to appear regularly in New York newspapers, mostly anonymously, occasionally with a byline.

p. 53

O. Henry: The pen name of US short story writer William Sydney Porter (1862–1910), many of whose stories are set in New York, which he always referred to as Bagdad-on-the-Subway. See also p. 201.

George M. Cohan: (1878–1942). An entertainer, playwright, composer, lyricist, actor, singer, dancer and producer who was an almost permanent fixture on Broadway during Roberts's New York years.

Tenderloin: Supposedly given its name by a police captain who, when transferred to the district, noted in anticipation of the higher bribes he would now receive: "I've been having chuck steak ever since I've been on the force, and now I'm going to have a bit of tenderloin." Many US cities have districts with this name: Roberts also describes the San Francisco version: see p. 88.

the Great White Way: A nickname – for its lights – for the section of Broadway in Midtown that includes the Theater District, between Forty-Second and Fifty-Third Streets.

p. 54

Tom Sharkey's saloon: Famous also for its prizefights, as painted by George Bellows (whom Roberts met). Sharkey (1873–1953), born in Ireland, was twice defeated by Jim Jeffries, the second time in a twenty-five-round fight in Coney Island in 1899 sometimes regarded as one of the greatest bouts of all time.

Tammany Hall: The New York political organization which acted as the Democratic Party political machine in the city, often controlling New York City and New York State politics while helping immigrants, most notably the Irish, get a foothold in the system. Eventually weakened in the 1930s, it ceased to exist in the 1960s.

p. 55

B.F. Keith himself: Benjamin Franklin Keith (1846–1914) was a US theatre owner, generally credited with the creation of vaudeville in the United States, which evolved by adopting the continuous variety show which ran from 10 a.m. to 11 p.m. every day. He was also involved in the early development of the film industry. He joined forces with Frederick Freeman Proctor in 1906, but the uneasy partnership was dissolved in 1910.

p. 56

Theodore Roosevelt: See note to p. 15.

p. 57

Judge Alton B. Parker: Alton Brooks Parker (1852–1926), lawyer, judge and the Democratic nominee for US president in 1904.

p. 58

Boss Charles F. Murphy: Charles Francis Murphy (1858–1924) was head of Tammany Hall from 1902 until his death, the most powerful boss in Tammany's history.

chippy-joints: brothels.

Big Tim: Timothy Daniel Sullivan (1862–1913) was a New York politician, businessman and criminal, one of the most colourful New York figures in the early twentieth century. He owned several theatres and was renowned for the lavish summer excursions to which he treated his constituents.

Little Tim: Timothy P. Sullivan (1870–1910) was not actually that little, but so called to distinguish him from his cousin, the 6-foot-4-inch Big Tim.

Dr Gertrude Kelly: A surgeon, philanthropist and suffragette, Kelly (1862–1934) emigrated from Ireland in 1873. She was outspoken in her support for Irish independence and helped establish the American Branch of Cumann na mBan, the Irish republican women's paramilitary organization.

p. 59
Incipit vita nova: [Latin]. New life begins.

Chapter 4. Adventure

p. 63
Guffanti's: At 274 Seventh Avenue, it opened in 1892.
Gonfarone's: On the corner of MacDougal and West Eighth Streets just north of Washington Square, Gonfarone's was a restaurant with attached hotel owned by the widow Caterina Gonfarone and run by her business partner Anacleto Sermolino. In 1919 it would be where the publication of Roberts's first book, *Pierrot Wounded*, would be celebrated at a dinner organized by his friend Salomón de la Selva (on whom see p. 210).
Renganeschi's: At 139 West Tenth Street, it features in a famous painting by John Sloan done in 1912.
Lion d'Or: At 59–61 West Twenty-Fourth Street.

p. 65
Little Johnny Jones: Sometimes regarded as the first American musical, featuring the well-known tunes "Give My Regards to Broadway" and "The Yankee Doodle Song", *Little Johnny Jones* had opened on Broadway in November 1904 and was revived there twice the following year, when Roberts and Florence would have seen it. George M. Cohan (see note to p. 53) directed and performed as part of the cast with the other members of The Four Cohans (Cohan, his parents and sister) and Ethel Levey, Cohan's wife.

p. 66
Beauregard: Pierre Gustave Toutant Beauregard (1818–1893), Louisiana-born engineer, soldier and politician, a Confederate general during the Civil War.
Bret Harte: (1836–1902). US author best remembered for his accounts of pioneering life in California and as the original Californian 'bohemian'.
Frank Norris: (1870–1902). US novelist who wrote predominantly in the naturalist genre: *McTeague* (1899) and *The Octopus: A Story of California* (1901) are two of his best-known works.
Stephen Crane: (1871–1900). US novelist, short story writer, poet and journalist. "The Blue Hotel" first appeared in his 1899 collection *The Monster and Other Stories*.

p. 67
legislator named Raines: Senator John Raines (1840–1909), Republican lawyer and politician. His infamous bill had been passed in 1896.

p. 69
Frank Stockton: (1834–1902). US writer and humourist, best known for his children's stories.

p. 70
Signora Volanti: Carolina Volanti (1866–1943) was a widow. Her daughter Emma would have been nineteen in 1909. Roberts stayed in touch with Emma.

p. 73
Southern Pacific Railroad: A huge railroad-building project had already criss-crossed northern Mexico in the previous three decades. The line between Nogales and Mexico City was the last link in the chain.

p. 76
Porfirio Díaz: Díaz (1830–1915) was president of Mexico for all but a handful of years between 1876 and 1911. The Porfiriato, as it is called, was a period of internal stability, economic growth and authoritarian politics, eventually ended by the Mexican Revolution.
jefe político: political chief.
General Forrest: Nathan Bedford Forrest (1821–1877) was a lieutenant general in the Confederate army during the American Civil War, remembered both as an innovative cavalry leader and as the first grand wizard of the Ku Klux Klan, the secret white supremacist vigilante organization.

p. 81
serious violence in northern Sonora: Nogales and Cananea had been the scenes of constant violence since the so-called Yaqui uprising in 1896. Mexican and US wars against the Yaqui continued until 1929. One of Roberts's earliest publications was an essay called "Tragedy of the Yaqui" (1908).
Colonel Kosterlitzky: Emilio Kosterlitzky (1853–1928) was a Russian-born soldier of fortune noted for his ability to speak most European languages. Deserting the Russian navy in Venezuela, he eventually fought in the Mexican Apache Wars and in 1885 was appointed commander of Porfirio Díaz's rural guard (*rurales*), which placed him at the centre of the wars against the Yaqui. During the Revolution he was captured in Nogales before moving with his family to Los Angeles. See Cornelius C. Smith Jr, *Emilio Kosterlitzky: Eagle of Sonora and the Southwest Border* (Glendale: Arthur H. Clark, 1970).
James Cashion: Born and raised in Canada, Cashion (1860–1936) moved to Kansas when he was nineteen. Starting as a mule driver in a construction camp, he steadily rose to a position of prominence as a railroad builder and was vice-president of Grant Brothers Construction Company.

Chapter 5. San Francisco

p. 87

Abe Ruef: For several years Ruef (1864–1936) was the political boss of San Francisco. Trained as a lawyer, he was the driving force behind the foundation of the Union Labor Party in 1901, with Eugene Schmitz as its mayoral candidate. Indicted in 1906, he was eventually convicted of bribery.

Eugene Schmitz: (1864–1928). Musician and politician elected mayor of San Francisco but who lost his position after being convicted on charges of corruption.

p. 88

Francis J. Heney: A US lawyer who had served as attorney general of the Arizona Territory between 1893 and 1895, Heney (1859–1937) worked extensively to prosecute those involved in San Francisco corruption, notably Abe Ruef. For his pains he was shot and nearly killed in 1906.

Hiram Johnson: Johnson (1866–1945) assisted Heney, taking over the prosecution after Heney was shot. He later became Theodore Roosevelt's running mate for the Progressive Party in the 1912 elections, served as governor of California, and was then a United States senator from 1917 to 1945.

Dr Edward R. Taylor: Lawyer and poet, Taylor (1838–1923) served as mayor of San Francisco between July 1907 and January 1910.

Tessie Wall: Teresa Susan Donohue (1869–1932), better known as Tessie Wall, owned and operated a number of brothels in San Francisco. She was married to gambler and political boss Frank Daroux, whom she attempted to kill in 1917 when he tried to divorce her. He declined to press charges.

chaffered: bantered.

Arnold Genthe: A self-taught photographer, renowned for his photographs of San Francisco's Chinatown and of the aftermath of the 1906 earthquake, Genthe (1889–1942) later moved to New York, where he photographed politicians and dancers in particular.

p. 89

Fremont Older: A San Francisco newspaperman known for his campaigns against civic corruption while editor of the *San Francisco Bulletin*, Older (1856–1935) later worked for William Randolph Hearst on the *San Francisco Call*.

p. 90

the great Biggy mystery: William J. Biggy (1859–1908) was San Francisco chief of police for the last two years of his life. During the graft prosecutions Biggy had held Abe Ruef in custody. Biggy was, however, criticized in the aftermath of Heney's shooting, first for allowing the excused juror who shot him to carry a small derringer, and second for allowing the killer to commit suicide under police watch. Falling out with the graft prosecution, Biggy was himself placed under surveillance. As Roberts reports, Biggy went overboard from a police launch during a nighttime crossing of San Francisco Bay from Belvedere to San Francisco after discussing matters with police commissioner Hugo Keil. His body was found floating in the bay two weeks later. Because Biggy, a devout Catholic, was considered an unlikely suicide, the coroner's jury returned a verdict of accidental death. The case remains unsolved. The launch from which he disappeared was being piloted by the only other man on board, police officer William Murphy, whom Roberts is therefore effectively fingering as Biggy's murderer.

p. 92
'Pinhead' McCarthy: Patrick Henry McCarthy (1863–1933) was an influential labour leader in San Francisco, who served as mayor from 1910 to 1912.
fencing: Both Ezra Pound and William Carlos Williams learned to fence in their youth, so Roberts's interest was not unusual among his generation of writers. Fencing is key to all three of his New Orleans novels.

p. 93
Owen Moran: (1884–1949). English bantamweight boxer.
Eddie Hanlon: (1885–1942). Lightweight boxer, local to San Francisco.
Stanley Ketchel: Stanisław Kiecal (1886–1910), known in the boxing world as Stanley Ketchel, the Michigan Assassin, was a Polish American professional boxer who became one of the greatest middleweight champions in history. He was murdered in 1910.
Billy Papke: Known as the Illinois Thunderbolt, Papke (1886–1936) had supposedly beaten Ketchel by punching him in the face when Ketchel stepped forward to shake his hand at the beginning of the bout, which may explain Ketchel's attitude during the fight Roberts witnessed. In 1936 Papke shot and killed his wife before turning the gun on himself.
Tom Corbett's: Tom Corbett (1868–1915) was brother to "Gentlemen Jim" Corbett, regarded as the father of modern boxing. Tom worked as an assistant to his brother and then as a boxing commissioner in California.
Jack London: An author and journalist born in and always associated with San Francisco, London (1876–1916) was one of the most commercially and critically successful writers of his day.
George Sterling: A Californian poet and bohemian, Sterling (1869–1926) was mentored by Ambrose Bierce and became a close friend of Jack London and Adolphe Roberts (who corresponded with him for many years). He committed suicide.
Ambrose Bierce: US journalist, short story writer and fabulist, Bierce (1842–after 1913) is best remembered for his satirical lexicon *The Devil's Dictionary*. He disappeared in Mexico while travelling with rebel troops during the revolution.
Sanguinetti . . . Coppa: Stefano Sanguinetti and Guiseppe Coppa were two of the best-known restauranteurs in San Francisco at this time. The fifty-cent dinner

would consist of seven courses. **The Poodle Dog** (possibly a mangled version of Le Poulet d'Or) had been a San Francisco landmark since 1849.

Bohemian Club: Gentlemen's club on Taylor Street founded in 1872 and extant.

p. 94

Diego Estrada Cabrera: Manuel Estrada Cabrera (1857–1924) was president of Guatemala from 1898 to 1920, ruling with an iron first and facilitating the establishment of the United Fruit Company in his country. He provided the model for the title character in Miguel Ángel Asturias's classic dictatorship novel, *El Señor Presidente* (1946). Estrada Cabrera had two legitimate children with his wife, Desideria Ocampo. Roberts's acquaintance in San Francisco in 1908, actually Diego Estrada Ocampo, contracted tuberculosis soon afterward and committed suicide in 1910. Given that his brother, Francisco, later committed suicide when he realized that his father had discovered his huge debts, Diego's ransom plan may have been a touch optimistic.

Nora May French: A talented and precocious writer, admired by many of the Californian bohemians, French (1881–1907) killed herself while staying at Carmel with Sterling and his wife Carrie in November 1907, but by taking cyanide, not leaping off a cliff. The collection Roberts refers to is *Poems* (San Francisco: Strange Company, 1910). A recent edition is *The Outer Gate: The Collected Poems of Nora May French*, ed. Donald Sidney-Fryer and Alan Gullette (New York: Hippocampus, 2009).

p. 95

'sourdoughs': Sourdough bread was a Northern Californian speciality, so 'sourdough' became a slang term for gold prospectors.

p. 96

Rex Beach: Beach (1877–1949) grew up in Florida but was drawn to Alaska at the time of the Klondike Gold Rush. After five years of unsuccessful prospecting, he turned to writing. *The Spoilers* was based on a true story of corrupt government officials stealing gold mines from prospectors: it became one of the best-selling novels of 1906. His later adventure stories were often turned into films. Beach shot himself in 1949 at his home in Florida.

p. 98

Lotta's Fountain: Named after the actress Lotta Crabtree. This and the monument to Stevenson are both still in place.

p. 99

Morant Bay in 1865: The Morant Bay Rebellion in 1865 is a key event in Jamaican history and one to which Roberts would often turn. Amid rumours that slavery might be restored, on account of worsening economic conditions, George William Gordon, a wealthy mulatto politician, began encouraging people to make their grievances known. After a scuffle in a courthouse in October 1865, arrest warrants were issued for several men – among them Paul Bogle, a follower of Gordon – for rioting, resisting arrest and assaulting the police. A few days later a protest march to the Morant Bay courthouse was met by a small and inexperienced volunteer militia. The crowd threw rocks and sticks; the militia opened fire, killing seven protesters. The protesters attacked, killing eighteen people, including white officials and militia, and taking control of the town. Governor Eyre sent government troops (led by Luke O'Connor, as Roberts notes) to hunt down the rebels and bring Paul Bogle back to Morant Bay for trial. The troops were met with no organized resistance but killed blacks indiscriminately, many of whom had not been involved in any rioting or rebellion: 439 black Jamaicans were killed by soldiers, and 354 more, including Bogle, arrested and executed. Despite having had little to do with the rebellion, Gordon – who had previously been critical of Eyre and his policies – was also arrested and executed. These events provoked fierce debate in Britain with public figures of different political affiliations lining up to support or oppose Eyre's actions. Opponents argued that he should be put on trial for his excesses. Eyre's opponents were men such as John Bright, Charles Darwin, John Stuart Mill, Thomas Huxley, Thomas Hughes and Herbert Spencer. Defending him were Thomas Carlyle, Charles Kingsley, Charles Dickens and John Ruskin. Eyre was twice charged with murder, but the cases never proceeded. As a result of the uprising, the Jamaica Assembly renounced its charter and Jamaica became a Crown Colony.

Bazaine at Metz: Marshall François Achille Bazaine (1811–1888) surrendered the last organized French army to the Prussians at Metz in 1870 during the Franco–Prussian war. **Marshal Patrice de Mac-Mahon, 1st Duke of Magenta** (1808–1893), fought at Sedan, which was also surrendered to the Prussians in the same year. He later served as chief of state of France from 1873 to 1875 and as the first president of the Third Republic, from 1875 to 1879. Paris was under siege from Prussian forces from September 1870 until January 1871, when **Wilhelm I** (1797–1888) was declared German emperor in the palace at Versailles. The Paris **Commune** then exercised control over the city for two months that spring before its bloody suppression.

Chapter 6. New York Heyday

p. 102

42, 60 and 61 Washington Square: All these houses have been demolished in the course of the development of New York University.

Horace Greeley: (1811–1872). US newspaper editor, liberal reformer and an outspoken opponent of slavery. The *New York Tribune* (which Greeley founded and edited) was the country's most influential newspaper from the 1840s to the 1870s.

William Jay Gaynor: (1849–1913). A well-respected and independent-minded politician who was mayor of the City of New York from 1910 to 1913, after serving as a New York Supreme Court justice.

Charles S. Whitman: Whitman (1868–1947) was well-known as New York district attorney for his prosecution of the police lieutenant Charles Becker for the murder in July 1912 of Times Square gambling house operator Herman Rosenthal in front of West Forty-Third Street's Hotel Metropole (owned by Tammany Hall leader, Big Tim Sullivan). Whitman later served as governor of New York from 1915 to 1918.

Madama's: See also p. 70.

p. 103

T. Victor Hall: Illustrator, painter and sculptor, born in Indiana, Hall (1879–1965) worked for most of his life in New York.

Henry Gallup Paine: (1859–1929). The author of *Handbook of Simplified Spelling* (1920).

p. 104

Blanche Schrack: Schrack (1881–1922) was later associated with the *Birth Control Review* that Roberts edited during his relationship with Margaret Sanger (see p. 138). When Blanche died of pneumonia in Pittsburg, Roberts wrote a short obituary for the *Birth Control Review*.

p. 105

A.B. Frost and Charles Dana Gibson: Arthur Burdett Frost (1851–1928) was indeed a highly regarded illustrator, graphic artist and painter. He lived in France between 1906 and 1914 and on his return to the United States worked mainly for *Life* magazine. Charles Dana Gibson (1867–1944) was best known for his creation of the 'Gibson Girl', an iconic representation of the beautiful and independent American woman at the turn of the twentieth century.

Franklin Booth: Though primarily a commercial artist, Booth (1874–1948) is still highly regarded for his detailed pen-and-ink illustrations.

Charles N. Sarka: (1879–1960). Painter, muralist, printmaker and illustrator.

Eugène Delacroix: (1798–1863). French Romantic artist and illustrator.

p. 106

Albert L. Scherzer: Although Robert G. Vosburgh has disappeared without trace, some of the work of Albert L. Scherzer (1882–1912) is still remembered and available.

Rudyard Kipling: Kipling (1865–1936) was at the height of his popularity in 1912: he had been awarded the Nobel Prize for Literature in 1907. Kipling's three thousand dollars would be around seventy thousand dollars today. **Richard Harding Davis** (1864–1916) was also a hugely successful writer at the time, renowned equally for his novels and his journalism. **Sir Gilbert Parker** (1862–1932) was a prolific Canadian-born writer who settled in England: he wrote historical novels, many about the history of Canada. On **Jack London**, see note to p. 93 and on **Rex Beach**, see note to p. 96. **Gouverneur Morris** (1876–1953) was the great-grandson of one of the writers of the US Constitution (who had the same name). He published some collections of stories during his lifetime, but is now almost completely unregarded.

Howard Chandler Christy: (1873–1952). US artist and illustrator famous for the 'Christy Girl', similar to a 'Gibson Girl'.

Harrison Fisher: (1877–1934). US illustrator whose work appeared regularly on the cover of *Cosmopolitan* magazine from the early 1900s until his death.

p. 107

Maison Petitpas: A boarding house and restaurant at 317–319 West Twenty-Ninth Street. See "Yeats at Petitpas'", in Van Wyck Brooks, *Scenes and Portraits: Memories of Childhood and Youth* (New York: E.P. Dutton, 1954), 169–88.

John Butler Yeats: Yeats (1839–1922) was sixty-nine when he moved to New York in 1908, so only just seventy when Roberts met him. Yeats sketched Roberts (see figure 11, p. 119).

p. 108

John Quinn: A second-generation Irish American lawyer in New York, Quinn (1870–1924) was an important patron of major figures of post-impressionism and literary modernism, and a collector of original manuscripts and artwork. He was particularly close to Joseph Conrad, W.B. Yeats and Ezra Pound, and was an organizer and spokesperson for the 1913 Armory Show. One of Roberts's friends, Jeanne Robert Foster (see pp. 109 and 212), worked closely with Quinn.

p. 109

Robert Henri: By this time Henri (1865–1929) was a well-established artist and teacher, committed to a realistic representation of urban life. In 1910, he had organized the Exhibition of Independent Artists, the first non-juried, no-prize show in the United States, which he modelled after the Salon des Indépendants in France, with pictures hung alphabetically to emphasize the egalitarian philosophy. Five of Henri's paintings were included in the Armory Show.

George Bellows: Bellows (1882–1925) had been a student of Henri's and was just coming to prominence at this time, similarly committed to urban realism – the Ashcan School as it would be much later termed.

John Sloan: Closely associated with Henri and Bellows, Sloan (1871–1951) painted *Yeats at Petitpas'* (now in the Corcoran Gallery, New York) around this time.

Boardman Robinson: (1876–1952). Canadian-US artist, illustrator and cartoonist, who worked on *The Masses* and *The Liberator*.

Alan Seeger: (1888–1916). Poet who fought and died in World War I serving in the French Foreign Legion. His nephew was the folk singer Pete Seeger. See also pp. 117, 165, 177, 191 and 197.

Joyce Kilmer: (1886–1918). Poet, journalist and literary critic killed at the Battle of the Marne in 1918.

Shaemus O'Sheel: (1886–1954). US poet, Irish nationalist, ardent communist, defender of Germany during World War II.

Jeanne Robert Foster: Born Julia Elizabeth Oliver in Johnsburg, New York, in the Adirondack Mountains, and married in her teens to a much older man, Foster (1879–1970) had a career as a fashion model before becoming a poet, literary editor and assistant to the collector John Quinn, through whom she met and made friends with many of the day's leading writers, including Ezra Pound, Ford Madox Ford and W.B. Yeats. She had a brief but troubled relationship with the English author and occultist Aleister Crowley. In 1932 she moved to Schenectady as a social worker. See Richard and Janis Londraville, *Dear Yeats, Dear Pound, Dear Ford: Jeanne Robert Foster and Her Circle of Friends* (Syracuse: Syracuse University Press, 2001).

Van Wyck Brooks: Brooks (1886–1963) was one of the great literary historians of the twentieth century. He wrote about this period of US writing in *The Confident Years: 1885–1915* (1952) and published a biography of one of the other regular diners, *John Sloan: A Painter's Life* (1955).

Allan Benson: Allan L. Benson (1871–1940) was a newspaper editor and author who ran for president in 1916 as the Socialist Party of America candidate.

Michael Monahan: (1865–1933). Irish-born literary critic and poet.

Robert W. Sneddon: (1880–1944). Scottish-born writer sometimes credited with writing the first vampire story.

Dolly Sloan: John Sloan met his wife Dolly, born Anna Maria Wall (1876–1943), in a brothel. Despite her sexual history and persistent alcoholism, they had a long and supportive relationship, marrying in 1901.

Jack London: See note to p. 93.

***John Barleycorn*:** London's autobiographical novel was published in 1913.

p. 110

William Butler Yeats: Irish poet and playwright, and one of the major literary figures of the twentieth century, Yeats (1865–1939) was a driving force behind the Irish Literary Revival, co-founding the Abbey Theatre, which he ran during its early years. In 1923 he was awarded the Nobel Prize in Literature.

according to George Moore: Novelist and art critic Moore (1852–1933) wrote about Yeats in his account of Dublin at the turn of the century: "Hail and Farewell, Ave" (1911).

p. 111
Marcel Duchamp: Roberts's lack of sympathy with non-figurative modern art perhaps explains the error in his typescript where he calls Duchamp (1887–1968) "Maurice". The Armory Show was the 1913 International Exhibition of Modern Art organized by the Association of American Painters and Sculptors. It ran in the **Sixty-Ninth Regiment Armory**, on Lexington Avenue between Twenty-Fifth and Twenty-Sixth Streets, from 17 February to 15 March, and is often regarded as a seminal event in the history of modern American art.

p. 112
Hedda Sars: Born Hedda Saari in 1886, she had come to New York in 1909.

p. 113
Katharine Hickey: See p. 213 and note.
Raymond Orteig: Having emigrated from the south of France aged twelve to join an uncle living in New York, Orteig (1870–1939) started working as a busboy and café manager but soon acquired the two hotels Roberts refers to, the **Brevoort** and the **Lafayette**. The Brevoort was demolished in 1954, the Lafayette in 1950.
Lüchow's: Established in 1882 when a German immigrant August Lüchow purchased the café where he worked as a bartender, the restaurant survived until 1986, with its original building finally demolished in 1995 after being gutted by a fire the year before.
Allaire's: Scheffel Hall at 190 Third Avenue in Gramercy Park was built in 1895 and named after Joseph Viktor von Scheffel, a German poet and novelist. It later became known as Allaire's, a name still inscribed on the building, now a fitness centre, which has been designated a New York City landmark.
Joel's: Joel's Bohemian Refreshery, on West Forty-First Street just off Seventh Avenue, was renowned for never closing and was famous for its chili con carne, which Joel Rinaldo (1871–?), born to Russian parents but also sometimes referred to as the son of a Garibaldian revolutionary, is supposed to have introduced to New York after several years living in Mexico City. The three upper floors of the building were the Hotel de Rinaldo.
The Monopol: On Second Avenue between Eighth and Ninth Streets.

p. 114
Mouquin's: The original Mouquin's was famous for having introduced French cuisine, such as *bouillabaisse*, to the United States. Henri Mouquin (1837–1933) was born in Switzerland to a family of hotel proprietors and came to the United States in 1854. In this second Mouquin's, in 1908, the group of artists known as "the Eight", led by Robert Henri (see p. 109 and note), plotted their artistic revolution. Madame Mouquin's onion soup was renowned as a hangover cure. The restaurant closed down in 1925, a victim of Prohibition.

p. 115

Charles Jaffé: Jaffé (c. 1879–1941) was a Belarus-born chess master and writer, nicknamed "the Crown Prince of East Side Chess" by the poet and chessmaster Alfred Kreymborg. Jaffé often played at the Stuyvesant Chess Club, hangout of chess hustlers and interesting characters, which was located on the Lower East Side. Jaffé indeed made much of his income through challenge games and odds games played there, so the Stuyvesant may well have been what Roberts calls "Karl's". Emanuel **Lasker** (1868–1941) was a German chess player, writer and philosopher who was World Chess Champion for twenty-seven years. Carl **Schlechter** (1874–1918) a leading Austrian chess master, tied a famous match with Lasker in 1910, the first person in many years to threaten Lasker's world title. Dawid **Janowski** (1868–1927) was a leading Polish chess master and subsequent French citizen. Frank James **Marshall** (1877–1944) was US chess champion from 1909 to 1936.

61 **Washington Square South:** Demolished in 1948. The room Roberts describes sounds remarkably similar to the one occupied by Don Hedger in Willa Cather's 1920 story, "Coming, Aphrodite!", which is described as a top-floor room of an old house on the south side of Washington Square with a big studio window: see *The Greenwich Village Reader: Fiction, Poetry, and Reminiscences, 1872–2002*, ed. June Skinner Sawyers (New York: Cooper Square, 2001, 126–27). Cather probably lived next door in number 60 in 1906, where Roberts also later lodged.

p. 116

Adelina Patti: (1843–1919), highly acclaimed opera singer, whose soprano voice earned her a fortune.

Mme Catherine Branchard: (1856–1937). She is often now referred to as Blanchard, although early newspaper reports agree with Roberts's spelling of her name. She was born Katharina Ruede Branchard in Sulz bei Laufenburg, a Rhine Valley town, and came to the United States in 1901. See "Madame Branchard and her 'House of Genius'", *American Notes and Queries* 5, no. 1 (April 1945): 3–7, for which Roberts supplied much of the information.

Alexandre Casarin: (c. 1845–1907).

Frank Norris: See p. 66 and note. Norris lived in New York from 1899 to 1902, the year of his death.

Gelett Burgess: (1866–1951). Artist and author, best known as a writer of nonsense verse.

Thompson Buchanan: (1877–1937). Novelist and playwright.

Eddie Townsend: Edward W. Townsend (1855–1942) invented the character Chimmie Fadden in his column for the *New York Sun* in the 1890s. Chimmie was an enterprising Irish tough who commented on New York slum life in colourful dialect. He became such a popular figure that Townsend was able to publish several volumes of stories and to pursue a Congressional career. Chimmie was adapted for both stage and screen.

Stephen Crane: See p. 66 and note. There is no evidence that Crane lived at the House of Genius.

p. 117

Alan Seeger: See note to p. 109. He spent four years in Mexico City right at the beginning of the century. From John Reed's "The Day in Bohemia" (1912):

> A timid footstep, – enter then the eager
> KEATS – SHELLEY – SWINBURNE – MEDIAEVAL – SEEGER;
> Poe's raven bang above Byronic brow,
> And Dante's beak, – you have his picture now;
> In fact he is, though feigning not to know it,
> The popular conception of a Poet.

Pico della Mirandola: Giovanni Pico della Mirandola (1463–1494). Renaissance philosopher renowned for his *Oration on the Dignity of Man* (1486), which is doubtless what Seeger admired.

p. 118

***Harper's*:** Two of the four may be eternal, but the *Century* folded in 1930, *Scribner's* in 1939.

Charlotte Collyer: Collyer's eyewitness account, "How I Was Saved from the *Titanic*", was published in the *Semi-Monthly Magazine* (26 May 1912). It has been widely reproduced as one of the first and most valuable eyewitness accounts. Since Roberts's name did not appear in connection with the original account, his role in writing it has never been recognized. Charlotte Collyer soon returned to England, only to die of tuberculosis in 1914.

p. 120

Ivan Narodny: As Roberts's account indicates, Narodny (1874–1953) was a strange character, perhaps the most mysterious that Roberts encountered. He had turned up in New York around the beginning of 1906 as a political refugee, having – he claimed in a *New York Times* interview (7 April 1906) – been involved in the aftermath of the Kronstadt rebellion and having had his home burned and his wife and children murdered by Cossacks. Prior to Kronstadt he had spent four years in the infamous St Peter and St Paul prison in St Petersburg. The contributor's note to one of his journal articles (presumably written by him) reads: "Ivan Narodny was a musical and literary critic for newspapers in his own country, Russia, when he was caught in the revolutionary movement. He was arrested and spent four years in solitary confinement and later has twice been forced to leave Russia. He came to America with Maxim Gorki and has since then been a contributor to American newspapers and magazines. He is a regular writer for *Musical America* and has published books on musical subjects" (*American-Scandinavian Review* 1, no. 5 [September 1913]).

Narodny must have known at least some English before reaching New York since he seems to have conducted interviews with newspapers in English and interpreted – again according to his own account – between Mark Twain and Maxim Gorki when the latter visited New York in April 1906: he does appear in photographs seated between them. He had announced himself with the book *Echoes of Myself: Romantic Studies of the Human Soul* in 1909, which seems to have fallen on deaf ears. He then worked as a journalist on *Russki Golos* and *New York American* as well as starting his own journal, the *Pilgrim's Almanac*. "The Apocalypse of Leo Tolstoy" appeared in the *Semi-Monthly Magazine* in February 1913, attached to Sunday newspapers across the United States. Once the World War broke out, Tolstoy's "vision" was remembered and reprinted, for example by Albert J. Edmunds as *The Vision of the World-War seen repeatedly by Leo Tolstoy from 1908 to 1910*, published in Philadelphia in 1914. Narodny had previously, in February 1911, also placed with the *Monthly Magazine* "The Last Interview with Count Leo Nikolaevich Tolstoy", conducted by "a favorite niece", that same Countess 'Nastasia Tolstoy; and in the *Semi-Monthly Magazine* itself in November 1912, "The Drama of My Life", about his imprisonment in St Petersburg. Narodny was a person of interest to the relatively new Bureau of Investigation (which became the Federal Bureau of Investigation). They concluded that his real name was Jaan Sibul, that he had been in prison in Estonia on charges of forgery, and that he had abandoned his family in Verro.

The Russian government was certainly capable of providing misinformation, but it seems that Narodny was even *persona non grata* among the Estonian exile community in the United States, and was involved in various shady financial deals at least until the early 1920s when his association with Robert W. Chanler's artistic salon provided him with a niche as an expert on Russian art – something which at least at first he probably knew very little about. He wrote a book about Chanler and was close to the Russian artist Nicolas Roerich who had a huge reputation in the mid-twentieth century, not least for designing the sets for Stravinsky's *Rite of Spring*. In 1936, after six years' study, Narodny announced that he had discovered the Key of Time, an idea he dubbed "chronosophy". By now he was living at 564 Riverside Drive in Upper Manhattan and owned a farm in Cornwall, Connecticut, his shady past well behind him. One of his children, Leo Narodny (1909–1999), became a well-known businessman in Dominica and Barbados. Roberts and Paine were surely right to be suspicious about Narodny. Tolstoy had an extensive family, but no grandniece called 'Nastasia. Her supposed covering letter to Narodny when she sent him the interview with Tolstoy states that it took place on 1 November 1910 – four days *after* Tolstoy left Yasnaya

Poliana on his last journey to Astapovo Station. The conclusion has to be that Narodny forged both pieces, as he had probably forged, or at least massively embroidered, his account of his imprisonment and release.

p. 121
William Griffith: Griffith (1876–1936) had an active career in the newspaper profession. His books of poems include *City Views and Visions* (1911), *Loves and Losses of Pierrot* (1916) and *City Pastorals* (1918).

Chapter 7. Pre-War Socialism

p. 122
The Fabians: The Fabian Society is a socialist society, still in existence. Founded in 1884 it soon attracted prominent writers and intellectuals such as Sidney and Beatrice Webb, George Bernard Shaw, H.G. Wells, Sydney Olivier, Virginia Woolf and Emmeline Pankhurst. Shaw visited Olivier in Jamaica in 1911.

p. 123
Francisco Ferrer: Ferrer (1859–1909) was a Catalan free-thinker and anarchist. He was exiled to Paris in 1885 and returned to Spain in 1901 to open what he called a "modern school". The school failed, but a book outlining his principles was translated into English. Following the declaration of martial law during the so-called Tragic Week in 1909, Ferrer was arrested, tried and executed by firing squad. After his death his educational ideas became popular in the United States, with the first and most notable Modern School formed in New York City in 1911.
some few were anarchists: Second Avenue was on the East Side, the lower part of which was home to Eastern European immigrants. There was traffic and overlap with the Village, but the East Side was more seriously political – often anarchist – in its interests.

p. 124
Emma Goldman: Goldman (1869–1940) was one of the leading anarchist figures of the period. Born in Kovno (present-day Kaunas, Lithuania), she emigrated to the United States in 1885 and was soon living in New York City, where she joined the anarchist movement in 1889, becoming a renowned lecturer on anarchist philosophy, women's rights and social issues. She was in her forties when Roberts knew her, but in her youth had been an attractive woman with many lovers. In 1919, Goldman was deported to Russia during the Red Scare. Disillusioned with the Bolshevik Revolution, she later lived in England, France and Canada, eventually dying in Toronto.
Ben Reitman: Trained as a doctor, Reitman (1879–1942) treated the down-and-out of US society, even performing abortions. In 1908 he and Goldman met and fell in love, spending eight years together despite Reitman's persistent infidelities.

Alexander Berkman: Goldman's early lover and lifelong friend, Berkman (1870–1936) planned to assassinate factory manager Henry Clay Frick as an act of propaganda of the deed during the violent Homestead strike against the Carnegie Steel Company. Berkman proved an incompetent assassin and Frick survived: Berkman was sentenced to twenty-two years in prison, serving fourteen. Despite Roberts's scepticism, Berkman's *Prison Memoirs of an Anarchist* is now considered something of a classic of the genre. Also deported in 1919, Berkman moved to France, where, suffering from ill health, he committed suicide.

p. 125

Nietzsche: Friedrich Nietzsche (1844–1900) was a philosopher, some of whose radical ideas appealed to anarchists, such as his hatred of the state and his anti-Christianity.

Kropotkin: Peter Kropotkin (1842–1921) was a Russian scientist, activist and anarcho-communist.

Dostoyevsky: Fyodor Dostoyevsky (1821–1881) was a novelist whose work explores psychological complexities within the context of the troubled atmosphere of nineteenth-century Russia.

Conrad: Joseph Conrad (1857–1924). Roberts was unusual in his enthusiasm for Conrad at this time, and unusually astute in recognizing the relationship between *Under Western Eyes* and *Crime and Punishment*.

Grand Duke Sergei of Russia: Grand Duke Sergei Alexandrovich (1857–1905) was a son of Emperor Alexander II of Russia. A conservative even by contemporary Russian standards, his policies when serving as governor general of Moscow made him a polarizing figure, and he was assassinated by a bomb at the Kremlin.

Empress Elisabeth of Austria: Elisabeth of Austria (1837–1898) was the wife of Franz Joseph I, and therefore both Empress of Austria and Queen of Hungary. Now regarded as something of a non-conformist and free spirit, she withdrew from public life following the suicide of her son Rudolf. She was murdered by an anarchist in Geneva.

King Umberto I of Italy: Umberto I (1844–1900) was a deeply conservative monarch loathed in left-wing and anarchist circles for his support of the massacre of demonstrators in Milan in May 1898 by General Bava-Beccaris. He was shot by anarchist Gaetano Bresci two years later, the killing planned – as Roberts notes – in Paterson, New Jersey.

p. 126

President McKinley: Six months into his second term as president of the United States, William McKinley (1843–1901) was assassinated during the Pan-American Exposition in Buffalo by Leon Czolgosz, who said he had been inspired by hearing a speech by Emma Goldman. Czolgosz was executed. Goldman wrote an essay in defence of the assassin, which attracted obloquy.

Max Eastman: US writer and activist. Eastman (1883–1969) was a leading socialist during the years before and after World War I, and was renowned as the editor of *The Masses*, where Roberts published some of his poems. His political views later turned sharply to the right, though he remained a maverick.
Allan Benson: See note to p. 109.
Norman Thomas: (1884–1968). Presbyterian minister, socialist and pacifist, who was six-time presidential candidate for the Socialist Party of America.
Eugene V. Debs: Debs (1855–1926) was a union leader, founding member of the Industrial Workers of the World (IWW), and several times presidential candidate for the Socialist Party of America.

p. 127
Meyer London: Born in Lithuania, London (1871–1926) was one of only two members of the Socialist Party of America ever elected to the US Congress.
Daniel DeLeon: DeLeon (1852–1914) was a Socialist newspaper editor, politician, Marxist theoretician and trade union organizer. He was a leading figure in the Socialist Labor Party of America from 1890 until his death.
Victor Berger: Berger (1860–1929) was a founding member of the Social Democratic Party of America and its successor, the Socialist Party of America. In 1910, he became the first Socialist elected to the US House of Representatives.
IWW: The Industrial Workers of the World (IWW, or the Wobblies) is an international trade union formed in 1905 with the idea that all workers should be united as a social class. Members could always belong to another union as well. Powerful in the 1910s and early 1920s, the IWW's influence subsequently declined, though it still exists, with its headquarters in Chicago.
Bill Haywood: William Haywood (1869–1928), known as Big Bill Haywood, was a founding member and leader of the IWW and a member of the Executive Committee of the Socialist Party of America, although his preference for direct action over political tactics eventually alienated him from the party. He was tried and acquitted for the murder of Frank Steunenberg in 1907 and was one of 101 IWW members convicted of violating the Espionage Act of 1917 during the "Red Scare". At this point he fled to what soon became the Soviet Union, where he spent the remaining years of his life.
Thompson: James P. Thompson (1873–1949) was one of the IWW's best-known speakers. Prominent at the Lawrence Textile Strike in 1911 (see p. 132 and note), he was arrested in 1916 and sentenced to twenty years in prison.

p. 128
***The Masses*:** An innovative and undogmatic socialist magazine, *The Masses* published high-quality writing and graphics from 1911 until 1917, when federal prosecutors brought charges against its editors for conspiring to obstruct conscription.
Colonel Edward M. House: Edward House (1858–1938), popularly known as Colonel

House though he had no military background, was a diplomat and presidential adviser who had enormous influence with Woodrow Wilson as his foreign policy adviser until 1919.

Mayor Gaynor: see p. 102 and note.

Woodrow Wilson: Thomas Woodrow Wilson (1856–1924) was the twenty-eighth president of the United States, from 1913 to 1921. Having trounced Taft and Roosevelt in 1912, Wilson won a narrower victory in 1916 and controlled US entry into World War I.

p. 129

Theodore Roosevelt: See note to p. 15.

President Taft: William Howard Taft (1857–1930) was the twenty-seventh president of the United States (1909–1913). Groomed by Roosevelt, he proved a disappointment, prompting Roosevelt to run against him in 1912. With the Republican vote split, Woodrow Wilson won easily.

p. 130

James E. Martine: See note to p. 45.

p. 131

Percy Stickney Grant: An American Protestant Episcopalian clergyman, Grant (1860–1927) was born in Boston and educated at Harvard. In 1893 he became minister of the Church of the Ascension of New York City, well known for his socialist opinions and for his open forum for the expression of all views. He was later involved in various controversies with his bishop and eventually resigned his rectorship.

Ernest Holcombe: Married to Grace Potter – social worker, journalist, free speech advocate, member of the Heterodoxy Club, and later psychoanalyst – Holcombe, an engineer, was reportedly a genial and welcoming figure.

Leigh Holdredge: Leigh Irving Holdredge (1879–?).

Berkeley Tobey: (1881–1962). A Greenwich Village bon vivant, Tobey was frequently married, on one occasion to the Catholic activist Dorothy Day. He worked as a journalist and was business manager of *The Masses*.

Paula Holladay: Born in Chicago in 1890, Polly ran a series of restaurants in the Village, of which this one in the basement of the Liberal Club was the most famous. 135 MacDougal Street was knocked down as part of the expansion of New York University.

p. 132

early in 1913: Actually October of that year.

Elizabeth Gurley Flynn: Labour leader, activist, socialist and feminist, Flynn (1890–1964) played a leading role in the IWW and was a prominent proponent of women's rights, birth control and women's suffrage. She died during a visit to the Soviet Union, where she was accorded a state funeral.

mill conditions at Lawrence: The Lawrence Textile Strike in 1912 was one of the biggest in US history. Immigrant workers in Lawrence, Massachusetts, led by the IWW, protested against the lowering of wages. The strike lasted more than two months and saw the children of strikers sent to New York and other cities to be cared for by sympathizers. The strike was successful in the short term, although the gains were later reversed.

p. 133

Lincoln Steffens: Steffens (1866–1936) was a New York reporter who campaigned against municipal corruption. He wrote *The Shame of the Cities* (1904), and is often associated with the term 'muckraking' with its original positive overtones.

New Forestry: This was probably Dr Herman de Fremery (1880–1968), who was employed by the Forestry Department of the American Museum of Natural History. He was married to the feminist Henrietta Rodman (1877–1923), and both were members of the club's executive committee.

p. 134

the Pagan Rout: Supposedly named by Floyd Dell: see his "Rents Were Low in Greenwich Village" (1947), in *The Greenwich Village Reader: Fiction, Poetry and Reminiscences, 1872–2002*, ed. June Skinner Sawyers (New York: Cooper Square, 2001), 257–66, at 261.

Webster Hall: Designed by Charles Rentz and built in 1886, Webster Hall was the venue for bacchanals of many kinds during this period. The hall, recently restored, still functions.

La Tierra de la Alegría: Based on a book by two young writers, José F. Elizondo and Eulogio Velasco, translated by Ruth Boyd Ober, Joaquín Valverde's operetta, *The Land of Joy*, was a huge success, running at the Park Theatre in Columbus Circle from the end of October 1917 to the end of January 1918, and then touring the country. It had previously been popular in Madrid, Paris, London, Buenos Aires and Havana.

Doloretes and Bilbao: Little is recorded about the life of Doloretes Falagan. Antonio Vidal (1885–1934) was born in Seville but brought up in Bilbao, hence his stage name. He is regarded as one of the greatest Spanish dancers.

p. 135

Winslow Homer: A New England landscape painter and printmaker, best known for his marine subjects, Homer (1836–1910) painted a series of canvases in the Caribbean.

my sister Ethel: Ethel Rovere was herself a published writer: in fact her story, "The Curse of God" won first prize in the *Public Opinion* short story competition in April 1939.

Helen Fulford: (1887–?).

p. 136
Sidney Olivier: See p. 26 and note.

p. 137
Auguste Comte: (1798–1857). Influential nineteenth-century figure, sometimes regarded as the first philosopher of science and as one of the founders of sociology. His *A General View of Positivism* (1848) was published in English translation in 1865.

p. 138
Kit Kat Club: Founded in 1881 at 61 East Twenty-Sixth Street, so it must subsequently have moved south.

Paterson: The 1913 Paterson, New Jersey silk mill workers strike, which lasted from 1 February to 28 July, was supported by many writers and artists from Greenwich Village, several of whom organized a pageant play at Madison Square Garden in which the events of the strike were reenacted. Despite these fundraising efforts, the strike ended in failure.

John Reed: John Silas "Jack" Reed (1887–1920) was a journalist, poet and socialist activist, best remembered for his first-hand account of the Bolshevik Revolution, *Ten Days that Shook the World* (1919), though he also wrote about the Mexican Revolution and was involved in the political and cultural life of Greenwich Village during Roberts's early years there.

Pat Quinlan: Arthur Patrick L. "Pat" Quinlan (1883–1948) was an Irish American trade unionist, journalist and socialist activist, best remembered for the part he played as an organizer for the IWW of the 1913 Paterson silk strike – an event which led to his imprisonment for two years in the New Jersey State Penitentiary.

Margaret Sanger: (1879–1966). Birth-control activist and sex educator who opened the first birth-control clinic in the United States, in 1916 in Brooklyn. As Roberts notes above, Sanger was involved in socialist and trade union activity, which brought her into contact with figures like John Reed and Emma Goldman, as well as with Roberts. After *The Woman Rebel* ran its course, she founded the *Birth Control Review* in 1917, which Roberts helped edit. Sanger's marriage had broken down in 1913, around the time she got to know Roberts. Her later lovers included Havelock Ellis and H.G. Wells. Unusually, Roberts does not admit to his romantic and sexual liaison with Sanger. Birth control was legalized in the United States in 1965, a year before Sanger's death.

p. 140
Camilla Farr: Given that Camilla Farr has left no documentary trace, there must be a suspicion that the name is a pseudonym.

p. 141
Inez Milholland: See p. 225 and note.
Edna St Vincent Millay: See p. 215 and note.

Chapter 8. Paris

p. 144
Paul Déroulède: (1846–1914). French author and nationalist politician.
Loubet: Émile François Loubet (1838–1929) was the eighth president of France (1899–1906), instrumental in the formulation of *entente* with Great Britain.
Adrien Machefert: (1881–1953). Californian painter and muralist.
Hotel des Ecoles: Man Ray and André Breton later lived here. It is now the Lenox Hotel.

p. 145
Café de la Rotonde: Located on the Carrefour Vavin, at the corner of boulevard du Montparnasse and boulevard Raspail, the Café de la Rotonde was founded by Victor Libion in 1911 and was soon a favourite watering hole of aspiring artists such as Picasso and Modigliani. It survives, much smarter than in Roberts's day.
Café du Dôme: This café had opened in 1898. Although its clientele overlapped with that of the Rotonde, it was widely known as "the Anglo-American café". It is now an upmarket fish restaurant.

p. 147
Hans von Kaltenborn: From 1928 H.V. Kaltenborn (1878–1965) became one of the best-known voices on US radio, renowned for his knowledge of world affairs.

p. 149
Mata Hari: Aged eighteen, Margaretha Geertruida Zelle (1876–1917) had married a Dutch colonial army captain, Rudolf MacLeod, who was living in the then Dutch East Indies (now Indonesia). Disappointed in her marriage, Margaretha studied local dance traditions and adopted the stage name Mata Hari. In 1903 she moved to Paris, where she performed as a circus horse rider, using the name Lady MacLeod, much to the disapproval of the Dutch MacLeods. Struggling to earn a living, she also posed as an artist's model, but soon began to win fame as an exotic dancer, often photographed nude or nearly so. Her reputation as a dancer began to decline around 1912, though by then she had become a successful courtesan who had relationships with high-ranking military officers and politicians. During World War I, since the Netherlands remained neutral, she was able to cross national borders freely, often travelling between France and the Netherlands via Spain and Britain. In 1916 she was arrested and interrogated in London, where she claimed to be working as a French agent, but the French soon identified her as a German agent and she was executed by firing squad on 15 October 1917. Most books about Mata Hari feature photographs "from the collection of W. Adolphe Roberts".
Louis Barthou: Jean Louis Barthou (1862–1934) was a French politician of the Third Republic who served as prime minister of France for eight months in 1913.

Gaston Doumergue: Doumergue (1863–1937) was a political contemporary of Barthou's who started as a radical but turned to the right. He served as prime minister from December 1913 to June 1914, and would later be both president of France (1924–1931) and again prime minister for several months in 1934 in a conservative national unity government.

Joseph Caillaux: Part of the same generation of politicians, Caillaux (1863–1944) had been prime minister in 1911 as leader of the Radicals. Forced to resign because of his secret negotiations with Germany, he fought the Three Years' Service bill and helped bring down the Barthou ministry in the autumn of 1913, returning to government as Doumergue's minister of finance. Still favouring conciliation with Germany, he was arrested, tried for treason, and sentenced to imprisonment and deprivation of civil rights; though he would later serve in several left-wing governments during the 1920s.

p. 150

Gaston Calmette: Calmette (1858–1914) had worked for *Le Figaro* since 1884 and been editor since 1894. His campaign against Caillaux had been long and virulent.

Mme Henriette Caillaux: Née Raynouard, Mme Caillaux (1874–1943) was a Parisian socialite best remembered for her killing of Gaston Calmette. Her affair with Caillaux had begun in 1907, while both were married to other people. Their eventual marriage in October 1911 made them one of the wealthiest couples in France.

Leo Clarétie: Journalist, literary critic and prolific novelist, Clarétie (1862–1924) is best remembered as Henriette Caillaux's first husband.

p. 152

T. Victor Hall: see p. 103 and note.

p. 153

Aïcha: For example, *Aïcha and Lorette* (1917) by Henri Matisse, now in a private collection. Aïcha Goblet was born in France to a Martinican father and French mother. She began her career as a circus performer and later worked as a dancer and actress.

p. 155

Revanche: Revenge. The movement to recover French territory lost to Germany in the Franco-Prussian War.

vegetable man's donkey: The painter was Roland Dorgelès (1885–1973) and the donkey – once used to transport fish but now retired – belonged to Frédéric Gerard, proprietor of the Lapin Agile (see note to p. 157). The donkey's painting, called *Et le soleil s'endormit sur l'Adriatique* [*And the Sun Set on the Adriatic*], was attributed to an imaginary Italian futurist called Jochim Raphaël Boronali and, after attracting favourable comment, sold for a good price. The imaginary futurist had also prepared a manifesto for the new school of Excessivism. See Jerrold Seigel, *Bohemian Paris: Culture, Politics, and the Boundaries of Bourgeois Life, 1830–1930* (New York: Viking, 1986), 346–47.

p. 156
Lascari: Salvatore Lascari (1884–1967). Sicilian American painter.
Henri Matisse: In 1914 Matisse (1869–1964) was painting pictures like his *View of Notre Dame* and *French Window at Collioure*, marked by blocks of colour.

p. 157
Lapin Agile: Famous Montmartre cabaret in the 18th arrondissement, a favourite spot at this time for struggling artists and writers, including Picasso, Modigliani, Apollinaire and Utrillo.
Aristide Bruant: (1851–1925). French cabaret singer, comedian and nightclub owner. His Montmartre club was called Le Mirliton.
Moulin Rouge: A Parisian cabaret built in 1889, near Montmartre, by Joseph Oller, it is best known as the birthplace of the modern form of the can-can. It remains a tourist attraction.
Toulouse-Lautrec: Henri de Toulouse-Lautrec (1864–1901). French post-impressionist painter who in his art had recorded many details of the bohemian lifestyle of Montmartre.
Moulin de la Galette: A windmill and associated businesses situated near the top of Montmartre.
apaches: Name given to members of one of the subcultures of the Parisian underworld in these years.
Naboth Hedin: (1884–1973). Swedish American journalist and author. Co-edited *Swedes in America 1638–1938* (1938) with Adolph B. Benson.

p. 158
Georges Clemenceau: (1841–1929). French journalist, physician and statesman. A member of the Radical Party, Clemenceau served as prime minister from 1906 to 1909, and again from 1917 to 1920. Leading France for most of the final year of World War I, he was one of the principal architects of the Treaty of Versailles at the Paris Peace Conference in the aftermath of the war. Roberts interviewed him in 1914 (see p. 152).
Maurice Barrès: French novelist, journalist, politician and agitator, Barrès (1862–1923) was known for his nationalist and antisemitic views. In 1906, he was elected both to the Académie française and as deputy, sitting with the conservative Entente républicaine démocratique.
René Viviani: (1863–1925). French politician, born in French Algeria, of left-wing sympathies, who served as prime minister for the first year of World War I.
President Poincaré: Raymond Poincaré (1860–1934) was a French statesman who

served five times as prime minister and as president from 1913 to 1920. He was conservative and anti-German in his views.

pourparlers: informal conversations before the beginning of formal discussions.

Alexandre Ribot: (1842–1923). French politician, four times prime minister, the last occasion being during the darkest French days of 1917.

p. 159

Jean-Jacques Waltz: Also known as "Oncle Hansi", or simply "Hansi", Waltz (1873–1951) was a French artist of Alsatian origin. He was a staunch pro-French activist, and was famous for his cute drawings, some of which contained harsh critiques of the Germans of the time. The full title of the book Roberts discusses is *Mon Village, ceux qui n'oublient pas [My Village: Those Who Do Not Forget]*. On his escape to France, Hansi joined the military as a translator when World War I broke out. In 1940, still wanted by the Gestapo for his militant works and his treason of 1914, he had to escape into Vichy France. He was attacked by the Nazis in Agen, and fled to Switzerland. Badly wounded as a result of this attack, he remained weak until he died in 1951.

p. 160

Murger's *La Vie de Bohème*: Henri Murger (1822–1861), son of a German immigrant to Paris, was a French novelist and poet, mainly remembered as the author of *Scènes de la vie de bohème* (1851), written from his own experiences as a desperately poor writer living in a Parisian attic. The book was the basis for Puccini's opera *La Bohème*.

Chapter 9. The Green Time Goes

p. 163

Franz Ferdinand: (1863–1914). Archduke of Austria-Este, he was from 1889 until his death heir presumptive to the Austro-Hungarian throne. His assassination in Sarajevo precipitated Austria-Hungary's declaration of war against Serbia, causing Germany and Austria-Hungary, on the one hand, and the countries allied with Serbia, on the other, to declare war on each other, starting World War I.

Sophie, the Duchess of Hohenberg: (1868–1914). Czech aristocrat and morganatic wife of Franz Ferdinand, she was assassinated with him in Sarajevo.

Antioch: The Siege of Antioch took place during the First Crusade in 1097 and 1098.

Kosovo: The Battle of Kosovo, also known as the Battle of the Field of Blackbirds, actually took place on 15 June 1389. (The date Roberts gives was often used earlier, but is the result of a mistaken back-projection of the not-then-adopted Gregorian calendar.) The Serbian army was routed by invading Ottoman forces about three miles northwest of modern-day Priština.

p. 164

Gavrilo Princip: Princip (1894–1918) was a member of the Yugoslav nationalist movement known as Young Bosnia. Given the maximum sentence of twenty years, he died in prison after contracting tuberculosis.

Franz Joseph: Franz Joseph I (1830–1916) was the emperor of Austria from 1848 until his death. His son, the Crown Prince Rudolf, committed suicide in 1889 and his wife, the Empress Elisabeth, was assassinated in 1898 (see p. 125 and note). He was indeed succeeded by his grandnephew Karl, who became Charles I, the last ruler of the Austro-Hungarian Empire.

p. 165

Alan Seeger: See note to p. 109.

Café Lavenue: "It was about half-past five on an October afternoon when Marya Zelli came out of the Café Lavenue, which is a dignified and comparatively expensive establishment on the Boulevard du Montparnasse." These are the opening lines of Jean Rhys's novel *Quartet* (1929), based on her years in Paris during the mid-1920s.

Closerie des Lilas: Another of the famous Montparnasse street cafés, frequented in earlier years by Zola, Cézanne and Baudelaire, and at this time by Apollinaire and Jarry, as well as Paul Fort. After the war the Closerie des Lilas would be favoured by US writers such as Hemingway, Fitzgerald and Pound. It survives.

Paul Fort: (1872–1960). French poet and playwright who supposedly played chess against Lenin in the Closerie des Lilas.

Rupert Brooke: English poet known for his idealistic war poems and his good looks, Brooke (1887–1915) died of an infected insect bite in Greece when part of the British Mediterranean Expeditionary Force.

Bal Bullier: Le Bal Bullier was a celebrated student dance hall in the Avenue de l'Observatoire.

Charles Péguy: (1873–1914). French poet, essayist and socialist who was killed in action.

p. 166

chypre **and** *santal***:** Chypre is the name of a family of perfumes characterized by the contrast between fresh citrus and oak moss. Santal is sandalwood.

"Sous les ponts de Paris": A popular song composed in 1914, with words by Jean Rodor and music by Vincent Scotto.

p. 167

Wilhelm II: The last German emperor, crowned in 1888, Wilhelm II (1859–1941) launched Germany on a bellicose programme of foreign affairs that culminated in his support for Austria-Hungary in the crisis of July 1914 that led to World War I. An ineffective war leader, he lost the support of the army, abdicated in November 1918, and fled to exile in the Netherlands.

p. 168
Maître Labori: Fernand Labori (1860–1917) was a French lawyer and politician. He had defended Dreyfus in 1899, surviving an attempt on his life.

p. 169
Jean Jaurès: (1859–1914). French Socialist leader assassinated at the outbreak of World War I.
Gustave Hervé: Originally a socialist and pacifist, imprisoned for his views, Hervé (1871–1944) embraced ultranationalism in 1912, creating a "national socialist" party which was soon transformed into French fascism.
Algeciras: The incident is more properly the Tangier Crisis, as Germany attempted to prevent France establishing a protectorate over Morocco. The Algeciras conference in 1906 tried to find a solution.
Agadir: In 1911, the arrival of a German gunboat, supposedly to protect the local German community, had triggered a crisis between France and Germany which allowed France, in 1913, to occupy nearly the whole kingdom of Morocco.

p. 171
Café du Croissant: At 146 Rue Montmartre. The café still exists.
Villain: Raoul Villain (1885–1936) was a French nationalist primarily remembered for his assassination of Jaurès. Astonishingly, after being incarcerated for the duration of the war, Villain was acquitted by a jury in March 1919. He was shot and killed in Ibiza in an incident at the beginning of the Spanish Civil War.

p. 173
Paul Bourget: A popular novelist and journalist, Paul Bourget (1852–1935) was in the offices of *Le Figaro* when Gaston Calmette was shot by Henriette Caillaux.

p. 174
Schoen: Wilhelm Eduard Freiherr von Schoen (1851–1933), German diplomat.
caisson: A two-wheeled cart carrying ammunition chests.
.75s: The French 75mm field gun, commonly regarded as the first modern artillery piece. Its official French designation was "Matériel de 75mm Mle 1897".
Gelett Burgess: See note to p. 116.

p. 176
the Schlieffen plan: Created by Count Alfred von Schlieffen (1833–1913) but modified after his retirement.
King Albert: Albert I of Belgium (1875–1934) had succeeded to the throne in 1909. He personally led the Belgian army.

p. 177
George Casmeze: Casmeze had an American father and a Turkish mother, and was born in England. He died in 1960.

Annotations ❧ 379

p. 178

a letter he wrote: See Alan Seeger, *Letters and Diary of Alan Seeger* (London: Constable, 1917).

taubes: Literally 'doves'. The first mass-produced German military plane.

Joffre: Marshall Joseph Joffre (1852–1931) had been made commander-in-chief of the French army in 1911.

p. 179

Marcel Sembat: (1862–1922). Socialist, journalist and politician. He was married to the fauvist painter and sculptor Georgette Agutte.

Jules Guesde: (1845–1922). Socialist, journalist and politician. He was close to Paul Lafargue and therefore to Lafargue's father-in-law, Karl Marx.

Bienvenu-Martin: Jean-Baptiste Bienvenu-Martin (1847–1943), Radical leader and cabinet officer.

p. 180

Gallieni: General Joseph Gallieni (1849–1916) had served in Martinique, the Sudan, Madagascar and Indo-China, as well as in the Franco-Prussian War. He was recalled from retirement to help defend Paris.

Kluck's big guns: Alexander von Kluck (1846–1934) was commander of the German First Army, which marched on Paris in the late summer of 1914.

p. 182

Georges Clemenceau: See note to p. 158.

p. 183

Thomasson: Raoul de Thomasson (1862–1939). Soldier and, later, military historian.

Chapter 10. World War I

p. 188

Coram Street: Just off Russell Square, well to the north of Soho, and therefore a much more salubrious area than Greek Street.

p. 189

Lord Kitchener of Khartoum: See note to p. 18.

p. 190

Café Royal: Started in Regent Street in 1865 by Daniel Nicholas Thévenon, a French wine merchant, the Café Royal was frequented by politicians, writers and celebrities, and was once renowned for its wine cellar. It closed in 2008. One of these bohemians Roberts saw might have been Jean Rhys, who frequented the Café Royal at this time.

p. 191

Alan Seeger: His sonnet 1 ends:

> Down the free roads of human happiness
> I frolicked, poor of purse but light of heart,
> And lived in strict devotion all along
> To my three idols – Love and Arms and Song.
> (Alan Seeger, *Poems*, with an introduction by William Archer [London: Constable and Co., 1917], 145.)

Roberts wrote a poem for Seeger called "To a Friend Fallen for France", collected in his *Pierrot Wounded* (1919).

p. 193

Boches: Derogotary French term for Germans, from *caboche* = cabbage, blockhead.

p. 195

Aristide Briand: Briand (1862–1932) served eleven terms as French prime minister during the Third Republic, including eighteen months during World War I.

p. 198

his beautiful poem: Seeger, *Poems*, 144.

memorial in Paris: On 4 July 1923, the president of the French Council of State, Raymond Poincaré, dedicated a monument in the Place des États-Unis to the Americans who had volunteered to fight in World War I in the service of France. The monument, in the form of a bronze statue on a plinth, executed by Jean Boucher, had been financed through a public subscription. Boucher had used a photograph of Seeger as his inspiration, and Seeger's name can be found, among those of others who had fallen in the ranks of the French Foreign Legion, on the back of the plinth. Also, on either side of the base of the statue are two excerpts from Seeger's "Ode in Memory of the American Volunteers Fallen for France" (one slightly misquoted), a poem he had actually written for a Decoration Day ceremony on 30 May 1916:

> Yet sought they neither recompense nor praise,
> Nor to be mentioned in another breath
> Than their blue-coated comrades whose great days
> It was their pride to share – ay, share even to the death!
>
> Hail, brothers, and farewell; you are twice blest, brave hearts.
> Double your glory is who perished thus,
> For you have died for France and vindicated us.
> (*Poems*, 170–72)

p. 199

Count Romanones: Álvaro de Figueroa y Torres-Sotomayor, 1st Count of Romanones (1863–1950), was the prime minister of Spain three times between 1912 and 1918.

Hedin told me in Paris: Roberts turned over his Parisian apartment to a distinguished quartet of US women writers: Solita Solano, Janet Flanner, Leda Bauerberg and Margaret Lee.
A voyage to the United States: Roberts returned to New York on the SS *Espagne*, which left Bordeaux on 23 December 1916.

Chapter 11. *Ainslee's* and Its Legend

p. 200
Robert Rudd Whiting: (1877–1918). Journalist and novelist.
exempted from military service: Roberts never explains just why he was exempt.

p. 201
O. Henry: See note to p. 53. O. Henry's first story, "Money Maze", was published in *Ainslee's* in May 1901.

p. 202
Al Jennings: Alphonso Jennings (1863–1961) was a famous, though inept, bandit, who eventually made a fortune as an adviser in Hollywood. His life story, as told to O. Henry in the Ohio Penitentiary, was supposedly the model for the writer's character the Cisco Kid in his 1907 story, "The Caballero's Way".

p. 203
June Willard: Her real name was Idalia Villiers-Wardell and she belonged to the Irish upper class. Her mother, Janie (or Jeanne) Villiers-Wardell, published *Spain of the Spanish* (1909) under her own name. Roberts visited them twice in Cannes in the period between the wars – a location which might suggest that the family had at least no financial need to be met through writing.
Olga Petrova: Petrova (1884–1977) was an actress, screenwriter and playwright. Born Muriel Harding on Merseyside, she had a career in music hall and theatre in England before moving to the United States and becoming a star of vaudeville with her fashionably Russian stage name. She then starred in a number of early films, most now lost, and wrote the scripts for several others. She left the film industry in 1918 but continued to act in Broadway productions. During the 1920s, she wrote three plays and toured the country with a theatre troupe. In her autobiography, *Butter with My Bread* (Indianapolis: Bobbs-Merrill, 1942), she describes her friend as "Adolphe Roberts of the Panlike visage and the mystic heart, literary in the best tradition and gifted with a genuine and generous delight in his fellow craftsmen" (301). She was also close friends with Solita Solano and Margaret Sanger. Roberts dedicated his second book of poems, *Pan and Peacocks*, to her.

p. 204

William M. Vander Weyde: (1871–1929). Now highly regarded as a pioneering photographer.

my second winter at *Ainslee's*: That is, 1918–1919. Shortly after this, Roberts hired Dorothy Parker to write theatre reviews for the magazine.

only daughter, Margaret: Margaret Worth Porter (1889–1927) married Oscar Cesare in 1916; they divorced in 1920.

Oscar Cesare: Swedish-born US caricaturist and painter, Cesare (1885–1948) sketched both Lenin and Trotsky on a visit to the Soviet Union in 1922.

p. 205

William Johnston: Journalist and novelist, Johnston (1871–1929) wrote an instant history of the Spanish-American War and a dozen novels with titles such as *The Apartment Next Door* and *Tragedy at the Beach Club*.

Frank Sullivan: (1892–1976). A humourist who would later make his reputation writing for the *New Yorker*.

Seward statue: At the southwest entrance to Madison Square Park, the seated bronze statue of the statesman William Henry Seward (1801–1872) – the purchaser of Alaska – was made by Randolph Rogers in 1876. Madison Square is formed by the intersection of Fifth Avenue and Broadway at Twenty-Third Street.

p. 206

Bryant Park: Between Fifth and Sixth Avenues and between Fortieth and Forty-Second Streets.

p. 207

Olive Tree Inn: Established by Henry Yates Satterlee (1843–1908), later bishop of Washington, while he was rector at the nearby Calvary Church.

p. 210

Solita Solano: Born Sarah Wilkinson in New York State, Solano (1888–1975) married young and travelled in the Far East with her engineer husband. Back in New York in 1908 she worked as a theatre critic and changed her name. In 1919 she began a relationship with the journalist Janet Flanner and the couple joined the Parisian lesbian coterie. During the 1930s and 1940s, Solano studied with G.I. Gurdieff, acting as his secretary.

Salomón de la Selva: De la Selva (1893–1959) was a Nicaraguan poet who lived in New York as a teenager. *Tropical Town and Other Poems* (1918) was published while he was in Europe, but all his subsequent work was in Spanish, including *El soldado desconocido* (1922), the only book of poems about World War I written in Spanish. His English grandmother was the daughter of the businessman Jonas Glenton, who had settled in Nicaragua in the early nineteenth century.

p. 211

Edna St Vincent Millay: See p. 215 and note.

Stephen Vincent Benét: Benét (1898–1943) was a poet, short story writer and novelist who won a Pulitzer Prize in 1929 for his book-length narrative poem about the American Civil War, *John Brown's Body*.

Rubén Darío: A Nicaraguan poet associated with the Spanish American literary movement of *modernismo*, Darío (1867–1916) had an enormous influence on poetry in Spanish. De la Selva acted as his guide when Darío visited New York in 1915, and with Thomas Walsh translated eleven of Darío's poems into English.

p. 212

Felixstowe, Suffolk: Coastal port where many British troops trained prior to deployment overseas. The Third Battalion of the Loyal North Lancashire Regiment was a "home" or "reserve" battalion, so de la Selva would have joined a different one when he was drafted to the front line.

Jeanne Robert Foster: See note to p. 109. The burial ground is in Chestertown Rural Cemetery in the Adirondacks.

George Sterling: See note to p. 93.

p. 213

His estranged wife: Carolyn Rand committed suicide by poison in August 1918.

B. Virginia Lee: (1902–?). Roberts's reference is to an article of hers called "The Last Phone Call of George Sterling", *Famous Lives* 1, no. 2 (1929): 93–95.

Richard Le Gallienne: (1866–1947). English author and poet long resident in the United States. *The Quest of the Golden Girls* (1896) was his best-known novel.

Ernest Dowson: (1867–1900). Poet and translator from the French. He died, penniless, of alcoholism.

Katharine Hickey: Katharine Amelia Hickey (1877–?). Roberts is slightly disingenuous here. Just before leaving for France he had had – as he mentions – a short-lived but passionate relationship with Camilla Farr, and immediately on his return he embarked on an equally passionate but rather longer-lasting one with Margaret Sanger, soon followed by his affair with Edna St Vincent Millay. Hickey was ten years older than Roberts and worked – like his first lover – as a milliner. The fact that he corresponded with her from Paris but that none of her letters survive in his papers suggests that this was the one relationship he really regretted and about which he felt some guilt.

Chapter 12. Edna St Vincent Millay

p. 215

Edna St Vincent Millay: During the 1920s and 1930s Millay (1892–1950) was one of the best known and highly regarded poets in the world, which is why Roberts devotes a separate chapter to his relationship with her.

many biographies: Not perhaps as many as Roberts anticipated. The most recent are Nancy Milford, *Savage Beauty: The Life of Edna St Vincent Millay* (New York: Random House, 2001), and Daniel Mark Epstein, *What Lips My Lips Have Kissed: The Loves and Love Poems of Edna St Vincent Millay* (New York: Henry Holt, 2001). Milford draws on Roberts's unpublished memoir about Millay, "Tiger Lily" (1952), which has extensive overlap with this chapter of his autobiography.

Mitchell Kennerley's *Lyric Year* contest: Mitchell Kennerley (1878–1950) was born in England. Arriving in the United States in 1896 he quickly worked his way into publishing, launching his own imprint in 1906 to publish literary criticism, modern drama, fiction and poetry. He produced elegant and often experimental books in small print runs. Later in life he opened and ran the Lexington Avenue Book Shop until his suicide in 1950. *The Lyric Year* (1912) was a "prize anthology" comprising one hundred poems by US poets chosen from – it was claimed – ten thousand submissions. One thousand dollars in prize money was divided among the authors of the three best poems chosen by a jury of Ferdinand Earle, Edwin J. Wheeler and W.S. Braithwaite. It was vigorously promoted by Kennerley and was extremely popular, but became hugely controversial because critical and popular sentiment declared loudly in favour of Millay's "Renascence", which had not been awarded a prize. It is sometimes claimed that the controversy launched modern poetry in the United States, signalling the obsolescence of an older regime of cultural valuation, though Millay's poem would soon seem formally unadventurous compared with those produced by the imagists and others in the following few years.

Ferdinand Earle: (1878–1951). A publisher, poet, artist and socialist, Earle (1878–1951) fell under Millay's sway in the course of some erotically charged correspondence about the prize anthology. It cost him his marriage.

p. 217

Harriet Monroe: (1860–1936). Editor and scholar. Her magazine, *Poetry*, begun in 1912, played a crucial role in the development of modernism.

"Daphne": A poem which later appeared in Millay's collection, *A Few Figs from Thistles* (1920). *Second April*, which Roberts mentions below, came out the following year.

The family: Norma (1898–1986) became her sister's literary executor and lived for the last twenty-five years of her life at Edna's house, Steepletop, in Austerlitz, New York. Kathleen (1900–1943) also became a writer of poetry and stories. She was estranged from her sisters at the time of her death. Cora Buzzell Millay (1863–1931) kicked out her profligate husband in 1900 and raised her three daughters on her own.

p. 219

False Armistice: 7 November 1918, with the real one following on 11 November.

p. 220

Provincetown Players: They began in makeshift fashion in Provincetown in July 1915 and in autumn 1916 took over the first floor of an apartment next door to the Liberal Club on MacDougal Street. The following year they moved three doors down the street, converting an old stable, where they staged some of Eugene O'Neill's early plays. See Brenda Murphy, *The Provincetown Players and the Culture of Modernity* (New York: Cambridge University Press, 2005).

Kit Kat ball: See p. 138 and note.

p. 221

Jacinto Benavente: Benavente (1866–1954) was a prolific Spanish playwright who won the Nobel Prize for Literature in 1922. *Los intereses creados* (1907), translated as *The Bonds of Interest*, is his most frequently performed play.

Floyd Dell: (1887–1969). Writer and critic and another of Millay's lovers. He wrote about her in his autobiography, *Homecoming* (1933).

A.E. Housman: (1859–1936). English classical scholar and poet, best known for his cycle of poems *A Shropshire Lad* with their wistful evocation of doomed youth in the English countryside.

p. 222

Tennyson's influence: Alfred Lord Tennyson (1809–1892). *Idylls of the King* was a cycle of twelve narrative poems (1856–1885). "Ilion" was written in 1830 as an experiment in quantitative measure when Tennyson was a student.

Swinburne: See note to p. 21. "I hid my heart" is the opening to his "A Ballad of Dreamland", first published in 1876.

p. 223

Meredith: George Meredith (1828–1909). Victorian novelist and poet. The phrase that Roberts quotes comes from a letter that Meredith wrote to the *Times* on the day of Swinburne's funeral (15 April 1909, 6).

Deems Taylor: Joseph Deems Taylor (1885–1966), composer, music critic and promoter of classical music. *The King's Henchman* – telling the story of a love triangle between King Eadgar, his henchman Aethelwold, and Aelfrida, daughter of the Thane of Devon – premiered on 17 February 1927 at the Metropolitan Opera in New York City to huge acclaim and was extensively performed throughout the country over the next few years.

translations from Baudelaire: Millay translated Baudelaire with George Dillon (who had earlier been her – much younger – lover): *Flowers of Evil* (1936).

p. 224

Arthur Davison Ficke: Ficke (1883–1945) was a conservative poet best remembered for his part in the Spectrist hoax in which he and Witter Bynner (see below) published *Spectra: A Book of Poetic Experiments* (1916), under pseudonyms, as a satire on Imagism. Nobody cottoned on, so two years later the authors came clean. An early admirer of Millay's poetry, Ficke became one of the loves of her life, as Roberts goes on to affirm, though their relationship was often thwarted, not least by his two marriages.

Stephen Vincent Benét: See note to p. 211.

Witter Bynner: Harold Witter Bynner (1881–1968) was a poet and scholar. One of the Spectrist hoaxers, along with Davison Ficke, he later studied and translated Chinese literature, which influenced his own poetry and brought him closer to Ezra Pound. He settled in Santa Fe where he befriended D.H. Lawrence as well as hosting Millay and many other writers and artists, including Willa Cather, Robert Frost, W.H. Auden, Carl Van Vechten and Thornton Wilder. Despite being gay, he proposed to Millay.

Ralph Hodgson: (1871–1962). English poet who later lived in Japan and the United States.

Louise Bogan: (1897–1970). Like Millay, she was born in Maine, but the daughter of a millworker. Bogan's poetry was polished and restrained, sometimes compared with the Metaphysicals, though her subject matter was contemporary.

Elinor Wylie: (1885–1928). Wylie was a poet and novelist, who had her red hair and tumultuous love life in common with Millay: they were good friends. Her third husband was William Rose Benét, Stephen Vincent's brother.

Amy Lowell: (1874–1925). A poet of independent means who became the spokesperson for the Imagist school, in the process quarrelling with Ezra Pound.

"To what purpose": This poem is called "Spring".

Edmund Wilson: Man of letters and author of, among many other books, *Axel's Castle: A Study in the Imaginative Literature of 1870–1930* (1931), Wilson (1895–1972) was another of Millay's lovers and long-term admirers. Roberts's "pleasantly" is presumably intended ironically: in a letter to Solita Solano he was scathing about Wilson's memoir, which was republished as the epilogue to his *The Shores of Light: A Literary Chronicle of the Twenties and Thirties* (New York: Farrar, Straus and Young, 1952).

Frank Crowninshield: (1872–1947). Journalist and art and theatre critic best known for developing and editing *Vanity Fair* between 1914 and 1935, making it a pre-eminent literary journal.

p. 225

Inez Milholland: A suffragist, labour lawyer, war correspondent and public speaker who greatly influenced the women's movement in the United States, Milholland (1886–1916) was married to Eugene Boissevain, who, after her death, married Edna St Vincent Millay. Like Millay, Milholland had attended Vassar.

Pieter Mijer: His relationship with Edna had started before she took up with Roberts. The only Millay biography that mentions Mijer is Norman A. Brittan's, drawing on Roberts's "Tiger Lily" essay (*Edna St Vincent Millay* [New York: Twayne, 1967], 42). The error Roberts notes occurs in Allan Ross Macdougall's collection of Millay's letters where, in a letter from Millay to Roberts (12 July 1919), Macdougall explains the reference to Pete as to Rollo Peters (*Letters of Edna St Vincent Millay*, ed. Allan Ross Macdougall [New York: Harper and Bros., 1952], 90). As Roberts rather tartly pointed put in a letter to Macdougall (8 December 1952 [Vassar, Edna St Vincent Millay Papers, 3.9]), she was actually referring to Pieter Mijer. Mijer was the key figure in the development of batik-making in New York during this period and author of *Batiks and How to Make Them* (1919), which ran to nine editions by 1931. Edmund Wilson mentions that when he met Millay in early 1920 she was "dressed in some bright batik" (*The Shores of Light*, 749). Mijer may have been the same Pieter Mijer (1881–1963) who competed in the individual épée event for the Netherlands in the 1928 Olympic Games.

bibelots: ornaments, trinkets.

Chapter 13. The *American Parade*

p. 227

Richard Duffy: (1873–1949). Translator from the French, close friend of Theodore Dreiser, and later agent to Emily Post.

R.R. Whiting: See p. 200 and note.

The Smart Set: Although founded in 1900 as a literary magazine, *The Smart Set* had its heyday under the editorship of H.L. Mencken and George Jean Nathan between 1914 and 1923. In an attempt to boost revenue, Mencken and Nathan began the pulp magazine *Parisienne* in 1915 as a place to publish surplus manuscripts deemed too inferior for *The Smart Set*. They repeated the trick with *Saucy Stories* in 1916. Mencken and Nathan later worked with publisher Alfred A. Knopf to start the *American Mercury*.

H.L. Mencken: Henry Louis Mencken (1880–1956) was one of the most influential journalists, editors and critics of the first half of the twentieth century, a true intellectual and debunker of all kinds of populist and religious nonsense.

George Jean Nathan: (1882–1958). Drama critic and editor. Nathan spent ten years in a relationship with the actress Lillian Gish.

p. 228

motion picture journalism: Among Roberts's claims to motion picture fame is that he conducted the first interview in the United States with Greta Garbo for *Motion Picture Magazine* in 1925. Already cultivating her reclusive image, Garbo conducted the interview from bed with Roberts in the next room. On this period, see Anthony Slide, *Inside the Hollywood Fan Magazine: A History of Star Makers, Fabricators, and Gossip Mongers* (Jackson: University Press of Mississippi, 2010).

p. 229

Witness Petrova: See p. 203 and note.

Norma Talmadge: (1894–1957). One of the most popular and best-paid screen actresses of the 1920s, she saw her career die with the end of silent pictures. Talmadge started a Hollywood tradition by accidentally standing in wet concrete outside Grauman's Chinese Theater.

not lured to Hollywood: Among Roberts's papers is a friendly letter from John Ford, who was an admirer of his writing, so Roberts would certainly have had a way in.

sensational detective fiction: *The Mind Reader: A Mystery* (1928).

p. 230

***American Parade*:** Forgotten for over eighty years, the *American Parade* has now had some recognition as a significant modernist journal. In an essay which brings together Roberts's journal and H.L. Mencken's *Smart Set*, Sharon Hamilton notes that *American Parade* made a point of promoting modernism from "both Americas"; that it attempted to reach a wide audience "through a tone characterized by wit and sophistication while experimenting with an eclectic mix of short stories, poems, and critical commentary"; and that it treated film, architecture, jazz, advertising and cartoons as worthy of serious critical attention (Sharon Hamilton, "American Manners: *The Smart Set* [1900–29]; *American Parade* [1926]", in *The Oxford Critical and Cultural History of Modernist Magazines*, volume 2, *North America 1894–1960*, ed. Peter Brooker and Andrew Thacker [Oxford: Oxford University Press, 2012], 224–48). In the opening number Roberts wrote this prospectus:

> THE AMERICAN PARADE comes into existence with the dawn of the second quarter of the Twentieth Century. It will march to the swift and splendid rhythm of its day, as that is realistically perceived in our western world.
>
> It will have no policy, in the sense of tabooing certain subjects and sanctifying others. But it will substitute personality for a policy. It does

not propose to be a scrap book of chaotic comment, or a literary SALON DES INDEPENDANTS.

Those who write for it will be free to use whatever material seems best to them, so long as they use it with clarity – so long as they portray the pageantry of our modern American life, which is glittering, hard-surfaced, and, above all, clear in its motivation.

There is a circus going by the door. This magazine is vastly interested in the circus, but has no scheme for reforming it. We shall cheer whatever is beautiful, or strong, or amusing in the big show, and leave the rest to the dullards.

Gamaliel Bradford: (1863–1932). Biographer, critic, poet and dramatist, scion of an early New England family. Author of 114 biographies, he was hardly a cutting-edge figure in 1926.

Woodrow Wilson: See note to p. 128. Roberts's essay was deeply critical of Wilson's actions with respect to Mexico.

p. 231

Orrick Johns: Johns (1887–1946) worked as a drama critic in St Louis before moving to New York in 1911, where he published poetry in leading modernist magazines such as *Others*. In the 1930s, he became an active member of the Communist party and was later the director of the Federal Writers Project in New York City.

Eleanor Ramos: See p. 233 and note.

Louise Townsend Nicholl: (1890–1981). Poet and editor.

Ethel Watts Mumford: From a wealthy family, Watts Mumford (1876–1940) studied painting in Paris and travelled widely. Well established as a writer by 1926, she had published novels, short stories, joke collections, songs, poems and essays, as well as painting and illustrating books.

Nunnally Johnson: A journalist, scriptwriter and film-maker, Johnson (1897–1977) later wrote the scripts for *Flaming Star* and *The Dirty Dozen*.

Poultney Bigelow: A journalist and author, Bigelow (1855–1954) travelled extensively, was London correspondent for several US publications, and was correspondent for the *Times* (of London) in Cuba during the Spanish-American War.

William Salisbury: That year (1926) Salisbury (1875–?) published a book-length study, *The Baltimore Phenomenon: An Estimate of H.L. Mencken as Critic and as Artist*. Roberts later wrote the foreword to Salisbury's futuristic novel, *The Squareheads: The Story of a Socialized State* (1929).

p. 232

Adolphe de Castro: Adolphe Danziger de Castro (1859–1959) was a journalist, lawyer, dentist and writer. Born in Poland, he emigrated to the United States in 1883, living mainly in San Francisco and New York. De Castro was a protégé of

Ambrose Bierce's, though they later fell out. His article in *American Parade* was followed by his book, *Portrait of Ambrose Bierce* (1929). Since he was widely regarded as at best a windbag and at worst a fraud, his theory about Bierce's death was never taken seriously.

Bernarr: Bernarr Macfadden (1868–1955) was an influential proponent of physical culture and founder of a long-running magazine publishing company. Born "Bernard", he changed his name because he thought "Bernarr" sounded like the roar of a lion. He founded *Physical Culture* magazine in 1899, and was editor until 1912. His huge publishing empire included *Liberty*, *True Detective*, *True Romances*, *Photoplay* and the tabloid newspaper the *New York Graphic*.

p. 233

The Haunting Hand: Ironically, not only is Roberts always credited as author of this book, published in 1926, but because of it, and because, being Jamaican, he is often assumed to be black, he is sometimes referred to as the first black author of a work of detective fiction.

Louise Rice: Rice (1880–?) was a journalist, feminist and author of books on cookery and graphology. She was a prolific writer of stories and founder of the Rice Institute of Graphology (1924) and the American Graphological Society (1926).

Eleanor Ramos: Ramos (1896–1948) published three stories in *The Smart Set* in 1921–22, one written with Roberts, and then the two pieces Roberts mentions in *American Parade*. Her subsequent stories through to 1937 appeared in *Marriage Stories*, *Sweetheart Stories*, and *Young Love*. In Mencken's only mention of her in his memoirs, he calls her a "hack" (*My Life as Author and Editor*, ed. Jonathan Yardley [New York: Alfred A. Knopf, 1993], 382). Her daughter, Dolores Ramos, had been born in 1916. In a letter to Roberts (24 June 1921) she wrote vehemently about not wanting another child, which may have been a factor in the breakdown of their relationship. Her husband, Ted Bourland, died in 1965. Roberts does not mention that his novel, *The Moralist* (1931), is clearly a *roman-à-clef* about his relationship with Eleanor Ramos.

p. 235

Grisette: Roberts wrote a poem about Grisette, called "The Cat", published in his *Pan and Peacocks* (1928), 15:

> No one of all the women I have known
> Has been so beautiful, or proud, or wise
> As this angora with her amber eyes.

p. 238

the fiction magazine for women: *Saucy Stories*, in which Roberts also published.

p. 239

G——H——: Probably Gladys Hall, a film journalist. A love letter from her is extant in Roberts's papers.

Chapter 14. The Lure of Travel

p. 241
Swinburne: See note to p. 21.

p. 242
Watts-Dunton: A keen and eventually successful writer, Theodor Watts-Dunton (1832–1914) was originally Swinburne's solicitor. Alarmed by Swinburne's alcoholism, Watts-Dunton moved the poet into his Putney home and looked after him for the last thirty years of his life.
Edmund Gosse: (1849–1928). English poet and critic, author of one of the first biographies of Swinburne.
T. Earle Welby: Thomas Earle Welby (1881–1933) was a prolific scholar of Victorian poetry.
Coulson Kernahan: (1858–1943). English novelist and critic.

p. 244
Naboth Hedin: See note to p. 157.
Kungsholm: Built in 1928, with an interior regarded as a masterpiece of art deco design, the ship first visited the Caribbean in 1929. In 1941 J.D. Salinger acted as its entertainment director.

p. 247
numerous friends: Roberts was also good friends with the Loynaz del Castillo family, true republican aristocracy. Enrique had fought with Antonio Maceo in 1896, and his children, Dulce María and Ernesto, were both distinguished poets. This was one of the best literary households in the city. It was where – also in 1930 – Federico García Lorca stayed when he visited Havana.
Dr Ramón Grau: Ramón Grau San Martín (1887–1969), Cuban doctor and founder of the Partido Auténtico, was president for four months in the heady days after the fall of Gerardo Machado in 1933, but was quickly forced out of office by Fulgencio Batista. He was president again from 1944 to 1948, but his regime was widely regarded as corrupt.
Conrado W. Massaguer: Brought up partly in the Yucatán, where he published his first caricatures, by the second decade of the century Massaguer (1887–1965) was publishing in Cuba and New York, often in magazines that he helped create, such as *Gráfico*, *Social* and *Carteles*. Opposed to the dictator Gerardo Machado, he went into political exile in New York at the end of 1931, returning to Cuba in 1935. Massaguer was particularly famous for his political cartoons, some of which were known around the world.

p. 248
Armando Maribona: (1894–1964). Cuban painter and caricaturist.

Abela: The Cuban painter and cartoonist Eduardo Abela (1889–1965) lived in France and Spain during the 1920s, where he got to know Alejo Carpentier. Back in Cuba he created for *Diario de la Marina* the character of "El Bobo" (The Fool) as a protest against the Machado government. He later returned to painting as well as serving as a cultural attaché to Mexico and Guatemala.

Antonio Gattorno: Gattorno (1904–1980) spent the early 1920s in Europe before becoming part of the Cuban artistic vanguard alongside figures like Wifredo Lam. His paintings of peasant life were taken as social critique. He lived the last forty years of his life in the United States.

López Méndez: Luis Alfredo López Méndez (1901–1996) was a Venezuelan painter who lived in Cuba during the 1930s.

José Antonio Fernández de Castro: Fernández de Castro (1887–1951) was a radical journalist, writer and scholar, renowned for his support for the literary vanguard in the pages of *Diario de la Marina*. He compiled the important anthology *La poesía moderna en Cuba* (1926).

Carmencita: Carmen Doucet Moreno (1868–1910) was a glamorous Spanish dancer known as "The Pearl of Seville". She became a New York celebrity in 1890 and may have been the first woman to appear in a motion picture in the United States.

La Argentinita: Encarnación López Júlvez (1898–1945) was one of the most successful dancers of that period, forming part of a cultural group that included writers such as Rafael Alberti and Federico García Lorca. Exiled by the Spanish Civil War, she settled in New York, dying – as Roberts notes – shortly after a triumphant flamenco spectacular at the Metropolitan Opera House.

p. 249

fandanguillo de Almería: Written by Gaspar Vivas Gómez (1872–1936), who was born in Almería, in southern Spain.

Mateo Hernández: Hernández (1884–1949) was one of the outstanding Spanish sculptors of the twentieth century. This spectacular piece called *Javanese Panther* was displayed in front of the Spanish pavilion at the 1925 Paris Exposition; it was later acquired by a US collector who gave it to the Metropolitan Museum of Art in New York, where it is frequently exhibited: Roberts saw it there in 1959.

Jacinto Benavente: See note to p. 221.

p. 250

Alexandre Dumas: (1802–1870). Prolific historical novelist, author of *The Count of Monte Cristo* and *The Three Musketeers*. One of his grandmothers was a black slave in Saint-Domingue.

Goncourt Brothers: Edmond de Goncourt (1822–1896) and Jules de Goncourt (1830–1870) were inseparable in life as in writing. They are remembered mainly for their diaries, which offer an intimate view of French literary society.

p. 251
Dance Magazine: As a result, Roberts became good friends with a number of distinguished dancers, including Eugenja Līczbinska and Natacha Nattova. Among his papers is a friendly letter from Martha Graham.

p. 252
Paul R. Milton: Two of the books published under Roberts's name were written by Paul Milton (1904–?), though with Roberts's collaboration. *Mayor Harding* (1931) and *The Strange Career of Bishop Sterling* (1932) are fictionalized versions of the scandal-ridden careers of New York mayor James J. Walker and Bishop James Cannon Jr of the Methodist Episcopal Church, South.
Robert Milton: (1885–1956). Born in Russia, Milton directed many Broadway plays between 1908 and 1940, as well as eleven films between 1929 and 1934.
La Argentina: Antonia Mercé y Luque (1890–1936).
Lew Leslie: Born in Russia, Leslie (1888–1963) was famous for his Cotton Club stage shows and Blackbirds reviews.

p. 253
the next issue of the Dance Magazine: Roberts's article was called "The Most Spanish of Dancers" (1930).
Mejías: Ignacio Sánchez Mejías (1891–1934) was the most famous bullfighter of his day. Widely admired, he associated with writers and artists. After his death, Federico García Lorca wrote the striking elegy, "Llanto por la muerte de Ignacio Sánchez Mejías" ("Lament on the Death of Ignacio Sánchez Mejías"). Sánchez Mejías had married the sister of his childhood friend José Gómez (Joselito), regarded as the best bullfighter of all time, but after Joselito's death – from a goring in the ring – he began an affair with Joselito's girlfriend, La Argentinita, with whom he had two children. It was she who introduced Sánchez Mejías to García Lorca as well as to other modern Spanish writers. Belieing Roberts's comment about his literacy, Sánchez Mejías wrote plays and an autobiography, as well as racing cars, playing polo and acting in films. In 1934 he returned to bullfighting – and died after being gored in the ring.

p. 254
Lord's Day Alliance: Founded in 1888, the Lord's Day Alliance is still active.
William A. Brady: Actor, theatrical producer and boxing promoter, Brady (1863–1950) lost a fortune in the Wall Street crash of 1929, but quickly made another one. Probably of Irish background, he was born in San Francisco.

p. 255
"Villanelle of a Spanish Dancer": Published in Roberts's collection *Pan and Peacocks* (1928).

Chapter 15. Freelance

p. 257
royalty cheque: Presumably *The Mind Reader: A Mystery* (1928).

p. 258
Felicien Rops: (1833–1898). Belgian artist and printmaker.

p. 259
pre-Raphaelite school: William **Holman Hunt** (1827–1910) and **Dante Gabriel Rossetti** (1828–1882), along with John Everett Millais, were the founders of the Pre-Raphaelite Brotherhood. Hunt became know for his religious paintings, but Roberts implies that his mother would not have appreciated Rossetti's more sexual imagery. George Frederick **Watts** (1817–1904) was a symbolist painter often associated with the Pre-Raphaelites.
Robert Henri: See note to p. 109.

p. 260
John Sloan: See note to p. 109.
George Luks: (1867–1933), **William J. Glackens** (1870–1938), **Everett Shinn** (1876–1933) and **Ernest Lawson** (1873–1939).
Franklin Booth: See note to p. 105.
Charles Sarka: See note to p. 105.
C.B. Falls: Charles Buckles Falls (1874–1960), children's author and illustrator.
T. Victor Hall: See note to p. 105.
Aristide Maillol: (1861–1944). French Catalan painter and sculptor. The original stone version of the monument to Cézanne is in the Musée d'Orsay in Paris. Cézanne's reputation is now rather higher than Maillot's, although a smaller version of the sculpture did sell in New York in 2009 for $1,426,500.

p. 261
that she was pregnant: Roberts moves the date of his daughter's conception and birth forward fourteen years, as is apparent from the final pages of the autobiography where she is still an adolescent in 1961. "Giulia" was not strictly an Italian, but born to an Italian family in Greenwich Village. Her husband worked in publishing and they had a son: Roberts fails to mention that he was the boy's godfather. Roberts had known the couple for some time, at least since 1931, so this Parisian episode was probably part of his intermittent affair with "Giulia", though the child was conceived in North America in the early months of 1945.

p. 262
Her full baptismal name: Roberts's paternal grandmother was called Eleanor Lind.
dedicated a book to her: *Lake Pontchartrain* (1946), Roberts's history of the New Orleans area.

p. 263

friendly reception by the critics: The prestigious *Times Literary Supplement* proferred some favourable words ("well worth reading for the sake of the information collected about Morgan"), even if these were couched in that quintessentially English tone of imperial condescension ([Edward W.O'F. Lynham], "Buccaneer and Governor", *Times Literary Supplement*, no. 1656 [26.x.1933], 723). Thoroughly positive was Henry E. Armstrong, "New Light on Sir Henry Morgan, Prince of Buccaneers", *New York Times*, 23 April 1933: BR12.

serious bearing on history: Crossed out in Roberts's typescript is the sentence that follows: "But I scarcely realised that my study of Morgan had stimulated my interest in political action to a point that had focussed my own attitudes." The sentiment is awkwardly expressed, but it makes clear the connection in Roberts's mind between his historical studies and contemporary West Indian politics.

"Self-Government in Jamaica": In *Sir Henry Morgan*, appendix B, 293–96.

Samuel Long: Long (1638–1683) was a Jamaican planter and politician who participated in the conquest of Jamaica and received large grants, ensuring himself a powerful position in the island's political life: duly elected a member of the assembly, he was chosen as speaker from 1672 to 1675, and appointed chief justice in 1674. He was renowned for speaking for the rights of the assembly over those of the governor. For trying to give the legislature control over the island's revenue, he was charged with treason, but the charges were dropped. Further resistance to imperial control led to his being arrested in 1680 and sent to be tried in London, where he was acquitted.

William Beeston: Beeston (1636–1702) arrived in Jamaica in 1660 and soon became both a wealthy merchant and a member of the assembly, where he worked alongside Samuel Long – and often in opposition to Henry Morgan and his supporters. His appointment as lieutenant governor in 1692 led to a change in his loyalties.

p. 264

George William Gordon . . . Edward John Eyre: On Morant Bay, see note to p. 99. Roberts's remarks may have been influenced by Sydney Olivier's revisionist account of the Morant Bay Rebellion, *The Myth of Governor Eyre* (1933).

p. 265

W.J. Gardner: (1825–1874). English missionary to Jamaica whose *A History of Jamaica* was published in London by E. Stock in 1873. The quotation is on p. 494.

Chapter 16. The Author at Fifty

p. 267

It was true I now had a daughter: This sentence is added in pencil as Roberts makes his typescript consistent. In fact the daughter would not be born for another ten years.

New York Times' critic: Catherine Young, "Grand Old Blackguard", *New York Times Saturday Review*, 17 May 1933, 586.

Current History: "British West Indian Aspirations" (1934).

p. 268

Sir Edward Denham: (1876–1938). British colonial administrator who served in the Gambia and British Guiana before his final posting as governor of Jamaica.

Luis Muñoz Marín: Roberts had been introduced to Muñoz Marín (1898–1980) and his fiancée, Muna Lee, by Salomón de la Selva when all four were young and aspiring poets in New York. Muñoz Marín eventually returned to Puerto Rico to take up a political career and was already, as Roberts notes, "a figure in Puerto Rico politics". His father, Luis Muñoz Rivera (1859–1916), had been a prominent politician too. In 1948 Muñoz Marín would become the first democratically elected governor of Puerto Rico, spearheading an administration that engineered profound economic, political and social reforms on the island, not least changing the status of Puerto Rico to that of an Estado Libre Asociado or "commonwealth". He was re-elected three times, serving a total of sixteen years as governor.

Muna Lee: When Roberts first met her, Muna Lee's (1895–1965) poems were being published in leading journals such as *Poetry* and *Others*, and she was translating poetry from Spanish. After her marriage to Muñoz Marín in July 1919, the couple lived on Staten Island before eventually moving to Puerto Rico, where she became a founding member of the Inter-American Commission of Women. Lee and Muñoz Marín were divorced before he became governor. In 1941, she would join the US State Department as an inter-American cultural affairs specialist. She and Roberts remained good friends and his novel *The Single Star* is dedicated to her. See *A Pan-American Life: Selected Poetry and Prose of Muna Lee*, edited and with biography by Jonathan Cohen (Madison: University of Wisconsin Press, 2004).

this speech: Given on 29 April 1936 to the Departamento de Historia y Ciencias Sociales at the University of Puerto Rico. Roberts also talked to students of English about the writers he had known.

Herbert George de Lisser: See note to p. 31.

p. 269

Pedro Albizu Campos: (1891–1965). Lawyer, politician and leader of the Puerto Rican Nationalist Party from 1930 until his death, Albizu Campos was imprisoned for twenty-six years for attempting to overthrow the US government in Puerto Rico. He had emerged as a national figure in the 1932 elections but, unlike his one-time colleague Muñoz Marín, was preparing for the paramilitary route toward independence.

p. 270

unconnected with politics: This was *Travel Magazine*, where Roberts published six long articles between 1934 and 1936.

Marcus Garvey: Garvey (1887–1940) had grown up in Jamaica at the same time as Roberts, though at St Ann's Bay on the north coast. Like Roberts, he was deeply influenced by his well educated father; and like Roberts, he left Jamaica as a young man to travel and ended up in New York – in Garvey's case in 1916. His Universal Negro Improvement Association became a huge but controversial organization, promoting black nationalism and a return of the African diaspora to its ancestral lands.

A.M. Wendell Malliet: Malliet (1896–1976) was a Jamaican-born journalist and later publisher. Active in New York–based West Indian politics, he wrote a number of pamphlets, including *The Destiny of the West Indies* (1927), and edited a number of usually short-lived journals, including *West Indian Affairs*. He later represented the Jamaica Labour Party in New York. In a 1940 letter to Roberts, Wilfred Domingo called him "a very petty and spiteful individual" (MS353.2.3.5).

Amsterdam News: One of the oldest African American newspapers in the United States, named for its original location on Amsterdam Avenue on the Upper West Side.

British Jamaicans Benevolent Association: This meeting took place on 15 July 1936. A prior meeting – probably arranged by Malliet – happened at a party earlier that month at the rather grand home of Judge James S. Watson at 117 West 120th Street in the heart of Harlem. Watson (1882–1952) had left Jamaica early in the century, become a successful lawyer in New York, and had recently been elected as the first black judge in New York State. He was also an amateur poet who acted as patron to writers of the Harlem Renaissance, including Claude McKay. McKay was at this party, but Roberts's key encounter there was with Wilfred A. Domingo, with whose name he may already have been familiar.

influential coloured physician: This meeting took place on 3 August 1936. The physician was Dr Lucien M. Brown (1895–1960), a friend of Judge Watson's. Brown was on the initial steering committee of the Jamaica Progressive League but soon took a back seat. Committee meetings on 10 and 17 August 1936 approved a declaration of principles prior to the public launch on 1 September 1936.

p. 271

The league was created: Neither of the two histories of the JPL written by its members are entirely satisfactory: Walter G. McFarlane, *The Birth of Self-Government for Jamaica and the Jamaica Progressive League 1937–1944* (1957; rev. ed.,

Kingston: [self-published], 1974), and John S. Young, *Lest We Forget* (New York: Isidor Books, 1981). The definitive account of the movement and its impact in Jamaica is Birte Timme, *Nationalists Abroad: The Jamaica Progressive League and the Foundations of Jamaican Independence* (Kingston: Ian Randle, 2015).

Ethelred Brown: Born in Falmouth, Edgar Ethelred Brown (1875–1956) had eventually relocated to New York in 1920, founding a community church in Harlem. In Jamaica he had helped organize the Negro Progressive Association and the Liberal Association, both of which were geared toward civil and economic rights for blacks. Brown's Harlem church was very much a forum for political debate: he chaired and encouraged heated discussions. Additionally, he was chairman of the British Jamaicans Benevolent Association and vice-president of the Federation of Jamaican Organizations. See Mark D. Morrison-Reed, *Black Pioneers in a White Denomination*, chapter 2, "A Dream Aborted: Egbert Ethelred Brown in Jamaica and Harlem", 3rd ed. (Boston: Skinner House, 1994), 31–111.

Wilfred A. Domingo: Before leaving Jamaica in 1910 Wilfred Adolphus Domingo (1889–1968) had worked in Kingston as an apprentice tailor and joined the newly formed National Club, through which he met Marcus Garvey, and in New York Domingo became one of the editors of Garvey's newspaper, *Negro World*. Meanwhile, however, Domingo had developed strong political ties with other black socialists which led to his split with Garvey. In the late 1920s and early 1930s Domingo prospered in business as an importer of West Indian foods while remaining an active presence in organizations such as the British Jamaicans Benevolent Association, which he had helped found in 1917. In 1925 his essay "The Black Tropics in New York" had appeared in the March edition of *Survey Graphic*, now considered the founding document of the Harlem Renaissance. Between them, therefore, Domingo and Brown had a wonderful array of connections throughout the Jamaican community in Harlem, exactly the sorts of connections Roberts needed. Just as important, Domingo and Brown were already committed nationalists who welcomed their association with this fellow Jamaican who arrived in Harlem as a fully fledged writer and historian. *"Look for Me All Around You": Anglophone Caribbean Immigrants in the Harlem Renaissance*, edited by Louis J. Parascandola (Detroit: Wayne State University Press, 2005), contains examples of Domingo's writing. As Roberts notes (see p. 305), Domingo tried to re-enter Jamaica in June 1941 but was arrested on board ship and placed in an internment camp, where he joined a number of Jamaican labour leaders. A lengthy campaign to secure his release from detention was launched by his associates in Jamaica and New York, with Roberts prominent among them, but Domingo was detained for twenty months and then forced to remain in Jamaica for an additional four years when the US government denied him a visa.

Jaime O'Meally: Originally James Augustus O'Meally. Born in Jamaica in 1891, he gave up his post as a teacher at Calabar College in Kingston to work with the Universal Negro Improvement Association, where he would have known Domingo. He was a delegate to the association's 1922 convention and was appointed to its League of Nations delegation, travelling as high commissioner general to Geneva, where he was not allowed to land, and later to Liberia. By January 1925 he had broken with Garvey and sued the Universal Negro Improvement Association for back salaries: he was awarded thirty-five hundred dollars in the courts. During the 1930s he worked for Domingo.

p. 272

O.T. Fairclough: Osmond Theodore Fairclough (1904–1970) was a black banker and one of the key figures behind the formation of the People's National Party (PNP) in September 1938. Fairclough had worked in Haiti's National Bank for eight years. Back in Jamaica he started *Public Opinion* in 1937; it ran till 1974.

Ken Hill: Ken Hill (1909–1989) was an outspoken and eloquent journalist, trade unionist and politician. Animated by the founding of the JPL in New York, Hill created the Jamaica National Movement at a meeting at the Collegiate Hall, Kingston, on 31 March 1937. His note in the *Gleaner* had appeared on 9 March. The Jamaica National Movement soon changed its name to the rather less ringing National Reform Association. Five hundred people attended a meeting on 28 April, though Hill's mobilizing efforts may have been affected by the accidental drowning of his father, Stephen A. Hill, also a journalist, on 16 May. The National Reform Association convened a large meeting on 10 August 1938 where Norman Manley made his first significant appearance on a political stage. But then, whereas the JPL supported the PNP but maintained its separate identity, the National Reform Association dissolved into the PNP. Hill stood unsuccessfully against Alexander Bustamante in the 1944 elections. He later had a spell as mayor of Kingston. Others involved in the National Reform Association included J.P. Dodds, Richard Hart (see note to p. 277) and H.P. Jacobs (see note to p. 277).

agent of a civic association: Possibly George Seymour of the Kencot Citizens' Association.

mayor of Kingston: Dr Oswald E. Anderson (1883–1948) was an early supporter of the Kingston JPL, though very much an independent spirit: see Henrice Altink, "A True Maverick: The Political Career of Dr Oswald E. Anderson, 1919–1944", *New West Indian Guide* 87 (2013): 3–29.

De Lisser: See note to p. 31. These remarks appeared in the *Gleaner* on 9 December 1937.

p. 273

a handful of persons: The two most significant were probably Walter G. McFarlane and Rupert Meikle. Walter George McFarlane (1896–1994) had been radicalized in North America, where he had trained and worked as a land surveyor, returning to Jamaica in 1933. His rambling and self-justifying book *The Birth of Self-Government in Jamaica* (1957, rev. ed. 1974) is vituperative about Norman Manley, with whom he had fallen out. He was awarded the Jamaican Order of Distinction (Commander Class) in 1993, at the age of ninety-six. In December 1935 – and so even prior to the founding of the JPL – Rupert E. Meikle had already written to the *Gleaner* asking it to reproduce Roberts's appendix from *Sir Henry Morgan* – which it did – and underlining that in Jamaica, "there is a group of young people who like myself feel that we cannot possibly go on being satisfied with this pseudo-Crown Colony Government and keep our self-respect as a people". He noted a move afoot among the Citizens' Associations for a wider constitution and for full representative government (16 July 1935). A year later, in another letter to the *Gleaner*, Meikle quoted extensively from Roberts's recommendations in his pamphlet *Self-Government for Jamaica* (21 December 1936). Meikle had founded the Quill and Ink literary club in Port Maria in 1932, contacting Roberts in November 1933 to ask him for books to help establish a library. He also became a prominent member of the National Reform Association and the League of Coloured Peoples.

the Jamaica Progressive League: Since Roberts's death, the JPL (New York) itself has gone through periods of crisis – some financial – and periods of quiescence. As of 2014 it survives, inasmuch as it has a website, but it seems inactive. The JPL (Kingston) also had long periods of quiescence before its (probable) demise. One of the last letters Roberts received, dated 13 August 1962, was from W.G. McFarlane, asking whether it was time to revive the organization. There was also an interesting burst of activity in the early 1990s, associated with McFarlane's remarkable longevity and the energy of the political scientist Dr Roy Edward Johnstone, who was appointed the new chairman in February 1991 (*Gleaner*, 22 February 1991, 31). The JPL (Kingston)'s main new plank was its push for a revised Jamaican constitution, more fitting for a truly independent nation. In late 1993 Johnstone announced that a forty-seven-page document entitled "A New Constitution for the Republic of Jamaica" had been presented to the government (*Gleaner*, 19 December 1993, 6A). It is unclear what, if anything, resulted, and Johnstone's death in 2001 seems to have initiated another period of quiescence; although if the current (2015) PNP government fulfils its promise to make Jamaica a republic – with a new constitution to match – then perhaps the PNP will again, as in the 1940s, have caught up with the proposals of the pioneering JPL. Meanwhile, 1993 also saw the centenary of the birth of Norman Manley. Walter G. McFarlane, ninety-six years old, noted that the founder of the Jamaican nation was in fact Walter Adolphe Roberts (*Gleaner*, 30 July 1993,

7). Prompted by McFarlane's letter, the journalist Terry Smith began a series of historical articles about "others who took the national stage", recalling the activities of Roberts and the JPL in the 1930s (*Gleaner*, 28 November 1993, 8A; 12 December 1993, 7B).

a large public meeting: On 15 December 1937 at the Metropolitan Hall, chaired by E.R.D. Evans.

p. 274

Arnold Lecesne: Lecesne (1877–1942) also voiced this view in letters to the journal *Public Opinion*: see Louis Lindsay, "The Myth of Independence: Middle Class Politics and Non-mobilization in Jamaica" [1975], Working Paper no. 6 (Kingston: Sir Arthur Lewis Institute of Social and Economic Studies, University of the West Indies, 2005), 100.

p. 275

Norman Washington Manley: See p. 286 and note.

p. 276

Frank Hill: (1902–1980). Nationalist, intellectual and maverick. The very idea of *The Upheaval* was ahead of its time. After the end of his political career Hill worked as a journalist before becoming the chairman of the National Trust and the chairman of the board of governors of the Institute of Jamaica under a Jamaica Labour Party government.

p. 277

Dick Hart: Richard Hart (1917–2013) followed his father, Ansell Hart, in qualifying as a solicitor in 1941. In 1937 he was a member of the National Reform Association and was also active in the trade union movement. He was a member of the PNP from 1938 to 1952, and on the executive committee from 1941 to 1952. He was briefly interned in 1942–43. After being forced out of the PNP, Hart occupied numerous roles within politics and the trade union movement. In 1965 he moved to England and wrote a number of valuable historical books.

Elsie Benjamin: Elsie Benjamin Barsoe (1911–1974). Her People's Theatre presented W.G. Ogilvie's *One Soja Man* in 1945 not under the patronage of the colonial administration, as was the custom, but, as its programme note said, "under the kind patronage of the Jamaican people". Benjamin played the nurse in the film of Richard Hughes's novel *A High Wind in Jamaica* (1965). She founded and edited the journal *Pepperpot* (1951–1967), which featured several pieces by Roberts, who acted as a consultant. They had been friends since 1937.

H.P. Jacobs: Hedley Powell Jacobs (1904–1985). Born in Yorkshire, Jacobs was a Fabian socialist who taught history at the Jamaica College and was president of the Jamaican Historical Society. He delivered the eulogy at Roberts's funeral, calling him "a moral force and an intellectual inspiration". But his was the advice in 1966, for which he was paid ten guineas, that the Institute of Jamaica should not publish *These Many Years* on the grounds that "the Institute would become a target for criticism if the book appeared under its auspices" (letter to C. Bernard Lewis, 28 November 1966 [MS353.13.1]).

Benjamin Disraeli: (1804–1881). British politician and writer. Disraeli coined the maxim in the biography of his friend and colleague: *Lord George Bentinck: A Political Biography* (1852).

Chapter 17. 1939

p. 278

ashore in Jamaica: Although clear about Semmes's racist views, which led him to remain a defender of the institution of slavery, Roberts is sparing in critical remarks about the Confederacy's naval hero. One of the few reprimands he offers is in connection with Semmes's short visit to Jamaica: "He did not greet Governor Edward John Eyre, the inept fanatic who two years later suppressed with unexampled brutality a minor disorder among the peasants of one parish, and called it a rebellion. Semmes was a realist. If he had talked with Eyre, he would have appraised the man and probably would have withheld the foolish compliment he pays him in his memoirs for 'nipping in the bud a widespread Negro insurrection'" (*Semmes of the Alabama*, 152).

p. 279

Lafcadio Hearn: Patrick Lafcadio Hearn (1850–1904) was a truly international writer, remembered for his books about Japan, as well as those about the West Indies and New Orleans, where he lived for ten years from 1877, working as a journalist. His writing about the city for national magazines helped establish New Orleans's reputation as a place with a distinct culture more akin to those of Europe and the Caribbean than to the rest of the United States.

George W. Cable: George Washington Cable (1844–1925), a writer native to New Orleans and now widely appreciated for the realism of his depictions of Creole life in the late nineteenth century.

Antoine's: Established in 1840 by Antoine Alciatore, this is still the most famous restaurant in New Orleans.

Pat O'Brien's: Established in 1933 on St Peter Street and still going.

worked hard: The next sentence ("Nada did the housekeeping") is crossed out in the typescript, indicating another of Roberts's lovers who did not make the final cut.

Tujague's: Established in 1856, on Decatur, and still thriving: famous for its shrimp remoulade and its beef brisket with horseradish. **Maylie's:** Established in 1876 on Poydras, closed in 1986. **Galatoire's:** Founded in 1905 on Bourbon Street and still going. **La Louisiane:** Founded in 1881 on Iberville and open again after some interruptions. **Broussard's:** On Conti and still open. **Arnaud's:** On Bienville since 1918 and still going.

p. 280
and grandson: Antoine's is still family-run – now on the sixth generation.
the last home of Semmes: Restored in the middle of the twentieth century, the home is now on the National Register of Historic Places.
Dr Toulmin Gaines: Marion Toulmin Gaines Jr (1897–1972). His father (of the same name) was the stepson of Oliver J. Semmes, Raphael Semmes's son.
strikes of some magnitude: On the labour rebellions in the British Caribbean, see O. Nigel Bolland, *On the March: Labour Rebellions in the British Caribbean, 1934–39* (Kingston: Ian Randle, 1995). On Jamaica, the study that pays most attention to the role of the JPL is Ken Post, *Arise Ye Starvelings: The Jamaican Labour Rebellion of 1938 and Its Aftermath* (The Hague: Martinus Nijhoff, 1978). See also, particularly for the rivalry between Manley and Bustamante, Colin A. Palmer, *Freedom's Children: The 1938 Labor Rebellion and the Birth of Modern Jamaica* (Durham: University of North Carolina Press, 2014).

p. 281
Sir Edward Denham: See note to p. 268.
Sir Arthur Richards: Arthur Frederick Richards, 1st Baron Milverton (1885–1978), was governor of Jamaica from 1938 to 1943, and later governor of Nigeria from 1943 to 1947.

p. 282
Lord Moyne: Walter Edward Guinness, 1st Baron Moyne (1880–1944), was an Anglo-Irish politician and businessman. From 1907 to 1931 Moyne had been a Conservative member of Parliament. In 1938, after his elevation to the peerage, he headed the commission Roberts mentions. After a year as colonial secretary, he worked during World War II for the British government in Cairo where, in November 1944, he was assassinated by Jewish terrorists. Completed in 1939, but only published in full in 1945, the Moyne Report (Report of the West India Royal Commission) exposed the awful conditions in which a large part of the population lived. Although ambivalent in its recommendations, the Moyne Report is usually seen as marking a turning point in official British attitudes toward the West Indies.
Stafford Cripps: Sir Richard Stafford Cripps (1889–1952) was a British Labour politician, one of the most prominent left-wing figures of the period.

p. 283
I concluded that my next book: In fact Roberts had already signed a contract with Bobbs-Merrill for a two-volume biography of Simón Bolívar, on which he quickly reneged in April 1941.

p. 284

Eileen Curran: Irish-born actress active in the republican movement in New York, Curran (1894–?) first came to prominence protesting outside the British consulate during Terence MacSwiney's hunger strike in 1920. She addressed the JPL in Harlem on 7 November 1938, alongside Arthur Schomburg, the Puerto Rican bibliophile whose collection now forms part of the New York Public Library.

p. 285

F.J. Makin: Makin wrote a book about his experiences in Jamaica: *Caribbean Nights* (London: Robert Hale, 1939). The *Standard* gave sympathetic coverage to the JPL, publishing Roberts's "Why I Demand Self-Government" (20 January 1939) and "Walter Adolphe Roberts: Patriot Man-of-Letters – A Pen Portrait" (19 August 1939) by Roberts's friend, A.E.T. Henry.

first big gathering: On 6 January 1939.

generous candour: This sentence originally read: "A generous candour toward friends is second nature with him." Roberts felt less well-inclined toward Manley by the time he revised his typescript in the late 1950s.

p. 286

Norman Washington Manley: (1893–1969). Jamaican statesman. A Rhodes scholar, Manley had become one of Jamaica's leading lawyers in the 1920s. First president of the PNP in 1938, he proceeded to dominate Jamaican politics over the next thirty years along with his cousin and rival, Alexander Bustamante. Manley would serve as the colony's chief minister from 1955 to 1959, and as premier from 1959 to 1962. He was a supporter of the island's participation in the Federation of the West Indies (see p. 335) but bowed to pressure to hold a referendum in 1961 which resulted in Jamaica withdrawing from the union.

Mrs Manley: Edna Swithenbank Manley (1900–1987). Jamaican sculptor. Daughter of an English cleric and his Jamaican wife, she married her cousin Norman Manley in 1921, and moved to Jamaica with him.

p. 288

Alexander Bustamante: Sir William Alexander Clarke Bustamante (1884–1977). Returning to Jamaica in 1932, Bustamante set himself up as a moneylender, but still managed to become recognized as the spokesman for various groups of striking workers. He founded the Bustamante Industrial Trade Union in 1938, and the Jamaica Labour Party in 1943, winning the first Jamaican elections held under universal suffrage and serving as the country's first chief minister and later, after independence, as its first prime minister (1962–1967).

p. 289

We will follow Bustamante till we die: The ten-stanza "Bustamante Anthem" was composed by S. Bigenoi of the Jamaica biscuit factory (Palmer, *Freedom's Children*, 174–75).

p. 290

Daniel O'Connell: (1775–1847). Irish political leader who campaigned the repeal of the Act of Union which combined Great Britain and Ireland.

Gladys Longbridge: (1912–2009). After her association with Alexander Bustamante began in 1932, Gladys Longbridge became a workers' and women's rights activist. She and Bustamante married in September 1962.

p. 293

Erasmus Campbell: Ethelred Erasmus Adolphus Campbell (1888–1969) was a barrister, biochemist, trade unionist and politician. He had worked in Panama and studied at Tuskegee, McGill and Edinburgh.

p. 294

at the old Race Course: The Race Course meeting Roberts refers to actually took place on Tuesday 21 February 1939, though a further meeting there on the Sunday (26 February) featured a dramatic (and short-lived) rapprochement between Bustamante and A.G.S. Coombs, founder in 1936 of the Jamaican Workers' and Tradesmen's Union, and therefore Bustamante's main competitor for the loyalty of the Jamaican working class. The Trades Union Council had been set up the previous day (25 February) during a meeting at Duke Street. The Bustamante Industrial Trade Union never affiliated, leaving it toothless.

N.N. Nethersole: Noel Newton Nethersole (1903–1959), known affectionately as Crab, was a keen cricketer, a solicitor and a leading light in the PNP. When Norman Manley became chief minister of Jamaica in 1955, Nethersole was his deputy and minister of finance.

p. 296

J.A.G. Smith: James Alexander George Smith (1879–1942), often known as 'Jags', was a civil servant, lawyer and long-standing black member of the legislative council. See Anthony Johnson, *J.A.G. Smith* (Kingston: Kingston Publishers, 1991).

p. 297

Smuts: General Jan Smuts (1870–1950) was a Boer War hero and a successful promoter of self-government for the Transvaal, and therefore an obvious figure for Roberts to identify with.

De Valera: Éamon de Valera (1882–1975), born in New York, with a Cuban father, and close friends with the Puerto Rican nationalist, Pedro Albizu Campos, is a similar figure to Smuts. Both became presidents of their countries.

series of articles: This series of articles contained an extraordinarily well-informed analysis of the world situation in 1939.

Chapter 18. The Act of Havana

p. 300

Pan American Union Building: At Seventeenth Street NW, Washington, DC, it is now home to the Organization of American States. Its library, the Columbus Memorial Library, moved in 1988 to the administrative wing of the Organization of American States at Nineteenth Street and Constitution Avenue, NW.

reviewed in flattering terms: Not only in newspapers. A leading academic journal, the *Hispanic American Historical Review*, wrote that Roberts "had covered his vast field better than any other writer in English has ever done before him" (rev. by Philip Ainsworth Means, 21, no. 1 [1941]: 83–85).

p. 301

West Indies National Council: Richard B. Moore was the vice-president of the West Indies National Council, while C. Augustin Petioni took over as president after Domingo returned to Jamaica. The PNP had given strong support to the council's actions in Havana.

p. 302

Hope R. Stevens: A native of Tortola, British Virgin Islands, and raised on Nevis, Stevens (?–1982) was an activist and attorney based in Harlem, a founding member of the National Conference of Black Lawyers, and a key figure in the pro-independence movement of several Caribbean islands including Barbados, St Kitts and Nevis. He had spent several years in the Dominican Republic before migrating to the United States in 1929.

text of my memorandum: See Roberts, "The Act of Havana" (1959).

p. 303

Cordell Hull: Franklin Roosevelt's secretary of state for most of World War II, Hull (1871–1951) was also instrumental in the establishment of the United Nations.

p. 304

Leopoldo Melo: (1869–1951). Argentine lawyer, diplomat and politician.

A.A. Berle Jr: Adolf Augustus Berle Jr (1895–1971) was a US lawyer, diplomat and politician.

denounced in a speech: At a school opening on 13 December 1940.

p. 305

interned in the concentration camp: It was indeed called a concentration camp.

p. 308

Lyle Saxon: (1891–1946). Saxon wrote six books about the history of New Orleans on which Roberts drew for his novels set in the city. He also worked to preserve the architectural fabric of the French Quarter. Saxon's fictionalized biography,

Lafitte the Pirate (1930), was adapted for the Cecil B. DeMille movie, *The Buccaneer* (1938).

p. 309

the Cabildo: The seat of colonial government on Jackson Square. The original building was burned down in 1788. Its replacement was used by the city council until the 1850s and then by the Louisiana Supreme Court, before becoming home to the Louisiana State Museum in 1911.

the Presbytère: On Jackson Square, it was begun in 1791 and now forms part of the Louisiana State Museum.

André Lafargue: (1879–1949). A lawyer who became secretary of the Alliance Franco-Louisianaise in 1925.

p. 310

Constance and Yvonne Le Mercier-du Quesnay: Constance (1903–1962); Yvonne (1907–1996).

Chapter 19. The Shaping of a Nation

p. 311

Eric Williams: Eric Eustace Williams (1911–1981) served as the first prime minister of Trinidad and Tobago from 1956 until his death. His historical works include *Capitalism and Slavery* (1944) and the wide-ranging *From Columbus to Castro* (1970). He shared Roberts's interest in a larger Caribbean perspective. See Selwyn Ryan, *Eric Williams: The Myth and the Man* (Kingston: University of the West Indies Press, 2008).

held by Howard: See Roberts's paper, given at this conference: "The Future of Colonialism in the Caribbean" (1944).

Captain John Huggins: Sir John Huggins (1891–1971) was governor of Jamaica from September 1943 to April 1951.

p. 313

the Democratic: The Jamaica Democratic Party won 4 per cent of the vote and no seats in the 1944 elections.

by a bush therapist: Dr Edward H. Fagan, who advertised himself as an electro-praetor. He later served as mayor of Kingston.

5 February 1945: It was around now that Roberts's daughter was conceived, presumably during this visit to New York to apply for his visa.

p. 314

in the pages of *Hansard*: Or see the verbatim accounts in the *Gleaner* between June and September 1945.

de Lisser, published in the *Gleaner*: 11 March 1943, 6.

Florizel A. Glasspole: (1909–2000). An early member of the PNP and a member of the House of Representatives from 1944 to 1973, when he became governor general, retiring in 1991.

concerned my nationality: Behind the juvenile bluster and political point-scoring – in this respect the Jamaican parliament exactly followed the London model – there was a serious point at issue: who had the right to call themselves Jamaican, and on what grounds? Roberts wrote a strong piece in *Public Opinion* called "I Am a Jamaican" (22 September 1945) in which he made the eminently postcolonial point that there was no Jamaican *citizenship* as such, and that therefore, born in Jamaica, he was a Jamaican unless he chose spiritually to give up the relationship to the land of his birth.

p. 315

Frank Pixley: Minister of education and social welfare under Bustamante, he lost his seat in 1949 and retired to private law practice, but was disbarred for stealing some of his clients' funds.

Isaac Barrant: (1907–1956). An uneducated but energetic and charismatic labourer who became minister of agriculture in Bustamante's government.

p. 316

The affair at Myrtle Bank: On the evening of Wednesday 7 August 1946. See the half-page report in the *Gleaner* (9 August 1946, 10) under the headline "Mr W. Adolphe Roberts Honoured at Dinner: Work as Journalist, Patriot, and Idealist Praised". *Public Opinion* welcomed him back with a series of articles, leading with "Roberts, at Last" (20 July 1946).

Ivan Lloyd: (1903–1993). A doctor and politician, he was one of the four original PNP members elected to the House of Representatives in 1944, where he acted as de facto leader of the opposition.

N.N. Nethersole: See note to p. 294.

W.G. McFarlane: See note to p. 273.

Philip Sherlock: Sir Philip Sherlock (1902–2000). Originally a schoolteacher, Sherlock joined the Institute of Jamaica in 1938. He was involved with the University of the West Indies from its inception in 1948, later serving as pro vice-chancellor and then vice chancellor. He wrote widely about West Indian history and culture, his final book being *The Story of the Jamaican People*, co-authored with Hazel Bennett (Kingston: Ian Randle, 1997).

T.E. Sealy: Theodore Eustace Sealy (1909–2001), born in British Honduras to a Barbadian father and a Jamaican mother, was educated in Jamaica and joined the *Gleaner*'s editorial staff in 1928, rising to become associate editor and then editor between 1951 and 1976.

Hugh Paget: Edward Robert Hugh Paget (1910–1981) studied history, and then worked for the British Council for thirty years, serving as its representative in

Jamaica, the Netherlands, Mexico, Poland and Australia. As the first representative in Jamaica, he helped to found the Jamaican Library Service.

p. 318

Noel Livingston: Sir Noel Brooks Livingston (1882–1954) and Roberts had been young men together, discussing literature and history, but Livingston had stayed in Kingston, forming a law firm in 1911 and becoming custos of the city in 1936. At the end of 1936 Roberts sent Livingston a copy of his pamphlet, *Self-Government for Jamaica*. The accompanying letter recalled how their paths had diverged. But Jamaica, Roberts wrote, "has never been out of my mind for long. . . . I have felt it to be my duty to raise the question . . . of an individualistic growth towards nationalism and self-government, without which no country can have a soul." He wrote that he would be glad of having Livingston's opinion – which he clearly never received. But Livingston did deposit the pamphlet, and the letter, in the National Library of Jamaica.

regular history department: For background, see Woodville Marshall, "History Teaching in the University of the West Indies", in *Before and After 1865: Education, Politics and Regionalism in the Caribbean*, eds. Brian L. Moore and Swithin R. Wilmot (Kingston: Ian Randle, 1998), 49–76.

José Martí: See note to p. 16. Martí had returned to eastern Cuba in May 1895. He was killed in a skirmish at Dos Ríos on 19 May 1895 and is buried in Santa Ifigenia cemetery in Santiago de Cuba.

p. 319

active historical society in Santiago: Roberts met a group of Santiago's leading intellectuals, including Fernando Boytel Jambú, the meteorologist, and Leonardo Griñan Peralta, author of books about Martí and Maceo.

p. 320

Sieur de Poincy: Phillipe de Longvilliers de Poincy (1583–1660) was a French nobleman and colonist. The poinciana (Caesalpinia pulcherrima) was named in his honour.

de Bougainville: Louis Antoine de Bougainville (1729–1811) was a French admiral and explorer who made the first French circumnavigation. The Battle of the Saintes in 1782 led to the French abandoning a planned invasion of Jamaica. The South American flowering plants now known as bougainvillea were described by Philibert Commerson, the botanist who accompanied Bougainville on his circumnavigation.

Céspedes: Carlos Manuel de Céspedes (1819–1874) was the leader of the first war of independence against Spanish rule, which he initiated on 10 October 1868 by freeing the slaves on his plantation at La Demajagua, just outside Manzanillo, in eastern Cuba. Elected first president of the insurgent Cuba, he was later deposed, and subsequently killed by Spanish soldiers.

Maceo: Antonio Maceo Grajales (1845–1896). Born into a reasonably affluent mulatto family in Santiago de Cuba, Maceo fought valiantly in the first war of independence and was a key military figure in the early part of the second, renowned for his personal bravery and tactical flair. He was killed in combat near Punta Brava. His mother and wife moved to Jamaica in 1878.

Máximo Gómez: See note to p. 16.

p. 321

for that matter: This is one of the most heavily reworked pages of Roberts's typescript, as if he were still struggling ten years later to make sense of the event.

Orden Nacional de Mérito: Eleven years later, Roberts was awarded the British equivalent, the Order of the British Empire.

p. 322

Touissaint l'Ouverture: (1743–1803). Leader of the Haitian Revolution, the second successful independence movement in America, which led to the transformation of a society of slaves into a free, self-governing black republic.

Simón Bolívar: (1783–1830). Born in what is now Venezuela, Bolívar was the pre-eminent political and military architect of Latin America's successful struggle for independence from the Spanish Empire. During his time in exile in Jamaica in 1815 (when he lived at 33 Princess Street), Bolívar wrote his *Carta de Jamaica* [*Letter from Jamaica*], regarded as one of his most important pieces of political writing. The Simón Bolívar Cultural Centre in Kingston is due to open in 2015.

p. 323

Ruth Angell: The Jamaican archives (Manchester VI/311) contain the marriage record for George Roberts and Ruth Angell, his second wife: "George Roberts of the parish of Manchester, Gent, and Ruth Angell of St Elizabeth, spinster, a person of colour, were married by licence 27/1/1830." There is no evidence that Roberts knew that one of his great-grandmothers was "a person of colour", though it would perhaps not have come as a great surprise to him, given his knowledge of Jamaican history. It may be possible to glimpse something of an ideological division between the more recently arrived Napier and King families on Roberts's mother's side, with their highly conservative, anglocentric, low church views, and the descendants of George Roberts and Ruth Angell, Adolphe's paternal great-grandfather and great-grandmother. George Roberts had ten children in all, and their descendants were spread over the northern parts of Manchester and St Elizabeth, small planters with mixed pens – coffee, sheep, cattle, pimento – a long way, physically and ideologically, from the owners of the huge sugar plantations in other parts of the island who were deeply embedded in the colonial administration.

Lookout: Lookout still stands, though much changed.

p. 324

Richard H. Rovere: Rovere (1915–1979) married Eleanor Burgess and they had three children: Ann, Elizabeth (Betsy), and Mark Rovere. In his last book, *Final Reports: Personal Reflections on Politics and History in Our Time* (Garden City, NY: Doubleday, 1984), Rovere refers to his uncle Adolphe as a "journeyman novelist and poet . . . an interesting though peripheral figure in the literary and intellectual life of the period" (12), a judgement perhaps owing something to the Elysian heights of the Hudson Valley where the family lived, and from where Rovere commented with some acuity on the political culture of Washington, DC. Rather like his uncle, however, Rovere had behind him a radical past as editor of the communist journal *The New Masses*. With his mother he had visited Roberts in Jamaica in 1939, accompanied by the glamorous Hollywood actress and screenwriter Ella Gerta Landry, who may have been a further romantic distraction for Roberts: they had certainly had a love affair in 1928.

p. 326

independent Jamaica: This is the first time Roberts uses this phrase instead of speaking of self-government. He clearly regards them as synonymous.

p. 328

driven from the party: The other two were Frank Hill and Arthur Henry.

Chapter 20. Full Circle

p. 331

Bolivarian Society of Jamaica: After years of dormancy the society became active again in the second decade of the twenty-first century. As well as his essay on Bolívar in *Caribbean Quarterly* (1950), Roberts wrote "That Jamaica May Remember: The Visit of Bolívar, the Liberator" (1959).

p. 332

Una Marson: Marson (1905–1965) was a pioneering black Jamaican feminist, with a career full of achievements despite a difficult life, marred by depression. Like Roberts she turned her hand to many forms of writing: journalism, editing, poetry, playwriting. She wrote for *Public Opinion*, which may be where Roberts first encountered her, and then worked for the BBC during World War II. She began the Pioneer Press, but left to live in Washington, DC, handing control to Roberts.

S.A.G. Taylor: Stanley Arthur Goodwin Taylor (1894–1981) was a Jamaican writer. As well as *The Capture of Jamaica* (1951) and *Pages from Our Past* (1954), he wrote the novel *Buccaneer Bay* (1952) and the historical work *The Western*

Design: An Account of Cromwell's Expedition to the Caribbean (1965). Roberts himself edited *The Capitals of Jamaica* (1955).

Redcam: See note to p. 24. *Orange Valley and Other Poems* appeared in 1951.

Clinton V. Black: Black (1918–1993) was the Jamaican government archivist: his dedication to the preservation of historical documents is said to have made the writing of Jamaican history possible. He was one of the first students from the region to be trained at the School of Librarianship and Archives at the University of London. After *Tales of Old Jamaica* (1966), he wrote *Historic Port Royal* (1970), and *History of Jamaica* (1988), which is still the standard short history of the island.

by me: *Sir Henry Morgan* was a shortened version of Roberts's 1936 biography. The sketches in *Six Great Jamaicans* (1952) were of Edward Jordon, George William Gordon, Enos Nuttall, Robert Love, Thomas Henry MacDermot and H.G. de Lisser, two of whom (Nuttall and Love) Roberts remembered from his childhood, and another two of whom (MacDermot and de Lisser) were lifelong friends.

Annie Palmer: The central character in the novel *The White Witch of Rose Hall* (1929), written by Roberts's friend Herbert de Lisser. Born in England to an English mother and Irish father, Palmer had been brought up in Haiti where she learned witchcraft and voodoo. Moving to Jamaica, she marries John Palmer, owner of Rose Hall Plantation, whom she murders along with two subsequent husbands and numerous slaves, before herself being murdered. The original mistress of Rose Hall was called Rosa Palmer, but she shared no attributes with her fictional namesake.

p. 333

Constantia Phillips: (1709–1765). An infamous courtesan who lived the last twelve years of her life in Jamaica, where she got through three husbands to add to the many she had had in England.

of divided historical interest: As well as writing *A Literature in the Making* (1956), John Ebeneezer Clare McFarlane (1894–1962) compiled the anthologies *Voices from Summerland* (1929) and *A Treasury of Jamaican Poetry* (1950). He became Jamaican poet laureate in 1952. McCulloch and Jeffrey-Smith's books were published in 1955 and 1956 respectively.

Musgrave Gold Medal: Edna Manley had been awarded the first in 1941. Roberts was only the third recipient.

p. 334

Douglas Judah: A lawyer who had a firm with N.N. Nethersole in the 1930s before both went into politics.

judge for myself: In a postscript to his note on this meeting, which he did not transfer to the autobiography, Roberts noted: "Manley, nevertheless, added shrewdly that perhaps Jamaica would have to meet its tests of courage after self-government had been attained" (MS353.5.5.6[B]).

p. 335
Grantley Adams: Sir Grantley Herbert Adams (1898–1971), Barbadian politician who was prime minister of the West Indies Federation from 1958 to 1962.

p. 336
my radio talks: The transcripts of Roberts's radio talks survive in his papers: MS353.5.5.4. His opposition to Federation did not mean that Roberts was reneging on his pan-Caribbean and pan-American perspectives. In the midst of the Federation debate he outlined ideas for a Caribbean league (incorporating all Caribbean countries, not just the English-speaking ones), which would itself form part of a pan-American league. Leagues, unlike federations, were based on co-operation between sovereign nations. See his "All Caribbean League" (1960).

p. 338
Hector Whistler: Painter, muralist and illustrator, Whistler (1905–1978) settled in Jamaica in 1948 and painted commissioned portraits of a number of officers of the University College of the West Indies.
Barbara Ferland: Born Barbara Lushington (1919–2003), she grew up in Jamaica, where she wrote and published poems from an early age, providing many of the songs for the first all-Jamaican pantomime, on which she worked with Louise Bennett. She was employed by the music department of the British Council in Kingston before moving to England, where, on her second marriage, she became Barbara Sheppard. Her collection, *Without Shoes I Must Run*, was published in 1994, and her poems appear in *The Penguin Book of Caribbean Verse* and the *Oxford Book of Caribbean Poetry*. One of them, "Expect No Turbulence", is also in *The Independence Anthology of Jamaican Literature*, selected by A.L. Hendriks and Cedric Lindo (Kingston: Ministry of Development and Welfare, 1962), 92.

p. 339
my own Nell: According to Roberts's changed birth date, Nell would have been in her late teens by now and hardly an issue; but in fact she was only seven or eight when Roberts met Barbara Ferland.

p. 340
Linda Mazini: (1836–1915), née White. She also wrote under the pseudonym Talmage Dalin. Her books include *In the Golden Shell: A Story of Palermo* (1872) and *Camilla's Girlhood* (1885).

p. 342
have to be lived: The typescript is dated 16 February 1962. Roberts would live only another seven months.

Index

Abbott, Lynn, 106
Abbott & Briggs, 104, 106
Abela, Eduardo
   Diario de la Marina, 248, 392
Act of Havana, 304
Adams, Sir Grantley Herbert
   first premier of West Indian Federation, 335, 413
African Blood Brotherhood, xxi
Agadir, 169, 170, 378
Aïcha. *See* Goblet, Aïcha
Aisne, 186, 191–192
Alaskan gold rush, 95–97
Albert I of Belgium, 176, 378
Albizu Campos, Pedro, 269, 396–397
Algeciras, 169, 170, 378
"All Caribbean League" (Roberts), 413
Allfrey, Phyllis Shand
   "In the Cabinet", xix
American Felt Company, 60, *61*, 63, 69
anarchism
   in New York, 124–126, 367
Anglican Church, 14–15
Anglo-American Caribbean Commission, 312
Antioch, Siege of, 163, 376
Arciniegas, Germán
   Biografía del Caribe (Caribbean: Sea of the New World), xv

art, 259–260
   futuristic, 259–260
   illustrators, 104–105, 138, 154–155, 372
   modern art
      at the Sixty-Ninth Regiment Armory, 110–111, 362–363
   Pre-Raphaelite school, 259, 394
art critics
   and the vegetable man's donkey, 155–156, 374–375 (*see also* Dorgelès, Roland)
Artistes Françaises, 154–155
Austria-Hungary, 166
   and Serbia, 168, 169

Baldwin, Stanley, 267
Baltimore
   districts
      Druid Hill Park, 43, 351
      Mount Royal, 42
   lodgings in, 41–42
   newspapers
      Sun, 42, 351
Bannerman Company, 48, 352
Baptist Church
   Particular Baptists, 33–34
Barrant, Isaac, 315, 408
Barrès, Maurice, 158, 375
Barthou, Jean Louis, 149, 373

Bastille Day, 1914, 166–167
Baudelaire, Charles, 223, 385
Bazaine, Marshall François Achille
 at Metz, 99, 359
Beach, Rex, 106, 361
 The Spoilers, 96, 358
Beauregard, Pierre Gustave Toutant, 66, 354
Beaux Arts, 155
Bedward, Alexander, xiv
 founder of Bedwardism, 350
 Particular Baptists, 33–34
Beeston, William, 263, 395
Belgian army, 176–177
Belgium
 museum at Namur, 258–259
Belgrade, 170
Bellows, George, 109, 361
Benavente, Jacinto, 249
 The Bonds of Interest, 221, 385
Benét, Stephen Vincent, 211, 224, 383, 386
Benjamin Barsoe, Elsie, 277, 401
Benson, Allan, 109, 126, 362
Berger, Victor, 127, 369
Berkman, Alexander, 124, 368
 Prison Memoirs of an Anarchist, 124
Berle Jr, Adolf Augustus
 US assistant secretary of state, 304, 406
Bienvenu-Martin, Jean-Baptiste
 French minister of labour, 179–180, 379
Bierce, Ambrose, 93, 357, 389–390
Bigelow, Poultney, 389
 "My Friend the Jew", 231
Biggy, William J.
 San Francisco chief of police, 90–92, 356
Black, Clinton V.
 Tales of Old Jamaica, 332–333, 412

Boer War, 17–18, 99, 346
Bogan, Louise, 224, 386
Bohemian Club, San Francisco, 93–94, 358
Boissevain, Eugene, 141, 387
Bolívar, Simón, 318, 322, 331, 410
Bolivarian Society of Jamaica, 331, 411
 celebration at the foundation of, 332
Bontemps, Arna. *See* Hughes, Langston, and Arna Bontemps
Booth, Franklin, 105, 260, 360
Bordeaux
 meeting with Clemenceau, 182–183
 press bureau, 181, 183
 temporary capital of France, 181–183
Bosch, Juan
 De Cristóbal Colón a Fidel Castro, xv
Bourget, Paul, 173, 378
Bourke, Kitty, 51–53, 59
Bourke, Margaret, 51, 51–53, 59, 63–64
Bradford, Gamaliel, 230, 389
Brady, William A.
 Playhouse Theatre, 254, 393
Branchard, Catherine, 116–117, 165, 198, 364
Brave Mardi Gras (Roberts), 305
Brereton, Bridget
 "Regional Histories", xv
British Colonial Office
 on federation of the British West Indies, 329–330
British Jamaicans Benevolent Association, 270, 397
"British West Indian Aspirations" (Roberts), 267, 396
British West Indian territories, 267
British West Indies
 federation of, 312
Brochu, Florence, 64–66, 65, 85, 101, 146
Brooke, Rupert, 165–166, 212, 377

Brooks, Van Wyck, 109, 362
Brown, Dr Lucien M., 397
Brown, Rev. Ethelred, xix, 271, 282, 398
Buchanan, Thompson, 116, 364
Burgess, Gelett, 116, 174, 364
Bustamante, Alexander, xix, xx, xxiii, 296, 314, 326–327
   background and education, 288–290, 404
   calls a general strike, 292–294, 405
   head of labour agitation, 281, 285
   interned, 299
   Jamaica Labour Party (JLP), xvii, xviii, 313
   labour unions, 287–288, 291–292
   on Norman Manley, 290
Bynner, Harold Witter, 224, 386

Cable, George Washington, 279, 402
Caillaux, Henriette
   killing of Gaston Calmette, 150–151, 374
   trial of, 167–169
Caillaux, Joseph, 158, 168–169
   French minister of finance, 149–151, 374
   Radical Socialists, 158
Calmette, Gaston
   editor of *Le Figaro*, 149–151, 374
Campbell, Erasmus, 293–294, 405
The Caribbean: The Story of Our Sea of Destiny (Roberts), xv, 283, 294–295, 300, *301*, 403, 406
Caribbean biography and autobiography, xix–xx
Carmencita (Carmen Doucet Moreno), 248, 392
Casarin, Colonel Alexandre, 116, 364

Cashion, James
   Grant Brothers Construction Company, 81–82, 355
Casmeze, George, 177, 378
Cayman Islands
   political situation in, 323
Cesare, Oscar, 204, 382
Céspedes, Carlos Manuel de, 320, 409–410
Cézanne, Paul, 260, 394
Chalmers, Stephen, 31, 349
Chamberlain, Joseph, xvii
chess
   in Café Monopol, 113, 114–115, 363–364
   in Karl's, 115, 364
Christy, Howard Chandler, 106
   'Christy Girl', 361
Churchill, Winston, 300
Clarétie, Leo
   literary editor of *Le Figaro*, 150, 374
Clemenceau, Georges, xiv, xvii, 158–159, 178–179, 182–183, 375
Cohan, George M., 53, 65, 351, 354
   "Little Old New York", 53, 352
the Cohans
   Little Johnny Jones, 65, 354
Collyer, Charlotte, and her daughter, Marjorie
   survivors of the *Titanic*, 118–120, *119*, 365
Comte, Auguste, 137, 372
Coney Island, 60, 62
Conrad, Joseph
   Under Western Eyes, 125, 368
Coppa, Guiseppe, 93, 357
Corbett, Tom, 93, 357
Coulthard, G.R., xx
Crane, Stephen, 116, 365
   "The Blue Hotel", 66, 354
Crawford, Pauline Brooks, 232–233

Creole Dusk (Roberts), 305
Cripps, Sir Richard Stafford, 282–283, 403
Crowninshield, Frank
    editor of *Vanity Fair*, 224, 386–387
Cuba
    Act of Havana, 304
    El Olimpo, 319–320
    French influences on, 320
    Havana, 245–248, 304, 320–321
        monuments to heroes, 245–246
        Stevens, Hope R., delegate to Havana conference, 302, 406
    Oriente Province, 318–320
    San Juan Hill, 319
    Santiago de Cuba
        by bus, 319
        historical society in, 319, 409
        social links with Jamaica, 319
    and the United States, 246–247
    War of Independence, 16, 319, 345
Cundall, Frank, 32, 350
Curran, Eileen
    in Harlem, 284, 404

Darío, Rubén, 211, 383
Davis, Richard Harding, 106, 360–361
de Castro, Adolphe, 232, 389–390
de la Selva, Salomón, xx, 210–212, *211*, 223, 382, 383
de Lisser, Herbert George, xx, 31–32, 349
    Daily Gleaner, 268, 314, 407
        on the Crown Colony system, 272–273
    The White Witch of Rose Hall, 412
de Thomasson, Commandant Raoul, 183–184, 379
de Valera, Éamon, 297, 405
de Wet, Christian Rudolf, 18, 347
Debs, Eugene V., 126, 129, 369

Deems Taylor, Joseph, 223, 385–386
Delacroix, Eugène, 105, 360
DeLeon, Daniel, 127, 369
Dell, Floyd, 221, 385
Denham, Sir Edward
    governor of Jamaica, 268, 275, 281, 396
Déroulède, Paul, 144, 170, 373
Díaz, Porfirio, 76, 355
Disraeli, Benjamin, 277, 402
Dixon, Alexander, 26, 348
Doloretes (Doloretes Falagan) and Bilbao (Antonio Vidal)
    Spanish dancers, 134, 371
Domingo, Wilfred A., xix, xxi, 284, 293–294, 316, 327, 329, 397, 398
    arrested and interned, 305, 406
    to Jamaica, 304
    letters censored, 305
    memorandum from Roberts, 302–304
    West Indies National Council, 301–302
Dorgelès, Roland
    Et le soleil s'endormit sur l'Adriatique, 374–375
Dostoyevsky, Fyodor
    Crime and Punishment, 125, 368
Douet, The Right Reverend, Bishop Charles Frederick, 14, 344
Doumergue, Gaston, 149, 158, 374
Downer, The Reverend George William, 8, 344
Dowson, Ernest, 213, 383
du Quesnay, Abbé Guillaume, 310
Duchamp, Marcel, 363
    Nude Descending a Staircase, 111
Duffy, Richard, 227, 387
Dumas, Alexandre, 250, 392
Durie, Walter Randolph, 24, 348

Earle, Ferdinand, 215, 384
Eastman, Max
    The Masses, 126, 369
Edward VIII, 267
Elisabeth of Austria, Empress, 125, 368
England, 173
    declared war on Germany, 175
    Felixstowe, Suffolk, 212, 383
    London, xxii–xxiii, 241–244 (*see also* Swinburne, Algernon Charles)
Estrada Cabrera, Diego, 94, 358
Estrada Cabrera, Manuel, 358
Europe
    incidents across, 158
Eyre, Edward John, 264–265, 395

Fabian Society, 26, 32, 122
Fairclough, Osmond Theodore
    Public Opinion, 272, 399
Falls, Charles Buckles, 260, 394
Farquhar, Giulia, 394
    affair with Roberts, 260–262, 339, 341
    daughter born, 262 (*see also* Roberts, W. Adolphe: and daughter "Nell")
Farquhar, Gordon, 260–262
Farr, Camilla, 140–141, 143, 157, 372, 383
Ferland, Barbara, xxiii, 338–339, *339*, 341, 413
Fernández de Castro, José Antonio, 248, 392
Ferrer, Francisco, 123, 367
Ficke, Arthur Davison, 224, 225, 386
Fisher, Harrison, 106, 361
Flynn, Elizabeth Gurley, xvi, 132, 370
Foreign Legion, 177
Forrest, Nathan Bedford, General, 76, 355
Fort, Paul, 165, 377
Foster, Jeanne Robert, 109, 212, 362, 383
Foster, Knox (headman), 9, *9*, 13, 16

France
    eastern front, 178–179
    elections in, 157–159
    government in Bordeaux, 179, 181
    Le Havre, 143–144
    military service in, 142–143, 149, 157–158, 171
    mobilization in, 172, 173–175, 177
    See also Paris
Franco-Prussian War, 99, 359
Franz Ferdinand, Archduke
    assissination in Sarajevo, Bosnia, 163–164, 376
Franz Joseph I, 164, 377
free verse school, 224, 385
French, Nora May, 94, 358
The French in the West Indies (Roberts), 305, 307, 310
Frick, Henry Clay, 124, 368
Frost, Arthur Burdett, 105, 360
Fulford, Helen, 135–136, 139
futuristic art, 259–260
Gallieni, General Joseph, 180, 379
Garbo, Greta, 387
García Iñiguez, Calixto, 16, 345
Gardner, W.J., 265, 395
Garland, Robert
    Telegram, 253
Garrett, Clara Maude, 21, 22, 25, 64, 347
Garvey, Marcus, 270, 285, 397
Gattorno, Antonio, 248, 392
Gaynor, William Jay
    mayor of New York, 102, 128–129, 130, 360
Genthe, Arnold, 356
    Street of the Gamblers, 88–89
Germany
    attack on Paris, 177–178
    declared war on Russia, 172

Gibson, Charles Dana
  'Gibson Girl', 105, 360
  'Gibson Man', 105
Glackens, William J., 260
Glasspole, Florizel A.
  People's National Party (PNP), 314–315, 408
Goblet, Aïcha, 153–154, *161*, 384
Goldman, Emma, xvi, 124, 125, 367
Gómez, Máximo, 16, 320, 345
Goncourt Brothers
  Edmond de Goncourt and Jules de Goncourt, 250, 392
Gordon, George William, 99, 264, 322, 358, 395
Gosse, Edmund, 242, 392
Grant, Percy Stickney, 131, 370
Grant Brothers Construction Company, 73–74, 76–77, 78, 81–82, 355
  and Mexican labourers, 75–76
Grau, Dr Ramón, 247, 391
Greater Antilles, 262
Greco-Turkish War (1897), 15, 344
Greeley, Horace, 102, 359
Griffith, William, 121, 209–210, 213, 367
Guaymas, 83
Guesde, Jules, 179, 181, 379
Guy, Robert C.
  editor of the *Daily Telegraph*, 36–37, 350–351

Haggard, H. Rider, 10, 344
Hall, Gilman, 209–210
Hall, Thomas Victor (Tom), 103, 145–146, 152–154, 170, 172, 178, 260, 360
Hamilton, Gerald, 31, 349
Hanlon, Eddie, 93, 357
"Hansi". *See* Waltz, Jean-Jacques
Hart, Richard (Dick), 277, 328, 401
Harte, Bret, 66, 86, 354

The Haunting Hand (Roberts), 232–233, 390
Haywood, William (Big Bill), 127, 369
Hearn, Patrick Lafcadio, 279, 402
Hedin, Naboth, 176, 244, 381
  Brooklyn Daily Eagle, 157, 375
Hemming, Sir Augustus, 26, 137, 348
Heney, Francis J., 88, 90, 356
Henri, Robert, 109, 259, 361
Henríquez Ureña, Pedro, xx
Henry, Arthur, 411
Hernández, Mateo, 249–251, 392
Hervé, Gustave
  La Guerre Sociale, 169, 378
Hickey, Katharine Amelia, 113, 139–140, 196, 213–214, *214*, 383
  marriage to Roberts, xviii, 213–214
  marriage to Roberts ends, 261
Hill, Frank, 411
  The Upheaval, 276–277, 401
Hill, Ken, xix, 276, 327–328
  Daily Gleaner, 272, 399
  National Reform Association, 272, 283, 399
Hodgson, Ralph, 224, 386
Holcombe, Ernest, 131, 370
Holdredge, Leigh, 131, 370
Holladay, Paula (Polly), 134, 370
  restaurant at the Liberal Club, 131–132, *133*
Hollywood, 72, 228–229, 388
Holman Hunt, William, 259, 394
Homer, Winslow, 135, 371
House, Colonel Edward M., 128, 369–370
Housman, A.E.
  A Shropshire Lad, 221–222, 385
Howard University
  conference on the Caribbean, 311–312, 407
Huggins, Sir John, 312, 314, 407

Hughes, Al, 95–98
Hughes, Langston, and Arna Bontemps
 The Poetry of the Negro 1746–1949, xxi
Hull, Cordell
 US secretary of war
  administration of colonies, 303–304, 406

illustrators, 104–105, 259–260
 Kit Kat Club, 138, 220, 372, 385
The Independence Anthology of Jamaican Literature, xiii
Indians, 75–76. See also Yaqui Indians
Industrial Workers of the World (IWW), 127–128, 369
Institute of Jamaica, xiii–xiv, 31, 333, 349
 public library at, 32
 West India Reference Library, 284
Ireland, 283–284, 334
Iremonger, Tom, xxiii
Italy
 Naples, 340
 Rome, 340–341

Jacobs, Hedley Powell, 277, 401–402
 Public Opinion editor, 405
Jaffé, Charles, 115, 364
Jamaica, 135–138
 August Town, 33–34
 Balaclava
  ancestors from, 323–324, 410
 Blue Mountains, 4, 343
 and citizenship, 314–315, 407
 Colonial Office, 37–38
  and the English official, 37–38
 Crown Colony system, 272–273, 312
 elections in, 312–313, 326, 333–334
 home rule for, 333
 and independence, xiii–xiv, xxii, 326, 411

 journalism in, 28 (*see also* Kingston: newspapers and magazines)
 Legislative Council, xvii, 25–27, 293, 296, 405
 middle-class, property owners, 275
  and a new political party, 326, 411
 Roberts, interviews, rallies and speeches, 315–316
 Royal Commission, 296
 and self-determination, 304
 and self-government, xvii, 267, 285
 Smith Constitution, 296
 speaking tour in, 272–275
 strikes in, 280–281, 292–294, 403
 suffrage, adult, 312–313
 suffrage, universal, 287–288, 297
 Trades Union Council, 293–294, 296, 405
 See also Bolivarian Society of Jamaica; Institute of Jamaica; Kingston; Manchester parish; Morant Bay; National Library of Jamaica; People's National Party (PNP); Poetry League of Jamaica
"Jamaica" (Roberts), 49, 352
Jamaica, Map of, 2
Jamaica Democratic Party, 313, 407
Jamaica Historical Society, xiii, 331, 408
 and Marlborough, Manchester Parish, 338
 Roberts made an honorary member, 318
Jamaica Labour Party (JLP), xvii, xviii, 313
 win the elections, 327
Jamaica Progressive League, xvi–xviii, xxi, xxii, 278, 282–283, 287–288, 296–297, 326
 in Boston, 311
 delegate to Havana, 301–302

Jamaica Progressive League (*continued*)
  flag of, *288*
  fundraising for PNP, 317–318, 326
  Kingston, 272–273, 400
    mass meeting at the Ward Theatre, 277
  Linstead township, 274
  memorandum by Roberts, 301–304
  New York, 270–272, 317–318, 397, 400
  Port Maria, 274–275
  and self-government, 285
Jamaica: The Portrait of an Island (Roberts), *337*, 337
Janowski, Dawid, 115, 364
Jaurès, Jean, 169, 171–172, 179, 378
  Socialists, 158
Jazz Age, 215
Jeffrey-Smith, May
  Bird-Watching in Jamaica, 333
Jeffries, Jim, 54, 353
Jennings, Alphonso, 202, 381
Joffre, Marshall Joseph
  commander of the French army, 178, 180, 183, 379
Johns, Orrick
  "An Idyll of the Province", 230–231, 389
Johnson, Hiram, 88, 90, 356
Johnson, Nunnally, 389
  "The Black Menace", 231
Johnston, William
  Sunday Editor, *New York World*, 205–209, 382
Judah, Douglas, 334, 412

Keats, John, 21
Keil, Hugo, 357
Keith, Benjamin Franklin, 55–56, 353
Keith and Proctor Theatres, 55
Kelly, Dr Gertrude, 58–59, 354

Kennerley, Mitchell
  Lyric Year contest, 215, 384
Kernahan, Coulson, 242, 391
Ketchel, Stanley, 93, 357
Kilmer, Joyce, 109, 362
Kingston, 3–4, 16–17, 326
  buildings
    Athenaeum, 31, 37, 349
    Headquarters House, 25, 348
    King's House (governor's mansion), 38, 351
  cafés
    Burke's Geisha Café, 31
  earthquake in, 68, 135
  getting about in, 28–29, 349
  Jamaica Club, 31, 349
  literary talent in, 31–32
  mass meeting at, 282
  newspapers and magazines
    Daily Gleaner, 10, 314, 316, 396, 398–399, 407, 408
      apprenticed to, 21–24
      article on fishermen, 28, 348–349
      assignments for, 25–28, 348–349
      contests in, 10
      a contributor to, 21
    Daily Telegraph, 34, 36
    Jamaica Times, 10, 23–24, 24
      a contributor to, 21
      and William Pringle Livingstone, 35–36
    Leader
      arrangement with the *Daily Telegraph*, 34
      article on Alexander Bedward, 33–34
      close of, 39, 351
      content of, 35

Index 423

fictional serials in, 39
as managing editor, 36–37
new weekly paper, 33
office space, 34–35
and William Pringle
Livingstone, 33–36, 39
Public Opinion, 272, 276–277, 405
and the People's National
Party, 314
Standard, 285, 297–298, 403–404,
405
at night, 30
Pioneer Press, 332, 332–333, 411
rioting in, 280–281
social life of, 31
Kipling, Rudyard, 106, 360
Kitchener of Khartoum, Herbert, Lord,
xvii, 18, 184, 347
Kosovo, Battle of, 163, 376
Kosterlitzky, Colonel Emilio, 81, 355
Kronstadt revolt (1905), 120–121, 365
Kropotkin, Peter, 125, 368
Kruger, Paul, 17, 346
Ku Klux Klan, 76, 355

La Argentina (Antonia Mercé y Luque),
252, 393
La Argentinita (Encarnación López
Júlvez), 392
in New York, 252–255
in Paris, 248–251
Labori, Fernand, 168, 378
labour disturbances, 280
labour unions, 287–288, 291–292
Lafargue, André, 309, 310, 407
Lake Pontchartrain (Roberts), 305
Lands of the Inner Sea (Roberts), 315
Lascari, Salvatore, 156, 374
Lasker, Emmanuel, 115, 364
Lawrence textile strike, 132, 371. *See also*

Paterson strike of mill workers
Lawson, Ernest, 260
Le Gallienne, Richard, 230
The Quest of the Golden Girls, 213, 383
Le Mercier-du Quesnay, Constance, 310,
407
Le Mercier-du Quesnay, Yvonne, 310, 407
Lebourg, Madeleine, 160–161, *161*, 162,
170, 178, 181, 184–186
Lecesne, Arnold, 274, 401
Lee, B. Virginia, 213, 383
Lee, Muna, 268–269, *269*, 396
Lenin, Nicolai, 126
Leslie, Lew
International Revue, 252, 393
Lewis, C. Bernard, xiii, 402
Liège, 176–177
Ligue des Patriotes, 144
Livingston, Sir Noel Brooks, 318, 409
Livingstone, William Pringle, 23, *23*,
41–42, 347
and the *Jamaica Times*, 35–36
and the *Leader*, 33–36, 39
and the Negro question in the
Southern states, 39
Lloyd, Dr Ivan, 316, 408
Lloyd George, David, 18, 346
Lobengula, 17, 346
London, xxii
Putney Heath, 241–244
London, Jack, xvi, 93, 94, 106, 123, 357,
361
John Barleycorn, 109–110, 362
London, Meyer, 127, 369
Long, Samuel, 263, 395
Longbridge, Gladys
Bustamante's secretary, 290, 405
López Méndez, Luis Alfredo, 248, 392
Lord's Day Alliance
and Sunday performances, 254, 393

Los Angeles, 72, 98
  Adolphus Sigismund Roberts in, 84
  Lotta's Fountain, 98, 358
  See also Hollywood
Loubet, Émile François
  President of France, 144, 373
Louisiana, 306
  Baton Rouge, 280
  See also New Orleans
L'Ouverture, Toussaint, 322, 410
Lowell, Amy, 224, 386
Loyal North Lancashire Regiment, 212
Luks, George, 260

Macaulay, Thomas Babington, 19, 347
MacDermot, Thomas Henry, 24, 32, 36, 68, 348. *See also* Redcam, Tom
Maceo Grajales, Antonio, 320, 410
Macfadden, Bernarr
  Physical Culture, 232, 390
Machefert, Adrien, 172, 373
  and Peggy, 144–146
Maclaren, Ian, 37, 351
Maillol, Aristide, 260, 394
Makin, F.J.
  editor of the *Standard*, 285, 404
Malliet, A.M. Wendell, 270–271, 397
Manchester Parish, 4–7, 9, 12–13, 337, 343
Manley, Edna Swithenbank, 286, 404
Manley, Norman Washington, xix, xx, 275–276, 276, 299, 304–305, 326
  action on strikes, 281
  attitude as chief minister, 334
  background and education, 286–287, 404
  on Bustamante, 296
  on Ireland, 412
  and labour unions, 291–293
  loses the election, 313, 407
  meeting with Roberts, 317, 327–328
  meetings in New York, 317–318
  People's National Party (PNP), xvi–xvii, 282–283
    attending meetings, 285–286, 287–288
  on Roberts's work, 316
  and West Indian Federation, 330, 334–336
Mantle, Burns
  Daily News, 253
Maribona, Armando, 248, 391
Marjorie, streetwalker, 67–68
Marlborough, Manchester Parish, 337–338
  Hall family at, 337–338
  Hector Whistler at, 338, 413
  and the Jamaica Historical Society, 331
Marshall, Frank James, 115, 364
Marson, Una
  editor of Pioneer Press, 332, 411
Martí, José, 16, 318, 320, 322, 345, 409
Martine, James Edgar
  US senator for New Jersey, 45, 130–131, 351
Martínez, Concha, 78–81
Marx, Karl, 127
  Das Capital, 122
Massaguer, Conrado W., 247, 247–248, 391
Mata Hari, 149, 373
Matisse, Henri, 156, 375
  Aïcha and Lorette, 374
Mayor Harding (Roberts), 393
Mazini, Linda, 340, 413
McCarthy, Patrick Henry (Pin Head), 92, 357
McCarty, Tom, 82–83
McCulloch, Dr W.E.
  Your Health in the Caribbean, 333

McFarlane, John Ebeneezer, Clare
  A Literature in the Making, 333, 412
McFarlane, Walter G., 316, 399–400, 408
McKay, Claude, xix–xxi, 397
  A Long Way Home, xix
  Banana Bottom, xxi
McKay, Thomas, xxi
McKee, Bill, 81, 98
  Grant Brothers Construction
    Company, 76–77, 78
McKinley, William
  shooting of, 125–126, 368
Meikle, Rupert E., 400
Melo, Dr Leopoldo
  Argentina's foreign minister, 304,
    406
Mencken, Henry Louis, 227, 387
Mendes, Alfred
  Autobiography, xix
Meredith, George, 223, 385
mestizos, 75–76
Mexican border, 73–74
Mexican labourers, 75–76
Mexico, 117
  Nogales, 73, 77–81
  Northern Sonora, 81, 355
  See also Grant Brothers
    Construction Company
Michelangelo, 259
Mijer, Pieter, 225–226, 387
Milholland, Inez, 141, 225, 387
Millay, Cora Buzzell, 219, 385
Millay, Edna St Vincent, xvi, xviii–xix,
  141, 203, 211, 217, 382–384, 385
  The Bonds of Interest
    actress in, 221
  contributor to *Ainslie's*, 216–217,
    218–219
  family of, 217–218, 219, 384
  and love, 224–226

memoir by Edmund Wilson, 224, 386
poetry, 216, 221–224
publications
  Aria da Capo, 220–221
  "Daphne", 217, 218, 384
  A Few Figs from Thistles, 218
  The King's Henchman, 223,
    385–386
  "Renascence", 215, 384
  Second April, 218, 224
  "Spring", 386
  The Seventh Stair, 219
sexual freedom, 225
translations from Baudelaire, 223, 386
in *Vanity Fair*, 224
writing fiction (as Nancy Boyd),
  218–219
Millay, Kathleen, 218, 385
Millay, Norma, 217–218, 220–221, 384
Milton, Paul R., 247, 252–253, 393
Milton, Robert, 252, 393
The Mind Reader (Roberts), 394
Mobile, 280
Monahan, Michael, 109, 362
Monroe, Harriet
  Poetry, 217, 219, 384
Montreal, 101–102
Moore, George, 110, 362
Moore, Richard B., xxi
The Moralist (Roberts), xviii–xix, 390
Moran, Owen, 93
Morant Bay Rebellion, 99, 268, 322, 350,
  358–359, 395
Moravian Church, 13, 344
Moreno, Antonio, 229
Morris, Gouverneur, 106, 361
motion picture journalism, 228–230, 388
Moyne, Walter Edward Guinness, Lord,
  282, 403
  and Royal Commission, 296

Mumford, Ethel Watts, 389
    on Prohibition, 231
Muñoz Marín, Luis, xx, 396
    and Puerto Rico politics, 268
Murger, Henri
    La Vie de Bohème, 160, 376
Murphy, Charles Francis, 58, 353
Murphy, William, 357

Napoleon III, 335
Narodny, Ivan, 365–366
    document by Tolstoy, 120–121
    memoirs of, 120
Nathan, George Jean, 227, 388
National Library of Jamaica, xxiii
National Reform Association, 283
'nationalist liberalism', 328–329
Negro villages, 5
Nethersole, Noel Newton, xix, 316
    People's National Party (PNP), 294, 405
New Orleans, 70–72, 278–280, 297, 300, 305–310, 310, 321
    Athénée Louisiannais, 309, 309–310
    bars
        Pat O'Brien's, 279, 402
    buildings
        the Cabildo, 309, 407
        Presbytère, 309, 407
    and coffee, 309–310
    Creoles in, 306
    districts
        Decatur Street, 309
        Garden District, 309
        Royal Street, 307–308
        St Ann Street, 307
        'Storyville', 309
        Vieux Carré, 279, 308–309
            bordellos in, 309
    and gambling, 309

    regional literature of, 308
    restaurants, 279, 402
        Antoine's, 279–280, 403
        Arnaud's, 279, 402
        Broussard's, 279, 402
        Galatoire's, 279, 402
        La Louisiane, 279, 402
        Madam Begué's, 279
        Maylie's, 279, 402
        Tujague's, 279, 402
    and seafood, 309–310
New York, 39–40, 47, 64, 100, 311, 313, 324, 407
    anarchism in, 124–126, 367
    bars
        Tom Sharkey's saloon, 54, 353
    boarding house, 51–53
    Brooklyn Bridge, 47, 352
    buildings
        Astor House, 47–48, 352
        brownstone houses in, 48
        business blocks, 48
        City Hall and City Hall Park, 47, 352
        Flatiron Building, 48, 352
        Grace Church, 48, 352
        New York World Building, 47, 352
        newspaper buildings, 48, 352
        Park Row Building, 47, 352
        Sixty-Ninth Regiment Armory, 110–111, 362–363
        St Paul Building, 47, 352
        Statue of Liberty, 60
        Tammany Hall, 54, 57–59, 353
        Trinity Church, 47, 352
        Webster Hall, 134, 371
    cafés and restaurants, 62–63, 354
        Allaire's, 113, 363
        Brevoort, 113, 363

Café Monopol, 113, 114, 363
Gonfarone's, 63, 354
Guffanti's, 63, 354
Joel's, 113, 363
Lafayette, 113, 363
Lion d'Or, 63, 354
Luchow's, 113, 363
Madama's, 70, 102–103, 111, 113–114, 355
Maison Petitpas, 107–114, 361
Mouquin's, 114, 363
Polly's Restaurant, 131–132, *133*
Renganeschi's, 63, 354
speakeasies, 62–63
table d'hôte, 62–63
districts
Battery, 47, 352
Bowery, 47, 53, 54, 352
Salvation Army in, 54
Broadway, 47, 53
'Great White Way', 53, 353
Bryant Park, 206, 382
Chinatown, 53
Columbus Circle, 53
Greenwich Village, xvi, 131–132, 220
Latin Quarter in, 215
Washington Square, 102, 115–116, 132, 325, 359, 364
Harlem, 53, 140, 403
Eileen Curran in, 284
Jamaicans in, 270–272
public meetings in, 282
Herald Square, 53, 57
Madison Square, 53, 204, 206
Tenderloin, 53, 352–353
Times Square, 53
Union Square, 48, 53, 352
exhibitions in
Irish arts and crafts, 108

flophouses
Olive Tree Inn, 207, 382
Washington House, 208–209
Harper & Brothers, 227–228
Kit Kat Club, 138, 220, 271, 385
Liberal Club, xvi, 131–134, 140
lectures and debates, 132–133, 371
Pagan Routs, 134, 371
La Tierra de la Alegría, 134, 371
lodgings in, 48–49
mother and sisters visit, 66–67
museums of art, 259
National Academy of Design, 259–260
newspapers and magazines
Ainslie's, xiv–xv, 200–201, 200–203, 210–213
and Edna St Vincent Millay, 216–219
American, 118
American Parade, xv, 230–232, 231, 240, 257, 259–260, 388
Amsterdam News, 270, 397
Atlantic Monthly, 118
Brief Stories, 227–228
Brooklyn Daily Eagle, 200–201
Century, 118, 365
Current History, 267, 395
Dance Magazine, 251–252, 393
La Argentinita article, 253, 257, 393
Everybody's, 118
Family Magazine Section, 118
Harper's Monthly, 118, 227, 365
The Masses, 126, 128, 369
McClure's, 118
Monthly Magazine Section, New York, 103–105, 106

New York (continued)
  newspapers and magazines (continued)
    Nation
      and Edna St Vincent Millay, 224, 386
    New York Times, 267, 395
    New York Tribune, 102, 104
    New York World, 205–209
    Physical Culture, 232, 389
    Scribner's, 118, 365
    Semi-Monthly Magazine Section, 118, 135, 139, 365
    The Smart Set, 227, 237, 387
    The Sun
      publishes Roberts's poem, 49
    Telegram, 253
    Travel Magazine, 270, 396
    Vanity Fair, 386–387
      and Edna St Vincent Millay, 224
  nightlife of, 53–56
  park-bench derelicts, search for, 212
  politics of, 102
  population of, 53
  Seward statue, 205, 382
  socialism in, 123–124, 136–136
    Branch One of Local New York, 126
  streetwalkers, 67–68
  theatre, 54–56, 103
  Theatre Guild, 220–221
  theatres
    Ethel Barrymore Theatre, 254
    Fifth Avenue Theatre, 55–56
    Playhouse Theatre, 254, 390
  winter in, 50–51
  writers and artists, 102–103
newspapers and magazines. *See under city of publication*
Nicholl, Louise Townsend, 231, 389

Nietzsche, Friedrich, 125, 368
Norris, Frank, 116, 364
  McTeague, 66, 354
  The Octopus, 66, 354
Nuttall, Enos
  Anglican archbishop, 32, 350

O. Henry (William Sydney Porter), 201–202, 209–210, 381
  "Bagdad-on-the-Subway", 53, 352
  daughter, Margaret, 381
  cash distributed, 204–209
  "Gift of the Magi, The", 205
  portraits of, 204
  stories about park-bench derelicts, 204–205
O'Connell, Daniel, 290, 405
Older, Fremont, 89, 92, 356
Olivier, Sydney Haldane, 1st Baron, xvii, 26–27, 32, 37, 68, 348, 367
  Fabian essays, 137
  and socialism, 136–137
O'Meally, James Augustus, 271, 399
Orden Nacional de Mérito: Carlos Manuel de Céspedes, 321, 410
Orteig, Raymond, 113, 363
Ortner, Eva, 149
O'Sheel, Shaemus, 109, 362
Owen, Wilfred, 212

Pacific Gas and Electric Company
  house paper, 89
Paget, Edward Robert Hugh, 316–317
  Jamaica Historical Society, 408
Paine, Henry Gallup, 106, 121, 360
  Monthly Magazine Section, 103–105
Palmer, Annie, 332–333, 412
Pankhurst, Emmeline, 367
Papke, Billy, 93, 357
Paris, 139, 142–146, 238–240, 248–251, 260–262

apaches, 157, 375
bombed by Germany, 177–178
buildings
    Grand Palais, 155
    Hotel des Ecoles, 144, 373
cabarets
    Aristide Bruant's, 157, 375
    Lapin Agile, 157, 375
    Le Bal Bullier, 165, 377
    Moulin de la Galette, 157, 375
    Moulin Rouge, 157, 375
cafés and restaurants
    Café de la Rotonde, 145, 152–154, 170, 373
    Café du Croissant, 378
        Jaurès shot in, 171
    Café du Dôme, 145, 373
    Café Lavenue, 165, 377
    Café Rotonde, 165
    Closerie des Lilas, 165
    Maison Leduc, 172–173
    Montparnasse cafés, 145–146, 172
districts
    Champs Elysées, 165
    Closerie des Lilas, 377
    Latin Quarter, 151
    Luxembourg Gardens, 164–165
    Montmartre, 156–157
    Montparnasse, 151–152
dragoons on the street, 170
newspapers
    censorship of, 176, 178–180, 183
newspapers and magazines
    Brooklyn Daily Eagle, 147–151, *148*, 156, 157, 159, 176, 181–183, 375
    Chicago Daily News, 146
    La Guerre Sociale, 169, 378
    Le Figaro, 149–151, 374
    L'Homme Enchaîné, 183
    L'Homme Libre, 179

New York Times, 146
    reports on the war, 173–174
Parker, Judge Alton Brooks, 56–57, 353
Parker, Sir Gilbert, 106, 361
Parker, Walter, 31, 349
Parks, Lucille, xxiii
Paterson, strike of silk mill workers, 138, 372
Patti, Adelina, 116, 364
Péguy, Charles, 165–166, 377
People's National Party (PNP), xvi–xviii, 283, 284, 286–287, 291–297, 301
    and Glaspole, Florizel A., 314–315, 408
    meetings in New York, 317–318
    in power, 333–334
    Public Opinion, 314
    purge of leftists, 327–328, 411
    routed in the elections, 313
    and self-government, 295–296
    and socialism, 311, 326–329
Petrova, Olga, *203*, 203
    Butter with My Bread, 381
Phillips, Constantia, 333, 412
Pico della Mirandola, Giovanni, 117, 365
Pitta, Brown (stockman), 12–13
Pixley, Frank, 315, 408
Plainfield, New Jersey, 43–46
    Daily Press, 43–45
Poetry League of Jamaica, xiii
Poincaré, Raymond, President of France, 158–159, 167, 170, 178–179, 181, 375–376
The Pomegranate (Roberts), 248–251
Poniersh, Clara (Sonia), 149
Porter, Margaret Worth, 204, 382
Porter, William Sydney. *See* O. Henry
Pound, Ezra, 357
Pre-Raphaelite school, 259, 394
Princip, Gavrilo, 166
    assassin of Franz Ferdinand, 164, 377

Progressive Party, 129–130
Provincetown Players, 220, 385
Puerto Rico, 266–270, 396
    and political conditions, 268–269
    speech on political conditions, 268–269, 396

Quinlan, Arthur Patrick (Pat), 138, 372
Quinn, John, 108, 109, 361

Radical Socialists, 158
Raines, Senator John, 67, 355
    Raines Law hotels, 67–68
Ramchand, Kenneth, xxii
Ramos, Eleanor, xviii–xix, 231, 236, 321, 390, 409
    assistant editorial post, 233, 238
    brother's death, 237
    The Exotic, 237–238
    novel rejected, 240
    publishing in *The Smart Set*, 237
    relationship with Roberts, 233–240
    and Ted Bourland, 239–240
    "The Red Waltz", 231–232
Raphael, 259, 393
Redcam, Tom (Thomas Henry MacDermot), 21, 24, 348, 412
    Orange Valley and Other Poems, 332
Reed, John Silas (Jack), 138, 372
Reitman, Ben, 124, 367
Revanche, 155, 374
Rhodes, Cecil, 17–18, 346
Rhys, Jean, xxi–xxii
    Smile Please, xix
    Voyage in the Dark, xxii
    Wide Sargasso Sea, xxii
Ribot, Alexandre
    Progressives, 158–159, 376
Rice, Louise, 233, 234, 390

Richards, Sir Arthur Frederick, 292, 298–299
    governor of Jamaica, 281–282, 297, 403
    and self-government movement, 304
Roberts, Adolphus Sigismund (father), xxi, 8, 16, 344
    careers, 3–4, 7–9
    illegitimate child of, xxii, 13, 344
    to the Isthmus of Panama, 68
    in Los Angeles, 83–84
    relationship with his wife, 3, 8, 9, 14–15
    in San Francisco, 85
    on socialism, 136
    travels of, 84–85, 99–100
    "Why Are the Churches Not Better Attended?", 10, 344
Roberts, Ethel Josephine (sister, later Rovere), 5, 135–137, 344, 371
Roberts, Field Marshal Frederick Sleigh, 17, 346
Roberts, Ivy R.F. (sister, later Steele), 5, 344
Roberts, Josephine Fanny (mother), 14–15, 266, 268, 344
    ends her marriage, 67
    to Halifax, Nova Scotia, 67, 70
    and puritanism, 14–15
    relationship with her husband, 3, 8, 9, 14–15
Roberts, W. Adolphe
    in 1917, *201*
    in 1922, *239*
    in 1939, *288*
    activities since the outbreak of war, 267
    Al Hughes, 95–98
    ambition to write books, 36–37

American Indian skull on his bookcase, 116–117
ancestors, 323–324, 410
with Antonio Moreno, 229
article on the Jamaica Nationalist Party, 282
with aunts at Mon Désir, Kingston, 22, 25
awarded Musgrave Gold Medal, 333, 412
awarded Orden Nacional de Mérito: Carlos Manuel de Céspedes, *321*, *321*, 409
and the Biggy mystery, 90–92
and Bustamante, 314–315
The Capitals of Jamaica, 332, 411
career, xiii–xv, xx–xxii, 20–21 (*see also newspapers and magazines under city of publication*)
    freelancing, 49, 257–258
and cat, Grisette, 235, 390
childhood, xvi, 3–7, 10–12, 13–14
and daughter "Nell", xix, 267, 339, *341*, 341–342, 395, 413
    use of grandmother's name, 261–262, 394
described by Petrova, 381
and detective fiction, 229–230, 388
discussion on his nationality, 314–315, 408
distributing cash to park-bench derelicts, 204–209
Domingo, memorandum to, 302–304
education, xiv, 7, 9–10, 18–19
encounter with a drunk, 98–99
encounter with a mountain lion/cougar, 75
and family
    at Berry Hill
        with sisters, 6
    with sisters and mother, *14*
    mother's death, 266, 268
    parents' relationship, 3, 8, 9, 14–15, 344
hobbies, 92, 233
    fencing, 357
Hopewell, St Ann, 136, 137–138
interest in art, history and poetry, 21, 258–260
and the Jamaica Progressive League, 284
Jamaican self-government, 267
La Argentinita, 248–251, 252–255
with Madeleine Lebourg and Aïcha in Paris, *161*
life threatened, 79–81
and loneliness, 42–43
Mandeville churchyard, 342
Norman Manley, 327–328, 334
military service, exempted from, 200, 381
Myrtle Bank Hotel
    dinner for Roberts, 315–316, 408
    menu from dinner for Roberts, *316*
Ivan Narodny, 120–121
naturalized US citizen, 297
publications
    "All Caribbean League", 413
    Brave Mardi Gras, 305
    "British West Indian Aspirations", 267, 396
    The Caribbean: The Story of Our Sea of Destiny, xv, 283, 294–295, 301, 403
        reviews of, 300, 406
    Creole Dusk, 305
    The French in the West Indies, 305, 307, 310

W. Adolphe Roberts (*continued*)
  publications (*continued*)
    The Haunting Hand, 232–233, 390
    "Jamaica", 49, 352
    Jamaica: The Portrait of an Island, 337, *337*
    Lake Pontchartrain, 305
    Lands of the Inner Sea, 315
    Mayor Harding, 393
    The Mind Reader, 394
    The Moralist, xviii–xix, 390
    The Pomegranate, 248–251
      dedicated to La Argentinita, 255
    Royal Street, 305, *307*, 310
    Self-Government in Jamaica, 263–265, 395, 409
    Semmes of the Alabama, 278, 280, 281, 402
    The Single Star, xiv, xv, 318, 319, 321, 329
    Sir Henry Morgan: Buccaneer and Governor, xv, xvii, xxi–xxii, 261–263, 267, 332, 412
    Six Great Jamaicans, 332, 412
    The Strange Career of Bishop Sterling, 393
    "Villanelle of a Spanish Dancer", 255–256, 393
  at Rawcliffe, Gordon Town, 294–295, *295*
  reading and early writing, 7, 10, 344
  relationships with women, xviii–xix, 94–95 (*see also* Bourke, Margaret; Brochu, Florence; Farquhar, Giulia; Farr, Camilla; Ferland, Barbara; Fulford, Helen; Garrett, Clara Maude; Hickey, Katharine Amelia; Lebourg, Madeleine; Marjorie, streetwalker; Martínez, Concha; Millay, Edna St Vincent; Ramos, Eleanor; Sanger, Margaret; Sars, Hedda)
  with Margaret Sanger, 139
  secretary of the Liberal Club, 131
  shorthand and typing, 21, 23, 43, 49–50
  sketched by John Butler Yeats, *109*
  spellings of "Adolphe", 343
  in Sunday magazines and papers, 50
  and the supernatural, 324
  at Swinburne's homes, 241–244
  Titanic survivors interview, 118–120, 365
  travel writing, xvi
  US South, 244
  verse and articles rejected, 49–50
  visa to Jamaica refused, 313–314
  visit to Henri Matisse, 156
  in Washington Square, *325*
  working for publishers, 232–233 (*see also* newspapers and magazines listed under city of publication)
Roberts family properties (pens)
  Berry Hill, Manchester Parish, 4, 5–7, *6*, 9, 12–13, 68, 337, 343
  Fairview, St Elizabeth Parish, 135–136
  Hanover, Manchester Parish, 4
  Lookout, Manchester Parish, 323, 411
  Mount Forest, Manchester Parish, 9, 12–13
Robinson, Boardman, 109, 361
Roosevelt, Franklin D., 300, 301
  conference of foreign ministers
    at Havana, 301, 303
    at Panama, 301
Roosevelt, Theodore, xvii, 16, 42, 56–57, 129–130, 345
Rops, Felicien, 258–259, 394
Rossetti, Dante Gabriel, 259, 394

Rovere, Richard H. (nephew), 324–325, 411
Royal Street (Roberts), 305, *307*, 310
Ruef, Abe, 87, 90, 92, 356

Sacramento, 88–89
Salisbury, William, 389
   "Mencken, the Foe of Beauty", 231
Salkey, Andrew, xxiii
Salon des Indépendants "Salon à Vingt Francs", 155, 156
Sampson, Rear Admiral William T., 16, 345
San Francisco, 83, 84–85, 98
   Adolphus Sigismund Roberts in, 99–100
   bohemia, 93–94, 358
   cafés and restaurants
      Coppa's, 93, 357
      The Poodle Dog and the Pup, 93, 358
      Sanguinetti's, 93, 357
      table d'hôte restaurants, 93
   and California boosterism, 86–87
   corrupt municipal government, 87–90
      graft investigation in, 88–91
      political leaders in, 92
   districts
      Chinatown, 85
      red light, 88–89
      tenderloin, 88, 92
   earthquake and fire, 66, 85, 86–87
   newspapers and magazines, 86
      Bulletin, 89
      Chronicle, 89
      Overland Monthly, 86, 94
   socialism in, 122–123
   sports, 92–93
   underworld, 97
Sánchez Mejías, Ignacio, 253–254, 393

Sanger, Margaret, xvi, *139*, 360, 372, 381, 383
   and the birth-control movement, 138–139
   Woman Rebel, 139
Sanguinetti, Stephano, 93, 357
Sarka, Charles, 105, 260, 360
Sars, Hedda, 112–113, 363
Saxon, Lyle
   biography of Jean Lafitte, *Lafitte the Pirate*, 308, 406–407
   Children of Strangers, 308
Scherzer, Albert L., 106, 360
Schlecter, Carl, 115, 364
Schley, Rear Admiral Winfield Scott, 16, 345
Schlieffen plan, 176, 378
Schmitz, Eugene, mayor of San Francisco, 87–88, 356
Schoen, Wilhelm Eduard Freiherr von, 378
   formal declaration of war, 174
Schrack, Blanche, 104
   Birth Control Review, 360
Sealy, Theodore Eustace
   editor of *The Gleaner*, 316, 408
Seeger, Alan, xvi, 109, 117, 165–166, 212, 362, 365, 379–380
   Foreign Legion volunteer, 177–178, 379
Self-Government in Jamaica (Roberts), 263–265, 395, 409
   Civil War in the United States
      liberation of slaves, 265
   constitutions and governments, 263–265
      freed slave uprising, 264
      the planter class, 263–265
      revenue to the Crown, 263
      Royal proclamation, 264
Selous, Frederick Courteney, 17, 346

Sembat, Marcel, 179, 379
Semmes, Father O.M., 278
Semmes, Raphael, 278, 280, 281, 402
Semmes of the Alabama (Roberts), 278, 280, 281, 402
Serbia, 166, 170
Sergei Alexandrovich, Grand Duke of Russia, 125, 368
Seymour, George
  Kencot Citizens' Association, 399
Shakespeare, William, 21
Shaw, George Bernard, 122, 367
Shelley, Percy Bysshe, 125
Sherlock, Philip, 316, 318, 408
Shinn, Everett, 260
The Single Star (Roberts), xiv, xv, 318, 319, 321, 329
Sinn Féin, 59
Sir Henry Morgan: Buccaneer and Governor (Roberts), xv, xvii, xxi–xxii, 261–263, 267, 332, 412
Six Great Jamaicans (Roberts), 332, 412
Sloan, Dolly, 109, 362
Sloan, John, 109, 260, 354, 361
Smith, James Alexander George
  Legislative Council, 296, 405
Smith, Thomas J., 147
  clerk at the *Brooklyn Eagle*, 156–157
Smuts, General Jan, 297, 405
Sneddon, Robert W., 109, 362
Socialist Labor Party, 127
Socialist Party of America
  in New York, xvi, xvii
socialists, 122–124, 158
  Fabian Socialism, 26, 32, 122, 137–138, 367
  in France, 158, 166, 168–169, 171, 179
    demonstration by, 171
    L'Humanité, 171
  in New York, 122–124, 126–128, 136–137
    Lower East Side, 126–127
  and the People's National Party (PNP), 311, 326–329
  San Francisco, 122–123
Solano, Solita, 210, *211*, 381, 382
Sophie, Duchess of Hohenberg
  assassination in Sarajevo, Bosnia, 163–164, 376
'sourdoughs', 95–96, 358
Southern Pacific Railroad, 70–72, 73, 355
  violence at the terminus, 81
Spanish dancing, 134, 248–256, 371, 392, 393
Steffens, Lincoln, 133, 371
Sterling, George, 93, 94, 212–213, 230, 357
  A Wine of Wizardry, 212
Stevens, Hope R.
  delegate to Havana, 301, 406
Stevenson, Robert Louis
  monument in San Francisco, 98
Stockton, Frank, 69, 355
The Strange Career of Bishop Sterling (Roberts), 393
Street & Smith, 201–202
  editorial offices in, 216
Sullivan, Frank
  New York World, 205–209, 382
Sullivan, Timothy Daniel (Big Tim), 58, 353
Sullivan, Timothy P. (Little Tim), 58, 353
Swinburne, Algernon Charles, 21, 125, 222–223, 241–244, 347, 385

Taft, William Howard, 129, 370
Tahiti, 97–98
Talmadge, Norma, 229, 388
Taylor, Dr Edward R.
  mayor of San Francisco, 88, 356

Taylor, Stanley Arthur Goodwin
   The Capture of Jamaica, 332, 411
   Pages from Our Past, 332
Tchaka, 17, 346
Tennyson, Alfred, Lord, 221–222, 385
   Maud, 21
Thomas, Norman, 126, 369
Thompson, James P., 127, 369
Tierra de la Alegría, La, 134, 371
Titanic
   sinking of, 118–120
   survivors of, 118–120, *119*
Tobey, Berkeley, 131, 370
Tolstoy, Count Leo, 120–121
Tolstoy, 'Nastasia, 120–121
Toulmin Gaines Jr, Dr Marion, 280, 403
Toulouse-Lautrec, Henri de, 157, 375
Townsend, Edward W., 116, 364–365
Tucson, Arizona, 73

Umberto I of Italy, 125, 368
United Artists, Long Island studio, 228
United States of America, 317
   military bases in the West Indies, 300, 304
   presidential campaign (1904), 56, 57
   presidential campaign (1912), 128–131
   and World War I, 200
   See also individual cities
Universal Negro Improvement Association, xxi, 397
University College of the West Indies, 318, 321–324, 331, 409

Vander Weyde, William M.
   photographer, 204, 382
   search for park-bench derelicts, 204–209
   the vegetable man's donkey, 155–156, 374–375 (*see also* Dorgelès, Roland)

Velázquez, Diego, 259
Villain, Raoul, 171, 378
"Villanelle of a Spanish Dancer" (Roberts), 255–256, 393
Virtue, Vivian, xxiii
Viviani, René, 158–159, 167, 170–171, 178–179, 181, 375
Volanti, Carolina 'Madama', 70, 103, 104–105, 355. *See also* New York *under* cafés and restaurants: Madama's
Volanti, Emma, 70, 103
von Kaltenborn, Hans, 147, 157, 373
von Kluck, Alexander
   German First Army, 180, 184, 379
Vosburgh, Robert G., 106, 360

Walker, Charles L. (Charlie), 136, 137
Wall, Tessie (Teresa Susan Donohue), 88, 89, 356
Waltz, Jean-Jacques (Hansi), 164, 167
   Mon Village, 159–160, 376
   trial in Germany, 167
Washington, DC, 42, 300, 405
Watts, George Frederick, 259, 394
Watts-Dunton, Theodore, 242, 391
Webb, Beatrice, 122, 367
Webb, Sidney, 122, 367
Welby, Thomas Earle, 242, 391
Wells, H.G., 367
West Indies, 267
West Indies cruise, 244
West Indies Federation, 312, 329–330, 333–336, 413
West Indies National Council, 301–302, 304, 406
Weyler y Nicolau, Don Valeriano, 16, 345
Wheeler, Joseph (Fighting Joe), 16, 345
Whistler, Hector, 338, 413
Whiting, Robert Rudd, 227
   editor of *Ainslie's*, 200–201, 381

Whitman, Charles S., 102, 360
Wilde, Oscar
   The Ballad of Reading Gaol, 125
Wildman and Treherne, 69–70
Wilhelm II, 167, 377
Willard, June, 381
   "The Riposte", 203
Williams, Dr Eric Eustace, 311, 312, 336, 407
   From Columbus to Castro, xv
Williams, William Carlos, 357
Wilson, Edmund
   memoir of Millay in the *Nation*, 224, 386
Wilson, Woodrow, 128, 129–130, 230, 370, 389
Woolf, Virginia, 367
Wylie, Elinor, 224, 386

Yaqui Indians, 81, 355
Yeats, John Butler, xvi, 212, 361
   at Maison Petitpas, 107–114
   on 'modern art', 110–111
   sketch of Roberts, *109*
   sketches by, 107
   and socialism, 123–124
Yeats, William Butler, 107, 110, 362

www.ingramcontent.com/pod-product-compliance
Lightning Source LLC
Chambersburg PA
CBHW021813300426
44114CB00009BA/158